MW01252297

WAKEFIELD PRESS

Croatians in Australia

Ilija Denis Šutalo was born in Melbourne in 1968. He completed his degree with honours (1991) and doctorate in chemical engineering (1996) at the University of Melbourne. Dr Ilija Šutalo received the international '2000 Extraction and Processing Science Award' in Nashville, United States for journal papers on extractive metallurgy and related sciences from TMS (Minerals Metals Materials Society). After a short period as a research fellow at the University of Melbourne, he worked in industry as a project metallurgist for Western Mining Corporation (now WMC Resources) at Olympic Dam. Since 1998 Dr Ilija Šutalo has been a research scientist at CSIRO in Melbourne. Currently, he is the team leader of the Medical Science and Liquid Particle Flow team at CSIRO Manufacturing and Infrastructure Technology. Dr Ilija Šutalo has published journal articles in the fields of mineral extraction and processing, fluid dynamics and medical science. He is currently undertaking a Masters of Business and Administration at the Australian Graduate School of Management (University of Sydney and University of New South Wales).

Ilija Šutalo has written articles on Croatian settlement in Australia in *The Australian People: An Encyclopedia of the Nation, Its People and Their Origins* (2001) and the *Encyclopedia of Melbourne* (2004). He was a curator of the exhibition, *Croatian Settlement in Victoria, The Untold Story* (1999), at the Immigration Museum in Melbourne. Ilija Šutalo was also a founder of the Croatian Historical Society Inc., which documents the history of Croatian settlement in Australia. He is also writing another book: *A Bibliography of Croatian Migrants*. His parents migrated to Australia from Croatia in the 1960s and he is the eldest of their five sons. Ilija Šutalo is married and has a son and daughter.

Croatians in Australia

Pioneers, Settlers and

Their Descendants

Dr Ilija Šutalo

Wakefield
Press

Wakefield Press
1 The Parade West
Kent Town
South Australia 5067
www.wakefieldpress.com.au

First published 2004
Copyright © Ilija Sutalo, 2004

Designed and typeset by Clinton Ellicott, Wakefield Press
Printed and bound by Everbest Printing Co Ltd, China

National Library of Australia
Cataloguing-in-publication entry

Sutalo, Ilija.
Croatians in Australia : pioneers, settlers and their descendants.

Bibliography.
Includes index.
ISBN 1 86254 651 7.

1. Croats – Australia – History. 2. Australia – Emigration and immigration – History.
3. Immigrants – Australia – History. 4. Pioneers – Australia. I. Title.

305.891823094

Contents

Foreword	
By Dr James Jupp, Australian National University	ix

1. Introduction	
Background	1
Researching early Croatian settlement in Australia	4
Why so little is known about these Croatian pioneers' lives	7
Interviews with descendants	9
History of Croatian migration	10

2. Geographical and Population Background	
Early Croatian settlers in Australia	15
How many Croatian pioneers came to Australia?	16
Origins and family background	18
Factors influencing migration	22
How the Croatian pioneers came to Australia	24
Statistics on Croatian pioneers and their family life	25

3. Patterns of Early Croatian Settlement	
Croatian settlements across Victoria	27
Geelong, Portarlington and Western district	29
Melbourne and surrounding district	32
Castlemaine district	40
Wedderburn and Inglewood district	43
Ballarat, Maryborough and Bendigo district	45
Redcastle, Costerfield and Goulburn Valley district	49
North-eastern Victoria, Woods Point and Gippsland district	51
Croatian settlements across Australia	54
Mobility	59

4. Pioneer Connections and Communities

Background 61
Multiple Croatian connections and friendships 62
Rites of passage 64
Croatian mining and business partners 67
Croatian communities 69
Societies, clubs and newspapers 70
Connections with the Catholic Church 71
Pioneer women 81
Poverty and disillusionment 87

5. Pioneers on the Goldfields

Early Australian goldfields 91
Gold discoveries by Croatian pioneers 94
Dalmatia and Sclavonian mines 98
Mining partners and mines named after Croatians 102
Connections between mining communities 104
Impact of Croatians on the goldfields 107

6. Pioneer Seamen and Fishermen

Prior seafaring experience 111
Croatian seamen visiting Australia 112
The wreck of the barque *Gange* 116
Warships 119
Croatian pioneer fishermen 120
Croatian pioneer seamen 128
Rescues and storms 133

7. Pioneers with Hotels, Wineries and Farms

Antonio Radovick, 'Father of Korumburra' 135
Hotels in gold mining towns 141
Metropolitan hotels 146
Banquets, balls and dances 148
Trojano Darveniza's Excelsior Vineyard 150
Other Croatian pioneers with wineries 154
Croatian wines at Australian international exhibitions 158
Croatian pioneers involved in farming 159

8. Pioneer Business Enterprise

Antonio Buzolich 167
Natale Vuscovich 170
Fortunato Poschich 171

Mattio Orlovich 172
Mattio Marassovich 175
Kosmos 177
John Terdich 178
John Sersic 180
George Bathols 182
Prospero Stanich 185

9. Beyond Pioneers 1891–1945

Descendants' contributions to Australian society 187
Descendants who fought for Australia 197
Enemy aliens and internment 200
Interwar Croatians and strikes 203
Clubs and community activities 209

10. Post-Second World War Settlement

Overview of Croatians in Australia today 211
Post-Second World War Croatian settlers 212
Employment 215
Community activities 217
Culture, language and the arts 222
Sport 224
Halls and sporting venues 226
Prominent Croatian Australians 229
Negative stereotypes attached to Croatians 231
Struggle for national recognition 233
Croatian celebration 237
Future prospects for the Croatian community 238

Appendices

Appendix 1: Table of Croatian pioneers in Australia 239
Appendix 2: Croatian pioneer letters 261
Appendix 3: Croatian halls and sporting venues 267

Acknowledgments 269
Notes 271
Bibliography 309
Summary in Croatian 321
Index 325

*This book is dedicated to my parents Nikola Šutalo and
Emilija Šutalo (nee Jukić) who made sacrifices to provide their children
with opportunities they never had. Their support, encouragement and
endless energy inspired me to write this book.*

Nikola and Emilija Šutalo's wedding day in Melbourne in 1967

Foreword

Croatians have been coming to Australia for at least 150 years. Today Australians of Croatian birth or descent number far more than 100,000, a figure which must remain somewhat elastic due to the differing criteria used for measuring ancestry. Regardless of exactness, this remains a major component of the multicultural society.

Ilija Šutalo has given us a very detailed and fascinating insight into Croatian settlers in the formative century up to the 1940s. With his unique collection of pictures he shows the lives of the mainly rural and working-class Croatians who helped to pioneer the Australian bush, to work in the mines and to develop agriculture.

This is a major effort, as so many left only a limited trace. Many were from Croatian villages, were illiterate and unable to speak English. They moved around rural districts, some of which have ceased to exist and in most of which the Croatian inheritance is either lost or even denied. This is one of the hardest research tasks, much more difficult than tracing official local histories or family histories of the majority of Australian immigrants who came from the United Kingdom and Ireland.

Croatians were always hidden within descriptions based on the dominant Austro-Hungarian empire and its successor, Yugoslavia. Not until the last fifteen years has it been possible to measure Croatian birth, ancestry and religion with any degree of accuracy. Yet we know that most of those described as 'Austrians' before 1914 were actually from the coast and islands of Croatia. Like those from the Greek islands, southern Italy or, indeed, the west of Scotland and Ireland, these immigrants were familiar with the sea and were willing to cross the world with more enthusiasm than those living further inland. The picture changes after 1945, but the original pioneers were linked to the outside world through their proximity to the sea.

Such a detailed analysis of Croatians has never before been attempted. Yet Croatians have certainly been here for 150 years and by the 1930s were well organised and conscious of their nationality. Dr Šutalo's work is an invaluable contribution to filling in the gaps in our knowledge of those many Australians who were not from the British and Irish mainstream, but without whom Australia could not have developed and grown.

Dr James Jupp
Australian National University

Dr James Jupp is the Director of the Centre for Immigration and Multicultural Studies at Australian National University. He received an Order of Australia Member award (AM) for his service to the recording of Australian history. Dr Jupp is recognised as Australia's leading academic commentator on migration.

CHAPTER 1

Introduction

Background

The history of Croatian-born immigrants in Australia is an 'untold story' since they were invariably recorded in official statistics as Austrians, Italians and Yugoslavs. Prior to the First World War, Croatians were usually known as Austrians or Italians. The interwar Croatians were usually referred to as Yugoslavs or Slavs, and occasionally as Italians. Croatians who settled in Australia between the Second World War and 1992 were still recorded in statistics as Yugoslavs, even though many identified themselves as Croatians. Since Croatian independence in 1992, the term 'Croatians' has become official and is used in the Australian Census, but the terms 'former Yugoslavs' or 'former Yugoslavs nfd (not further defined)' are also used in official statistics which adds confusion.[1]

To date, very little has been written about the lives of Croatian pioneers in Australia, and those few about whom something is known have not normally been identified as Croatian, a situation constituting a significant gap in our knowledge of Australian pioneer and migration history. This account is designed to show the human aspect of Croatian pioneers including their successes and failures. It identifies the communities of Croatian pioneers living in Australia in the second half of the nineteenth century and describes their contribution to this country's development – which was significant in the wine, fishing and mining industries. This account also summarises the history of Croatian settlement in Australia to the present.

In this study, a pioneer in the Australian context is defined as a settler who arrived in Australia by 1890. Although the main topic of the book is Croatian pioneers of Australia, there are frequent references to Croatians in other settler societies, including New Zealand, Canada, United States of America, South Africa and some South American countries. Croatians in these countries participated in similar activities, occupations and had experiences similar to those in Australia. The comparisons with Croatians in other countries are given when they throw light on the experiences of Croatians in Australia. For example, each of these countries had a large influx of immigrants and gold rushes. The comparisons place the Australian pioneer and migration story in a much broader context.

A book such as this holds great significance for the large number of people of Croatian birth and ancestry in Australia. According to the 2001 Australian Census there are 51,909 Croatian-born people living in Australia and 105,747 people of Croatian ancestry in Australia. However, Price (2001) estimates that there are currently about 146,000 people of Croatian ancestry in Australia, representing approximately 0.8 per cent of the Australian population; other references quote a figure of between 200,000 and 250,000. However, the number of Croatians in Australia is larger than indicated by the 2001 census because a large number of Croatians born in Bosnia-Herzegovina were not included, and other Croatians were coded as Yugoslav-born.[2] The 2001 census stated that there were 69,851 Croatian-speakers in Australia and revealed that 19.3 per cent of people from Bosnia-Herzegovina who lived in Australia spoke Croatian at home. If the number of Croatian speakers born in Bosnia-Herzegovina, Yugoslavia and Slovenia is added, the total would be 58,325 Croatians in Australia.[3] However, this figure is still a conservative estimate as it does not include Croatians from Yugoslavia and Bosnia-Herzegovina who stated they spoke South Slavic nfd (not further defined) or English at home. In the 2001 census, 6027 people in the Yugoslav-born category stated that they were Western Catholics and spoke South Slavic nfd or English at home. At least half of these would be Croatian.[4] If one adds these Croatians, a more accurate estimate of the number of Croatians in Australia is 61,338.[5]

This number does not include the Croatian-born who consider themselves Italian and who stated in the census that they were born in Italy. These Croatian-born are also known as Giuliano-Dalmati or Italo-Croatians, since in the interwar period Italy ruled parts of Croatia (Istria, Rijeka, Zadar, islands of Cres, Lošinj and Lastovo). In *Giuliano-Dalmati in Australia: Contributi E Testimonianze Per Una Storia* (ed Cresciani 1999), which details the lives of 30 prominent members of the Giuliano-Dalmati community in Australia, 57 per cent are Croatian-born and many have ethnic Croatian surnames like Bradicich, Francetich, Mircovich and Velcich. The majority (52 per cent) of the 21 Giuliano-Dalmati clubs and associations in Australia include Croatian place names such as Fiume (Rijeka), Chreso (Cres) and Zara (Zadar) as part of their title. Between 1949 and 1952 about 6000 Giuliano-Dalmati born in Croatia came to Australia as refugees.[6]

Similarly, the number of Croatians in Australia does not include the Croatian-born ethnic Serbs who classified themselves as being born in Yugoslavia in the census. The majority of ethnic Serbs in Australia were born in Croatia or Bosnia-Herzegovina.[7] Croatians in mixed marriages with Serbs or Bosnian Muslims also often stated they were born in Yugoslavia. The controversial tennis player, Jelena Dokic, who previously played for Australia, was born in Osijek in Croatia to a Croatian mother and Serbian father. She often stated she was born in Belgrade.

The accuracy of statistics on the number of Croatians and Croatian-born in

Australia is an important issue, since in the past it has usually been hidden or underestimated. The 1996 Australian Census was the first time Croatian-born immigrants were recorded separately from immigrants from other parts of the former Yugoslavia. Until then, Croatians were recorded as Yugoslav-born. Between 1871 and 1911 Croatians in Australia were coded under Austrian-born in the Australian Census. The Kingdom of Serbs, Croats and Slovenes was established in 1918 and renamed Yugoslavia in 1929. From the 1921 to 1991 census Croatians were coded under Yugoslavs or Yugoslav-born. Even after Croatian independence many Croatians in Australia continue to state they are Yugoslav-born in official documents. Hence, it is not surprising that many Croatian-born people stated in the 1996 census that they were former Yugoslavia nfd-born and Yugoslav-born in the 2001 census.[8]

The history of Croatian residency in Australia is summarised in table 1. By 1890 over 850 Croatians had lived in Australia. In 1891 there were 440 Croatians in Australia, which increased to 720 in 1921, to 3413 in 1933 and 5020 in 1947. In the interwar period Croatians constituted 86 per cent of the Yugoslav-born in Australia. Immediately after the Second World War the Yugoslav-born population almost quadrupled from 5866 in 1947 to 23,126 in 1954. During this period, most of those recorded as Yugoslav-born migrated under the Displaced Persons Scheme and half of them were Croatians.[9] So by 1954, there were at least 14,700 Croatians in Australia and they constituted 64 per cent of the Yugoslav-born population. In the 1960s and 1970s when Yugoslavia opened its borders, large numbers of Croatians came to Australia. Yugoslav-born immigration increased dramatically, peaking in 1970 and 1971, then decreased until it stabilised in the mid-1970s. As a result, the Yugoslav-born population in Australia increased from 49,776 in 1961, 129,816 in 1971, 149,355 in 1981 to 161,076 in 1991. During this period the percentage of Croatians from the Yugoslav-born number gradually decreased, principally due to an increased number of Macedonians arriving from the late 1960s. In 1991 there were at least 52,900 Croatians in Australia, or a third of the Yugoslav-born population in Australia. In the 1990s Croatian refugees arrived from Croatia and Bosnia-Herzegovina.

By comparing the number of Croatian-born in table 1 with Australian Census data, it was found that, from 1947 to 1981, Croatian-born usually ranked as the seventh largest overseas-born migrant group in Australia from a non-English-speaking country behind Italy, Greece, Germany, Netherlands, Poland and Malta. The exceptions to this are the years 1961, when Croatian-born was ranked ninth due to larger numbers of Hungarian-born and Austrian-born, and 1966, when Croatian-born was ranked eighth due to a larger number of Hungarian-born. In 1973 a new immigration policy which did not discriminate on the basis of race was introduced and formally ended the 'White Australia' policy. This resulted in a large increase in Asian migration to Australia, which decreased the Croatian-born ranking. By the 2001 census the numbers of overseas-born people from Vietnam, China, Philippines, India, Malaysia, Lebanon and Hong Kong were all higher than the Croatian-born group.

Year	Number of Croatians in Australia	Percentage Croatians from Census	Australian Census	Number
1871			Austria-Hungary	610
1881			Austria-Hungary	1,024
1891	440 (250[a])		Austria-Hungary	1,639
1901			Austria-Hungary	1,914
1911			Austria-Hungary	2,774
1921	720[a]	87%	Jugo Slavia	829
1933	3,413	86%	Yugoslavia	3,969
1947	5,020[a]	86%	Yugoslavia	5,866
1954	14,700	64%	Yugoslavia	23,126
1961	22,000	44%	Yugoslavia	49,776
1966	26,500	37%	Yugoslavia	71,277
1971	43,600	34%	Yugoslavia	129,816
1976	48,900	34%	Yugoslavia	143,591
1981	50,200	34%	Yugoslavia	149,335
1986	51,100	34%	Yugoslavia	150,032
1991	52,900 (58,000[b])	33%	Yugoslavia	161,076
1996	56,300		Croatia[c]	47,015
2001	61,338		Croatia[d]	51,909

a C. Price, *Southern Europeans in Australia*, 1963, p. 11.
b L. Paric et al. *Croats in the Australian Community*, 1996, p. 81
c The 1996 census did not include Croatians born in other countries in the former Yugoslavia or classified as being born in former Yugoslavia nfd.
d The 2001 census did not include Croatians born in other countries in the former Yugoslavia or classified as being born in Yugoslavia.

Table 1: Number of Croatians in Australia estimated from the Australian Census

Researching early Croatian settlement in Australia

Another major reason for the scarcity of information about Croatian pioneers in Australia relates to the political situation at the time when these pioneers migrated – Croatia was then part of the Austro-Hungarian Empire. Consequently, official sources labelled Croatian pioneers as Austrians. In the Austro-Hungarian Empire, Croatia was divided into the administrative districts of Croatia and Slavonia, Dalmatia and Istria. Croatia and Slavonia were under Hungarian control, while Dalmatia and Istria were under Austrian control. Under Austro-Hungarian rule, Italian was used as the official language of administrative and legal bodies in Dalmatia and Istria. Given the long history of Venetian rule on parts of coastal Croatia up until 1797, Croatians were also labelled as Italians. As most Croatian pioneers came from Croatia's southern coastline – Dalmatia – they were sometimes referred to as Dalmatians or as being born in Dalmatia. Similarly, some were known as Sclavonians or Slavonians, a term used to describe Croatians from the interior region of Croatia called Slavonia.

Croatian pioneers were repeatedly and inaccurately referred to as Austrians or Italians in newspaper articles. In some areas of Australia where Croatians settled, the newspaper reporters called the same group of Croatian pioneers Austrians *and* Italians. For example, both *The McIvor News* and *The McIvor Times* referred to the Croatians working on the Sclavonian reef in Redcastle in Victoria as Austrians and Italians.[10] In fact, Croatian pioneers did not associate with German-speaking Austrians in Australia; they did not have mining claims together, nor did they attend each other's weddings. Croatians and Austrians have completely different customs, traditions and languages. Croatian pioneers maintained ties with other Croatian settlers in Australia. They tended to concentrate in certain areas and formed communities and networks.

Croatian pioneers were recorded on marriage and naturalisation certificates as being born in Austria, Dalmatia, Trieste, Italy, Gulf of Venice, Sclavonia, Slavonia, Illyria, Adriatic Gulf and Hungary. Italian forms of the names of the birthplaces of the pioneers, such as Fiume (Rijeka), Ragusa (Dubrovnik), Brazza (island of Brač) and Lesina (island of Hvar), were also often used, adding confusion.[11] Although it was common for Croatian pioneers to be referred to as being born in Trieste, other records would reveal the actual town in Croatia where they were born. For example, Joseph Catarinich's naturalisation certificate stated he was born in Trieste, Austria, but in fact, he was born in Malinska on the island of Krk. Trieste was the best known town in the area which may account for this discrepancy. Thirty-five years later, during the First World War, an intelligence inquiry into enemy aliens by the Wynyard Police stated that Joseph Catarinich was born in Croatia.[12]

This study draws on extensive research carried out in Australia, Croatia, Austria, New Zealand, the United States and Italy. Most of the references used in this book come from the second half of the nineteenth century. The range of sources used include newspaper articles, naturalisation certificates, marriage certificates, death certificates, wills and probates, mining records, historical societies records, shipping records, cemeteries, hospitals, inquests, archives, museums, libraries, personal letters of the Croatian pioneers, and Catholic Church records in Croatia and Australia. The references have not been limited to English; useful sources were in Croatian, Italian, German, Latin and Polish. Throughout this book newspaper articles that mention Croatian settlers have been used extensively to support this research. Locating references in the newspapers in towns where Croatians lived was a tedious process since each page of the newspaper had to be searched. In this way fragmented sources were amalgamated to reconstruct the story of Croatian immigrants in Australia.

Official Australian records can be misleading or incorrect. Marriage, death and naturalisation certificates often contain errors, and the year of birth determined using death, marriage and naturalisation certificates sometimes varied by several years. Nicholas Jasprizza's naturalisation certificate stated he was born in Abolstein, Lower Saxony, but in fact he was born in Janjina on the Pelješac Peninsula. Moreover,

Croatian pioneers occasionally lied about their age when they were married, stating they were younger than they actually were. From a sample of 23 Croatian pioneers whose year of birth as indicated by their Croatian baptism certificates was compared to that determined from their Victorian marriage certificates, it was found that 29 per cent had lied about their age at the time of marriage. They were in fact from four to eight years older than the age they stated on their marriage certificate.[13]

Differences in spellings of surnames made it extremely difficult to follow Croatian pioneers' movements around Australia. For example, Natale Vuscovich's (Božo Vušković) surname in newspaper articles and rate books was spelt Vuscovih, Vuscovitch, Wiskiwitch and Vascovitch. In this book the most common spelling of the Croatian pioneers' surnames used in Australia is used. As shown above, the correct Croatian spelling of the pioneer's name is placed in brackets if known. Careful attention has been given to avoiding an overestimate of the Croatian presence by counting different spellings of the same person's surname as separate pioneers.

Pavle Vidas

Most Croatian pioneers' surnames were Anglicised to enable them to be pronounced properly or because the Croatian pioneers were illiterate. The most common change was for surnames ending in 'ić'; they were modified to end in 'ch', 'ck' or 'itch'. Sometimes the surnames were changed depending on how the person writing the surname on behalf of an illiterate pioneer interpreted it; for example, Trče became Torchie, Bošković became Boscovich, and Poščić became Poschich. The Croatian alphabet has 30 letters, but no Q, W, X, or Y.[14] In a number of cases these non-Croatian letters were used to obtain the correct pronunciation. Similarly, the Croatian given names were often replaced by their English or Italian equivalents, for example, Ivan became John or Giovanni. Some Croatians used Anglo-Saxon surnames such as Golden, McNish, Melford, Neil, Phillips, Vincent and Abbott to enable an easier integration into their new environment or to avoid discrimination. Obviously, it was more difficult to trace the lives of these Croatians, especially if they moved to another area of Australia.

The Croatian pioneers of Australia were largely illiterate. Almost half (48 per cent) of the Croatian pioneers in Victoria could not sign their name on their marriage certificates. As a consequence, little written correspondence exists between the Croatian pioneers. Only several letters and a few diaries detailing aspects of their lives in Australia exist. The Croatian traveller, Pavle Vidas from Hreljin, lived in Australia from 1889 to 1894. His diary details how he met and sometimes worked with Croatians in Adelaide, Melbourne, Sydney, Lismore, Nyngan, Hobart and Broken Hill. For example, in Sydney Vidas stayed in Frederick Rossich's hotel (Rossich was from the island of Premuda near Zadar) with 20 other Croatians. On the ship to Australia Vidas had met another 22 Croatians. He also lived in Argentina, Brazil, Canada, United States, South Africa and Panama where he maintained close ties with Croatian settlers living there.[15]

Why so little is known about these Croatian pioneers' lives

As noted earlier little is known about these Croatian pioneers because there has never been a comprehensive study on their lives and contribution to Australian society. Australian historians have typically tended to ignore Croatian pioneers. Histories of Australian towns that mention prominent (Croatian) pioneers rarely mention their birthplace. For example, *The History of the Shire of Korumburra* (1988) and *The Early Days of Korumburra* (1979) both describe the important contributions Antonio Radovick made to the development of the town. But neither of these books states where he was born.[16] Sometimes it was noted that they had come from Austria, or from Dalmatia in Austria. For example, *The Jubilee History of Victoria and Melbourne* (1888) stated that Trojano Darveniza was born in the Province of Dalmatia in Austria, and in *Rich Earth, History of Young New South Wales* (1977) Nicholas Jasprizza was identified as being a native of Dalmeith (Dalmatia), Austria.[17] Many Croatian pioneers lived in towns and communities on the Victorian goldfields, towns such as Redcastle, Costerfield, Grant, Buckland and Yandoit, all towns which no longer exist. Very little has been published on these towns and where it has, the Croatian pioneers are usually completely ignored or no mention is made of where they were from originally.

To illustrate this, we can consider James Flett's *History of Gold Discovery in Victoria* (1979). Flett noted that one Andrea Franktovich made a statement to a Select Committee of the Victorian Parliament about his discovery of the Redcastle goldfield. However, Flett left out one important point: the name of the site of the gold discovery – Sclavonia Reef. This is an unfortunate omission as 'Sclavonia', the name of the reef, refers to Andrea Franktovich's birthplace. Further, Flett refers to a goldfield discovery by Yanicle who was the Croatian pioneer, Luke Yannich, without mentioning his nationality. Admittedly, the 'Yanicle' spelling was an unusual spelling of Yannich's surname and this helps to hide his origins. However, Yannich had gold mines named after Dalmatia in the same area and, surprisingly, these were not mentioned. On another occasion Flett incorrectly spelt 'Sclavonians' as 'Selavonians' when he was quoting from a newspaper article, and this mistake, like his other omissions, hides the Croatian connection.[18]

Although over 850 Croatian pioneers settled in Australia by 1890, the history of their settlement in Australia is largely unresearched. Only four studies have touched on the subject. In 1978 Neven Smoje first mentioned Croatian pioneers in his article on the shipwreck of the Croatian barque, *Stefano*. In 1988 he detailed the lives of several Croatian pioneers in his article, 'Early Croatian Settlement in Western Australia', in the first edition of *The Australian People: An Encyclopedia of the Nation, Its People and their Origins*. In the same book Marin Alagich mentioned several Croatian pioneers who settled in eastern Australia.[19] Mate Tkalcevic detailed the lives of several additional Croatian pioneers to those mentioned in the above in his book, *Croats in Australia: An Information and Resource Guide* (1988). Mary Stenning listed the names of Croatian pioneers in three booklets printed between 1996 and 1999. However, in her registers of supposedly Croatian pioneers she had included many non-Croatians, for example, Irish, Scots, French, Swiss and Germans. Furthermore, in her register of Croatian pioneer marriages in Victoria before 1890, almost half were not Croatian-born. In addition, she did not normally identify where the Croatian pioneers were from.[20] A *Bibliography of Croatian Migrants* currently being complied by Ilija Šutalo contains a literature review of all published works on Croatians in Australia and will not be repeated here.

Previous studies on early Southern European migration to Australia, such as *Southern Europeans in Australia* and *The Method and Statistics of Southern Europeans in Australia*, both by Charles Price and published in 1963, relied primarily on naturalisation records. However, if in this present study naturalisation records were the only sources used, then over half of the Croatian pioneers would have been missed. Many unnaturalised Croatian pioneers contributed to and lived out their lives in Australia. Price claimed that, for Southern Europeans, naturalisation records covered two-thirds to three-quarters of the adult male settlers in the period 1904 to 1946, of whom two-thirds settled permanently.[21] However, for the Croatian pioneers, the percentage naturalised was considerably lower: in Victoria less than 40 per cent of Croatian pioneers were naturalised. Of these, over 85 per cent remained in Victoria permanently. Another six per cent were naturalised in other Australian states and New Zealand, but most of these did not remain in Victoria permanently. Naturalisation records were also inadequate in providing a better understanding of the Croatian pioneers' successes and failures. More details on Price's study are discussed in chapter 2.

Croatian sources that deal with migration or genealogy usually omit the overwhelming majority of Croatians who settled in Australia prior to 1890. *Iseljenici Otoka Brača* (1982) by Klement Derado and Ivan Čizmić is the most comprehensive study on Croatian migration from the island of Brač. These authors listed only 8.3 per cent of the Croatians from Brač who settled in Victoria prior to 1890. Nenad Vekarić, a notable Croatian genealogist and expert on the surnames of the Pelješac Peninsula, has listed in several books almost all the births from this area and the Croatians who migrated from the region. From my research I was able to determine that, of the Croatians who were born on the Pelješac Peninsula and migrated to Victoria, he gives only 14 per cent as migrating to Victoria.[22]

Croatian surnames are a means of identifying Croatian descendants, but in most instances when the surname disappears, so does the Croatian connection. At least every second Croatian pioneer's surname died out in Victoria with the death of the pioneer. Over 28 per cent of the early Croatian settlers never married. This figure could be even higher since, at the time of death of some Croatian miners, it was unknown whether they were married. Many of the miners who lived in certain communities remained unmarried. Of those who were married, about 15 per cent died childless and another 15 per cent died with only female descendants. Other Croatian surnames died out when the male descendants lost their lives fighting for Australia during both World Wars. Bartholomew Millich's only male heir, Cosmo Millich, died from wounds sustained in France in the First World War. Both of Victor Lusic's sons fought for Australia during the First World War. One son, Victor, was killed in action at Gallipoli, and although the other, Matthew, returned to Australia, the surname has since died out. If Victor Lusic had not been killed in Gallipoli, then the Lusic surname may still exist in Australia today. However, not all the Croatian pioneers' surnames have died out – some such as Gercovich, Mercovich, Juratowitch and Terdich are widespread.

Interviews with descendants

Between 1993 and 2004 I corresponded with over 180 descendants of Croatian pioneers of Australia. The majority knew very little or nothing about their Croatian ancestors and most were unaware of any Croatian connection. From the initial group of descendants, I eventually narrowed the group down and conducted 53 interviews with third-generation (grandchildren) to fifth-generation descendants (great-great-grandchildren). The selection criteria for interview were that the descendant generally possessed a more detailed knowledge about their Croatian ancestor. The details of each interview were recorded in a questionnaire. The majority (55 per cent) of the interviewed descendants knew their ancestor was born in Dalmatia or Croatia, 22.5 per cent assumed they were born in Austria and about 22.5 per cent did not know where their ancestor was born. A quarter of the descendants knew that their Croatian ancestor had some contact in Australia with people who were born in the same region of Europe. Most descendants knew at least one of the occupations their Croatian ancestor had in Australia. Surprisingly, given the current interest in family histories, half of the interviewed descendants did not know when their Croatian ancestor had come to Australia. They often confused the Croatian pioneers' sons with the original pioneer.

Most of the interviewed descendants did not know when their Croatian ancestor was born and 47 per cent did not know when their ancestor had married and died. The majority of the interviewed descendants knew that their Croatian ancestor had descendants who fought for Australia during the First World War. Some of the descendants believed that their Croatian ancestor possessed a good formal education when they were in fact illiterate.

History of Croatian migration

Croatians have a long history of migration. In the sixteenth century Croatian refugees fleeing from the Turkish (Ottoman) onslaught settled in Austria (Burgenland), western Hungary, Italy (Molise), Slovakia, Czech (Moravia), and Romania. Croatian speakers who are descendants of these refugees still live in these countries. Burgenland alone has 45,000 of these citizens who speak unique Croatian dialects which have incorporated non-Croatian words from the local languages.[23] Since the 1950s almost half of the population from the three Molisan-Croatian-speaking towns in Italy have been lost to chain migration. There are 2000 first-generation speakers of Molisan-Croatian left in the world, almost half of whom have emigrated to Western Australia. In 1998 Molisan-Croatians in Australia formed the Molisan Croatian Cultural Association of Western Australia.[24] Croatians who were mining and commercial entrepreneurs settled in Kosovo (Janjevo region) prior to the Turkish invasion. They numbered several thousand before the 1990s when ethnic Albanians forced them to leave. Most of these Janjevo Croatian refugees settled in Croatia.

Although a small number of Croatian missionaries, explorers and seamen had settled in North and South America between the sixteenth and nineteenth centuries, it was not until the nineteenth century that the first wave of Croatian migrants arrived and formed communities. Before 1890 Croatians almost exclusively from Dalmatia and other coastal regions of Croatia had settled in California and Louisiana, Argentina, Chile, Australia, New Zealand, Peru, Canada and South Africa. Almost all of these Croatian settlers were single men on arrival and usually married into other ethnic groups, but many never married. In their adopted countries some were seamen, fishermen and farmers as they had been in Croatia, but others mined, were merchants or ran other businesses. As we will see in chapter 4 some of these communities of new settlers formed Croatian societies and established newspapers to keep their culture alive.

The first Croatian community in the United States was established in Louisiana in the 1830s, where Croatians found employment on the New Orleans waterfront as seamen and then as saloon keepers and fruit dealers. Others became pioneers in the oyster fishing industry in the Plaquemines Parish on the Mississippi Delta.

The Californian gold rush, which began in 1848, attracted many Croatians. The main Croatian community was established in San Francisco where most Croatians ran businesses such as saloons, although some also became fishermen. By the 1870s, Croatians were farmers in the Santa Clara, San Joaquin and Pajaro Valleys in California. Croatian farmers were so successful in growing apples, grapes and figs in the Pajaro Valley that the region was known as 'New Dalmatia'. Their greatest contribution was to the apple industry, particularly in Watsonville. Croatians also settled in Sacramento, San Jose, and Los Angeles. In the 1860s and 1870s, the silver boom in Nevada also attracted many Croatians, with some becoming rich from the silver mines, although many made their fortunes from owning saloons and restaurants. Croatians emigrating to Canada mainly went to British Columbia where they worked as gold miners and salmon fishermen.[25]

In Argentina, Croatians primarily settled in Buenos Aires where they worked as sailors and seamen in river and maritime shipping; some became owners of shipping companies. Others settled in the Argentinean province of Santa Fe, where their main communities were in Rosario and Acebal; here they were mainly farmers. In southern Chile, most Croatians settled in Punta Arenas and were seamen and merchants. Many had been gold miners during Chile's nearby Tierra del Fuego gold rush in the 1880s and 1890s before settling in Punta Arenas. In northern Chile, the largest settlement of Croatians was in Antofagasta where they were primarily merchants, but Croatian occupations also included miners, managers and owners of Chile's nitrate mines. In Peru the largest Croatian community was in Callao where they were seamen and merchants.[26]

Croatians arrived in New Zealand during the Otago gold rush in the 1860s and became gold miners. Later, Croatians worked as Kauri gum diggers on New Zealand's North Island. Croatians in South Africa initially worked as seamen, but many later worked in the Kimberly diamond mines in the 1870s and 1880s and in gold mines.[27] In later chapters we will see that before 1890 there were many similarities in the lives of Croatian pioneers in Australia and those of other Croatians migrating to other overseas countries.

By the 1880s Croatians had begun to emigrate on a larger scale and from a larger area of Croatia. Emigration had spread to the Modruša-Rijeka county, across to the Karlovac and Zagreb districts and subsequently to the rest of Croatia. Between 1890 and the beginning of the First World War, between 350,000 and 400,000 Croatians emigrated overseas. The majority of these migrants came from Croatia and Slavonia (68.3 per cent), with the remainder coming from Dalmatia (18.8 per cent) and Istria (12.9 per cent). The largest number from Croatia and Slavonia came from the Zagreb county, which lost a quarter of its population to emigration. During this period the overwhelming majority of Croatians migrated to the United States, followed in descending order by Argentina, Chile, New Zealand and Australia. Most inland Croatians migrated to the United States where they primarily settled in the industrial centres in Pennsylvania, Illinios, Ohio and New York and worked in the mines and steel mills. Their largest settlement was in Pittsburgh. They were more numerous and better organised than earlier Croatian arrivals and established many societies, Catholic parishes and newspapers. On the eve of the First World War, Croatians from Dalmatia and coastal Croatia still constituted the majority in many overseas Croatian communities. In Australia and New Zealand, they predominantly came from central Dalmatia and Croatian islands. In Chile they came from Dalmatia, especially the island of Brač, in Argentina from Hvar, Kotor and Dubrovnik districts, and in Peru from the Dubrovnik district.[28]

In the interwar period, over 104,000 Croatians migrated overseas. Half migrated to South America (Argentina, Brazil, Uruguay, and Chile) due to the immigration restriction quotas imposed by the United States. The largest number of these migrated to Argentina. The remainder migrated in descending order to the United States, Canada, Australia and New Zealand. Over 47,000 Croatian migrants returned to Croatia during the interwar period, most of whom left the United States immediately after the First World War to help rebuild the country no longer under Austro-Hungarian control. During the Depression there were also more Croatian returnees than arrivals to South America, New Zealand, Australia and Canada. Although women started to migrate before the First World War, the interwar period is characterised by a much larger number of Croatian women migrating. On the eve of the Second World War, Croatian immigrants became concentrated in certain regions: the majority of Croatians who were in the United States lived in the eastern states of Pennsylvania, Ohio, Illinios and Michigan; in Canada the majority lived in Ontario; in Australia the majority lived in Western Australia, while in New Zealand the majority lived in Auckland.[29]

In the period from 1939 to 1948, about 250,000 people left Croatia. Most fled as refugees from Communist Yugoslavia at the end of the Second World War and went via displaced persons camps in Austria, Italy and Germany to the United States, Canada and Australia. This large flow of people leaving Croatia to escape Communist Yugoslavia also included ethnic Italians, Germans and Hungarians. A number of Croatians who had been in the Ustasha (Ustaša) government and armed services (which collaborated with Germany and Italy during the Second World War) fled to Argentina. After this initial surge of departures immediately after the war, Croatians essentially stopped migrating to South America.[30] Many Croatians continued to escape illegally from Yugoslavia until the mid-1960s.

Most post-Second World War Croatian migrants were anticommunist and were opposed to Yugoslavia's Communist Government which came to be Serb-dominated. Many actively supported the struggle for more autonomy for Croatia or an independent Croatia. While many pre-war Croatian migrants had supported the Yugoslav Communist movement (Tito and the Partisans), the Yugoslav Communist Government's break with Moscow, their dictatorial nature and partisan massacres of

Croatians convinced many pre-war Croatian migrants to withdraw their support of the Yugoslav regime.

From 1965 when Yugoslavia opened up its borders allowing its workers to seek temporary employment abroad, Croatians have been working as 'guest workers' in Western Europe to meet labour shortages. With this move the Yugoslav Communist regime hoped to combat rising unemployment and to obtain valuable hard currency for the Yugoslav economy. By the 1970s, European migration had overtaken overseas migration. Before the 1990s Croatians migrated for political as well as economic considerations. By 1991 more than 500,000 Croatians (including members of their families) had worked as guest workers in Western European countries, North America and Australia. According to the 1991 Croatian Census, 71.4 per cent of the guest workers and their families were living in Western Europe, and the overwhelming majority of these were in Germany, followed by Switzerland, Austria, France and Sweden. In terms of Croatian emigration, Australia was ranked second after Germany, with the number of Croatian workers abroad (a total of 10.3 per cent). Over two-thirds of the guest workers had been working abroad for over ten years and are, in reality, permanent rather than temporary migrants.[31]

According to the 1991 Yugoslav Census there were 761,000 Croatians in Bosnia-Herzegovina, 156,000 Croatians in Serbia and Montenegro (Vojvodina and Kotor) and 56,000 Croatians in Slovenia. Between 1991 and 1995 during the invasion of Croatia by Serbia and the Yugoslav National Army and the war in Bosnia-Herzegovina, large numbers of Croatians (from Croatia, Bosnia-Herzegovina and Serbia and Montenegro [Yugoslavia]) were forced to flee into Western European countries. With the break-up of Yugoslavia, the number of Croatians in Bosnia-Herzegovina and Yugoslavia (Vojvodina and Kotor) has been dramatically reduced. It is estimated that, during these wars, about 300,000 Croatians emigrated, many of whom returned to Croatia after regions of Croatia were liberated.

After the formation of the Kingdom of Serbs, Croats and Slovenes in 1918 (later renamed Yugoslavia), the number of Croatians in Kotor and Vojvodina decreased substantially. In 1871 Croatians constituted more than 70.2 per cent of Kotor's population (Tivat, Prčanj and Lastva had over 90 per cent Croatians), but by 1991 this decreased to eight per cent (with a total of only 4910). However, Serbian rule since 1991 has forced many more Croatians to leave Kotor, and some of them have settled in Croatia.[32] Between 1945 and 1948 over 200,000 Serbians were settled into Vojvodina and have gradually increased their influence in the area, and since 1991, Serbian rule has forced at least 30,000 Croatians to flee the region. In the Bačka and Srijem regions of Vojvodina, Croatians are continually intimidated by the Serbian authorities who attempt to persuade them to identify themselves as Bunjevci and Šokci rather than Croatian, in order to decrease the number of Croatians in the Vojvodina population statistics.[33]

The number of Croatians now living outside Croatia is estimated at over two million, the largest number being in the United States, followed by Germany, Australia, South America (Argentina, Chile) and Canada. The 2000 United States Census estimate of 374,241 people of Croatian ancestry living in the United States is too low since many stated they were of Yugoslav ancestry. The largest number of people of Croatian ancestry live in Pennsylvania, followed by Illinios, Ohio, California, and New York. In Canada the majority live in Ontario, while in Australia most Croatians live in Victoria and New South Wales. Croatians abroad have established Croatian community halls, sporting clubs, social clubs and Catholic parishes. They have also formed Croatian language schools, soccer clubs, folkloric groups and tamburica orchestras. During the invasion of Croatia by Serbia and the Yugoslav National Army and the war in Bosnia-Herzegovina, Croatians abroad sent humanitarian and financial aid to Croatians in Croatia and Bosnia-Herzegovina. More details on the activities of post-Second World War Croatians in Australia will be given in chapter 10.

The Croatian communities outside Croatia and Bosnia-Herzegovina vary in different countries. Between the Second World War and the 1980s most educated professional Croatians migrated to Germany and other European countries, and those who emigrated overseas went to the United States and Canada. However, since the mid-1980s, educated professional Croatians have also been migrating to Australia. Interestingly, the children of Croatian settlers in Australia and Canada are often bilingual and have better Croatian language retention than those in the United States. Germany has the largest number of Croatian-born immigrants followed by Australia, while the United States has the largest number of people with Croatian ancestry. Many Croatians in Germany and other Western European countries have homes or holiday houses in Croatia and Bosnia-Herzegovina. Typically, they visit Croatia annually on their summer holidays. Not surprisingly, Croatians in Australia and New Zealand visit Croatia far less frequently, mainly due to the high travel costs associated with overseas travel. Now that Croatia is a sovereign state Croatians in the diaspora are forming links and business and cultural relationships with Croatia and their new homelands.

CHAPTER 2

Geographical and Population Background

Early Croatian settlers in Australia

Croatians have been arriving in Australia since the early 1800s. In the early years they often came as sailors and deserted their ships to stay in Australia. As we have already seen, many of these early Croatian pioneers changed their surnames when they arrived in Australia; thus, their presence in Australia has largely gone unnoticed and their patterns of settlement difficult to reconstruct.

Stefano Posic (also spelt as Posich, Possech and Powseitch) was a convict of Croatian descent who was transported to Australia in 1813. He was born in Sicily to Croatian parents. Posic was charged with larceny for stealing from a dwelling in England and was transported as a convict to Sydney under the name, Stephano Haskitt which he later changed to John Stanton. In 1819 Posic was given a 'ticket-of-leave'. He married an Irish woman, Mary Stanton, and they raised four children in Castle Hill near Sydney. The register at St John's Church in Parramatta records his name as Stefano Posich. He died in Sydney on 29 August 1861.[1]

George Dominick, born in Dalmatia, married an Irish woman, Mary Coffey, in Sydney on 7 April 1842. They had seven children. Dominick was previously a ship's carpenter on the barque, *Ann Gales*, that sailed between London and Sydney. He had a small vineyard in Sydney, but during the gold rush he moved with his family to Coolac near Gundagai. He pursued various occupations in Coolac and was a miner, farmer, vigneron and wine shopkeeper. He had the first vineyard in the Coolac district, made a variety of wines and opened a wine shop on Sydney Road, Coolac, where travellers could buy wine as well as have a meal. Also a successful miner, he employed men to work on his farm and in his mine.

George Dominick from Dalmatia, a pioneer of Coolac near Gundagai, New South Wales

Dominick died on 13 October 1888.[2] His grandson, Frederick Dominick, fought for Australia during the First World War and is commemorated on the Coolac War Memorial.

Early Croatian pioneer arrivals to Victoria include Matthew Florio from Bol on the island of Brač who arrived in 1848 and Joseph Postich from Volosko who arrived in 1849. Girollamo Florio from Bol, George Rismondo from Rovinj and Matthew Tripovich from Tivat in Kotor all arrived in Victoria in 1851. Croatian pioneers who arrived in Victoria in 1852 include Natale Starcevich from Kraljevica, Nicholas Tadich from the island of Vis, John Gobbie from the island of Korčula, Dominico Francovich from Dalmatia and Bartholomew Mercovich from Trpanj. There have also been Croatians living in South Australia, Queensland, Tasmania and Western Australia since the 1850s.

How many Croatian pioneers came to Australia?

Few Croatians had settled in Victoria prior to its establishment as a colony on 1 July 1851. However, the first wave of Croatian migration to Victoria took place that year, and was attributable to the discovery of gold. These Croatians arrived in Australia on ships (usually from England) or by deserting ships on which they served. By 1854 there were over 60 Croatian settlers in Victoria. Most were miners, working the goldfields with varying degrees of success. After the thrill – or disappointment – of the goldfields had worn off, many became seamen, labourers, fishermen, publicans and storekeepers. In 1861 the number of Croatians in Victoria was 151, in 1871 was 142, in 1881 was 172 and in 1891 was 178. In 1881, Victoria and New South Wales each had approximately 172 Croatians, followed in descending order by South Australia, Queensland, Tasmania and Western Australia.

By 1890 over 850 Croatians had settled in Australia. Of these, 180 arrived between 1840 and 1859; 186 between 1860 and 1869; 145 between 1870 and 1879; and 339 between 1880 and 1890. When it comes to the year of arrival, a number of inaccuracies have been identified, since if no arrival date was available, then the year the Croatian pioneer was first mentioned in records (mining records, newspaper articles, marriage certificates etc.) in Australia was used instead. Many Croatian pioneers first mentioned in records in Australia in the 1860s were gold miners who, in all probability, arrived in the 1850s. Similarly, some of the Croatians first mentioned in the 1880s actually came earlier. This number of over 850 Croatian settlers does not include the seamen who came for short visits to Australia; nor has the Australian-born generation been included in this number. Also not included in this count are Croatian pioneers who changed their surnames upon arrival from fear of being caught for deserting the ships on which they served, or who came during the early stages of the Victorian and New South Wales gold rushes where the records are incomplete, and have yet to be identified as Croatians.[3] The flow of Croatian immigrants was not evenly distributed and depended on the opportunities and economic conditions in Australia at the time. For example, the largest number of Croatian pioneers to settle in Victoria arrived in the ten years following the discovery of gold in Victoria in 1851 when Australia's population tripled. Fewer Croatians came in the 1870s. During most of this decade Victoria had a net negative migration (all nationalities). While 850 Croatian settlers up to 1890 is not an enormous number, their contribution to the development of Australia was significant in that they discovered goldfields, became successful businessmen, publicans and farmers.

The most detailed previous estimate of early Croatian settlers in Australia has been carried out by Price (1963) in his comprehensive study on Southern Europeans in Australia. He estimates that there were 250 Croatians in Australia in 1891, 720 in 1921 and 5020 in 1947. Croatians constituted 4.2 per cent of the Southern European population in 1891 which increased to 8.3 per cent by 1947. However, his estimate of 250 Croatians living in Australia in 1891 is too low. Careful examination of naturalisation records, marriage certificates, mining records and newspaper articles has revealed that at that time there were over 440 Croatians living in Australia. Price's estimate also gives us no indication of the Croatian population in Australia during the population explosion accompanying the Victorian gold rush. Price also claims that no Croatians settled in Victoria from the islands of Brač, Hvar and Vis prior to 1939. However, this claim appears to be unjustified since my research has shown that the islands of Brač and Hvar were areas of high migration from Croatia to Victoria prior to 1890. There were four times more Croatians in Victoria from the islands of Brač and Hvar prior to 1890 than Price estimated for the whole of Australia up to 1896. Similarly, Price underestimated the number of Croatians in Victoria from Rijeka up to 1896. In reality there were three times more Croatians in Victoria from Rijeka prior to 1890 than he estimated for Australia prior to 1939.[4]

In 1881 there were over 172 Croatians in Victoria, which, according to Victorian Census statistics, was a greater number than stated in the census from Greece, Spain, Portugal or Belgium. Croatian pioneers constituted one per cent of the Victorian population who were born in non-English-speaking regions of Europe.[5] Furthermore, they constituted between 53 and 71 per cent of the migrants in Victoria who had come from the Austro-Hungarian Empire. In 1882 the Austrian Consulate carried out a register or census of 108 people from the Austrian Empire living in Victoria, listing their names, birthplaces, occupations and where they lived. Included in this register were 77 Croatians (who constituted 71 per cent of the former Austrian subjects registered as living in Victoria). However, in 1882 there were an additional 95 Croatians living in Victoria who were not included in this register. Some of them lived in isolated locations so were missed. It seems reasonable to suggest that other Croatians who had not signed the register did not maintain contact with the Austrian Consulate.[6]

Origins and family background

Croatian settlers who came to Australia by 1890 came from the culturally rich coastal regions and islands of Croatia, especially from Dalmatia. Almost a third were born on islands chiefly from the islands of Brač, Lošinj and Hvar. In Victoria, New South Wales and South Australia, the largest number of these settlers came from the Rijeka/Bakar and Dubrovnik districts. They mainly came from small coastal towns and villages. The origins of those Croatians who settled in Australia by 1890 are shown in table 2. The birthplaces of all the individual Croatian pioneers can be found in appendix 1.

Town/Island	%	Town/Island	%
Istria (excluding Rovinj)	2.1	Split	1.2
Rovinj	3.5	Island of Šolta	0.2
Opatija/Volosko	1.7	Island of Brač	8.6
Rijeka/Bakar district	17.9	Island of Hvar	5.8
Island of Krk	2.9	Island of Vis	3.5
Island of Cres	1.2	Island of Korčula	1.4
Island of Lošinj	5.0	Island of Lopud	0.2
Island of Susak	0.2	Island of Mljet	0.6
Island of Unije	0.2	Island of Šipan	0.2
Island of Olib	0.4	Makarska/Omiš districts	1.2
Island of Premuda	0.2	Imotski district	0.4
Crikvenica/Novi Vinodolski	0.4	Baćina	0.2
Krivi Put/Otočac	0.6	Pelješac Peninsula	7.8
Island of Iž	0.4	Trnovica/Lisac/Majkovi	1.9
Zadar	0.8	Dubrovnik district	11.1
Island of Zlarin	1.4	Kotor district	5.1
Šibenik	0.4	Dalmatia unspecified	10.1
Trogir	0.4	Slavonia	0.8

Table 2: Origins of Croatian settlers as a percentage of the overall number that came to Australia by 1890

There seemed to be no clear chain migration pattern to Australia from Croatia except for a small group of settlers from the island of Brač and the Pelješac Peninsula. Between 1853 and 1857, four Croatian pioneers with the surname Lussich (Lukšić), who were born in Sutivan on the island of Brač, arrived in Victoria. Even though they had lived in various regions around Victoria, by 1881 most had settled in Portarlington. That same year another John Lussich had joined his relatives in Portarlington. He was born after the first four Lussichs had migrated to Victoria. Several years later in 1888, a Victor Lusic arrived in Victoria from Bombay and Jerome Lussick, who was born in Sutivan in 1874, arrived in Melbourne in 1890. The various Lussich families maintained close ties in Victoria: they were each other's marriage witnesses, children's baptism witnesses and they attended each

Map of Croatia showing the towns where the Croatian pioneers in Australia were born

other's funerals. In Victoria the Lussichs also associated with other Croatians from the island of Brač, including Mark Grussich, Paulo Arnerich, Pietro Jassich and Natale Vuscovich. Some of these Croatians may have been related. For example, Mark Grussich's (Marko Grušić also spelt Grubšić) mother's maiden name was Lussich, so he may have been related to the Lussichs living in Victoria. Mark Grussich lived in Geelong in the 1860s, where he had at least five children. During this period, John and Dominick Lussich also lived in Geelong and maintained contacts with him. The

Jerome Lussick in Geelong. Jerome Lussick is on the left side of the photograph and, according to his descendants, the older person on the right is a Lussich relative living in Victoria.

Lussichs in Victoria did not restrict their personal contacts to Croatians from their own region, they maintained contact with Croatians from as far south as Dubrovnik and Kotor, and as far north as Istria. The Lussich chain migration was not limited to one clan either, as there were Lussichs from the Imbre and Slavić clans.

I have discovered there were 53 documented cases where a brother, father or cousin followed his Croatian relative to Australia prior to 1890. There were even more cases where Croatian settlers had the same surname and were born in the same town in Croatia as other compatriots in Australia, so they may have also been related. There were several Margitichs (Margitić) from the Bakar district who settled across South Australia, Victoria and New South Wales before 1890, and whose occupations included a fisherman, miner, labourer, restaurateur and cabman. They all maintained ties with other Croatians in Australia and some lived within Croatian communities in Australia. On occasions, the Croatian pioneers' blood ties are not immediately obvious. For example, Seraphin Bersica (Serafin Beršić) and Taddeo Gamulin (Tadija Gamulin) were cousins who were born in Jelsa on the island of Hvar. Matteo Gargurevich (Mate Grgurević) and Matteo Cravarovich (Mate Kravarević) were also cousins, from Mokošica in Dubrovačka Rijeka. Both Gargurevich and Cravarovich were mining on different Victorian goldfields in the 1860s, but as yet we have no evidence that they were mining together.[7]

Croatian pioneers in Australia associated with Croatians from the whole coastal region of Croatia. The origins of the pioneers in the Croatian communities in Australia were not limited to particular towns or islands along the Croatian coast. The Croatians from southern Dalmatia mixed with Croatians from Istria in the north. Hence, Croatian migration to Australia prior to 1890 cannot be categorised solely under the classic 'campanilismo' migration theory often used by academics when analysing migrant settlement patterns and migration chains. 'Campanilismo' refers to attachment to one's bell tower or home town and the identity shared by the home town.[8] The settlement patterns of Croatian pioneers in Australia were more complex as they were also influenced by issues of national identity (other Croatians from further afield) not just those relating to local community or home town.

Croatian pioneers of Australia were descendants of Croatian families with long associations with the Croatian land, traditions and customs. As we have seen, they were not ethnic Austrians or Italians. Most of these Croatian families had lived in the same town or area for hundreds of years before the Croatian pioneers had migrated to Australia. For example, James Zibilich's (Jakov Cibilić) ancestors were recorded as fishermen in Duba on the Pelješac Peninsula as far back as 1504, while the Lussich (Lukšić) surname has been mentioned in Sutivan Catholic Church records on the island of Brač as far back as 1623.[9]

Most coastal Croatians in the first half of the nineteenth century were illiterate but versatile peasant farmers, seamen and fishermen and often also traders.[10] The majority of Croatian pioneers' fathers were farmers and vignerons who worked on the land, while over a quarter were sea captains and seamen. Other common occupations for their fathers were labourers and carpenters. Sometimes they were multi-skilled: Vincent Zarich's father was a shoemaker, but he also worked as a skipper, artist and labourer.[11] Even though farming was the primary occupation of most Croatian pioneers' fathers and brothers in Croatia, many had been seamen when they were younger. The families of two Croatian pioneers from the Pelješac Peninsula are used below to demonstrate their connection with seafaring. John Bundara (Ivan Bundara) and Antonio Bundara (Antun Bundara) were born in Žuljana on the Pelješac Peninsula and settled in Victoria in the 1860s. They were the two eldest of five male children of Kolendin Bundara. John Bundara was a seaman from approximately 1856 to 1858, before he arrived in Victoria from Liverpool in 1860. The other three male children of Kolendin Bundara who remained in Croatia were seamen for an average of seven years each.[12] Similarly, Paul Dominick (Pavao Domančić), who was born in Stankovići near Orebić on 30 March 1849, was a seaman from 1863 until his arrival in Victoria in 1874. He had at least three brothers who were seamen, each on average, for 21 years.[13]

Many Croatian pioneers brought valuable skills with them to Australia. Some Croatian pioneers who were seamen prior to arrival, worked as sea captains, sailors and fishermen in Australia. Others may have had experience in certain trades such as carpentry and stone masonry. Emilios Rossely was a carpenter in Victoria, like his father in Croatia. George Bathols (Jure Vidulić) was primarily a carpenter and labourer in Australia, but he also had stone mason experience that may have been acquired from his father who was a stone mason and carpenter in Croatia. As will be shown later, George Bathols crafted a small bluestone chest for a competition for the Melbourne International Exhibition of 1880. Some Croatian settlers who had experience as vignerons in Croatia found employment in wineries in Australia or established their own wineries.

Factors influencing migration

In the nineteenth century Croatians migrated for mainly economic reasons. There was not enough fertile land along the coast and rapid population growth placed added pressure on the limited resources and employment opportunities. Between 1840 and 1890, the population in Dalmatia increased by 32 per cent, rising from 399,000 to 527,000. However, this rapid population growth was not accompanied by parallel industrial development. There was a lack of capital investment in Croatia by the Austro-Hungarian regime; manufacturing industry in the cities was neglected and insufficient employment opportunities were created. Limitations were imposed on industrial development and on the fishing and shipping industries. All in all, migration offered a viable alternative to the very low wage of farm labourers.[14]

Over 80 per cent of the population along the Croatian coastline worked in agriculture, mostly in subsistence farming. The demise of the 'zadruga' or communal farm, together with the division of the father's estate among his sons and unmarried daughters, resulted in the size of the farms being reduced to smaller plots. The average holding of land was less than an acre and a half, which meant that the profit margins were extremely low. Moreover, the Austro-Hungarian regime did little to promote the use of modern agricultural methods to Croatian peasants which would have assisted in making farming more profitable.[15]

There were additional reasons for the depressed economic status of Croatia. The Austro-Hungarian regime deliberately designated Trieste (and to a lesser degree Rijeka) as a major port, due to its closer proximity to Vienna, a strategy which dramatically diverted trade and decreased the shipping industry along the rest of the Croatian coast. Moreover, the lack of capital investment made it impossible for this industry to make the transition from sail to steam, a transition which was taking place in other parts of the world at that time. The fishing industry was restricted by heavy taxes. Sir John Wilkinson, an English traveller visiting Trpanj on the Pelješac Peninsula in 1847, commented on how heavy duties on the salt restricted the fishing industry. He wrote:

> The quantity of fish caught for salting is very great, and the village purchases annually 35,000 florins worth of salt for this trade; which would be greatly increased, were it not for the heavy duties on that article. Salt, indeed, has always been subjected to a rigid monopoly in Dalmatia; it often led to serious disputes with other neighbouring states; and the exclusive privilege of selling it … has been scrupulously maintained by the Austrians.[16]

Avoiding military service also constituted a reason for Croatian migration. According to Emily Balch in *Our Slavic Fellow Citizens* (1910), 'Every man in Austria and Hungary must serve his three years, and he is forbidden to marry till after his liability to this service is past'.[17] Still other Croatians emigrated because of political and cultural repression under Austro-Hungarian rule. Although Dalmatia and Istria had their own parliaments under Austro-Hungarian rule, the overwhelming majority of the population was not allowed to vote. In Istria for example, only eight per cent of the population could vote. The extremely biased electoral system allowed the Italian minority (which constituted only 3.1 per cent of the population in Dalmatia in 1890) to acquire a majority in the Dalmatian parliament.[18] The Italians controlling the parliaments in Dalmatia and Istria concentrated on remaining in power rather than improving the economic situation of these regions. In Dalmatia and Istria, Croatians were constantly exposed to Italianisation; in inland Croatia they were exposed to Magyarisation and Germanisation under Austro-Hungarian rule. The Hungarians in particular attempted to impose the Hungarian language on Croatians.

The imposition of heavy taxes along with general economic neglect by the

Austro-Hungarian regime kept most Croatian peasants poor. Some Croatians opted for loans in an attempt to improve their situation, but these loans carried extremely high interest rates.[19] Many Croatians who were seamen or who had migrated sent back money to help their families in Croatia or to repay their loans. Some hoped to return one day as successful migrants who could buy land or open a small business.

As noted previously, before 1890 most Croatians migrated to the United States of America, while others migrated to South America, Australia, New Zealand, Canada and South Africa, with the lure of the gold rush being an obvious impetus in the decision of early Croatian pioneers to select Australia as a destination. News of success stories of Croatian migrants on the goldfields in California spread rapidly in Croatia. When gold was discovered in New South Wales and Victoria, many Croatians left for the goldfields hoping to have the same success as their lucky compatriots in California. News about the Australian gold rushes had reached Croatia through correspondence of Croatians serving on ships or adventurers visiting Australia. The brig, *Splendido*, under Ivan Visin and the barque, *Lorenza*, under Karlo Poščić – both Croatians – docked in Melbourne in the 1850s. Tomo Skalica's account of his visit to the New South Wales goldfields, which was published in the Croatian periodical, *Neven*, in 1856, may also have acted as an incentive for Croatians to migrate to Australia.

Yet other Croatian pioneers came to Australia as adventurers or to escape a scandal. One such person was Kosmos from Rijeka whose story is detailed in chapter 8. His father was an extremely wealthy man. However, Kosmos fell out of his father's favour after having a romantic affair in Paris. As a result of these problems Kosmos went to try his luck on the Victorian goldfields, with the hope of returning to his sweetheart a wealthy man.[20] Other Croatians came to join relatives or friends in Australia, who had described the excellent opportunities in Australia.

How the Croatian pioneers came to Australia

Croatian pioneers arrived in Australia on ships, usually from England. In contrast to many of the early British settlers who came as assisted passengers, Croatian pioneers served on the ships or they paid their own way. A typical sea vessel that brought migrants to Australia during the Victorian gold rush was the 1293-ton ship, *Queen of the East*. She embarked with 390 passengers from Liverpool on 15 June 1854, arriving in Melbourne three months later. Croatian pioneers who disembarked from the *Queen of the East* in Melbourne include Nicolo Baladinivinsh, Simon Chillivish, John Lussich, Guivani Perorish, Nicolo Perorish and John Vukasovich. Similarly, another ship from Liverpool, the *Morning Light*, arrived in Melbourne on 13 August 1859. Croatians among the passengers were Nicolo Gevirosick, Nicola Guovich, Nicolo Milderwick, Stephen Paulussy and Pietro Pandwick.[21] The Croatians who came as crew on ships and disembarked in Australian ports were either released from service or had deserted their ships. On 20 January 1865 George Bathols (Jure Vidulić) arrived in Port Melbourne as part of the crew on the steamship, *Golden Empire*, a 1218-ton steamship carrying around 320 passengers, which had departed from Liverpool a few months earlier. He had completed his service on this steamship.[22]

In the 1880s numerous vessels with Croatian captains and crew sailing under the Austrian flag arrived in Australia. As chapter 6 will demonstrate, on occasions Croatians from these vessels stayed in Australia. Naturalisation papers and death certificates reveal that, during the Victorian gold rush, many Croatians also came to Victoria overland from the nearby colonies of New South Wales and South Australia.

Statistics on Croatian pioneers and their family life

The physical characteristics of the Croatian pioneers in Australia are exceedingly difficult to pinpoint as there is very little documented evidence on these early settlers. The average height (albeit using a very small sample of 28) of Croatian pioneers in Australia was 173 cm and they typically had brown hair and brown or blue eyes. However, variations within this sample included light blue through to dark brown eyes, fair to dark hair, and fair to dark complexions. These physical characteristics are similar to those identified by Price using a larger sample (119) of Croatians from central Dalmatia who came to Australia between 1890 and 1940, where he found the average height of 177 cm. On average, these Croatians were slightly taller than their English counterparts whose average height was 171 cm.[23]

At the time of marriage, the average age of Croatian pioneers in Victoria was 34 years, while the average age for their wives was 26. For approximately a third of the marriages, the male partners were over ten years older than their wives and a fifth of the married Croatian pioneers had married widows. In the marriages that were not childless, the average number of children born was five. However, some families had a high mortality rate in keeping with society at large: Martin Pasquan had six children but only one survived past childhood.

The Croatian pioneers who were married in Victoria were usually married according to Roman Catholic rites (59 per cent). The breakdown of the religious denomination of the other Croatian pioneer marriages are: Church of England (11 per cent), Presbyterian (10 per cent), Methodist (7 per cent), register of marriages (7 per cent) and other denominations (6 per cent). Most Croatian pioneers married women of Irish, English or Scottish descent. Their wives were born in Ireland (30 per cent), Victoria (26 per cent), England (24 per cent), other Australian colonies (7 per cent), Scotland (6 per cent), Croatia (2 per cent) and other European countries (5 per cent). Because so few Croatian women came to Australia prior to 1890, only 2 per cent of Croatian pioneers had Croatian wives.

The average age of Croatian pioneers in Australia at the time of death was

63 years, which, according to the 1871 Victorian Census was several years higher than the life expectancy of Victorian males. The number of years Croatian pioneers lived in Australia before they were naturalised varied significantly from two to 67 years. It is possible that many Croatian pioneers were not naturalised early as they were undecided whether or not they would be permanent settlers. Some were transient migrants and moved on to other settler countries like New Zealand, or as was more common for Croatian settlers in the United States, they returned to Croatia after working overseas for several years.

Antonio Wolfe (Ante Vuković) from Dubrovnik with four of his children. He arrived in 1852 and was a gold miner in the Tumbarumba district in New South Wales

CHAPTER 3

Patterns of Early Croatian Settlement

Croatian pioneers settled across Australia, the majority establishing themselves in Victoria and New South Wales. In the Victorian gold mining districts, their main settlements were at Wedderburn, Inglewood, Epsom, Redcastle, Crooked River, Maryborough, Daylesford, Yandoit, Buckland, Woods Point, Ballarat and Bendigo, where many of them tried their luck at various goldfields before settling in Melbourne – about a third of all the Croatian pioneers in Victoria finally ended up in Melbourne. There were also settlements of Croatians in Portarlington and Geelong. A number of Croatian settlers moved to the New Zealand goldfields or other Australian colonies after spending time on the Victorian goldfields to which some of them subsequently returned.

Croatian settlements in the various colonies of Australia are considered in this chapter, with particular emphasis on those in Victoria, since most of the Croatian pioneers settled there, while others lived for some time in Victoria before moving to other states.

Croatian settlements across Victoria

For the purposes of this study Victoria is divided into seven geographical districts or areas. These districts are as follows:
- Geelong, Portarlington and Western district
- Melbourne and surrounding district
- Castlemaine district
- Wedderburn and Inglewood district
- Ballarat, Maryborough and Bendigo district
- Redcastle, Costerfield and Goulburn Valley district
- North-eastern Victoria, Woods Point and Gippsland district.

All but the Melbourne and the Geelong, Portarlington and Western districts were principally gold mining areas. This chapter provides a general overview of the occupations and numbers of Croatian pioneers within these regions and other regions of Australia.

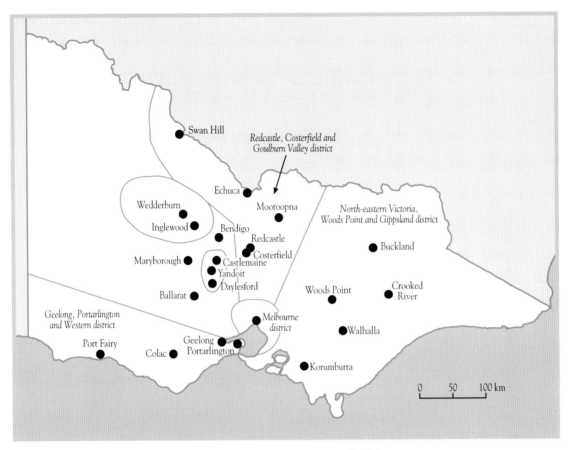

Map of Victoria showing the seven geographical districts

Melbourne and Geelong were already established towns when gold was discovered in Victoria. In 1851 Victoria's population was about half that of New South Wales, but within a few years, with people flocking to the Victorian goldfields, its population exceeded that of New South Wales. The main towns on the Victorian goldfields were Ballarat, Bendigo (formerly Sandhurst) and Castlemaine (formerly Mount Alexander). Ballarat was the first to attract worldwide attention, but Bendigo became known as 'The Golden City'. Bendigo produced more gold than anywhere else in Victoria, but the majority of the gold was extracted from deep quartz mines. Most of Castlemaine's gold was alluvial, so once the deposits were worked out, the town was no longer a significant gold mining centre. Other important gold mining areas in Victoria include Beechworth, Walhalla, Maryborough, Wedderburn, Stawell and Creswick.

Between 1853 and 1861 Australia produced one-third of the world's gold, creating enormous wealth in Victoria, particularly in Melbourne, a situation which obviously had a huge impact on the development and growth of the city. In 1861, Melbourne with 123,000 residents was Victoria's largest town followed by Geelong (23,000) and the mining towns of Ballarat (22,000), Bendigo (13,000) and Castlemaine-Chewton

(13,000). Several other mining towns, including Creswick, Maldon, Inglewood, Maryborough, Beechworth and Amherst had populations of between 2000 and 5000. The three Western ports and Kyneton also had populations of over 2000. But by the end of the decade, Ballarat and Bendigo had surpassed Geelong's population. In 1871 the populations of the four main towns in Victoria were 191,450 in Melbourne, 28,600 in Bendigo, 27,200 in Ballarat and 21,500 in Geelong.[1]

Geelong, Portarlington and Western district

The first sales of Geelong town allotments were made in 1839. The following year, *The Geelong Advertiser*, regional Victoria's oldest morning newspaper, was first published and the first ship loaded with wool left Geelong for London. In 1849 the town of Geelong was incorporated, so by the time the first three Croatians were married in Geelong in 1852, it was an active town. Australia's first country railway (Geelong to Melbourne) was built in 1857. Geelong was a major wool sales and wool exporting centre in the nineteenth century.

The Geelong, Portarlington and Western district Croatian community in the 1850s was centred in Geelong. Most of the Croatian pioneers in Geelong were involved in the fishing or shipping industries. They were captains of ships, fishermen, sailors and they also used their boats to rescue drowning people as will be described in chapter 6. Some later changed their professions: Fortunato Poschich became a successful greengrocer in Geelong and Vincent Florio had a marine store. Most of these Croatians came from the island of Brač, but others came from the Rijeka district. About ten Croatian pioneers made Geelong their permanent home, but others had lived in, or visited Geelong occasionally for specific purposes. Croatians in other parts of the district, such as Portarlington and Port Fairy, maintained links with St Mary's Catholic Church, Geelong, while some others visited Geelong from the Steiglitz goldfields, 38 kilometres away. For example, Bartholomew Mercovich who was mining at Steiglitz had his daughter baptised in St Mary's Catholic Church Geelong on 21 February 1859.[2]

Portarlington was a small seaport town from which growers in the district could transport their products to Melbourne or Geelong. But Portarlington was also known for being a recreational and tourist town where visitors enjoyed the sandy beach, sea bathing, gardens and beautiful scenery. The surrounding countryside was agricultural. In 1879 the population of Portarlington numbered about 300 persons.[3]

In the early 1870s Croatians began to settle in Portarlington, the first five Croatian settlers having arrived in Australia in the 1850s. In 1882 there were at least ten Croatian pioneers living in the township.[4] Croatian pioneers continued to migrate to Portarlington from Croatia and other parts of Victoria, and by 1890, at least 19 Croatian pioneers had lived and established a Croatian community there. Some had previously lived in Geelong so they maintained ties with Croatian relatives and friends in that town, and they also had links with Croatian fishermen elsewhere in Victoria. In Portarlington all of the Croatians at some stage were involved in the fishing industry.

The early Croatian migrants in Portarlington came from various regions along the Croatian coast, a third being from the island of Brač. In Portarlington there were six Croatians from the island of Brač, three from the Pelješac Peninsula, one from Split, one from Dalmatia, one from the island of Zlarin, three from Bakar, two from Plomin in Istria, one from the island of Lošinj and one from the island of Susak. A number of Croatians in the Portarlington community had many and close contacts with other

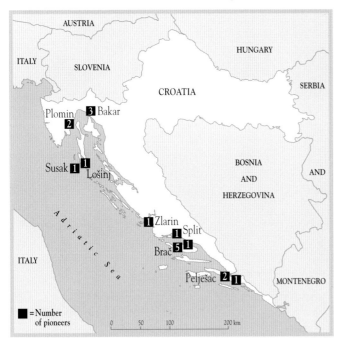

Map of Croatia showing where the Portarlington Croatians were born

Croatians in Victoria, some of whom were born as far south as Dubrovnik and as far north as Istria. Croatian pioneers in Australia had established links with other Croatian pioneers from the whole Croatian coastline. Thus, it is obvious that these Croatian pioneers were bound together by more than just their village of origin. There is evidence that John Lussich, for example, had connections with another 21 Croatians in Victoria, while Gregory Pavletich had connections with another 16 (these connections will be described in chapter 4). However, the actual number of close contacts with other Croatians would probably have been higher, as there were other Croatians living in Portarlington at the time. A group of four Croatians from Račišče on the island of Korčula came to Portarlington after 1907 and became involved in the Croatian pioneer community. One married a Croatian pioneer's daughter, and Jerome Florio, the son of a Croatian pioneer from Geelong, worked as a fisherman with the Portarlington Croatians.

Even though the Portarlington Croatian community consisted of only 19 pioneers (five per cent of the Portarlington population), their presence was felt in town, as they were all fishermen, they lived near each other and their children all attended the same school. *The Geelong Advertiser* in the 1880s and 1890s referred to most of the fishermen in Portarlington as 'foreigners'. Careful examination of the Portarlington rate books reveals that almost all of these were actually Croatian.[5] The Croatian fishermen in Portarlington contributed significantly to the Portarlington fishing industry at the time as chapter 6 will demonstrate.

Although fishing was the primary source of income for most of the Portarlington Croatians, some also worked as farmers and labourers or leased out properties to supplement their income. Natale Lussich had become extremely prosperous in Portarlington, but due to failing health he had to leave Victoria (possibly to return to Croatia). On 10 January 1884 all of his property went on sale by auction. Part of the advertisement in *The Geelong Advertiser* reads as follows:

> The whole of his valuable property, consisting of – allotment of land in Newcombe Street, nearly opposite the jetty, and close to the Park, upon which is erected a Milliner's shop and ladies' waiting room; also a cottage of three rooms, now used as a hairdressing establishment, both doing a capital business. A large underground water tank. One first class mare with filly at foot by Landsman, and in foal to Baron of Glenlee, together with dray, and a splendid set of cart harness, Also, three allotments of land fronting Clare Street and the Esplanade, opposite the baths. These properties being some of the most valuable in the township, and the owner being about to leave the colony through ill-health, has fully resolved to dispose of the same.[6]

Other Croatians who had lived on Newcombe Street include John Lekovich, Dominick Lussich and Gregory Pavletich.[7] Natale Lussich was previously a successful miner in the Redcastle and Costerfield Croatian communities where he made a small fortune. Several Croatians in the Geelong and Portarlington communities had previously been miners with Croatian partners on goldfields. The Portarlington Croatians maintained links with various Catholic churches in the district. They were family men; they married and raised children. In Portarlington there lived at least 22 Croatians prior to the First World War. Almost half of these Croatians left Portarlington and went to live in Melbourne, although Croatians from Melbourne also visited Portarlington. Later chapters will present more details on some of the Croatians (including Dominick Lussich, Natale Lussich, Natale Vuscovich and Joseph Zagabria) who lived in Portarlington. In Port Fairy there were a couple of Croatian fishermen, Natale Vuscovich and Andrew Radoslovich, who maintained many links with the Portarlington Croatian community. More information about these two will also be given later in this account.

Croatian pioneers also lived in inland regions of this district, areas such as Colac and Casterton. Unlike the Croatians who lived in coastal towns of western Victoria, Croatians in Colac and Casterton were principally labourers, an example being Matthew Tripovich (Mate Tripović), who was born in Tivat Kotor. He arrived in Victoria in 1851 on the ship *Agnes* from Liverpool. After spending time on the goldfields he settled in Colac where he worked as a labourer.[8] John Monkivitch (Ivan Monković) who was born in Dubrovnik in about 1845, owned 150 acres at Barongarook near Colac. His occupations were timber cutter, carter and labourer.

Both these pioneers married and raised families in Colac. Some of John Monkivitch's descendants maintained a successful butcher shop in Colac for many years.[9] In the 1970s, Matthew Tripovich's grandson, John Tripovich, was a prominent parliamentarian in the Australian Labor Party.

Melbourne and surrounding district

The wealth of Victorian gold had transformed Melbourne into a dynamic metropolis, 'Marvellous Melbourne', bigger than Sydney, and the undisputed financial capital of Australia. Many splendid public buildings were built from money earned through gold mining. The era from 1851 to 1890 came to be known as the 'Golden Age'. The Exhibition Buildings stand today as one of the monuments of the 'Golden Age', its great dome a symbol of the confidence and wealth of the city. Other buildings from the 'Golden Age' include Parliament House, cathedrals, Government House, Old Treasury buildings and the Princess Theatre. By the 1880s, land in Melbourne was booming, with rapid city expansion which saw the trebling of housing construction in Melbourne. However, by 1891 the boom was over and a devastating depression had begun.[10] Melbourne's population decreased between 1854 and 1857 from 45,250 to 29,100 as many residents left for the goldfields. In 1861 the population was 123,000 and increased to 191,450 in 1871. During Melbourne's boom the population increased from 262,400 in 1881 to 474,400 in 1891. As a result of the 1890s depression the population of Melbourne increased by less than 10,000 between 1891 and 1901.[11]

Over 130 Croatians had settled in Melbourne and the surrounding district between 1851 and 1890. Some had been gold miners on the Victorian goldfields before settling in Melbourne. Unlike other Croatian gold-seeking hopefuls, most Croatian pioneers who settled in Melbourne came in the 1870s and 1880s rather than in the 1850s and 1860s. In Melbourne, the highest concentration of Croatian pioneers was in South Melbourne (formerly Emerald Hill); other important areas include Carlton, Brunswick, Footscray and North Melbourne (formerly Hotham). Their main occupations in descending order were seamen, labourers, publicans, restaurateurs, fruiterers and fishermen. In Melbourne many Croatian pioneers were labourers for only a short period before they established their own businesses. An example of a Croatian working his way up was Thomas Zuzulich (Tomislav Cuculić) who was born in Kukuljanovo near Bakar on 11 December 1856. He arrived in Melbourne in 1883 and initially worked as a labourer.[12] From 1892 onwards he lived on Edward Street, Brunswick. In 1898 he had a ham and beef shop at 166 Sydney Road, Brunswick, and from 1911 onwards he had a coffee stall on the same road.

In South Melbourne most Croatian pioneers were seamen. Due to the higher concentration of Croatians in South Melbourne, Croatians had restaurants and dining rooms in the area. In the early 1890s Frank Cucel managed dining rooms at 63 Clarendon Street, South Melbourne. His friends, Margitich, Musich and Pavletich, managed a restaurant close by at 88 to 92 Moray Street, South Melbourne. Cucel later had a restaurant at Murray Street, Perth. Croatian pioneers lived in South Melbourne from the 1860s until after the First World War. Victor Lusic married Julia Hurley at St Joseph's Catholic Church, Port Melbourne, on 19 January 1893. Their marriage witnesses were the Croatian Paul Dominick and his wife Lucy, who also lived in South Melbourne.[13] Croatian pioneers who lived in South Melbourne mixed with Croatian settlers from different parts of Croatia who arrived at a later date. For example, Joseph Lucich, who was born in Opatija and arrived in Victoria in 1862, was friends with Samuel Pulisic (Pulišić) from Labin in Istria who arrived in Melbourne 42 years later and married Lucich's stepdaughter. After Lucich's death on 14 August 1918, Pulisic continued to live in his home at 77 Gladstone Street, South Melbourne.[14] Some South Melbourne Croatian pioneers moved to other suburbs, such as Brunswick and Richmond, while others left Melbourne to join Croatian friends in other parts of Australia. For example, Jacob Stiglich moved to Korumburra to join his friend Antonio Radovick while a couple went to Western Australia to start new businesses.

The Croatian pioneer Matthew Beovich once said to his son, the future Archbishop of Adelaide, 'Whatever you do, make sure you work for yourself'.[15] Croatian pioneers opened small businesses, had their own fishing boats and gold mines, suggesting they enjoyed having the independence associated with being self-employed. Some of the businesses managed by Croatians in Melbourne in the 1850s and 1860s include boarding houses and fruit shops. Thomas Pavletich (Tomislav Pavletić), who was baptised in Bakar on 9 December 1821, arrived in Victoria in 1853. From 1856 to 1858 Pavletich managed a boarding house at 45 Little Bourke Street and in 1859 managed a similar establishment at 219 and 221 Bourke Street. A couple of years later he was a general dealer and lived in Faraday Street, Carlton. John Gasparo (Ivan Gašper) who was born in Selca on the island of Brač, managed a boarding house at 232 Lonsdale Street from 1865 to 1869.[16]

An early Croatian arrival to Victoria was George Rismondo (Jure Rismondo) who was born in Rovinj and arrived in Australia in 1851. From 1859 to 1863 Rismondo was a fruiterer on Leveson Street, North Melbourne, subsequently becoming a fruiterer at 172 King Street and then at Sandridge Road, South Melbourne. In 1871 he ran a restaurant at 170 Elizabeth Street. From 1873 to 1877 Rismondo managed the Criterion restaurant situated at 134 Bourke Street. In 1877 he made a short visit to Europe. In the early 1880s Rismondo lived at 213 Bourke Street and was a restaurant keeper before he returned to Rovinj.[17]

From 1879 to 1885 Matteo Gargurevich had various businesses on Napier Street, Fitzroy, such as a grocer shop and woodyard business, hay and corn store. For the next decade Gargurevich was a grocer and provision dealer at 495 Lygon Street, North Carlton. In the years 1889 to 1892, he was also a fruiterer and greengrocer at 111 Victoria Market building near Queen Street. Later, Matthew Beovich, John Cucel and Victor Lusic were fruiterers at Eastern Market, Bourke Street.[18]

It is worth mentioning more details on Matthew Beovich (Mate Beović) who was born in Supetar on the island of Brač on 14 December 1861 and arrived in Victoria from Hong Kong in 1884. In St Francis Catholic Church, Melbourne on 26 April 1893 Beovich married Elizabeth Kenny. They had four children and Croatians were godparents to three of them. Matthew Beovich's marriage witness was a fellow Croatian, Vincent Zan (Zaninović). Beovich also maintained contacts with Buzolich, Lusic, Mercovich and Radich. Originally he was a caterer and had his own restaurant in Melbourne, but he was a fruiterer from 1895 until his death on 2 July 1933. Matthew Beovich died while assisting at Sunday Mass.[19] Beovich's family were devout Catholics – his son later became the Catholic Archbishop of Adelaide while his daughter Vera became a nun.

Some Croatian pioneers were entrepreneurs. Antonio Buzolich (Buzolić) was a miner, shipwright, publican and was involved in other businesses, including the Buzolich Patent Damp Resisting and Anti-Fouling Paint Company Limited and Buzolich hat shops. The Buzolich family sales logo was 'Buzolich's HATS look well ahead'. Other Croatians incorporated their names into their businesses' names. Martin Pasquan (Martin Paškvan) had dining rooms called Pasquan's Hotel at 60 Bourke Street in 1888. Previously he managed hotels in several locations in Melbourne.[20] In the 1880s John Terdich (Ivan Terdić) managed Tardy's [Terdich] Railway Dining Rooms on Little Collins Street. The following decade Vincent Zan (Zaninović) established the Zan Bros & Co. broom manufacturing business at 43 Capel Street, North Melbourne. Other occupations of Croatian pioneers in Melbourne include: storekeeper, fish and oyster saloon keeper, sawdust merchant, sack merchant, wood and coal merchant, builder, carpenter, tobacconist, cabdriver, barman and brick burner.

Prior to 1900 there were 19 Croatian fishmongers in Melbourne and Sydney. Some were fishmongers on currently well-known streets in Melbourne such as Martin Pavletich's business at 186 Chapel Street, Prahran, and John Radich's business at 390 Lygon Street, Carlton.[21] Radich was married to Eliza Duffy in St Brigid's Catholic Church in North Fitzroy in 1888. The marriage witness was Bartholomew Mercovich's son, Anthony. Radich had a brother Peter who also came to Australia.[22] Croatians also had oyster saloons in Sydney, Melbourne, Brisbane, Fremantle and Port Fairy.

In the 1880s and 1890s, the majority (59 per cent) of Melbourne householders were renting. At this time a number of Croatian pioneers in Melbourne, Sydney and Adelaide were highly mobile which suggests they were probably also renting their homes. For example, Paul Dominick (Pavao Domančić) moved eight times in South Melbourne in a 15-year period between 1896 and 1911. From his arrival in Victoria in 1874 to his death on 11 November 1923 he had moved at least 20 times in Melbourne. Others, such as publicans, were mobile because they were managing different hotels. However, from will and probate records we do know that many Croatian pioneers purchased their homes in Melbourne.[23]

Matthew Beovich's wedding day in 1893

Matthew Beovich together with his wife and two eldest children in about 1899.
His son on the left side later became the Catholic Archbishop of Adelaide

John Radich with his family

Paul Dominick with his family in about 1896

Most of Melbourne's seafaring Croatian pioneers were sailors rather than fishermen. However, there was a Croatian fishing community in Sandringham while other Croatian fishermen worked out of Dromana, Rosebud and Hastings. In outlying areas of Melbourne, such as Ringwood and Burwood, the Croatians were farmers and fruit growers. Sandringham, Ringwood and Burwood have since become suburbs of Melbourne.

Today there are many descendants of the Melbourne Croatian pioneers who have retained Croatian surnames living in Melbourne. Streets named after Croatian pioneers or their descendants include Tripovich, De Murska and Bundara Streets. By contrast, in Spearwood, Western Australia there are 28 streets and ten parks named after Croatians who lived in Spearwood in the first half of the twentieth century. Croatian pioneers' surnames are inscribed on tombstones – some like Antonio Radovick's are very impressive – in various cemeteries in Melbourne. There were at least 25 Croatian pioneers buried in Melbourne General Cemetery, of whom 11 have tombstones with their names inscribed on them.[24]

In 1889 the Croatian traveller, Pavle Vidas, described his first impressions of Melbourne:

It is a respectable and clean city. We are staying there for one day so we proceed to the city. In the city the buildings are large and beautiful, and the top of the Post Office was like a balloon, and that balloon is electrically lit up and the whole city glows in the night, just like it is day. All of the people there are clean and healthy and living there were also our Croatians. When we entered the city in the steamship all of the people were staring at us and at the strapped sandals that some of the Banovci or Bunjevci [Croatians] were wearing. We then went to a pub where English women courteously serve and make conversation sweet as honey while you spend, but when you stop spending they then will not even look at you … Thus, these Banovci stayed in Melbourne, as they had met a Croatian, who had found them a job somewhere to saw wood, so we parted. I then departed on the same steamship for Sydney in New South Wales and arrived there safely. I had with me a companion, also from Hreljin, and together we went with the steamship to the shore and then into the town of Sydney. Sydney is a large city, but is not cleaner or more beautiful than Melbourne. Sydney is covered with more vegetation.

Pavle Vidas later found work in a vineyard in Lilydale near Melbourne. A Scotsman called Fulton owned the vineyard and had the best land in Lilydale. He was a widower and had two daughters. As Fulton was not at home, his older daughter gave Vidas the job. The next day they went to work, cleaning and pruning vines, and in the afternoon the landowner turned up. Fulton's daughter told him that they had hired a workman, then he called Vidas and asked rudely:

'what countryman are you?,' and I tell him that I am Croatian. However, as he did not know of that I told him that I was Austrian. Good, he tells me and along the way he asked me if I readily drink wine. I replied to him that I drink a little, as his older daughter behind his back shook her head so that I do not say a great deal. This landowner was a big drunk, however, he told me he had enough property and money so that he lived off the interest and drank. Disgustingly he never gave his daughters any money for them to buy anything, but they secretly sold wine from the cellar and they spent this money on themselves.

Fulton would always go to town and to Melbourne to drink where he would get arrested for drunkenness. When he was arrested in town Vidas would be sent by the daughters to bail him out. When drunk, Fulton would yell and swear, calling his daughters disgusting names. Vidas could not tolerate this drunk landowner any more so he resigned which surprised Fulton. 'When I told him [about the resignation], he gets angry and asks, why am I not at all afraid of him, so I tell him: "I am from that place where the people are not afraid of anyone on earth, even the dead". Whereupon he pays me my wage and goes off to Melbourne.'[25]

Castlemaine district

The main concentration of permanent Croatian settlers in the Castlemaine district was in Yandoit. Today Yandoit is no longer a gold mining town and only a few houses remain where once the town stood. Croatians lived in this area from the late 1850s, with at least 12 Croatian pioneers settling here.[26] Some of them had mined on other goldfields before settling in Yandoit. All the Croatian pioneers in Yandoit had been miners at some stage; however, many of them turned to farming later in life when gold mining became less profitable. This Croatian community was tight-knit and family-oriented and they maintained considerable contact between one another through the 1860s to 1880s. They had combined mining claims and attended various functions together and Croatian pioneers and their children owned properties close to each other. For example, Antonio Pavich had one property which was across the road from Mark Busanich's property and another property nearby; Thomas Mavorvitch had a property nearby and Mark Belanich had two properties which were bordered by Peter Mavorvitch's properties.[27] The Croatian pioneers in Yandoit maintained links with St Mary's Catholic Church in Castlemaine and most were buried in Sandon Catholic Cemetery. They also supported the wider community by signing petitions to improve conditions at the local school.[28]

The Croatians who had taken up residence in Yandoit came from different parts of the Croatian coast. For example, Antonio Passalick was born on the island of Vis to the south, while Giovanni Ivanussich was born in Brseč in Istria. A typical Croatian pioneer in Yandoit was Antonio Pavich (Ante Pavić), who was born on the island of Zlarin. He arrived in Victoria in 1854 on the ship *Mercy* from London.[29] Pavich was married twice in St Mary's Catholic Church in Castlemaine. In 1862 he married an Irish woman, Mary Hayes, in St Mary's Catholic Church and they had eight children. The witness to the marriage was a fellow Croatian, James Pollich. Pavich who was a miner in Yandoit kept in close contact with other Croatians in Yandoit. In the 1860s he was the godparent to three of Antonio Passalick's children who were baptised in St Mary's Church.[30] Pavich attended Mark Busanich's funeral along with three other Croatians. Similarly, when Giovanni Ivanussich was buried in the Sandon Catholic Cemetery on 9 February 1894, he was the burial witness.[31] Giovanni Ivanussich left all his assets in Brseč, Croatia and Australia to his relative from Croatia, Antonio Ivanussich, who lived in Western Australia. After Pavich's wife died he married Mark Belanich's widow. Pavich died in Yandoit on 29 January 1909 and was buried in the Sandon Catholic Cemetery.[32]

The Mount Alexander goldfields, where the town of Castlemaine was later established, was an important goldfield in the 1850s. During the gold rush there were Croatian pioneers in Castlemaine, most of whom were miners, although some were involved in businesses apart from mining. For example, in March 1856 Giuseppe B who was born in Dalmatia, worked as an assistant in a beer brewing business next to the highway in Castlemaine.[33] In the early 1860s Thomas Pavletich managed the Universal Boarding House located on Lyttleton Street, Castlemaine. In 1862 or 1863 he moved to Dunedin, New Zealand, with his wife and two children during the Otago gold rush. Later, he named his hotel in Dunedin, the Universal Hotel.[34] In 1890 Joseph Marich (Josip Marić) helped revive mining activities in Taradale by establishing the Victoria Junction Gold Mining Company. As an experienced and trusted mine manager, he helped convince investors to invest into his proposed company, which later proved to be successful.[35] In contrast to the Yandoit Croatian community where most of the Croatian pioneers remained for the rest of their lives, the Castlemaine and Daylesford Croatians usually moved on.

Near the end of 1853, Seweryn Korzelinski, a Polish patriot, and his gold mining party camped at the Jim Crow diggings near Daylesford. They set up their tents on top of a hill between two deep gullies. Korzelinski wrote in his diary that around them

Antonio Pavich standing in the doorway of his miner's hut on the Victorian goldfields with his son on the bicycle

A cartoon drawn in around 1865 depicting life at Matteo Benussi's Star and Garter Hotel and on the goldfields

were the tents of 'Dalmatians, Italians, French – mainly from Mauritius . . . further on Swiss, Spanish and Germans'.[36] In gold mining circles it seems Croatians from Dalmatia were known as a distinct group, separate from Austrians or Italians. Another group of 11 Croatian miners lived in the Daylesford area. Some of these later became storekeepers, bakers and publicans. Matteo Benussi (Mate Benussi) who was born in Rovinj in 1832, was involved in various businesses in Daylesford while still pursuing mining activities. From 1854 he mined at various goldfields such as Yandoit, Fryer's Creek, Bendigo, Muckleford, Sebastopol, Jim Crow Diggings and Dry Diggings, Daylesford. Benussi married an English woman and they had nine children. He was one of the more prominent and successful Croatians of the area. In 1859 Benussi purchased the Wombat Flat Bakery in King Street, Daylesford and he was the licensee of the Star and Garter Hotel in 1865. In 1866 he sold the bakery which traded under the name, Benussi and Company. He then worked as a miner for around a year. Subsequently, Benussi ran a bakery and cake shop until 1893, before he sold these premises and moved to Geelong to live with one of his sons. Matteo Benussi was also the Grand Master of the Loyal Hand of Friendship Lodge in Daylesford in 1877 and 1886. He died at Noble Street, Geelong, on 16 December 1896.[37]

Wedderburn and Inglewood district

The Wedderburn district is famous for the numerous gold nuggets found there. In fact Croatians were amongst those who found nuggets – and became very wealthy. In the early 1860s Croatian pioneers owned quartz claims in the Inglewood mining district – a couple had 'Slavonia' in their names. There were over 38 Croatian miners in the Wedderburn and Inglewood district. Some of these miners later had their own small wineries on the southern side of Wedderburn when the gold became scarce. Most of the Croatian pioneers in the Wedderburn and Inglewood district remained bachelors, while others who married had no descendants. With very few descendants in this district, the Croatian pioneers' presence in the area was completely forgotten after their deaths. Many bachelor Croatians lived a lonely existence as they became older and some resorted to heavy drinking.

Most of the Croatian pioneers of Wedderburn lived on the southern side of town, on or near the Wedderburn to Kingower Road, owning about a third of the properties in this area. Other Croatians also lived in southern Wedderburn, but did not own land. In southern Wedderburn, the Croatian pioneers, Ignatio Billich, Stefano Celovich, Andrew Petrasich, Antonio Petrasich, W. Petrasich (Vid Mlican), A. Petrosich, Thomas Rossi and John Volich, all had properties near each other. Many Croatians were neighbours, for example: W. Petrasich was A. Petrasich's neighbour; Thomas Rossi's property was neighbouring Stefano Celovich's and Ignatio Billich's properties. Two of John Volich's properties bordered one of the Rossi family properties.[38] The Wedderburn Croatian community consisted of Croatians from

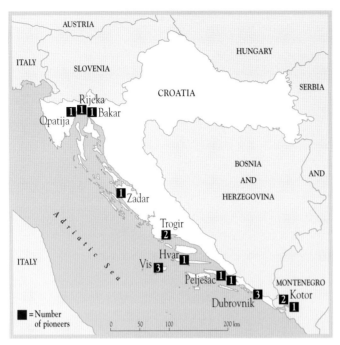

Map of Croatia showing where the Wedderburn Croatians were born

different regions of the Croatian coast.[39]

An example of a Wedderburn Croatian was Antonio Petrasich (Ante Petrašić) who was born in Komiža on the island of Vis. He arrived in Victoria in 1863 on the ship *Laurenzo* from Trieste. Up to 1895 Petrasich had various mining claims in the Wedderburn area. He was unmarried, and by the 1890s he had a small vineyard on his property on the southern side of Wedderburn. Antonio Petrasich died on 17 December 1911 and was buried in the Catholic section of the Wedderburn Cemetery. Prior to his death he had a two-roomed hut on his land and his nephew, Andrew Petrasich, lived with him.[40]

Dalmatian Road near McIntyre named after Croatian pioneers

Gregory Ferentza

McIntyre and Moliagul were important areas of Croatian mining activity, especially between 1877 and 1881. During this period two mining companies were formed by Croatians – the Dalmatia Gold Mining Company and the Maximilian Gold Mining Company – which mined two deep shafts in the area. Due to flooding problems these mines were closed before any real profit could be made. Today, Dalma*tian* Road, Dalma*tion* Road and Dalma*tion* Springs are reminders of the Croatian presence in this area.

Croatian pioneers also lived in other nearby mining towns, such as Dunolly, Waanyarra, St Arnaud and Stuart Mill. However, these Croatians had no surviving biological descendants; for example, Gregorio Ferentza (Grgur Ferenca) who was born in Trpanj on the Pelješac Peninsula came to Victoria in 1854 on the Croatian brigantine *Splendido* from Callao, Peru. Initially he was a miner, but in the 1870s he selected land in the Stuart Mill area and began farming. In 1885 Ferentza married a widow, who had ten children, in St Patrick's Roman Catholic Church, St Arnaud. He died on 23 April 1904 without leaving any children of his own. There were also two Croatians who settled in the Charlton area.[41]

Ballarat, Maryborough and Bendigo district

Ballarat was one of the richest alluvial goldfields ever discovered in the world, its eventual output exceeding 750 tons. This enormous wealth was reflected in such impressive buildings of the city as St Patrick's Catholic Cathedral, Ballarat City Hall, Post Office and the railway station. There were hundreds of hotels in the district. The Ballarat district was also the scene of the Eureka Stockade rebellion in 1854 where miners clashed with police. At its gold mining peak in 1868, the Ballarat goldfield supported a population of 64,000 and 300 mining companies. However, a recession soon afterwards caused a dramatic decrease in population. By the late 1860s the shallow deposits were exhausted. Companies were then formed to extract gold from deep quartz mines. Ballarat's richest mine (and Victoria's second richest mine), the Band of Hope and Albion Consols mine, produced approximately 740,746 ounces (22.5 tons) of gold between 1868 and 1908.[42]

There were at least 38 Croatian pioneers living in Ballarat or surrounding mining towns such as Buninyong, Creswick, Clunes, Blackwood, Smythesdale and Steiglitz. Over half of the Ballarat Croatians eventually moved onto other goldfields. A miner who remained in the Ballarat area for his entire life was Vincent Gercovich (Vicko Jerković) who was born in Starigrad on the island of Hvar on 5 October 1834. He came to Victoria on 12 April 1860 and he had various occupations in the Ballarat district, such as wood carter, woodsplitter, miner, labourer and tollgate keeper. He married an English woman and they had a large family. Gercovich died on 7 August 1900 and 11 of his 12 children outlived him.[43] Other Croatians in the area were primarily miners, such as Luke Sellovich who arrived in Australia in about 1855. He

Vincent Gercovich with his wife and 11 of his children

lived in South Australia for two years and the rest of the time in Victoria. Sellovich had mined in various goldfields such as Epsom, Cockatoo, Alma and Ballarat. He married an English woman, Elizabeth Dingle, and they had five children. Luke

Vincent Gercovich

Sellovich died on 26 November 1885 and was buried in the Ballarat Cemetery.[44]

The Croatian community in Maryborough and nearby Moonlight was comprised of 13 Croatians from different parts of coastal Croatia, for example, from Kotor, Dubrovnik and the island of Lošinj. There were also individual Croatian miners in Avoca, Amherst, Alma and Majorca. Vincent Zarich (Vicko Zarić) who was born on 6 December 1827 in Starigrad on the island of Hvar, was a miner in Moonlight. He arrived in Australia in approximately 1857. During his time in Australia he lived for six years in South Australia before moving to Victoria. Zarich married an English woman and they had at least four children. He was a miner at Adelaide Lead, and Moonlight Flat near Maryborough. Zarich registered the alluvial prospecting claim, Dalmatian, situated at Moonlight Flat in 1878. He died in Maryborough on 15 August 1879; his surviving children were between three months and four years old.[45]

A Croatian character worth mentioning who lived in the Stawell area was Vincenzo Bercich (Vicko Berčić) who was born in Rijeka in 1830. He was one of the pioneers of Pleasant Creek near Stawell who arrived during the early alluvial days; he also kept a general store at Silver Shillings.[46] In 1855 Bercich married a German woman in the German Church in Melbourne. He was also actively involved in mining in the Stawell area and had shares in various mining companies. In 1868, Bercich opened a store on Patrick Street, Stawell. In the early 1870s he was an agent for Broadbent Bros & Co. Railway and General Carriers.[47] Unfortunately on 18 April 1875 Bercich was involved in a serious road carriage accident between Stawell and Great Western. A couple of months later his leg was amputated above the thigh and he died in Stawell on 15 June 1875. His death notice in *The Pleasant Creek News* mentioned that 'Bercich was a native of the city of Fiume [Rijeka], a seaport on the Adriatic, in that part of Croatia'. This newspaper also detailed that, during the funeral of Vincenzo Bercich, 'Almost all business places were partially or wholly closed as a mark of respect to the deceased, who had been so long and deservedly esteemed by the residents in the town and throughout the surrounding district. He was held in the greatest estimation by the old alluvial miners on this field, to whom he and his respected widow many times showed acts of friendship that are not likely to be seen forgotten'.[48]

Bendigo was the most productive of all the Victorian goldfields, producing 830 tons of gold. Most of its output came from rich, deep quartz mines and the very rich Victoria Quartz mine at a depth of 1400 metres was for many years the world's deepest gold mine. However, the workers in the quartz mines saw little of this wealth – until the end of the nineteenth century they only earned £3 a week. In 1865 there were 53 hotels in Bendigo and 39 hotels in the surrounding district.[49] In 1858, the Croatian, James Mandelick, was proprietor of the Prince of Wales Hotel in High Street, Bendigo. Another hotel, the Shamrock, a landmark in Bendigo, is also noted for a Croatian connection. Every famous visitor to Bendigo, including members of the royal family, stayed at the Shamrock, and in 1875, a crowd of over 6000 admirers gathered outside the Shamrock to honour the Croatian soprano, Ilma de Murska (Ema Pukšec), after her performance at the Royal Princess Theatre. She caused such a great sensation that the crowd would not disperse until she sang *The Last Rose of Summer* from the balcony.[50]

There were 44 Croatian pioneers living in the Bendigo district, which includes Epsom, Eaglehawk, Huntly, Elysian Flat and Whipstick, although most Croatians who settled in Bendigo had previously mined in other regions of Victoria. A typical example was Dominico Francovich who was born in Dalmatia. He arrived in Victoria around 1852, and prior to his arrival, he had been a sailor.[51] As a miner, Francovich moved to various goldfields, including Ballarat, Mount Korong, McIntyre,

Bercich's surname on a shop in Stawell

BROADBENT BROS. & CO.,
RAILWAY AND GENERAL CARRIERS.
*FORWARDING AND COMMISSION
AGENTS,*
RAILWAY STATION, BALLARAT,
91 Flinders Lane, Melbourne,
AND
MOORAMBELL WHARF, GEELONG.
————
V. BERCICH, Patrick-street,
Agent for Stawell and surrounding Distrtct

Newspaper advertisement with Bercich's surname

Maryborough, Majorca and Bendigo. He was married twice and had a total of six children. From around 1871 to 1873, Francovich lived at Honeysuckle Street, Bendigo and he died on 20 November 1873.[52] A few of the Bendigo district Croatians settled in Huntly. Spirodine Tussup (Špiro Tušup), for example, who was born in Dalmatia and arrived in Australia in about 1860 was a Huntly settler. Tussup married an Irish woman and they had nine children. He was initially a miner in Huntly and Bendigo, but later he became one of the pioneer fruit growers of Huntly. Spirodine Tussup died on 16 August 1916.[53]

Between May 1860 and October 1863, there were many unclaimed letters in Epsom for 28 different Croatian pioneers, suggesting that most of these Croatians had moved on to other goldfields.[54] At least five Croatian pioneers from Epsom later went to the Gippsland goldfields, four to Redcastle and Costerfield, one to Ballarat, four to New South Wales and two to the New Zealand goldfields.

Spirodine Tussup

Redcastle, Costerfield and Goulburn Valley district

The Redcastle, Costerfield and Graytown gold mining towns have since disappeared. However, these towns are of particular interest to this account as there was an important Croatian presence in them in the 1860s and 1870s. Croatian pioneers were there from the first discovery of payable gold by Andrea Franktovich in Redcastle in 1859, right through to the 1880s by which time these towns were in decline because gold production had decreased considerably. Over 35 Croatians lived in the Redcastle and Costerfield area during the height of mining activity in the early 1860s. This figure includes miners who later went to Whroo, Rushworth, Murchison and Avenel. A couple of Croatian miners from Redcastle, who subsequently settled in Avenel, turned to farming. Several later left the Redcastle and Costerfield district and settled in Portarlington, Geelong and Melbourne. Croatians were at the forefront of town development in Redcastle and Costerfield, a number of them managing some of the main hotels in these towns. Antonio Geronevitch, for example, managed the All Nations Hotel in Redcastle, while Frank Golden (born in Starigrad on the island of Hvar) managed the Costerfield Family Hotel. In the 1870s, Natale Lussich, after attempting to revive Costerfield by mining antimony, moved to join the Croatian community in Portarlington. Numerous gold mines in the area were named after Croatian pioneers or their birthplace, Dalmatia and Sclavonia. The gold discoveries by Croatians and gold mines with Croatian names will be detailed in chapter 5, and the publicans described in chapter 7.

In the Goulburn Valley district the main settlement of Croatians was in Mooroopna where, from the 1870s, they were vignerons and farmers. Those who were vignerons or had wine shops in Mooroopna included Trojano Darveniza, Thomas Milovitch and Seraphin Bersica.[55] Trojano Darveniza's Excelsior Vineyard was the most successful vineyard managed by a Croatian pioneer in Australia prior to the First World War and is described in greater detail in chapter 7. Darveniza also initiated chain migration of Croatians to Mooroopna. Seraphin Bersica (Serafin Beršić), who was born in Jelsa on the island of Hvar, was from the early 1880s, a vigneron in Mooroopna. He arrived in Victoria in 1855 and upon his arrival he began mining – mainly in the Daylesford area. Bersica married an Irish woman and they had ten children. In 1872 he registered the Dalmatia tunnel at Stony Creek in the Daylesford mining district. After his first wife died he married again late in life. He died on 15 October 1916 and was buried in the Mooroopna Cemetery.[56] Bersica maintained friendships with other Croatians, including Taddeo Gamulin, Thomas Milovitch, Trojano Darveniza and later Croatian migrants to Mooroopna.

Another Croatian pioneer, Emilios Rossely, who was born in Dubrovnik, settled in Youanmite. Rossely was an excellent tradesman and was well known in the district for his skill in furniture making and carpentry. He built many houses in the Youanmite, Katamatite, Tungamah and Burramine districts. Rossely also built halls and churches, such as St Mary's Catholic Church in Youanmite in 1884. This church still stands today and sustains a small congregation. Rossely met his future wife, Agnes Ferguson, at a dance which was held in the church before it was blessed. They had ten children, three sons and seven daughters. Emilios Rossely died in 1928.[57]

Emilios Rossely

There was a handful of Croatians who lived in Echuca. A couple were mariners who worked on the river boats of the Murray River, one was a fishmonger and another was a miner. Joseph Bautovich (Josip Bautović) from Dubrovnik lived in Kerang, Swan Hill and also in towns across the Murray in New South Wales. After spending five years in South Australia, he arrived in Victoria in 1870. Bautovich had 12 children. He had various jobs such as boundary rider, labourer and farmer. He finally settled on a farm at Tyntynder adjacent to the Murray River, north of Swan Hill. Bautovich died on 22 November 1930 and was buried in the Swan Hill Cemetery.[58]

North-eastern Victoria, Woods Point and Gippsland district

Beechworth was the main gold mining area in north-eastern Victoria. However, most Croatians in this area mined in Buckland. Buckland is famous for the Buckland River Riots that took place on 4 July 1857, in which Europeans disgracefully attacked Chinese diggers because they felt the Chinese were mining gold that was rightfully theirs. In Buckland the Chinese diggers were in the overwhelming majority, out-numbering the Europeans 4 to 1. Europeans resented that Chinese diggers were mining on new fields rather than on abandoned land.[59] So far it is unknown whether any Croatians were mining in the region at the time of the riots. Nicholas Paulussy, who was born in Dubrovnik, was a miner in Buckland as early as 1860. Apart from his mining ventures with other Croatians, he was also a storekeeper.[60] There were at least 12 Croatians living in Buckland in the 1860s and all of them had worked in mining claims with Croatian partners. Stephen Paulussy's crushing plant operated in Buckland for decades and was a centre of mining activity, most of which took place in the vicinity of Clear Creek. Austrian Creek, which is located near Lower Buckland and runs into Clear Creek, was named after these Croatian pioneers who, as we have already seen, were commonly held to be former Austrian citizens. Today nothing remains in Buckland except the Buckland Cemetery, where the names of a few Croatian pioneers are inscribed on tombstones.[61]

Croatians were among the last miners in Buckland. James Zibilich had lived in the Buckland valley for close to 50 years and never left the area. Previously he had mined with other Croatians in Epsom and Crooked River. In addition to mining, Zibilich was a vegetable gardener growing many varieties of vegetables. He was a very close friend of fellow Croatian Stephen Paulussy. James Zibilich never married, and died on 20 April 1922 in Upper Buckland at the ripe old age of 90 years and was buried in the Paulussy family plot in the Buckland Cemetery.[62] Frank Entra (Franjo Kentra), who was a miner with other Croatians at Clear Creek near Buckland, later owned and managed the main hotel in Yackandandah.

In the 1860s there were at least 16 Croatian pioneers in the Woods Point area. Although not high in numbers, these Croatians played an important role in mining in the area. They discovered gold, initiating gold rushes, formed mining companies and owned hotels. Mattio Marassovich, who will be described in more detail in chapter 8, later managed the main hotel in Woods Point. In addition to the gold mining companies established with Croatian partners, individual Croatians were shareholders in mining companies with miners of other nationalities. For example, in 1864 Paulo Arnerich (born on the island of Brač) and another ten shareholders formed the Austrians Amalgamated Gold Mining Company; the following year Francis Nicolich (born in Dalmatia), together with another 18 shareholders formed the Hungarian Gold Mining Company. Since the other shareholders in these companies had Anglo-Saxon names, the names of these companies suggest that Croatians had important roles in these companies. In fact, Paulo Arnerich had the largest number of shares in the Austrians Amalgamated Gold Mining Company. These mining companies had considerable capital, over £15,000 each, owning quartz-crushing machines and tramway tracks.[63] Woods Point is still a small town; however, apart from Mattio Marassovich's name inscribed on his tombstone in the cemetery, today there is little in the area to indicate a Croatian pioneer presence. Almost all of the Croatians from Woods Point moved to other areas in Victoria or went to the New Zealand goldfields. Another Croatian pioneer buried in this cemetery was Antonia Germano (Ante Germano) who was born in Dalmatia. He died in Woods Point on 28 January 1864 where he had been working as a miner. The next day he was buried by his Croatian neighbour, Nicolo Anticevich.[64] In 1874 John Bundara was married in Walhalla and his marriage witness was his brother, Antonio Bundara.

In the mining district of Gippsland the Croatian pioneers were primarily involved in gold mining. Some owned hotels on the goldfields, others became farmers when the gold rushes receded. The Paynesville, Lakes Entrance, Tarraville and Port Albert Croatian pioneers were primarily involved in the fishing industry. In each of these towns there were between one and two Croatians who were fishermen. The Gippsland Croatian fishermen arrived in Victoria later than the gold miners.

In Gippsland the main goldfield was Walhalla. In contrast to most other important Victorian goldfields, the rich Walhalla goldfield was not discovered until 1863. Today, the old gold mining town of Walhalla is a tourist attraction, but not much remains from this once bustling gold rush town. Many of the buildings were relocated to other towns when the railway finally reached Walhalla. The buildings were dismantled, put on the train and then transported. The railway reached Walhalla after the main gold rush period was over. Of the mountain gold towns, Walhalla was the most successful, with several very profitable companies. One of these, the Long Tunnel Mine, produced more gold than any Victorian mine and paid £1.2 million in dividends before the end of the nineteenth century.[65] From the 1860s to 1900s there were several Croatian miners who lived in the Walhalla district. But most moved on to Melbourne, Portarlington or other goldfields. However, Francis Nicolich remained in Walhalla for the rest of his life. In the 1860s he was mining at Sailor Bills Creek north of Woods Point. Nicolich married an Irish woman, Sarah Ryan, in Walhalla in 1873. The marriage witnesses were the Croatian, Michele Augustinvich, and his wife Bridget. Francis Nicolich died in Walhalla in 1882 and was buried in the Walhalla Cemetery. He left behind a widow and seven young children to mourn his loss, with the youngest child only five weeks old.[66]

In the 1860s there were thriving gold mining towns in the Crooked River area, such as Grant and Talbotville, but today nothing remains of these once-booming towns. The primary reason for their demise was a decline in gold returns, but other reasons include inhospitable conditions due to location, and poor roads which led to high transport costs. Dargo is the only town in the region that has survived. In Gippsland a handful of Croatians were also miners in the Omeo area.

Croatian pioneers played an important role in gold mining in the Crooked River mining district. However, very little of their presence or mining contribution to the Crooked River district has ever been recorded. In October 1864 a reporter for *The Gippsland Times* visited a group of Croatian miners at the 25 Mile Creek, which is the right-hand branch of the Crooked River. The reporter stated that: 'The upper portion of this auriferous stream is nearly all taken up by "Austrians, Italians and Sclavonians". I encroached upon the hospitality of the latter countrymen [Sclavonian] for one night, and to Messrs Bundara and party I am much indebted for their kindness and information'.[67] The reporter stayed with the Croatian brothers, John and Antonio Bundara (who were born in Žuljana), and their mining party. John and Antonio Bundara lived amongst Croatians in Woods Point, Portarlington and Melbourne. The Croatian miners were constructing flood ditches and were building a hut which indicated that they had planned to stay in the area for a while. There were about 120 miners at work on a 13-kilometre section of the creek near Bundara's claim. Careful examination of the Crooked River mining district register of claims and water rights revealed that Croatian surnames greatly outnumbered Austrian or Italian surnames.[68] This suggests that it is likely that many of the miners referred to as Austrians and Italians were actually Croatians.

There were at least 28 Croatian pioneers who mined for gold in the Crooked River mining district between 1864 and 1890. Some of these stayed for a short time before they proceeded to other goldfields or to Melbourne. Others such as Nicholas Lasich and Peter Albich, remained in the Crooked River district into the twentieth century. Nicholas Lasich was born in Dubrovnik and arrived in Victoria from Liverpool in 1859. Lasich and Ellen Lusk were married on Mt Grant, Crooked River on 23 April 1866 by a Catholic priest. The witnesses were a fellow Croatian pioneer, Nicolo Anticevich, and his wife. Nicholas and Ellen Lasich had nine children. Lasich had gold mining claims with other Croatian pioneers in the Crooked River mining district during the 1860s and 1870s. For example in the 1870s, he had claims with Matteo Gargurevich and Matteo Perich. Lasich also mined in the Dargo region. In the 1880s however, he acquired 110 acres of land in Dargo where he also pursued a farming life. Lasich died in Dargo on 18 August 1906. Descendants with the Lasich surname lived on a property near Dargo until 1995.[69]

One of last permanent miners in the Crooked River area was Peter Albich (Petar Albić), who was born on the island of Lošinj on 25 March 1830. In about 1864 he arrived from Glasgow on the ship, *Three Bells*. He lived in Woods Point for one year, after which he settled permanently in the Dargo, Crooked River and Talbotville districts where he was a gold miner. He had numerous mining claims in the Crooked River mining district, most of which were located near Talbotville. One of his claims at Good Luck Creek was named after him. Peter Albich died a bachelor in Talbotville on 27 December 1914 and was subsequently buried in the Talbotville Cemetery.[70]

One of the people most influential in the development of Korumburra into a prosperous town was the Croatian pioneer, Antonio Radovick, whose contribution will be discussed in greater detail in chapter 7. Today, as a reminder of him, one of the main streets in Korumburra is called Radovick Street and there is Antonio's Bar in the Korumburra Hotel. Histories of Korumburra and the surrounding district have never mentioned his birthplace.[71] Other Croatian pioneers living in Korumburra include Steffano Radovick, Jacob Stiglich and Rocco Zagabria. There were also Croatians in other inland Gippsland towns such as Bairnsdale, Boggy Creek, Walpa, Lindenow and Budgeree. Frederick Roderick (Jerolim Kos) who was born in Baška on the island of Krk was a farmer in Lindenow. He arrived in Adelaide in 1881 and was married in Port Adelaide a couple of years later. Roderick moved to Victoria in 1886. He had ten children, one of his sons Frederick was killed while on active service with the AIF.

Croatian settlements across Australia

As we have seen, the Victorian and New South Wales gold rushes led to the first wave of Croatian immigration to Australia. Croatian gold miners in New South Wales mainly settled at Gulgong, Sofala, Lambing Flat, Grenfell, Grafton, Mudgee, Hill End, Araluen, Gundagai and Temora. In the 1870s there were at least 22 Croatians in Gulgong. Most of the Croatians in New South Wales lived in Sydney and the highest

Frederick Roderick with his wife

concentration of them lived in the city centre as well as in Drummoyne, Glebe, Petersham and Woolloomooloo. After trying their luck on the goldfields many Croatians worked as seamen, publicans and/or restaurateurs, labourers, farmers and fishermen throughout what were then the main economic centres of Australia. Croatians also worked as labourers constructing railways throughout Australia.

Almost all the Croatian seamen in New South Wales lived in Sydney, and most of them had arrived in the 1870s and 1880s. In 1887 Croatians ran 15 per cent of the oyster saloons in Sydney and were seven per cent of the fishmongers in Sydney. There were nine oyster saloons run by Croatian pioneers in Sydney. For example in the 1880s, Frederick Rossich had an oyster saloon in Sydney as did Matthew Sepich from Rijeka, although Sepich subsequently established an oyster saloon in South Brisbane. Mathew Jvancich (Mate Ivančić) who was born on the island of Olib was a fishmonger in Sydney. He had been a seaman on board a ship that arrived in Sydney in 1883, but after breaking his leg, stayed on. Jvancich was married twice in Sydney. He had a fruit shop and was also a wood and coal merchant in Campsie. Jvancich died on 3 November 1935 and was survived by five children.[72] Another Croatian storekeeper in New South Wales was Francis Frank from Volosko who established a grocery shop in North Botany. Nicholas Anticevich (Nikola Antičević) was also a Croatian fishmonger in Sydney who was born on the Pelješac Peninsula. He arrived in Sydney in about 1880; his cousin John Harlovich had arrived there a couple of years earlier. Anticevich had close friendships with other Croatian pioneers in Australia; in 1892 he was witness to the wedding of another Croatian, Stefano Dedo, in St Patrick's Catholic Church Sydney. In 1895 Anticevich was married in the same church and his marriage witness was the Croatian Andrew Tverdeich (Tvrdeić). Anticevich's fishmonger business on George Street in Sydney was highly successful and traded under the name 'A. Nicholas & Co.'. His brother later joined him in Sydney.[73] Anticevich subsequently took on the role of helping Croatians migrate to Warriewood. In 1881 Frederick Rossich from the island of Premuda arrived in Sydney. He had various occupations in Sydney, including fishmonger, cook, boarding house keeper, oyster saloon keeper and wine retailer. He was also married in St Patrick's Catholic Church in Sydney in 1884 and the witness was another Croatian, Frank Milach. In 1885 Rossich was living in Argyle Street, Sydney, his Croatian neighbours included Matthew Sepich and Peter Baric-Ravich. Peter Baric-Ravich kept a boarding house on Argyle Street.[74] In the Catholic section of the Rookwood Cemetery in Sydney, 15 Croatian pioneers are buried, of which 40 per cent have the town in which they were born inscribed on their tombstones.[75] Croatians in Australia also named their homes after their birthplaces. For example, in Sydney Nicolla Raicovich called his residence 'Ragusa' (Dubrovnik) and Marino Petrich and Matteo Babare called their residences 'Dalmacia'.

A Croatian pioneer who lived in regional New South Wales was Vincent

Mathew Jvancich's wedding day in 1901

Mathew Jvancich with his wife and children

Chernich (Vicko Cernić) who was born in Rijeka. He was a seaman who had jumped ship in Melbourne in 1876. Chernich made his way to Bega where he worked initially as a farm labourer before he learnt cheese- and butter-making. Chernich worked in the NSW Creamery Co. in Yarrangung and later at the Bega Cooperative factory. He married Ellen Adams in 1885 and they had four children. After living for over 26 years in the Bega district, Chernich moved to Sydney where he ran a produce store. He died in Sydney on 9 October 1944. In 1880 Chernich received two letters in Croatian from his mother in Rijeka. Her letters detailed the economic hardships they were enduring; she also expressed a wish to hug Vincent once again before she died.[76] Nicholas Juratowitch (Nikola Đuratović) from Dubrovnik arrived in Australia in 1860. He married an Irish woman in Singleton the following year. They subsequently had 16 children. Juratowitch who worked as a mail contractor died in South Singleton in 1896.[77]

After the discovery of the silver-lead deposits in Broken Hill in 1883, Croatians began to settle there and worked in the silver-lead mines. From the late 1880s Croatian women began accompanying their husbands from Croatia, and by the early 1890s there were about 150 Croatians in Broken Hill. They wrote to their relatives in Croatia and assisted them in their migration to Australia. This was the first large-scale chain migration of Croatians to Australia.[78]

The majority of Croatian pioneers in South Australia were seamen and usually

56

lived in Port Adelaide and Adelaide, examples in the 1850s being Nicholas Bonacich from Milna on the island of Brač and Prospero Covacevich from Dalmatia. Most Croatians who settled in Adelaide in the 1870s and 1880s were initially employed as seamen and later became wharf labourers. Peter Vranat was a Croatian who followed this path. He was born in Dubrovnik and arrived in Adelaide in about 1883. He was initially a seaman on several vessels in Adelaide before he became a wharf labourer. Vranat was married twice and had one son. Unfortunately, on 7 December 1923 Vranat was severely injured at work when a beam fell on him and he died a few days later. The executor of Vranat's will was another Croatian, Matteo Guratovich, who was born in Dubrovnik and arrived in Australia in 1874. Guratovich was a seaman who resided in Port Adelaide.[79] Another Croatian in Adelaide was Christie Dubricich (Dubričić) who was born in Kastav near Rijeka. In 1880 he married an Irish woman in Adelaide and they had 11 children. Dubricich was also a seaman in South Australia before

Vincent Chernich in sailor's uniform

becoming a wharf labourer. Dubricich died in 1926. Some of his children went by the name of Dubricich, while others were known by the name of Dubrich. His son Francis was killed in action during the First World War as an Australian Ambulance driver.[80] Other Croatians in Adelaide and Port Adelaide were publicans and wine merchants. Croatian pioneers who lived in Port Pirie were primarily labourers, while those Croatians who lived in Port Augusta and Port Lincoln worked as seamen and fishermen.

Croatians were attracted to Queensland by the gold rushes, especially Charters Towers and Palmer River in the 1870s and Mount Morgan in the 1880s. Charters Towers became Queensland's biggest city outside Brisbane and had its own stock exchange. Mount Morgan had one of the richest single gold mines in the world.[81] Quite a number of Croatian miners stayed on the Queensland goldfields for many years. Nicholas Sabadina (Nikola Šabadin), from Dubrovnik, who arrived in Australia in 1859 was a miner in Queensland. He was married in the 1870s and subsequently had 11 children. By 1890 he was mining in Ravenswood in Queensland and later at

Christie Dubricich with his wife

Broughton near Charters Towers. Sabadina lived in Queensland for over 50 years. The largest concentration of Croatians in Queensland was in Townsville and they were predominately seamen. There were also Croatian farmers in Bundaberg. In contrast to the other states, few Croatian pioneers settled in Queensland's capital city. Nicolas Sparozvich (Nikola Sparožvić), who was born in Omišalj on the island of Krk, was a seaman in Maryborough. In 1880 he married Matilda Bayford and they subsequently had six children. Sparozvich was the well-known boatswain of the steamer *Llewellyn* and was the pilot of the Port of Maryborough. He also built model ships that have been passed down to his descendants. Sparozvich died in Maryborough on 22 August 1910.[82]

Most of the Croatian pioneer settlers in Tasmania arrived in the 1880s. The majority of them moved to Victoria where some of them settled in already established Croatian communities. The Croatian pioneers in Tasmania mainly lived in or near Launceston, Hobart and Burnie. Croatian seamen traded between Melbourne and northern Tasmania. An early Croatian settler to Tasmania was Nicholas Bonnitcha from Dubrovnik who arrived in Hobart in 1856. He was married twice in Tasmania and had eight children by his first wife. Bonnitcha worked as a seaman in Tasmania. He died in 1913 and was survived by six children.[83]

Croatians who settled in Western Australia prior to 1890 for the most part lived in Fremantle, Perth and Albany where they were seamen and farmers. For example, Nicholas Gableish (Nikola Gabelić) who was born in Vrboska on the island of Hvar was married in Fremantle in 1879. He settled in Albany in the 1880s. At first Gableish used a ketch to ferry passengers to and from sailing ships in the harbour. However, around 1888 he turned to market gardening and dairying. He died in 1935 and was survived by six children.[84]

Mobility

Some Croatian pioneers were highly mobile, especially the gold miners, as will be shown in chapter 5. Others such as John Margitich (Ivan Margitić), who was born in Bakar on 24 June 1852, moved around Victoria depending on where the work was. He disembarked in Melbourne on 14 October 1883 after coming from the East Indies on the brig, *Zero*. Margitich lived in Nagambie for ten months, Sale for ten months, Narnar-goon for nine months and Walhalla for three years, before he settled permanently among the Croatians in Portarlington. Another example of a peripatetic Croatian pioneer was George Ivanusic. He had previously lived in New Zealand, moving to Queensland for 22 years, then three years in New South Wales and for the rest of the time in Bendigo and Melbourne.[85] Other Croatians were experienced travellers before arriving in Australia. Antone Rerecich who was born in Veli Lošinj on the island of Lošinj on 19 January 1860 had lived in South Africa and New Zealand before coming to Victoria in 1886. In the early 1890s he was a fisherman in Port Albert, subsequently moving to Western Australia. His grandson, Ray Gabelich, was the legendary Australian Rules footballer whose football achievements in the 1950s and 1960s will be described in chapter 9. Croatians were highly mobile and moved to

Nicholas Gableish in front of his property in Albany. He is on the left side of the photograph, two of his sons and other family members are also in the photograph

other states when they found available work there. An example of one such Croatian was the gold miner, Nicolla Raicovich from Dubrovnik, who first landed in Wellington, New Zealand. Raicovich arrived in Sydney in 1874 where he remained for four years. He then moved to Stanthorpe (Queensland) for two years, returning to New South Wales for several years, before travelling to the goldfields around Kalgoorlie in Western Australia. Nicolla Raicovich died in Sydney on 16 May 1914.[86]

In the 1860s over 20 Croatians moved from Victoria to the New Zealand goldfields during the Otago gold rush. About a third stayed permanently in New Zealand, the rest returned to Victoria. From 1861 to 1863, about 50,000 adult males left Victoria for New Zealand.[87] Two Croatian pioneers who returned, Trojano Darveniza and Antonio Radovick, were later among the most successful Croatian pioneers in Australia. There were several other Croatian pioneers who spent some time in New Zealand, but it is unknown whether they were involved in gold mining on the South Island. Many Croatians who were Kauri gum diggers on New Zealand's North Island later settled in Australia. Because they had generally left Croatia after 1890, the Kauri gum diggers who settled in Australia were generally not pioneers, but they still had contacts with the Croatian pioneers.

Newspaper advertisement for James Mandelick's hotel in Bendigo in 1858

Newspaper advertisement for George Sabadine's boarding house on the Home Rule goldfield in New South Wales in 1872

CHAPTER 4

Pioneer Connections
and Communities

Background

The Croatian settlers who came to Australia prior to 1890 were almost without exception single men; therefore there was a large gender imbalance. It was not until 1913 that any formal Croatian societies or organisations were established. However, they did form Croatian communities – they worked and ran businesses together, socialised and lived together – and maintained ties with other Croatian settlers in

Australia. There is written evidence that over 54 per cent of Croatian settlers had connections with other Croatian settlers in Victoria. However, the real figure is probably much higher, since they very often had mutual friends, lived in the same towns or had mining claims near one another. As noted earlier, they were each other's marriage witnesses, attendees at funerals and godparents to each other's children. They sometimes travelled great distances to be a marriage witness or to be present at a funeral of a Croatian friend. For example, Andrew Radoslovich (Andrija Radoslović), who was born on the island of Lošinj in 1865, regularly travelled 250 kilometres from Port Fairy to Portarlington for various Croatian functions there.[1] Croatian settlers were partners in mining claims, had fishing boats together and managed restaurants together. Since only several Croatian women had migrated to Australia prior to 1890, marriage with Croatian women was rare. Thus, Croatian pioneers often quickly assimilated into

Andrew Radoslovich with his wife Mary Ann and his son Charles

the Australian community. Moreover, Croatian pioneers spoke English with their wives and children. The fact that Croatian pioneers were distributed throughout Australia in search of gold and work also hastened their assimilation. Nevertheless, some preferred to work with other Croatian pioneers so they could readily communicate in their native Croatian language.[2]

Multiple Croatian connections and friendships

Many Croatian pioneers had multiple connections and friendships with other Croatian pioneers in Australia. Cosmo Antich (Kuzma Antić), who was born in Bakar in September 1831, had documented connections with at least 20 other Croatian pioneers. He disembarked in Melbourne on 14 April 1857 from the ship, *Oliver Lang*. Antich had mining claims with other Croatian pioneers in the Crooked River mining district, and in 1879 he had a river claim at Middle Dargo with Luka Margitich and Nicholas Stipicich. The following year Antich registered a race claim in Bull Town adjoining Peter Albich's claim. The same year Antich and Stipicich had a bank claim together at Middle Dargo.[3] Cosmo Antich signed a register on behalf of 17 Croatian pioneers living in Victoria in 1882 for the Austrian Consulate in Victoria.[4] At that time most of these Croatian pioneers lived among other Croatians in Yandoit, Wedderburn and Maryborough. Antich lived mainly in Victoria for about 36 years, visiting and residing in other states for short periods. He then moved to Western Australia where he was a miner and wood carter for a further 17 years prior to his death. Antich died an unmarried man in the Wellington Dam area near Worsley, Western Australia in 1909.[5]

Other Croatian pioneers, such as John Lussich (Ivan Lukšić), lived in more than one Croatian community in Australia. There is written evidence that he had close ties with at least another 21 Croatians in Victoria. He lived in Redcastle, Costerfield, Woods Point and Portarlington. Lussich was born in Sutivan on the island of Brač. In March 1853 he arrived in Victoria on the barque, *Galatea*, from Sydney.[6] On his arrival in Victoria he worked as a gold and antimony miner with varying degrees of success and had Croatian partners in his mines. In May 1861 Lussich crushed 42 tons of quartz obtained from the Slavonian Reef at Redcastle which produced 85.5 ounces of gold. Five months later he registered an antimony and gold mining company called Lussich and Party in Costerfield.[7] In 1862, while mining in the Redcastle area, John Lussich was the marriage witness to the Croatian, Antonio Geronevitch.[8] On 29 August 1862 Lussich applied for a six-acre antimony mining lease in Costerfield. His mining partners were the Croatians, Antonio Bundara, Natale Lussich, N. Laisch, Niccola Mitrovich and Gregory Cristilovich. Another four Croatian pioneers, Pietro Jassich, Michele Marinovich, George Marinovitch and Bogden Slocovich, ran the adjoining antimony claim. The following year Lussich and his Croatian partners had a gold mine in Costerfield. Within two years he had moved to Woods Point where he was a miner in the No. 1 East Champion Quartz Mining Company. Other Croatian miners in this mining company were Paulo Arnerich, Antonio Bassich, Steffano Beban and Antonio Vizulin (Viculin).[9]

By 1870 Lussich had arrived in Portarlington and immediately started to work as a fisherman, where he continued to work while his health lasted. Lussich was married to an Irish woman, Mary Wilson, in St Patrick's Catholic Cathedral, Melbourne, on 23 December 1871. She had been a widow since 1868 and had five children from her first marriage. His best man was a fellow Croatian from the island of Brač, Natale Lussich. John and Mary Lussich had one child together, Katina. Dominick Lussich became the godparent of Katina on 10 August 1873 in St Mary's Catholic Church, Geelong.[10] In 1876 John Lussich's wife was the marriage witness for the marriage between her sister and the Croatian, Nicholas Torchie, in St Mary's Catholic

John Lussich with his wife

Church, Geelong. Five years later John Lussich and his wife were the marriage witnesses for John Lussich Slavich in the same church. Joseph Catarinich's nephew, Hugh Manson, married John Lussich's daughter. Another Croatian, Jerome Lussick, was a godparent to John Lussich's granddaughter, Veronica Manson.[11] John Lussich was in poor health for the last several years of his life; he died on 15 May 1904 in Portarlington. He was interred in the Portarlington Cemetery and one of the pallbearers was Joseph Zagabria, a fellow Croatian.[12] John Lussich and his family were also friends with Gregory Pavletich's family. In 1908 Lussich's wife attended Annie Pavletich's wedding, while his daughter was the godparent to Gregory Pavletich's granddaughter.[13] During John Lussich's time in Portarlington there were another 11 Croatian pioneers living there, and it is highly likely he knew some of them as they had mutual Croatian friends.

Another Croatian pioneer in Portarlington, who maintained friendships with at least 16 Croatians in Victoria, was Gregory Pavletich (Grgur Pavletić) who was born in Bakar on 7 March 1844. He had arrived in Victoria on the ship, *Neray*, from Mauritius in 1873.[14] Pavletich was the godparent to Nicholas Torchie's son in 1879, while Natale Lussich was the godparent to Torchie's daughter. Gregory Pavletich married Ellen McMahon at St Mary's Catholic Church, Geelong, on 9 August 1886. The marriage witness was a fellow Croatian, Natale Vuscovich. Gregory and Ellen Pavletich had six children in Portarlington. The godparents of four of these children were either Croatian or had Croatian connections. Pavletich's wife and Vincent Margitich were Joseph Zagabria's marriage witnesses in St Thomas' Catholic Church, Drysdale.[15]

Pavletich was a fisherman in Portarlington, but he also did some farming. His neighbours were Vuscovich and Zagabria.[16] In 1908 two of Gregory Pavletich's daughters were married at St Patrick's Catholic Church, Portarlington. Croatians and their families attended his daughters' weddings. As a gift at the wedding of Augustina Pavletich, Joseph Zagabria's son, Thomas Zagabria, gave bread plates, while Andrew and Mary Ann Radoslovich from Port Fairy gave a linen cushion and tablecloth; John Lussich's wife gave a cheque.[17] Pavletich's youngest daughter, Ellen Pavletich, married a Croatian, John Lekovich, in 1920.[18] Gregory Pavletich died in Portarlington on 14 April 1929.[19] He was also friends and fished with Croatians, Dominick Lussich, John Margitich and Dominic Tarabochia, and Croatians who came to Australia after 1907, including Mati Botica, Ivan Franich, Mate Franich, John Lekovich and Marko Simunovich.[20] Other Croatians with more than ten documented close associations with Croatian pioneers will be mentioned later and include five other Croatians, Antonio Buzolich, John Grandi, Natale Lussich, Stephen Paulussy and Antonio Radovick.

Rites of passage

Marriages and baptisms, in addition to being a time for celebration, were times for re-acquaintance with fellow Croatians. These functions assisted Croatian pioneers to maintain ties. Having a fellow Croatian at their wedding or child's baptism was a symbolic gesture, given the great distance from their native Croatia, and may have been comparable to having a relative there. The Croatian pioneers were very proud when their best man or child's godparent was a fellow Croatian – someone who could understand their Croatian language, customs, traditions and their yearning for their families back in Croatia.

Of a sample of 100 early Croatian settlers who were married in Victoria, 30 per cent had a Croatian marriage witness. Another 30 per cent had a family member on the spouse's side as a marriage witness. Joseph Catarinich had at least three documented connections with other Croatian pioneers through weddings. Catarinich married Margaret McKenna in St Francis Catholic Church, Melbourne, in 1877. The marriage witness was fellow Croatian pioneer, Frank Millawich. Joseph Catarinich was the marriage witness to Jacob Stiglich who was married in St Patrick's Catholic Cathedral, Melbourne, in 1883 and also to Antonio Catarinich who was married in St Peter and Paul's Catholic Church, South Melbourne in 1897.[21]

Two Croatian pioneers, Dominick Lussich and Martin Pavilach, will be used to illustrate Croatian connections through baptisms. Dominick Lussich's wife and John Lussich became the godparents to John Grussich in St Mary's Catholic Church, Geelong in 1864. John Lussich became the godparent to three of Dominick Lussich's daughters in the same church between 1867 and 1873, while Dominick Lussich became the godparent to John Lussich's daughter. Martin Pavilach had Croatian pioneers and their wives as godparents to three of his children at St Mary's Catholic Church, Castlemaine, between 1876 and 1883. The surnames of the Croatian godparents were Belanich, Mavorvitch and Passalick. Other marriages and baptisms with Croatian pioneer witnesses will be mentioned later to further illustrate the close links which Croatian migrants maintained.[22]

The Croatian women who settled in Australia prior to 1890 usually accompanied their husbands to Australia. However, by the 1890s, single Croatian women started to arrive in Australia in larger numbers, and by the mid-1890s, there were marriages between Croatian-born in Broken Hill with Croatian-born witnesses. The trend

Martin Pavilach

of Croatian settlers from Australia returning to Croatia to marry or marriage by proxy was uncommon in Australia before 1890.

Croatian pioneers gave each other comfort and support when fellow Croatian pioneers or members of their families died. Funerals of Croatian pioneers were an extremely sorrowful time for other Croatian pioneers who knew them – apart from losing a cherished friend, there was a realisation that the size of their Croatian community may be diminishing. There could also have been an awareness that the Croatian migrant's dream of returning a wealthy person to their birthplace would not be realised. Funerals were also a time to reminisce about earlier days when they were young and to think about their families back in Croatia; they also provided opportunities for catching up on the news of other Croatian migrants in Australia. From the United States we know how important this rite of passage was for Croatians. There Croatian settlers were better organised, forming mutual benefit societies and collecting funds for the burial of their deceased Croatian friends. In the United States in fact, some of these societies made it compulsory for their members to attend funeral processions of deceased members.[23] By way of example, the Croatian Slavonic Mutual and Benevolent Society purchased a section of the San Francisco Cemetery in 1861 to provide a burial site for its members, priests and poor Croatians who were unable to pay for their burial sites. In Australia some Croatian pioneers became members of mainstream benevolent societies.

Mark Busanich (Marko Busanić), who was born on the island of Lošinj, died in Yandoit on 18 July 1871. At his funeral the Croatians living in the Yandoit district turned out in force as a sign of respect and also as an expression of membership of a Croatian community or extended family. Mark Belanich, who was also his mining partner, buried Busanich in the Sandon Catholic Cemetery. The witnesses at his funeral were fellow Croatian pioneers, Mark Belanich, Peter Mavorvitch, Antonio Pavich and Martin Pavilach. Some other Croatian pioneers in Victoria who were buried by a fellow Croatian, had Croatian pallbearers or had a Croatian informant who signed their death certificate, include John Borcich, Stefano Celovich, Antonia Germano, Giovanni Ivanussich, John Lussich and George Zaninovich. Croatians also buried family members of other Croatian pioneers. For example, Natale Lussich buried Paulo Arnerich's daughter, Mary Ann, in Woods Point Cemetery in 1866.[24] The pattern of Croatian settlers being present at funerals of other Croatians was repeated across Australia. For example, Nicholas Sitanich (Cvitanić) from the island of Brač was mining at Palmer River, Queensland, when he died on 27 May 1874. The witnesses at his funeral were his Croatian mining partners, Matteo Marincovich (Mate Marinković) and Peter Mijch (Mijić). Similarly, when Marko Marienovich died in Sydney Hospital in 1887, the witness on his death certificate was Natale Matich's wife. Her sister was married to another Croatian, Matthew Sepich.[25]

In the Lussich family plot in the Catholic section of the Geelong Eastern Cemetery are buried Dominick Lussich, his brother John, wife Kate and daughter Johanna. A section of the tombstone inscription reads, 'in loving memory of Dominick Lussich the beloved husband of Kate Lussich who died 22nd June 1922 age 87 years and 7 months a colonist of 65 years a native of Dalmatia R.I.P'.[26] Dominick Lussich's second wife, Kate, died in 1906 in Portarlington. She was interred in the Lussich family plot and among the coffin bearers was Victor Lusic, a Croatian from the island of Brač, who lived in Melbourne.[27] Successful Croatian pioneers Antonio Radovick and Trojano Darveniza also had Dalmatia as their birthplace inscribed on their tombstone. However, in Australia, Lussich, Radovick and Darveniza also maintained links with Croatians from regions of coastal Croatia other than Dalmatia. Trojano Darveniza's tombstone had some words such as 'uspomena' [in memory], 'rodjen na' [born on] and 'umro na' [died on] in the Croatian language, the inscription reads 'in memory of Trojano Darveniza born Dalmacia 1838 died Mooroopna 1927 uspomena Trojano Drveniza rodjen na 20.VIII.1838 umro na 5.X.1927 R.I.P'.[28] George Sabadine (Šabadin) died on the Gulgong goldfields in New South Wales on 9 May 1873 and was buried in the Catholic section of the Gulgong Cemetery. On his tombstone was inscribed that he was 'Native of Cannaliracusa Dalmazia' [Dubrovnik Dalmatia]. In 1872 Sabadine had a boarding house nearby at Home Rule.[29]

Anton Margitich (Ante Margitić) from Bakar came to Australia in about 1861. He died in the Alfred Hospital in Melbourne on 14 September 1892 and was subsequently buried in the Catholic section of the St Kilda Cemetery. Inscribed on his tombstone over a century ago were the following words in Croatian 'Lezi Namiru Ostani Zbogom' [Lay in peace and stay with God].[30] Anton Margitich bequeathed his brother, Luka Margitich who lived in Sydney, over £75, which was held in the Bank of Victoria. Luka Margitich sent the letters of administration of Anton Margitich's estate to John Terdich, a Croatian friend, on 17 September 1892. Terdich and another Croatian pioneer, Frank Cucel, were the valuers of Anton Margitich's property.[31]

In the Catholic section of the Buckland Cemetery the Paulussy family plot is located where three Croatian pioneers, Stephen Paulussy, Stephen Pandrige and James Zibilich were buried. All three are buried next to each other in the same family plot. Samuel Tadich was buried alongside his brother, Nicholas Tadich, in the Burwood Cemetery.[32]

Croatian mining and business partners

Typically, Croatian pioneer miners had mining claims with one or two Croatian partners, although some companies consisted of up to nine Croatian shareholders. More details on the Croatian mining contacts are discussed in the following chapter. A typical miner was Stephen Paulussy who was born in Dubrovnik. In 1859 he came to Victoria as a paying passenger along with four other Croatian pioneers.[33] Paulussy had several claims in the Buckland area with a Croatian friend, Stephen Pandrige, in the years between 1865 to 1880. Some of these claims had other Croatian share-holders, such as Michele Augustinvich, Steffano Brsiza, Nicholas Paulussy, John Perovich and James Zibilich.

Over a 23-year period, from 1866 to 1889, Stephen Paulussy and his partners, under the name Paulussy and Company, crushed at least 4637 tons of quartz in the Buckland mining district which was registered in the *Reports of the Mining Surveyors and Registrars* to yield a total of 1916 ounces of gold. Today this gold would be worth in the vicinity of $785,560.[34] Paulussy's crushing plant was one of the main (of 19) crushing plants in Buckland and frequently produced the highest quarterly yield of gold in Buckland. This plant was still operating in 1895 after almost all the other crushing plants in the area had ceased operation.

In 1885 Stephen Paulussy and the Croatian pioneer Steffano Brsiza erected a crushing plant on the site of the old Harp of Erin Reef. They made a battery of four stamp crushers, driven by a 7.5 kilowatt water wheel.[35] Paulussy married Catherine O'Brien, the widow of his Croatian partner, Stephen Pandrige, in Myrtleford in 1885 in a Catholic ceremony. Paulussy's two children lived until their seventies but had no descendants. Stephen Paulussy was still mining when he died in Upper Buckland on 24 January 1909.[36]

The personal connections of some Croatian miners with other Croatians spanned over half a century. John Grandi from Dubrovnik had friendships with another 12 Croatians in Victoria. These ties spanned from his arrival in Australia on a ship with

Paulussy's Mill in the Buckland mining district

other Croatian passengers in 1853 until his death in 1907. In the 1870s Grandi worked in gold mines in the McIntyre district with other Croatian miners. These mines, whose names reflect their Croatian connections, include the Dalmatia claim, Dalmatia quartz claim, Dalmazia Reef quartz prospecting claim, Dalmazia Reef quartz cooperative prospecting claim, Archduke Maximilian Dalmatian Reef quartz claim and Dalmazia Quartz Gold Mining Company. He later mined in Wedderburn with other Croatian miners.[37] Grandi was admitted to the Inglewood Hospital on 18 March 1907. The following day he died from senile decay. His Croatian friend, Baldosa Trobog, died in the same hospital on the same day.[38]

Croatians also ran businesses together and maintained fishing boats together. For example, Anton Margitich had been involved in a restaurant business with Croatian partners: from 1890 to 1891 Margitich and Pavletich ran a restaurant at 88–92 Moray Street, South Melbourne; the following year it was run by Margitich and Musich. In 1892 Anton Margitich was also a cabdriver in Melbourne, while his brother Luka was a cabdriver in Sydney. In 1904 Luka Margitich died as a result of a collision between a tram and the cab he was driving on Parramatta Road, Sydney.[39] In 1889 Vincent Zan and Plancich registered a trademark with letters ZP as their broom company logo. In 1901 the Croatian pioneers, Natale Starcevich and Antonio Filess, who lived in New South Wales, patented an improved automatic railway coupling device.[40]

Croatian communities

As noted in the previous chapter, some Croatian communities had over 15 Croatian pioneers living there at one time. The existence of these communities was often very noticeable. For example, Croatians constituted 39 per cent of fishermen in Portarlington, and in Wedderburn, they all lived on the southern side of town. Croatian pioneers moved between these communities or developed new areas, depending on available work opportunities. Croatian pioneers lived together on the goldfields and shared houses. By living together they could save money more quickly and in these situations they would also be more comfortable – speaking their native Croatian language, eating familiar food and retaining some of their Croatian customs. For example, Antonio Catarinich had lived with his brother Joseph Catarinich and family at 210 Nelson Road, South Melbourne for almost a decade in the 1890s.[41] There were numerous other cases where a Croatian pioneer lived with a Croatian relative or friend.

In relation to later Croatian arrivals, there were many instances where later migrants mixed with the earlier pioneers, and several cases where later migrants married daughters of Croatian pioneers.[42] On occasions, Croatian pioneers and their families looked after older Croatian pioneers in their time of need. They comforted them and imparted a sense of family, even if they were not relatives. For example, a few weeks before his death, Natale Vuscovich was living in Victor Lusic's home at Clarendon Street, South Melbourne. Vuscovich left all his assets to Lusic who paid for his cemetery plot.[43] The Croatian pioneer, George Ivanusic, died in Thomas Zuzulich's home at 30 Edward Street, Brunswick on 2 July 1917, where he had lived for at least the last few years of his life. Ivanusic left Zuzulich over £529 in his will.[44] Dominick Lussich's daughter had been nurse and housekeeper to her uncle, John Lussich, for the last six years of his life.[45]

In cities Croatians tended to congregate in certain areas. For example, numerous Croatians lived on George Street, Sydney. Among these residents were the confectioner, James Joseph from Dalmatia, the fishmonger, Nicholas Anticevich from Pelješac, and the labourer, Joseph Calafatovich also from Pelješac. Croatians managed boarding houses in Sydney and would often have up to 20 Croatian boarders staying there at the one time. In 1910 Croatians ran the Dalmatinska Gostiona (Dalmatian boarding house/hotel) on Crescent Street, Sydney. The Dalmatinska Gostiona business card read in Croatian 'Naj Bolja Svratiste u Sydney. I Svako Parni Brod Bitice Docekan' (The best boarding house/hotel in Sydney and every steamship will be welcomed). Some of the Croatian proprietors were Zan (Zaninović), Kosovich, Gojak, Pivach and Doša.[46]

The extended family, kinship and the greater sense of belonging were very important to the early Croatian settlers. The Croatian *zadruga* or communal household traditions provided the foundation for the strong emphasis on the extended family. According to Balch writing in the United States about Slavic migrants (1910), in the Croatian *zadruga* the household and farm were owned and worked as a family cooperative rather than individually. The communal nature of the *zadruga* in Croatia dominated social relationships, it was characterised by strong patriarchy and a clear division of labour.[47] Although Croatian pioneers were almost always single men on arrival, loneliness was not always a problem. They sometimes had brothers, cousins and other Croatian settlers to make them feel comfortable in their foreign surroundings. On many occasions Croatians who fell under the umbrella of the extended family in Australia were not necessarily related by blood. Being born in the same region or on the same island was adequate. As we have seen, Croatian pioneers not only maintained friendships with people from their own native village or district, but also with Croatians from other parts of Croatia further afield, as well as corresponding with their compatriots in other states. For example, Mattio Marassovich who lived in Woods Point received a letter from John Cvitanovich (Ivan Cvitanović), a fellow Croatian who was working in the Western Australian gold mines in Kalgoorlie in 1897, where at the time there was a concentration of Croatians. However, when a number of Croatians in a given community died, loneliness became a greater issue. This was especially evident for single Croatian miners who lived alone on the goldfields after the gold rushes had long past.[48]

Societies, clubs and newspapers

While Croatians in Australia established no formal clubs, societies or newspapers prior to 1913, it is interesting to consider other communities of Croatians living outside Europe who did. The first Croatian society formed in North America was the Slavonic-Illyric Mutual and Benevolent Society established in San Francisco in 1857. Other early Croatian societies include the Slavonic Charitable Society in New Orleans (1874), Slavonian Benevolent Society in Callao, Peru (1871), and Dalmatia No. 5, a volunteer firefighters association in Iquique, Chile (1874).

It was only in the 1890s that Croatians began to join fraternal or mutual benefit societies in large numbers. These societies provided Croatian immigrant industrial workers with insurance benefits in case of illness, accidents or death while supporting Croatian cultural and social activities within their communities. Included amongst these societies are the Croatian and Dalmatian Club in San Francisco (1893), Croatian Fraternal Union in Pittsburgh (1894), Croatian Slavonian Benevolent Society in Los Angeles (1895) and the Croatian Charitable Society in Pisagua Chile (1896). The Croatian Fraternal Union is now the largest Croatian organisation outside Croatia with over 90,000 members. Another important Croatian organisation in the United States is the Croatian Catholic Union. In 1907 the Croatian Benefit Society was formed in Dargaville, New Zealand, while the first Croatian society formed in Australia was the Croatian Slavonic Society established in Western

Thomas Pavletich's portrait

*Ane Milkovitch just before she left Croatia in
a Croatian embroidered dress*

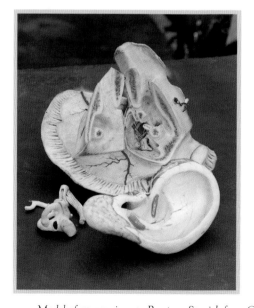

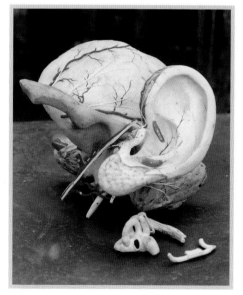

Model of an ear given to Prospero Stanich from Queen Victoria in recognition for treating her ears

Examples of ships that visited Australia in the second half of the nineteenth century and had a majority of Croatian seamen.

Model of the brig Splendido

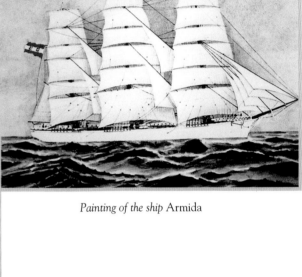

Painting of the ship Armida

Model of the corvette Helgoland

Model of the frigate Novara

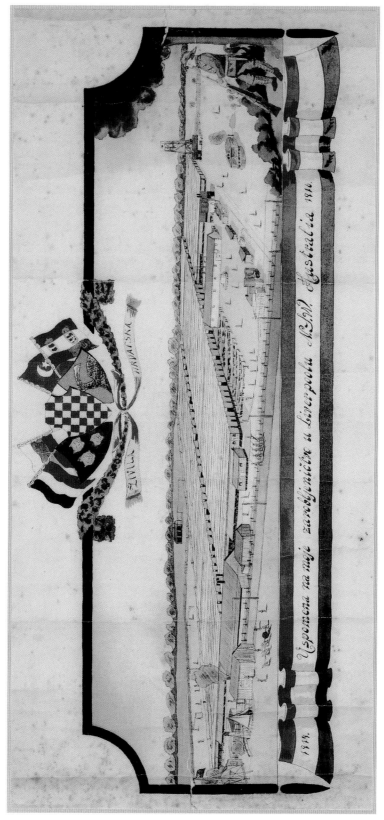

A painting of the Liverpool Camp by a Croatian internee during his internment in the Liverpool camp during the First World War. In the painting, from left to right, are the coats of arms of Dalmatia, Croatia, and Bosnia. In the painting the words, 'Živila Hrvatska' (Long live Croatia), are written.

Melbourne-based Croatian folkloric group Hrvatska Zora (Croatian Dawn) in the Croatian Catholic church in Sunshine, Melbourne in 2004

Melbourne-based Croatian folkloric group Mladi Hrvati (Young Croatians) in the 1980s

Croatians thanking Australia for recognition of Croatian independence on the steps of the Victorian parliament in 1992

Sydney-based Croatian folkloric group Lindo

'Sydney Symphony' painting by Charles Billich, the official artist of the Sydney Olympics and Australian Grand Prix

Wollongong-based Croatian folkloric group Zagreb performing at the Croatian folkloric festival in the Sydney Town Hall in 1998

Sydney-based Croatian folkloric group Braća Radić (Radić Brothers) at the Đakovački Vezovi folkloric festival in Croatia

Students attending the Croatian student conference in Mt Eliza, Victoria in 1989

Students attending the Croatian student conference in Bundeena, Sydney in 1990

Australia in 1913. Details on the activities of the Croatian Slavonic Society will be presented in chapter 9.[49]

The establishment of Croatian language newspapers and magazines by Croatian settlers was important as they kept Croatian immigrants informed of community activities in their new countries and of events in Croatia. Some of these newspapers became the mouthpieces of Croatian immigrant societies, providing information on community activities and Croatian politics. Croatian settlers established three newspapers in San Francisco between 1859 and 1885, and three newspapers in Buenos Aires in the 1880s. However, little is known about them apart from the fact they existed. In the 1890s several Croatian immigrant newspapers were established in the United States, the main ones being *Danica* (Morning Star), *Narodni List* (People's News) and *Napredak* (Progress). *Narodni List*'s daily circulation reached 24,000 in 1915. Between 1899 and 1913 the three main Croatian immigrant newspapers published in New Zealand were *Bratska Sloga* (Fraternal Unity), *Napredak* (Progress) and *Zora* (Dawn), and in 1914, the latter claimed on its front page that it was 'the only Croatian newspaper in all Australasia'.[50] Croatian pioneers in Australia maintained links with communities in New Zealand who were also predominantly from the same regions of Croatia. Many Croatian pioneers in Australia were still alive when these newspapers were printed, and some of them may well have read these newspapers.[51]

Connections with the Catholic Church

It appears from records that Croatian pioneers who were practising Catholics or who had ties with the Catholic Church maintained more connections with other Croatians. Of the Croatian settlers' marriages in Victoria where there was a Croatian marriage witness, over 83 per cent were celebrated according to Catholic rites. The local Catholic church was the meeting place for a number of Croatian communities. Over 55 per cent of the early Croatian settlers who were married in Victoria were married according to Catholic rites. Croatian pioneers generally had a Catholic upbringing prior to their arrival in Australia. However, in some instances when they married non-Catholics in Australia, they stopped practising their faith or converted to other religions. Some Croatians who were married according to other rites, still remained practising Catholics and were buried in Catholic sections of cemeteries.[52]

Many Croatian pioneers and their descendants played an active role in local Catholic churches. However, their contribution to the development of the Catholic Church in Australia has remained largely unresearched and unrecorded. They collected funds, donated funds and helped maintain churches. They were married, baptised, attended mass, sang in choirs, played the church organ and had their requiem masses in Catholic churches. For example, Jacob Stiglich's daughter was a Catholic Sunday school teacher in Korumburra.[53] Children of Croatian pioneers attended Catholic schools and some were awarded Catholic school scholarships.

Many of the descendants of the Croatian pioneers became Catholic nuns and priests. The most highly distinguished of these, Matthew Beovich, became the Archbishop of Adelaide. The main areas in Victoria where there was a concentration of practising Catholic Croatian pioneers and their families were Geelong, Portarlington, Melbourne and Yandoit.

Many children of Croatian migrants joined the public service due to its being non-discriminatory on the grounds of religion. For example, Archbishop Beovich stated in 1980:

> By the time I'd reached 16 I might have, in the normal way, gone to a seminary. But financial considerations prevented this. So I went to work as a junior clerk in the Public Service for about five years. In those days we Catholics were second-class citizens. There were many jobs that weren't open to us. But the public service was. Entrance was by examination. They didn't ask your religion. But those are days long gone.[54]

Archbishop Matthew Beovich who was consecrated on Sunday 7 April 1940 was the Catholic Archbishop of Adelaide from 1939 to 1971; he was the eighth Archbishop of Adelaide and the first Australian-born Archbishop of Adelaide. He was well respected and known for the assistance he gave to post-war migrants who came to South Australia. Beovich was also involved in expanding the Catholic education system in Australia, believing it to be of the upmost importance. The new archbishop celebrated the first mass after his consecration to over 2000 Catholic school and college students in St Francis Xavier's Cathedral. In 1942 Archbishop Beovich established St Francis Xavier's Seminary for priests, the first in South Australia, and Aquinas College, a residential college of the University of Adelaide in 1950; he also established the Catholic Family Welfare Bureau.[55]

Archbishop Beovich helped Croatian refugees migrate to Australia. On 13 October 1954 at the Catholic Immigration Centre in Wakefield Street, Adelaide, he welcomed 25 Croatian refugee youths who had come by rail to Adelaide from Melbourne. At the train station a crowd of Croatians associated with the Adelaide Croatian Club greeted them. Some months earlier these young people had made their escape

Archbishop Beovich and his sister who was a nun

Archbishop Beovich

from Communist Yugoslavia. Four of them had rowed all the way to Italy in a small dinghy without food or water and without even a compass to guide them. According to *The News*, Archbishop Beovich commented: 'that more than 70 years ago a Croatian youth left Dalmatia … from where the boys have come, and migrated to Australia, where he married an Australian girl. These two people became my father and mother'.[56] Although Archbishop Beovich could only say a few words in Croatian, he tried to help the Croatian Catholic community in South Australia whenever he could.

Bartholomew Mercovich had four descendants who became Catholic nuns and another two became priests. One of these, Sister Catherine Teresa Mercovich, was a religious superior who led a group of nuns to establish the first Good Samaritan Sisters group in Japan in 1948. She spent the first few years in Nagasaki visiting the sick and operating a clinic for the poor. Later Sister Catherine Mercovich went to Sasebo where she established and was principal of Seiwa Girl's High School. After her death, graduates of Seiwa donated funds for a memorial plaque to be erected in her honour in Melbourne's Northcote Convent.

An important Catholic priest of Croatian descent, who was not born in Australia but in Cobh (formerly Queenstown), County Cork, Ireland in 1867 and who contributed to the early days of the Catholic Church in regional Victoria, was Monsignor Edward Goidanich. His father, Gabriele Goidanich (Gojdanić), who was born in Veli Lošinj on the island of Lošinj, was a Croatian ship's captain who settled in Cobh in the 1850s where he worked as a shipping agent and married an Irish woman, Arabella O'Sullivan. Edward Goidanich was educated in Ireland and some of his fellow students, Daniel Mannix (later Archbishop Mannix) and Maurice O'Reilly (later Monsignor O'Reilly), were destined to make important contributions to the Catholic Church and the Irish cause in Australia. After being ordained a priest, Goidanich arrived in Australia in 1891 where he worked as a priest in country areas like Swan Hill, Charlton and Ararat, where he helped build several new churches. During the First World War, Goidanich served for two years as chaplain to the Sixth Brigade in Gallipoli, Egypt and France. He was wounded in Gallipoli and later received the Military Cross for his service in the Australian Imperial Force (AIF). Goidanich was Dean of Ararat from 1930 to until his death in 1948.[57]

Almost all of the Croatian pioneers in the Geelong and Portarlington district considered themselves Catholics. There were at least 12 marriages with Croatian-born husbands in St Mary's Catholic Church Geelong prior to 1887. The first Catholic church in Geelong, St Mary's of the Angels, was a wooden church built in 1842. Within five years, a larger stone building was erected. By the early 1870s an even larger church had been built, although the existing spire and towers were not added until the 1930s.[58] A number of Croatians, for example, Joseph Postich, Matthew Florio and Girollamo Florio, were married in this church as early as 1852. Matthew Florio's marriage witness was Girollamo Florio. Almost half of the Croatian pioneers married in this church lived or later settled in Portarlington. As a return trip from Portarlington to St Mary's Catholic Church Geelong was 62 kilometres, it would be reasonable to suggest that, since these Croatians and their families regularly made the journey to practise their faith, they were devoted Catholics. By travelling to Geelong they could also interact with Croatians in Geelong. For example, Dominick Lussich who lived in Portarlington could visit his brother John Lussich in Geelong. There were at least 20 children with Croatian-born fathers baptised in St Mary's Catholic Church Geelong prior to 1890, and nine of these had a Croatian-born godparent.[59]

From the 1890s the Portarlington Croatians became more involved in the activities of the St Thomas' Catholic Church, Drysdale, which was closer to Portarlington. Ten of the early Croatian settlers' children were baptised in this church. After St Patrick's Catholic Church in Portarlington was completed in May 1895, the Portarlington Croatians and their families became an integral part of St Patrick's Catholic Church community in Portarlington.[60] They helped collect funds for the church and hall, attended Sunday school and Catholic district picnics, and also gave assistance to the parish priests whenever possible. For example, Dominick Lussich was a pallbearer for many Catholic funerals in Portarlington while John Lussich, on Sunday morning of 29 July 1899, had an accident at St Patrick's Catholic Church while helping the Catholic priest. According to *The Bellarine Herald*, 'John Lussich was harnessing the Rev. Father Cusack's horse to buggy, when something startled the animal. It plunged forward knocking Mr Lussich down and rendering him unconscious. The horse dashed through one fence, but failed at a second, and was captured. Mr Lussich was found to be severely bruised, but the horse and vehicle were uninjured'.[61] Descendants of the Croatian pioneers continued to support St Patrick's Catholic Church well after all the Croatian pioneers in the district had passed away.

Drawing of John Lussich

Many Croatian pioneers attended mass in St Francis Catholic Church on the corner of Lonsdale and Elizabeth Streets in Melbourne, which is the oldest Catholic church in Melbourne. The first Catholic mass in Melbourne was celebrated in an unroofed store in 1839, and the same year a collection was taken up for a more suitable place of worship. The first mass was celebrated in St Francis Catholic Church on 22 May 1842, three years almost to the day since the first mass in the unroofed store. St Francis was the home of Melbourne's first bishop and a temporary cathedral. Here priests were ordained and a Catholic school was also built. St Francis Catholic Church was built in Gothic style and has beautiful stained glass windows. Prior to 1894 there were at least 12 Croatian settlers who were married in St Francis Catholic Church.[62]

Other Croatian pioneers were married and attended mass in numerous Catholic churches in Melbourne including: St Patrick's Cathedral; St Peter's and Paul's, South Melbourne; St Ignatius', Richmond; St Brigid's, North Fitzroy; St Joseph's, Port Melbourne and so on. Some of the Catholic churches in which Croatian pioneers were married in Sydney include St Patrick's, St Mary's Cathedral, and St Francis. Before 1899 there were 15 Croatian pioneers married in St Patrick's Catholic Church in Sydney; a third of these had a Croatian marriage witness. The Catholic Church also supported Croatians in their time of need. Both Antonio Bundara and Natale Vuscovich, who at one time lived in Portarlington, died in the care of the Catholic nuns at the Convent of Little Sisters of the Poor in Northcote, Melbourne.[63]

Croatians in Yandoit were also practising Catholics, and St Mary's Catholic Church, Castlemaine, played an important role in their lives. There were 25 baptisms of children with Croatian-born fathers in St Mary's Catholic Church before 1883. Eleven of these children had a Croatian-born godparent. Sandon Catholic Cemetery had at least six Croatian pioneers buried there.[64] Other Croatian pioneers who lived in Yandoit were buried in Catholic sections of other cemeteries.

Antonio Radovick played a prominent role in establishing a Catholic church in Korumburra. In the early days of Korumburra, Catholic mass was celebrated in Radovick's Korumburra Hotel. According to *The Great Southern Advocate*, Antonio Radovick was the chairman and local treasurer of the committee formed in 1891 to raise funds to build a Catholic church in Korumburra. He generously donated an altar and funds for the church, and committee meetings were held in his hotel. In 1894 Radovick opened a fund-raising bazaar in aid of the Catholic church where his daughters worked at various stalls.[65] On 28 April 1895, St Joseph's Catholic Church in Korumburra was officially opened and blessed by Archbishop Carr. The wooden church was built in a Gothic style and could accommodate 300 people. After his sermon Archbishop Carr commented: 'it is not customary, in fact I always avoid making reference to the part any person takes in assisting in church matters. On this occasion, however, I cannot pass over the great assistance rendered on behalf of the church by Mr Radovick and the members of his estimable family'. During the opening ceremony Antonio Radovick's daughter played the organ.[66] Antonio Radovick continued to assist the Catholic community in Korumburra. He was president of the committee that organised Catholic Sports while another committee member was his Croatian friend, Jacob Stiglich.[67] *The Great Southern Advocate* wrote that, after Antonio Radovick's death, Father Keating, the priest at St Joseph's, 'paid tribute to Mr Radovick's generosity and liberality towards the church on all occasions, and asked the prayers of those present for the repose of his soul'.[68]

It seems that in isolated towns and mining communities the Catholic church was a means of bringing social, spiritual and cultural fulfilment to Croatian pioneers and

Opening of St Joseph's Catholic Church in Korumburra

their descendants. The Catholic church played a vital role for Croatian pioneers and their families in the Dargo, Buckland, Walhalla and Gulgong regions. Catholic priests would perform marriage ceremonies and give spiritual guidance for Croatian pioneers in isolated mining communities. In Dargo, the Catholic school, for a brief

THE EXFORD HOTEL,
RUSSELL STREET, MELBOURNE.

A. RADOVICK wishes to draw the attention of his friends in SOUTH GIPPSLAND to the above well-known and long-established Hotel. It is centrally situated in the heart of the Metropolis, and visitors will find there the comforts of a home, combined with the strictest attention. Business men will also be well suited, the establishment being so well known and accessable from all parts of the city.

THE KORUMBURRA HOTEL.
(SEVENTY ROOMS.)

This Handsome and Commodious Hotel is replete with every modern convenience, and affords comfortable and recherche Accommodation for Visitors.

Baths. Billiards. Good Stabling.
SADDLE HORSES ON HIRE.

Only the most superior brands of Ales, Wines and Spirits kept.

CUISINE SANS REPROCHE.

A. RADOVICK, Proprietor.

Antonio Radovick and advertisements for his hotels

period, replaced the state school due to the strong Catholic presence there. Stephen Paulussy's family in Buckland were practising Catholics; his daughter Ellen was a member of the Catholic Women's Social Guild. *The Alpine Observer* commented that Ellen Paulussy together with her cousin Clara Walsh, who used to live with the Paulussy family, freely cleaned and took care of the garden of the Catholic Church in Bright for many years.[69]

On many occasions the Catholic upbringing of Croatian pioneers still exerted an influence even when they changed religions. Even though John Markovich was married in a Church of England ceremony and attended Church of England services, he was a Catholic by background. Two brass candlesticks on the St Nicholas Church of England Church altar in Lakes Entrance were donated to the memory of John Markovich. These candlesticks were previously locked away by the Anglican clergy as it was believed that they resembled the Roman Catholic style too much. However, for at least the last decade, the brass candlesticks have been displayed on the altar.[70]

Early Croatian settlers in other states were also devout Catholics. For example, Nicholas Jasprizza who arrived in Australia in 1860 donated a life-size statue of the Blessed Virgin to St Mary's Catholic Church in Young, New South Wales. The impressive statue is still an important focal point of the church today.[71] In Western Australia a Croatian pioneer named his winery 'Sveta Marija' (Holy Mary). Croatian pioneers attended mass, were married and had their children baptised in St Joseph's Catholic Church, Townsville. For example, the Croatian pioneers Joseph Sabadine, John and Jacomina Comandich were godparents to two of Joseph Vidulich's children in this church between 1880 and 1890.[72]

The Catholic Church in Australia was linked to and dominated by the Irish. Through the influence of the Catholic Church, and perhaps because some wives of the Croatian pioneers were born in Ireland or were of Irish descent, many Croatian pioneers were sympathetic to the Irish cause. It could be that they felt that the Irish had been exploited by foreign powers in a similar way as the Croatians. In 1894 Antonio Radovick provided everything at his own expense for the St Patrick's Day Celebrations banquet in Korumburra. *The Korumburra Times* noted that about 50 gentlemen representing all beliefs and religions attended the celebrations.[73] Croatian pioneers and their families were always willing to give assistance for St Patrick's Day Celebrations and the Irish Famine Relief Fund. For example, in Costerfield, Bartholomew Mercovich's daughter, Kate, together with Mary, the wife of the Croatian pioneer Frank Golden, collected money and food for the St Patrick's Day Sports in 1878.[74] Croatian pioneers and their descendants were members of various Catholic organisations and lodges such as the Hibernian Australasian Catholic Benefit Society, Australian Holy Catholic Guild and Irish National Foresters. At Jacob Curlizza's funeral in Sydney in 1885 for example, his cousin Lawrence Glaninich, as well as members of the Australian Holy Catholic Guild were present. Curlizza (Čurlica) was born in Mokošica. In 1884 he was Vincent Yannich's marriage witness in St Patrick's Catholic Church, Sydney. Similarly, a branch of the Irish National Foresters (INF) participated in Jacob Stiglich's funeral cortege. According to *The Great Southern Advocate*, he was well known by the early settlers in Korumburra and was regarded as 'the friend of everyone'.[75] Some of these lodges, such as the INF Daniel O'Connell Branch, South Melbourne, had pro-Irish inclinations.

Thomas Pavletich lived in Victoria before moving to New Zealand. On 22 August 1875 he wrote a letter to the editor of *The Otago Daily Times* complaining of the way a Daniel O'Connell Centenary Banquet was held. The banquet was supposed to have been held in the memory of Daniel O'Connell, but very few words were said to memory of Daniel O'Connell or of his liberal views. Pavletich stated he had great respect for Daniel O'Connell, so he detested the fact that all the speeches given had been presented from the conservative Presbyterian viewpoint. More people, he believed, should have been allowed to have their say. Pavletich said he would keep his money in his pocket and not attend such conservative functions in the future.[76] The editorial was somewhat cynical of Thomas Pavletich, referring to him as a porcine benefactor – a reference to the fact that he was considering establishing a piggery in or near Dunedin. They sarcastically stated that the public had missed a treat by not hearing Pavletich speak at the O'Connell Centenary Banquet. They also made fun of his forward-thinking suggestion, 'That the railway authorities should issue season tickets according to the class for every line, so as persons could travel anywhere with one ticket', rather like today's Eurail Passes.[77]

Thomas Pavletich

Dunedin was originally settled in 1848 by the Otago Association with exclusively Scottish immigrants. Thus the town was largely Scottish and conservative Presbyterian in character. However, the Otago gold rush began in 1861 and the population of Dunedin began to change. Gold miners like Thomas Pavletich were more liberal in their political views than many of Dunedin's earlier citizens. Pavletich, being a Catholic and having an Irish wife, supported Daniel O'Connell's view for Ireland to be independent of Britain. However, a Croatian speaking on Irish affairs was not highly regarded in Dunedin. By way of another example of Croatian support for the Irish cause, Mattio Orlovich was a member of a committee formed in Gulgong in 1875 to celebrate the centenary of Daniel O'Connell's birth.[78]

Matthew Beovich's diary revealed that he was very interested in Ireland, Irish culture and Irish politics. His maternal grandparents were Irish. In 1918 Beovich received a letter from his old high school friend Arthur Calwell, who later became Minister for Immigration. In the letter Calwell mentioned their disgust that Irish sympathisers were interned. Censors used this letter to recommend that Lieutenant Calwell be dismissed from the Australian Military Forces because of his Irish sympathies.[79]

On 22 June 1923, Matthew Beovich, when planning his journey home from Rome to Australia, wrote in his diary: 'I fear I must cut out Dalmatia'. However, he still managed to visit Ireland for three weeks. Beovich's reason for not going to Dalmatia was explained in a letter he wrote 58 years later (five months before his death on 24 October 1981). By travelling to Croatia he had wished to learn more about his family in Croatia. He wrote: 'I had hoped to visit Dalmatia but advisers in Rome said there was still a shortage of food there after the war and visitors would only aggravate the position'.[80]

Croatians who settled in Australia between 1890 and the First World War and their descendants also maintained strong links with the Catholic Church. For example, Fred Franich's daughter was a nun and his son, Ivan Franich, was granted an Archbishop's scholarship at St Colman's Central Scholarship School in Fitzroy, Melbourne. The following year he was granted a scholarship for the Victoria Parade Christian Brothers College.

As a young priest in the early 1930s, Father Launcelot Goody (later Archbishop of Perth) went to Split in Croatia to learn Croatian to enable him to more effectively serve the many Croatian Catholics in Western Australia at the time. He celebrated mass in Croatian to Croatian settlers in Spearwood, Midland and Kalgoorlie–Boulder. Father Goody built the Catholic church in Spearwood with the assistance of the Croatian community in the area. In 1934 Father Milan Pavlinović, a Croatian missionary in New Zealand, visited Australia at the invitation of Bishop Fox and celebrated Catholic mass for Croatian communities in Broken Hill, Kalgoorlie–Boulder, Perth, Spearwood, Fremantle and Sydney.[81]

Today Croatian migrants and their descendants still attend Catholic masses, are baptised, confirmed and married in some of the same Catholic churches throughout Australia frequented by Croatian pioneers. Mass, weddings, baptisms and confirmations are celebrated in the Croatian language in a number of these Catholic churches, including St Mary's, Geelong; St Patrick's Cathedral, Melbourne; St Mary's Cathedral, Sydney; and St Alipius', Ballarat. Many Croatian immigrants and their descendants have been married and confirmed in Croatian language services in St Mary's Catholic Church, Geelong. In the second half of the twentieth century Melbourne's St Patrick's Cathedral has been an important place for Croatians to conduct vigils in support of democracy and peace in Croatia.

The first Croatian Catholic parish outside Europe was founded by Croatian migrants in Pittsburgh in 1894 and the next year they completed building their own church. By the time of the First World War, 22 Croatian Catholic parishes had been established in the United States. Today there are 73 Croatian parishes outside Europe. The United States has 33 Croatian parishes, Canada 19, Australia 14, South America (Argentina, Venezuela, and Peru) three, New Zealand two and South Africa one. Further details on the Croatian Catholic parishes in Australia will be given in chapter 10. There are 121 Croatian Catholic parishes in Western European countries. Over 70 per cent of these are in Germany, where there are 85; Switzerland has 13, Austria eight, France four, Sweden four, Belgium two and Britain, Netherlands, Norway, Denmark and Luxembourg each have one parish. Croatian Catholic churches are also maintained in Bosnia-Herzegovina and Yugoslavia (Vojvodina and Kotor), and Slovenia has Croatian parishes. There are also Croatian churches in Austrian Burgenland, western Hungary and Romania.[82]

Pioneer women

As noted earlier in this chapter, several Croatian women settled in Australia prior to 1890. Ursula Zan (Uršula Zaninović) came with her husband Vincent (Vicko), three daughters and two sons to Australia in 1889. They were all born in Starigrad on the island of Hvar.[83] For a decade they had a thriving broom factory, Zan Bros & Co., in North Melbourne before moving the business to Drummoyne, Sydney where it was called Excelsior Broom Factory.

The Zan family Excelsior Broom Factory in Sydney

The Zan (Zaninovich) family in Sydney

One of Ursula Zan's daughters, Manda, was a fine singer and actress, and at one time toured New Zealand.[84] Manda Zan married Michael Canny in 1909 at St Mary's Catholic Cathedral, Sydney. The marriage witness was her sister Clara. Manda returned to Melbourne where she had two sons and lived out the rest of her life. Her husband became the Railway Commissioner of Victoria. Clara Zan never married and lived with her parents. After her death she was buried in the same plot as her father's uncle, George Zaninovich (Jure Zaninović).[85] He had arrived in Victoria in about 1861 and was a gold miner in Majorca. George Zaninovich had joined Vincent Zan's family in Sydney a few years before his death on 30 August 1906. The witness to his will was Marino Petrich.[86]

Manda Zan on her voyage to New Zealand,
she is on the right side

Mary Zaninovich married a fellow Croatian, Gasper Marohnic (Gašpar Marohnić), in St Mary's Roman Catholic Church, West Melbourne, on 4 November 1895. The witnesses to the marriage were Maximillian Pasquan (Paškvan), the son of the Croatian pioneer, Martin Pasquan, and Mary's sister Clara. Mary and Gasper Marohnic later went to live in San Francisco where they joined

Above and below: Manda Zan's wedding breakfast

the already well-established Croatian community which boasted six Croatian societies. From 1850 to 1900 there were over 250 Croatian fishermen in San Francisco and over 100 restaurants, saloons and fruit shops managed by Croatians on Davis Street, San Francisco. The Slavonic-Illyric Mutual and Benevolent Society hall was also on Davis Street. Gasper Marohnic and Mary Zaninovich were both buried in the Croatian section of the San Francisco Cemetery.

This was not the Zan's family's first connection with Croatians in San Francisco. Vincent, together with his brother, had managed the Zan Brothers broom factory, also on Davis Street, before returning to Croatia to be married. Later Vincent with his wife and children rejoined his brother in the United States before coming to Australia. The Zan family were friends with other Croatians such as Matthew Beovich, Marino Petrich and P. Plancich.[87]

Lena Vodanovich (Vodanović) and her husband Gerald, who were born on the island of Vis, arrived in New South Wales in 1885. They were fishmongers and had an oyster shop in Sydney. Apart from a 15-year period in Western Australia, they spent most of their lives in Sydney.[88] Another Croatian-born woman pioneer settler was Susan Pascoe who was born in Dubrovnik in approximately 1865. She was married to an Englishman, Joseph Morris, on 21 December 1886 in Melbourne. At the time she was living on Union Street, Brunswick; her occupation was listed as home duties.[89]

Other Croatian women visited Melbourne (and other coastal cities) when they accompanied their Croatian captain husbands on trading trips. Mrs Tarabochia came on the barque, *Triade Tarabochia*, in 1886 and Nilla Ivancich (Ivančić) came on the barque, *Gange*, in 1887. Both these barques had Croatians among the crew. During the shipwreck of the *Gange* (described in chapter 6), Nilla Ivancich remained calm and courageous in extremely dangerous circumstances. The seas were rough and the *Gange* was taking in water. *The Age* detailed how she was almost thrown overboard, 'only one woman on board, the captain's wife, who had a very narrow escape. She was in bed at the time the vessel struck, and barely succeeded in reaching the deck before her cabin was swamped. She had to escape with nothing but her night dress upon her, and remained wrapped in a blanket in the chart room. While seated there a heavy sea swept over the vessel, bursting through the chart room and carrying Mrs. Ivanchich to the fore part of the ship, where she was fortunately grasped by the second mate, and saved from being washed overboard'. After spending the night on the stranded vessel, Nilla Ivancich and all others on board were saved by a lifeboat. She was 18 years old and on her honeymoon.[90]

The most famous Croatian woman to visit Australia was the highly distinguished soprano, Ilma De Murska (Ema Pukšec), who was born in Ogulin. Ilma De Murska had sung in concert halls throughout the world, in cities such as Florence, Vienna, London and New York. In 1875 she performed in 13 well-attended concerts in the Melbourne Town Hall, and concerts in Ballarat and Bendigo. In the following year she gave 12 performances at the Melbourne Opera House, the operas being *Lucia di Lammermoor*, *La Sonnambula*, *Il Trovatore* and *Faust*. She also performed at Geelong's Mechanics' Hall.[91] Her tours were a great success, although they were also accompanied by scandal. She married twice during the tour (once in Sydney and once in New Zealand) while apparently still being married in Europe.[92] In Sydney she drew audiences of 3000 to 4000 to the Exhibition Building. In 1876 *The Argus* described her performance in the opera *Faust* in glowing terms, writing: 'she is exceptionally gifted as a singer, we find in Mademoiselle Ilma de Murska such a grand union of powers, both natural and acquired, that their application to the interpretation of this famous part is an event in a lifetime to have witnessed, and having been once seen is never to be forgotten'.[93] *The Australasian Sketcher*'s compliments on De Murska's performances were even more generous: 'Of her success since she has been in Victoria there is but one opinion, namely, that great as it may be, it is only the recognition of her talents which is her just due, and no more, and that she is the greatest singer who has ever visited us, so ought her success here be the greatest on record'.[94] Ilma De Murska died in Munich in Germany on 14 January 1889.[95] De Murska Street, in Prahran, was named in her honour. In the late 1870s and 1880s in the Creswick region, there were successful De Murska gold mines also named after her.[96] In 1901 another Croatian opera singer, Bassich, was extremely popular during a successful season throughout Australia.[97]

Another early Croatian female arrival was Perena Rocchi (Roki) who was born on the island of Vis and arrived in Australia in 1895. She was one of the first Croatian women to settle on the Western Australian goldfields. Her maiden name was Rastovich (Rastović). Perena Rocchi's husband, Luke, was also born on the island of

Ilma De Murska, a highly distinguished soprano

Perena Rocchi with her children in 1912

Vis and they had six children before he died in Kalgoorlie in 1907. She spent three years in Broken Hill, six months in Adelaide, six years in Boulder and the rest of the time in Spearwood in Western Australia where, against the odds as a widow, she purchased a property and became a market gardener. The Perena Rocchi Reserve near Spearwood was named in her honour.[98]

Since there were only several Croatian women who settled in Australia prior to 1890, a number who settled in Mooroopna and Bendigo in Victoria before the end of the First World War will also be mentioned. These women were predominantly the wives and female children of Trojano Darveniza's brothers, for example, his brother John (Ivan) Darveniza's family, including wife Clara Devcic (Jele Devčić), two daughters and son arrived in Victoria in 1894.[99] His brother, Mato Darveniza, and some members of his family arrived in Australia in 1909. Mato brought a bride from Croatia for his son, Peter (Pero). Ane Milkovitch (Ane Miljković) and Peter Darveniza were married in 1910 at St Brendan's Roman Catholic Church, Shepparton. They subsequently had nine children. According to *The Shepparton News*, the 'bride was handsomely attired in white silk, and wore the customary veil and coronet of orange blossoms'. The bridesmaid was Peter Darveniza's cousin, Mary Darveniza, and the wedding party was held at John Darveniza's residence.[100] The Croatian women in Mooroopna also had contact with other Croatian pioneers and their families.

A few Croatian women settled in Bendigo. Francesca Radic (Radić), who was born in Malinska on the island of Krk on 29 June 1879, was one of them. She disembarked in Melbourne in 1907 and a couple of years later she married a Swiss widower, James Maranta, but they had no children.[101] She and her husband managed the Suburban Hotel on White Hill Road, Bendigo. Francesca Maranta's niece, Maria Kovacevic (Marija Kovačević), who was born in Rijeka, arrived in Australia in 1912 and joined her aunt in Bendigo. Maria Kovacevic never married and died in her aunt's home in 1919 at the age of 26. Their relative, Katerina Kavacevih, whose maiden name was Radich, also lived in Bendigo.[102]

Poverty and disillusionment

Not all Croatian pioneers made their fortunes or were successful in Australia. Some were forced to live a life of economic hardship and poverty. Their disillusionment with life in Australia was further fuelled by loneliness, especially felt by poor elderly single male Croatian pioneers. Growing up in the traditional Croatian way where family and kinship were of utmost importance presented a sharp contrast to the life some Croatian pioneers led in Australia, a life without family or support. As we have seen, occasionally Croatian pioneers corresponded with relatives in Croatia to ease their loneliness. Others resorted to alcohol.

Croatian pioneers in Victoria and New South Wales who lived in poverty were typically old single miners who could not find enough gold to support themselves. Ladies' benevolent societies gave assistance to struggling Croatian pioneers. For example, Louis Fabrio (Luka Fabrio), who was born in Starigrad on the island of Hvar, and was a miner at Moonlight Flat, Victoria, received assistance from the Maryborough Ladies' Benevolent Society. He was found dead in his home in 1900 by the grocer's assistant who was supplying him with some provisions – through the kindness of the Maryborough Ladies' Benevolent Society. John Antoniwich was another Croatian who received assistance from a similar society. Both he and his wife were sick for the last few years of his life. Fortunately, the Ladies' Benevolent Society of Echuca gave them assistance during this time of need, also contributing to his burial costs after he died on 12 August 1885 in Echuca. Similarly, Catholic nuns in Melbourne assisted destitute Croatians. Descendants of Croatian pioneers also assisted the Ladies' Benevolent Societies. For example, Antonio Radovick's daughter was secretary of the Ladies' Benevolent Society in Korumburra.[103]

Struggling miners with families were often forced to seek other forms of employment when their gold mining was not profitable. For example, Gaspar Blossage, who was born in Rijeka, was for several years a miner in Bendigo and Huntly, but had to seek employment elsewhere to support his family. In April 1877 Blossage left his home in Huntly and went to work at Whiteley's Saw Mill in Echuca East. Blossage was in a desperate economic situation with his wife and children nearly starving in Huntly. On 6 May 1877 he was found lying dead in his bed in his hut. A post-mortem examination of Blossage's body revealed that he had died from heart disease, but it was also found that he had no food in his stomach. According to his fellow workers, Blossage sent all the money he earned to his needy family, while he went without. Blossage never complained to anyone about his illness.[104]

A Croatian who died in the bush without support or company was Andrea Guircovich who was born in Opatija. He died near his mine in the Wedderburn district in July 1888. His body was found several days after his death in the fireplace of his tent. His head had been burnt beyond recognition and cats had eaten the uncovered parts of his body.[105]

In the Wedderburn Croatian community alcohol was a problem. Some miners became heavy drinkers late in life. Ignatio Billich (Bilić), who was born in Trogir, was a miner and vigneron in Wedderburn who died from alcohol poisoning. Billich, like other Croatians in the area, made his own wine. In 1892 he was taken to court on the charge of illegal sale of liquor. Billich was given the lowest fine possible for the offence – £25 in default of one month's imprisonment. As he could not afford to pay the fine he was sent to Castlemaine gaol for one month. It was recorded that Billich, on entering prison had a bullet mark behind his right ear, he had lost several teeth in his upper and lower jaws, there was a long scar on his left arm and a tumour on the back of his neck. He died on 12 October 1900 in Wedderburn from a heart attack as a result of alcohol poisoning. Billich was found dead on the roadside where he had been lying drunk from the previous night.[106]

For some impoverished miners, asylums and hospitals seemed a good alternative to their miners' huts where meals were not guaranteed. At least 17 Croatian pioneers were admitted to asylums in Victoria between 1855 and 1906, in most cases reportedly suffering from mania and dementia. The majority of the Croatian pioneers admitted to asylums were miners. James McNish, who was born in Dalmatia, spent six months in the Kew Asylum in 1877 as a patient suffering from dementia. The examining doctor believed that his being a loner in the mining industry was the cause of his dementia. Some Croatian patients in asylums had hallucinations, heard voices, and were incoherent and noisy. Croatians in asylums usually had no visitors.[107] Croatians were also sent to hospital for treatment of illnesses and treatment of injuries they suffered in accidents. For example, both Fortunato Poschich and Antonio Scopenage were admitted to the Geelong Hospital for amputations after being involved in accidents. Poschich's accident occurred while working as captain of a schooner. Scopenage was injured when he was hit by a train attempting to cross the railway lines in Geelong.[108]

The impact of the Australian environment on some Croatian immigrants was harsh. For example, the last couple of decades of Luke Yannich's life on the Omeo goldfields and Peter Albich's life on the Crooked River goldfields must have been extremely lonely as most of the other miners had already left these isolated goldfields and both were single. Other Croatians lived in similarly remote and harsh regions of Australia, enduring the tropical and rugged aspects of the Palmer River goldfields in Queensland, while others had the heat and dust of the Kalgoorlie goldfields in Western Australia to contend with.

Croatian pioneers, in the main, were law-abiding members of the community, the crime rate being very low amongst them. Careful examination of Victorian police gazettes and court session records revealed that the Croatian pioneers' most common crime was selling alcohol without a license. However, this may have been due to a cultural difference, since in Croatia vignerons would often sell small volumes of alcohol without a license. Other crimes include using obscene language in public, wife desertion, having no means of support and petty theft.

In their own communities Croatians tended to resolve any disputes or grievances which arose in the community by themselves. For example, on Christmas Eve in 1875 in the Wedderburn mining community, Stefano Celovich stabbed a fellow Croatian, Matteo Baillich, during a brawl. To the astonishment of the Crown, in the case of the Queen versus Celovich, the stabbed Baillich dropped all charges just before the trial. Instead, he had accepted £40 out of court from the defendant as compensation for the injury.[109]

The most common crime committed against Croatian pioneers was theft. This was especially prevalent against Croatian publicans. Gold watches were the most common item stolen from Croatian pioneers. Some of the more interesting items stolen from Croatian pioneers include a telescope 61 cm long and a brown sealskin rug, both of which were stolen from Fortunato Poschich.[110]

The main causes of death amongst Croatian pioneers in descending order were heart attacks and heart disease, phthisis (pulmonary tuberculosis), pneumonia, bronchitis and senile debility. The medical assistance for unbearable pain was virtually non-existent apart from alcohol. A number of Croatian pioneers inflicted injuries upon themselves while suffering terminal illnesses in an attempt to relieve the pain. In 1896 Dominic Milovitch stabbed himself in the stomach while he was a patient in Maryborough Hospital, Victoria. The wound was about 20 cm long across his stomach, from which his intestines protruded. Milovitch had not been attempting suicide but was trying to relieve the pain. He had complained on numerous occasions about the pain he had to endure. The wound subsequently became infected and he died.[111]

In many instances, letters from Croatia gave details of the economic hardships the pioneers' relatives in Croatia were experiencing. Apart from failed crops and lack of well-paid jobs, the family based in Croatia had the added burden of educating younger brothers and sisters, finding the dowry for any sisters, supporting the parents in their old age, paying funeral expenses and so on. In some of these letters, relatives in Croatia also asked for financial aid to ease their burden. Mattio Marassovich received these kinds of letters from both a brother and sister on the island of Vis. One of his sisters begged him to send financial assistance to enable her to supply the dowry necessary for her only daughter's marriage. She also asked for Mattio or his son to be her daughter's best man by proxy at the wedding. In a similar vein, Mattio's brother asked him to forgo his paternal inheritance as his brother had paid the dowry for their three sisters' weddings, paid off their father's debts and restored their parents' home.[112]

It was common for Croatian pioneers to leave assets in their will for their relatives in Croatia. Even though some of these pioneers had their own children and wives in Australia whom they were supporting, they still set something aside for their families in Croatia. For example, Thomas Zuzulich left the majority of his assets to his wife and children in Australia, but he still left £50 to his sister Paulina in Croatia. Similarly, Dominick Lussich left his assets to his daughters in Victoria and relatives on the island of Brač.[113]

The flow of money was not one-sided. Croatian pioneers in Australia also received money from their share of inheritances in Croatia. Antonio Bogovich (Ante Bogović) was expecting money from his share of his family farm in Croatia, but died a hero in an accident before it arrived. In 1906 he was sitting on the veranda in front of Smith's store in Yapeen in Victoria when he noticed a horse on the run and out of control. The horse was dragging a baker's cart and had raced onto the road. Although 68 years old, Bogovich quickly ran out in front of the horse and attempted to grab the reins, and with his stick, turn the horse. He was struck by the horse and thrown to the ground. Bogovich was killed instantly as a result of a knock received on his head. It was believed that the horse was originally startled by a gun shot.[114] Some of the older Croatian miners may have wanted to return to Croatia, but their poor financial state and old age prevented this. They may have also been ashamed to return to Croatia not having made their expected fortune.

CHAPTER 5

Pioneers on the Goldfields

Early Australian goldfields

Croatian settlers were involved in all aspects of mining: alluvial, quartz, prospecting for nuggets, operating crushing plants, and working in deep mine shafts. They were shareholders in mining companies and were mine managers. They also worked as publicans, storekeepers, woodcutters and labourers on the goldfields. Croatian pioneer miners followed each other to the various goldfields. As we noted earlier, they had mining claims together, typically with one or two Croatian partners. The most frequent occupation of the Croatian pioneers in Victoria was that of a gold miner – it was about four times more common than labourer and seaman.

Although life was hard on the goldfields, some Croatian pioneers stayed on the goldfields for many years, with several remaining miners in Victoria for over 50 years. At least 23 Croatian pioneers were still mining at the age of 50 years or older.[1] In a number of settlements, almost no Croatian pioneers were married. They lived in miners' huts and died without family comfort or support. Croatian mining communities across Victoria differed greatly. For example, in the Yandoit mining community most Croatians were married and raised families. However, in the Wedderburn area the Croatians very rarely married and if so, it was late in life.

The news of gold discoveries in Australia caused an unprecedented acceleration in the flow of migrants to Australia. Edward Hargraves, who had earlier mined in California, received the reward for the discovery of gold on 7 April 1851 at Ophir, New South Wales. Ten weeks later, another miner who had returned from California, James Esmond, discovered gold at Clunes, Victoria. This was not the first discovery of gold in Victoria, but the first of significance.[2] The excitement and hysteria that gripped people when gold discoveries became known was extraordinary. Ships bringing people to Melbourne lost their crew who 'jumped ship' and proceeded to the diggings. The gold miners came from all parts of the world and from every social class, determined to strike it rich and to return home wealthy. Unlike previous migration to Australia, which was almost exclusively British, there was a large influx of people of other nationalities. These included the Chinese, Germans, Americans, Italians, Croatians and many others. Many gold miners came to the Victorian goldfields from other Australian states. In fact, the Victorian gold rush had an enormous impact on South Australia – half of its male population had left for the goldfields by the end of 1851.[3] Many of the Croatian gold miners had lived in South Australia and New South Wales before arriving on the Victorian goldfields. Most walked to the goldfields carrying what they could on their backs, while the few who could afford it, bought a horse or booked a passage with a bullock team or coach. The roads to the goldfields were atrocious: they were wet and muddy in winter, dry and dusty in summer.

While mining on the Californian goldfields, the Croatian traveller, Tomo Skalica, who was born in Slavonski Brod, heard that: 'in Australia are very rich newly proclaimed goldfields, where every miner can earn with certainty and without a large amount of effort two ounces of gold daily'. When he arrived in San Francisco he was astonished by the number of miners waiting to board a ship bound for Australia. In 1853 Skalica arrived in Sydney and made his way to the New South Wales goldfields; he was one of thousands who came to Australia from the Californian goldfields. His account of this journey was published in the Croatian periodical *Neven* in 1856. Unfortunately, his account in *Neven* ended with his arrival on the goldfields. Skalica did not make his fortune on the goldfields and actually returned home to Croatia penniless in 1855.[4] If his failure on the goldfields had been published in *Neven*, then perhaps it may have deterred other Croatians from making the journey to Australia.

Conditions on the goldfields varied according to a miner's experience, skill, capital and equipment. Most of the early gold finds came from alluvial deposits, which were easy for a poor man to find and mine, the alluvial gold being found in sand and gravel near or in creek beds. After an alluvial goldfield was discovered, the miners would stake a claim. In creek beds they would pan for gold or use a rocking cradle to separate the heavier alluvial gold from the lighter sand and gravel. When alluvial deposits became exhausted, they dug shafts into the ground using picks and shovels to locate gold, most of which was found in quartz reefs. However, more skill and capital was required to follow the vein of gold in quartz, and water was a hazard in the deep mine shafts. In the 1850s the average shaft depth was 37 to 49 m and took several months to sink.[5] Companies which could afford necessary equipment and steam engines were formed to mine the gold found deep in the ground. These companies normally paid the miners' wages.

Before they could mine, miners required a gold license which cost 30s per month. But when the average earnings of miners dropped significantly, many could not afford to pay the high license fees. Resentment of the fee and the constant harassment by police to produce the license led to the famous battle at Eureka Stockade in Ballarat on 3 December 1854. Even though Eureka was a disaster, it gave the miners a political voice. The license fee was subsequently abolished and a miner's right of £1 per annum was introduced. All those who held a miner's right were allowed to vote at parliamentary elections.[6]

Life on the goldfields was extremely rugged. Many goldfield towns were temporary settlements of tents or bark dwellings, only a few of them becoming more permanent. For example, in 1864 a census of the number of dwellings and inhabitants within a radius of four kilometres around Woods Point revealed that the majority of the 1573 inhabitants lived in tents. There were 390 tents; 216 weatherboard houses and stores; and 114 log and slab houses.[7] Food supplies were expensive, of poor quality and could not always keep up with the rapid rise in population. The miners' diets usually consisted of mutton, damper and black tea; some went without vegetables for months at a time. Gold miners had a proven self-reliance, as evidenced by the fact that they made their own makeshift huts and mended their own clothes.[8] The clothes and possessions of Matteo Perich were typical of miners on the Victorian goldfields. He dressed in coloured moleskin trousers, flannel shirt, a dark tweed tac coat and vest, a soft, light-brown, wide-a-wake hat, a red silk scarf and a cotton handkerchief. On his back he carried two blue blankets wrapped in a bundle. In addition, Perich had a tobacco pouch, a pair of scissors, a towel, two combs, a looking glass, a purse and a piece of scythe stone.[9] Miners also wore heavy boots, and attached to their leather belts was a fossicking knife; many wore a sailor's coat and cap. They also carried axes, firearms, tents, pans and pots. A miner's social background was concealed by his rugged appearance. Miners worked on their claims six days a week.[10]

Drunkenness, burglary and violent crimes were occasionally a problem on goldfields, especially in the early days on new goldfields. Armed bushrangers occasionally attacked miners on the main roads surrounding the diggings.[11] For example, in May 1873 Natale Lussich was held up by two robbers. They stole the money he had received selling gold in Heathcote earlier that day. Later in the week the same thieves attacked and robbed another man. In the months prior to the robbery Lussich had crushed at least 14 tons of quartz to yield 36.3 ounces of gold (worth approximately £145), so it is presumed that he was carrying a substantial amount of money when robbed.[12] On two occasions in the 1870s, Australia's most famous bushranger, Ned Kelly, and his gang took shelter in Trojano Darveniza's winery. Darveniza let the men drink from his cellars and fed the men and their horses.[13] Gambling also flourished on the goldfields.

The price of mining equipment varied from one mining centre to another. For example, in December 1868, double-ended picks ranged from £2 8s to £3 per dozen in Ballarat, while in Buckland they were double that price, at £4 16s per dozen. Long-handled shovels varied from £3 to £4 per dozen in Ballarat, while in Woods Point they were £5 5s per dozen.[14]

The Victorian mining population peaked in December 1858 with 147,358 European miners and 26,321 Chinese miners. In 1857 during the gold rush there were almost twice as many males as females in Victoria. From 1853 to 1861, Victoria had been producing about a third of the world's gold. By the early 1860s however, most of

Victoria's great rushes had ceased, with the easier alluvial goldfields becoming a thing of the past. From 1853 Victoria's gold production declined, and from the late 1850s to the late 1870s, it had decreased to about a quarter of the 1850s figure. The quantity of gold produced in Victoria from 1851 to 1867, was 35,178,193 ounces; in New South Wales from 1851 to 1867 it was 7,929,688; in Queensland from 1860 to 1867 it was 128,711; and in New Zealand from 1853 to 1867 it was 3,746,214 ounces.[15] From 1851 to well into the twentieth century, Victoria was Australia's leading gold producer. Gold mining is still an important source of income for Australia; however, most of the gold produced in Australia today comes from Western Australia.[16]

Gold discoveries by Croatian pioneers

Andrea Franktovich (Andrija Franotović), from the island of Korčula, discovered a payable goldfield at Redcastle in December 1859. On 2 May 1862 he proved to a select committee of the Legislative Assembly that he had discovered the Redcastle and Sclavonian Reef. He subsequently received a £100 reward for his discovery.[17] Before he made this discovery, Franktovich had mined throughout Victoria. One of his mining partners at the time was Antonio Geronevitch from Dubrovnik, who later opened the All Nations Hotel in Redcastle. Both miners came to Victoria in 1853. Geronevitch came from San Francisco which suggests that he may have been a miner in California before arriving in Victoria. Franktovich and his Croatian partners had invested a considerable amount of capital up front before it became obvious that the Redcastle goldfield would be profitable. They had seven tons of quartz carted a distance of 20 kilometres to the nearest crushing plant at Heathcote which cost £22 15s. From this quartz Franktovich obtained 34.35 ounces of gold, a considerable amount. The gold would have sold for about £137. (According to Serle the average salary of a miner in 1859 was £80 per annum.) Other miners in Redcastle were not prepared to invest in carting quartz to Heathcote at such a high price without certain knowledge that the goldfield would be payable. Franktovich and party had also prospected for two months on other reefs and abandoned them, although some of them were later worked with payable results.[18]

In August 1861 Franktovich's Slavonian Company proceeded against John Clarke at the Redcastle Police Court for encroachment of a quartz claim. A few months later the case was heard at the Court of Mines where the Slavonian Company was rewarded £235 damages.[19] A dispute between Andrea Franktovich and John Clarke over who had discovered the Redcastle goldfield continued. In the Victorian Parliament, the select committee of the Legislative Assembly appointed to inquire into claims of prospectors and discoverers of new goldfields determined that Franktovich had discovered a payable goldfield at Redcastle. Franktovich's statement before the Victorian Parliament on 2 May 1862 was possibly the first statement by a Croatian to the Victorian Parliament, a section of which has been reproduced below.[20]

Mr Andrea Francktovick, examined.

561. By the Chairman. – Are you a miner? – I have been a miner for the last eight or nine years.

562. Where have you been mining? – Right throughout the colony.

563. In various places? – In various places.

564. Do you claim to be the discoverer of a gold-field? I do.

565. What is the name of it? – Of Redcastle and Sclavonia Reef.

566. When did you discover Redcastle? – I discovered it in December, 1859.

567. December? – In December, 1859. And I did not know what the ground might turn out, and I did not apply to the warden.

568. Were you at that time an alluvial miner or a quartz miner? – A quartz miner.

569. It was quartz you discovered at Redcastle in December, 1859? – Yes.

570. Was there any person there before you? – Yes.

571. How do you make yourself a discoverer if there were people before you? – For a payable gold-field.

572. If other people tell this Committee that they had discovered payable gold in August, 1859, would it not be the case? – I did not see the gold, nor was aware of it.

573. If they tell the Committee that payable gold was discovered at Redcastle in August, 1859 – long before you were on the ground – would it be the case? – Not to my knowledge.

574. By Mr McLellan. – Did you know Mr Clarke, on the Redcastle Reef? – Redcastle Reef?

575. At Redcastle, on any of the reefs there? – I know he had a reef not eastward. It was called Spring Creek; and he shifted from there to Redcastle, and had a business place there. He used to keep a little bit of a store – a country shanty – on the road, to make the best of his living, and when he had nothing to do he used to work prospecting.

In chapter 1 we saw that when Flett quoted Franktovich's statement about the Redcastle gold discovery in his book, *The History of Gold Discovery in Victoria* (1979), he omitted the line referring to the Sclavonian Reef. In the context of the quote above, this is an extraordinary omission.

In the early 1860s the Sclavonia Reef in Redcastle was yielding, on average, five ounces of gold for every ton of quartz crushed, increasing in richness with increase in depth. In the first half of 1864 at least 160 tons of quartz were obtained from the Sclavonian Reef at depths of up to 82 m, yielding 1697 ounces of gold. These were extremely good average returns of 10.6 ounces of gold per ton of quartz. Croatians also obtained similar returns on the other three main reefs in Redcastle.[21]

Another Croatian pioneer, Bartolomeo Citanich, claimed to have discovered the nearby Graytown payable goldfield in early spring 1868 but was never officially acknowledged or rewarded for his discovery. (Albert Corbett and co-workers were rewarded £400 for discovering the Graytown goldfield in October 1868.) Citanich wrote to the local newspaper on 3 December 1870 stating that he was the person who had discovered the goldfield a few weeks before the other party.[22] Citanich had five Croatian mining partners in the district. One of these was Dominic Milovitch (Dominik Milović) from Dalmatia with whom, in 1870, Citanich registered the Maximilian Quartz claim in Redcastle.[23] In 1888 the Croatian pioneer, Luke Yannich from Dalmatia, and Alfred Lucas discovered payable quartz reefs at Mountain Creek about 6.5 kilometres north-west of Omeo. In July 1888 they received £300 reward for discovering this new goldfield.[24]

At new rushes those who quickly took claims on newly discovered reefs increased their prospects of success. In January 1865 there was a rush of about 400 people to a new goldfield at Black River. According to *The Mountaineer* correspondent visiting the Black River goldfields, of all the mining claims, Radevich (Radovich) and Party were the first to strike a reef in their claim 'No. 1. South'. They then proceeded to clear away the timber and would not allow anybody to touch the stone in the reef as it was believed to be saturated with gold.[25] In any event it is unknown how much gold they found. Charles Radovich also associated with other Croatians; for example, in 1860 one of his mining partners in Redcastle was John Metrowich.[26]

In the Wedderburn district Croatian pioneers found gold nuggets weighing up to 330 ounces of pure gold. Stefano Celovich, who was born in Dalmatia, was mining in the Wedderburn area from the early 1860s. About 1.5 kilometres south of Wedderburn he found five gold nuggets at a depth of 4 m close by some old workings. The gold nugget sizes varied from four to 26.2 ounces, the largest of them being found on 30 November 1875 and the rest a few days later. Apart from the wealth realised from mining, Celovich was also a successful vigneron.[27] He died in Wedderburn on 16 October 1891. Thomas Rossi (from Zadar) was a witness at the burial and the executor of his assets. Stephen Celovich left all of his property to his wife, Antoinette Celovich, but in the event of her death, it would then go to Thomas Rossi. He also left John Volich (from Kotor) a bundle of fence wire.[28]

After his discoveries of gold nuggets Stefano Celovich sent for his nephew Constantino (or Costa) Celovich who subsequently arrived in 1886. On 7 May 1889 Constantino Celovich discovered a nugget weighing 336 ounces, of which 330 ounces were pure gold. The nugget was called 'The Opossum' and was found at a depth of 3.5 m at O'possum Point, about a kilometre south of Wedderburn. It was worth approximately £1400 and was exhibited in the window of the Bank of Australasia. *The Wedderburn Express* reported that:

the exhibiting of the nugget created a deal of excitement, and was soon the means of drawing a crowd, who passed some very complimentary remarks on the handsome speck, and congratulated the lucky finder. The nugget is of a smooth character, and almost perfectly clean, and is of a flat description with a number of smooth lumps on it. It is the intension of Mr Celovich to take the valuable lump to the Royal Mint after it has been some time on view in the window of the local Bank.[29]

The nugget was the ninetieth largest nugget found in Victoria; however, this nugget contained much more gold than many of the larger nuggets.

The largest gold nugget officially confirmed was discovered by two Cornish miners, John Deason and Richard Oates, at Moliagul on 5 February 1869. The nugget, named the 'Welcome Stranger', yielded over 2248 ounces (69.92 kg) of pure gold. In the weeks following the discovery of the large gold nugget Celovich found several smaller gold nuggets varying in weight up to 12 ounces. As a result of Celovich's discovery, at least 60 miners rushed to O'possum Point. Most of these miners worked in pairs, pegging their claims all around the original discovery site. By the end of May 1889 this rush had led to the discovery of several other smaller gold nuggets weighing up to nine ounces.[30] In 1890 another Croatian, Antonio Petrovitch, discovered in the same region, a 36-ounce gold nugget at a depth of 2.5 m this nugget yielded over 32 ounces of pure gold.[31] All these nuggets were found on the southern side of Wedderburn where the Croatian community lived.

A Croatian gold miner who had an interesting association with both the discovery of gold in California and Australia was Matthew Ivancovich. Apart from his mining adventures he was also a ship's carpenter and deck officer. In the 1840s Ivancovich was a sailor on a British merchant ship that sailed from Southhampton to Sydney. Among the cargo was a flock of sheep. When the ship docked in Sydney repairs were required. While waiting for the repairs to be completed, Ivancovich volunteered to assist in driving the sheep to the tableland, about 160 kilometres west of Sydney. The round trip took about eight days. He then proceeded to San Francisco to visit his brother John.

Ivancovich, who was working for Captain Sutter to help build a dam at Sutter's Fort on the Sacramento River, was present when gold was discovered there. Sutter employed men to build a sawmill, and in the newly constructed millrace, his foreman, James Marshall, discovered gold in January 1848 which resulted in the famous Californian gold rush. The following year, on the Californian goldfields at the Stanislaus river mines, Ivancovich noticed that Edward Hargraves was having difficulty operating the gold pan and cradle and showed him how to operate the device. The two men had both been sailors, and since Ivancovich had also recently been in Australia, they soon became friends. Later, Ivancovich and Hargraves discussed the similarity of the rocks and contour of hills in Australia and California. Hargraves decided to return to Australia to look for gold and asked Ivancovich to accompany him. They returned to Australia on the barque *Emma*, arriving in Sydney on 7 January 1851. The following month Hargraves set out from Sydney on horseback to cross the Blue Mountains; Ivancovich walked as he was afraid of riding a horse.

On 12 February 1851 Edward Hargraves found five specks of gold at Lewis Point Creek near Bathurst. The area later became known as Ophir. He immediately travelled to Sydney to announce his discovery and apply for a reward. Ivancovich was not impressed by the find and assessed that the areas they had mined were much poorer compared to the average diggings in California. Ivancovich decided to return to California and went to Sydney where he found work on a coastal merchant vessel trading between Melbourne and Sydney.

Payable gold was actually discovered by John Lister and William Tom at the junction of Summerhill Creek and Lewis Ponds on 7 April 1851. These two men washed four ounces of gold, worth more than £12, which was a payable field. Hargraves had shown John Lister, James Tom and William Tom how to build the cradle and how to use the pan and cradle. But he was in Sydney when they discovered the payable field. Hargraves received all the glory and almost all of the rewards. The New South Wales Parliament gave Hargraves over £10,000 and, after they had petitioned, gave John Lister, William Tom and James Tom £1000 between them.[32]

Later that year, while in port in Melbourne, Ivancovich met Croatians going to the Victorian goldfields and decided to accompany them. He first mined in Ballarat and then tried his luck in the Bendigo region. Even though he was successful in Ballarat, the cost of living was very high, so at the end of his mining career in Australia, he was not rich. Ivancovich subsequently returned to California where, apart from a mining stint in British Columbia, he mined for the rest of his life.[33]

Dalmatia and Sclavonian mines

We have already observed that, as most of the pioneers came from Dalmatia, the southern coastal region of Croatia, they were sometimes described as 'Dalmatians'. Another term used to describe Croatians was 'Sclavonian'. Croatian miners were proud of their origins, and in 1856 on one occasion they wore Croatian national costume on the goldfields at a farewell celebration for the Polish patriot, Seweryn Korzelinski. There were also Scottish Highlanders and some Englishmen in national costume at the celebrations at Quartz Mountain, about five kilometres from Alma.[34]

There were at least nine gold mining claims or reefs named Dalmatia and several others named Sclavonia or Slavonia throughout the Victorian goldfields. As noted previously, mining claims were named after the Croatian miners themselves or the town where they were born. Careful examination of mining records has revealed that, from 1860 to 1891, Croatians worked in over 500 mining claims in Victoria. Since Croatian pioneers were involved in so many mining claims, only the claims particularly named after Dalmatia, Sclavonia, Slavonia and the pioneers themselves will be used to highlight the types of mines they generally worked. Croatian miners who had Dalmatia and Sclavonia mines occasionally named their mines 'Maximilian' and 'Francis Joseph', also suggesting an attachment to the Habsburgs.[35] In the 1860s and 1870s in the United States, there were also Slavonian gold and silver mining companies worked by Croatians. In Peru Croatian miners owned gold, silver, copper and lead mines named after towns and regions of Croatia. For example, the names of some of their silver mines include Dubrovnik (1886), Zadar (1899), Dalmacia (1902) and Slavonia (1906).[36]

In the late 1870s two mining companies were formed by a group of Croatians north of Mount Moliagul in the McIntyre region. They were called the Dalmatia Gold Mining Company and Maximilian Gold Mining Company. The main shaft of Dalmatia mine still exists and is situated near Dalmatian Road, but the Maximilian mine shaft has been filled in. Before they formed the gold mining companies, Croatian pioneers had owned quartz prospecting claims in the area. In 1861 Croatians Crewechich and Lazarawitch originally discovered gold in the area about half a kilometre north of Moliagul Cemetery and this resulted in a gold rush. The goldfield was named Cemetery Flat.[37] Originally worked in the 1860s, the area had yielded quite good returns with as much as seven to ten ounces of gold per ton, but unfortunately the quartz had to be carted about 32 kilometres to be crushed.

The two Croatian companies – the Dalmatia Gold Mining Company and the Maximilian Gold Mining Company – were the largest known mining companies established by any group of Croatian pioneers on the Victorian goldfields. Unlike previous mining companies formed by Croatians, most of the work was tendered out. For example in October 1878, John Buzolich, the mining manager of the Dalmatia Gold Mining Company, requested tenders for driving a 55 m tunnel along the reef of the claim and for constructing a water dam.[38]

On 15 August 1877, Croatians Stephen Beriza, John Buzolich, John Grandi and John Muscardin formed the Dalmatia quartz claim. In March 1878, with 12 additional shareholders, the Dalmazia Reef quartz prospecting claim became a cooperative. One of these shareholders was Antonio Buzolich.[39] By June 1878 the Croatian miners and their partners had spent over £1150 on sinking four shafts and had found payable gold at the Dalmatia Quartz Reef. A full box of quartz specimens from the Dalmatia and Maximilian claims was brought to Dunolly for display. The quartz pieces were as large as 23 to 26 centimetres square and they had considerable gold on their exterior.[40]

The Dalmatia Gold Mining Company, No Liability was registered on 10 July 1878 and covered about 24 acres near Mount Moliagul. The company had 24,000 shares worth £1 each, owned by 17 shareholders and the Croatians, Stephen Beriza, Antonio Buzolich, John Buzolich, John Grandi and John Muscardin, owned over a quarter of the company.[41] A trial sample of ten tons was sent to a crushing machine at Bendigo and produced 1.35 ounces of gold per ton of quartz. The Dalmatia Gold Mining Company purchased a winding plant at St Arnaud and a crushing plant near Wehla. It had 24 heads of stamp crushers in four batteries and two good boilers.[42]

By March 1879 the depth of the shaft was 37 m. The south drive was 10 m long

The Dalmatia Gold Mining Company mine shaft today

with a 1.2 m thick quartz reef, while the north drive was 5 m long with a 1 m thick quartz reef. Gold could be seen in the quartz in both drives and the mine was expected to produce good yields. At the 30-m level a drive east along the quartz reef was over 3.5 m. A couple of months later there had been enough rain to start the stamps on the crushing plant. Quartz taken from the 30-m level produced payable returns of 0.5 ounces of gold per ton.[43]

In 1880 the Dalmatia Gold Mining Company received a £250 loan from the Victorian Government (as part of the prospecting vote of £20,000 passed by the Victorian Parliament) to assist them in further prospecting of the reef.[44] By June 1880, as a result of excess water in the mine, they were forced to stop sinking the shaft. Instead an attempt was made to make a cross-cut drive at the 41.5-m level. However, the company stopped work soon afterwards due to the water problem and lack of adequate pumping machinery. As a result they put their mine on the market.[45]

Overall, this company was not as successful as others, but it gave employment to many miners. The operation of this mining company proved that these Croatian miners had sound business and management skills. They arranged tenders, employed miners, purchased and transported large mining equipment, and knew how to apply for and receive government mining grants.

On 21 May 1878, nine Croatian pioneers (Stephen Beriza, Antonio Buzolich, Fiovaranti Buzolich, John Buzolich, John Grandi, Vincent Lazarovich, John Muscardin, Theodore Petcovich and James Polorineo) and another three shareholders formed the Archduke Maximilian Dalmatian Reef quartz claim.[46] The Maximilian Gold Mining Company, Limited which was on the Dalmatia line of the reef was registered on 5 September 1878. Out of a total of 17 shareholders, six were Croatian.[47] By January 1879, the shaft's total depth was 19 m, but the influx of water at this depth was so excessive, it allowed the contractors to request the cancelling of the contract. Another couple of attempts were made to make the shaft deeper, but each time, after a short period of work, they were forced to stop due to the influx of water. Towards 1880 all work on the Maximilian Gold Mining Company shaft had halted at the final depth of 22 m.[48] In 1876 Mattio Bussanich and partners worked on a gold mining claim on the Prospector's Maximillian Reef on the Little River Goldfields, New South Wales.[49]

Another miner, Niccola Mitrovich, was granted miner's rights on a quartz claim he named No. 1 North Slavonia Reef in the Inglewood mining district on 18 June 1860. The following month, three Croatian pioneers (Stanislaus Gazettick, Charles Miarlorick and Francesco Glinbich) became his partners. This was not the only time Niccola Mitrovich had mining claims with fellow Croatians. In the early 1860s, Mitrovich, together with another five Croatians, registered gold and antimony mines in Costerfield. In 1876 Mitrovich and the Croatian pioneer Frank Golden registered the Morning Star quartz and antimony claim in Costerfield.[50] The Croatian miner changing his surname to Golden suggests he dreamt of making a fortune on the goldfields. It is unknown what his real surname was but his mother's maiden name was Politch (Polić).[51] A quartz claim, the No. 1 South on the Slovian Reef near the No. 1 North Slavonia Reef, was worked by the Croatians, Nicholas Siglich, James Pollich and Gregory Prolich.[52]

Like other miners on the Victorian goldfields, Croatians were highly mobile. They travelled to payable goldfields or where there were new gold rushes. For example, Antonio Harlovich from Dalmatia moved to various goldfields trying his luck on new claims. He sometimes worked in claims with Croatian partners, including Frank Entra, Guro Herzgovich and Stephen Pandrige in the Buckland district.[53] The following is a brief summary of Antonio Harlovich's travels. He was in Epsom in 1860, Whipsnake Gully near Whipstick in 1861, from 1865 to 1867 he was at Mount Livingstone, Pioneer Hill and Swift Creek, all near Omeo. In 1867 he was also at Thingers Reef and Hayes Point in the Yackandandah South mining subdivision, and from 1867 to 1870 he was at Clear Creek near Buckland. Shortly after the first payable gold had been found in Whipsnake Gully by George Bavins in February 1861, Harlovich applied for a prospecting claim in the area. In about 1875 Harlovich moved to the Georgetown goldfields in Queensland. There he was a miner and storekeeper until he died in 1909.[54] In 1865 Antonio Harlovich had a mining lease called the Dalmatin Quartz Mining Company near Omeo, and 20 years later, Luke Yannich had a mining lease, the 'Dalmatia' claim, nearby.[55] Between 1883 and 1885, Yannich and party crushed at least 179 tons of quartz obtained from the Dalmatia claim which yielded over 166.5 ounces of gold. The Dalmatia claim and Dalmatia reef are at Mountain Creek, which is about 6.5 kilometres north-west of Omeo. By June 1886 the depth of the Dalmatia claim had reached 21 m. In 1892 Luke Yannich registered another Dalmatia claim, in the Omeo district.[56]

Natale Lussich also named mines after Dalmatia and after himself. He was born in Sutivan on the island of Brač and arrived in Melbourne in about 1857.[57] There is documented evidence that Lussich had contacts with at least another 11 Croatians in Victoria. From about 1862 to 1874, he had varying degrees of success in gold and antimony mining in the Redcastle and Costerfield area; however, during this time he also mined in Woods Point which supported a community of Croatian miners. In 1870 Lussich acquired a third of the Francis Joseph Quartz claim in Redcastle. Dominic

Milovitch was already the owner of another third of the claim and other Croatians who were shareholders in the same claim at some stage were Bartolomeo Citanich, George Luchinovich and Louis Spallatrino.

In the early 1870s, Lussich acquired miners' rights on the Lussich and Company Quartz situated on the Lussich and Company Line Reef; on New Dalmatia Quartz, located on the New Dalmatia Reef; on Good Content Quartz, on the New Dalmatia Reef and on San Juan (Sutivan) Quartz, situated on the San Juan (Sutivan) Reef in the Redcastle mining district. The San Juan Quartz claim was named after Natale Lussich's birthplace. The town name 'Sutivan' originated from Sv. Ivan (Saint John) or San Juan in Spanish.[58]

An example of a typical crushing by Natale Lussich occurred in the first couple of weeks in March 1872 when he crushed 12 tons of ore in Redcastle and received 19 ounces of gold, a profitable yield. In December 1872 Lussich had the top payable mine in the Heathcote district, situated about three kilometres from Redcastle. He had one reef about 15 cm thick speckled with gold, and another with a thickness of greater than 1 m. It was expected this gold mine would produce one ounce of gold per ton of ore. By 1876 he had moved to Portarlington and was paying rates on a one-acre allotment of land previously owned by John Lussich.[59]

Mining partners and mines named after Croatians

Miners quickly learned that working in a team, especially with three or four miners on one shaft, offered the best chance of success. One dug the shaft, another hauled up the earth on a pulley, one cradled and another cooked for his colleagues. Sometimes they had to cart the quartz to water so that they could actually use the cradle. Moreover, in terms of forming teams, there was a tendency for miners to gravitate towards their own national group. Croatians were no exception, and each large goldfield had a Croatian presence. Some Croatian immigrants suffered from language difficulties and experienced social dislocation, so by working together they were able to find companionship amongst fellow Croatians. It was common for Croatian miners to have multiple Croatian mining partners. In general, there were between one and eight Croatian partners in their mining claims.

In many mining areas Croatian pioneers often named their mining claims after themselves, especially in Redcastle. These include Lussich and Party (1861), Marinovich and Party (1861), Lazzarovich and Company (1865), Spallatrino Company quartz claim (1868), Borsich and Company quartz claim (1869), Marcovitch's (Mercovich's) Quartz claim (1870), and as seen earlier, Lussich and Company Quartz (1871). In this section further examples of Croatian miners on various goldfields working together and maintaining links with other Croatians will be given.

Michele Marinovich (Marinović), who was born in Trpanj on the Pelješac Peninsula arrived in Australia in 1859. In 1861 he registered the Marinovich and

Party antimony and gold mining company in Costerfield. In 1862 Marinovich and Louis Spallatrino applied for a nearby 2.2-acre antimony claim which they called Marinovich, Spallatrino and Company. They were the original discoverers of the claim on 6 June 1861 and had been working since then. By June 1862 other Croatian mining partners in the company were Gregory Cristilovich, Pietro Jassich, Spiro Lazzarovich, George Marinovitch and Bogden Slocovich.[60]

Louis Spallatrino from Split arrived in Victoria in about 1856. He had Croatian mining partners on various goldfields. Spallatrino was mining in Redcastle from 1861 to 1863, Sailor Bills Creek in 1866, Mt Pleasant in 1867 and again in Redcastle from 1868 to 1869. Spallatrino and fellow Croatian Ivan Nicolich registered a claim at Sailor Bills Creek in 1866. Francis Nicolich later became a shareholder in this claim. Other Croatians had claims nearby; for example, Francis Petrich, Francis Nicolich, and party held the Hungarian prospecting claim.[61] In 1868 Spallatrino returned to Redcastle where he registered three claims, the Louis Company Quartz on the Dalmatian Reef, Louis Company Alluvial and Spallatrino Company Quartz. The following year he registered more claims with George Luchinovich and Dominic Milovitch.[62]

A typical miner within the Croatian community in Yandoit was Peter Mavorvitch (Petar Mavrović or Maurović) who was born in Brseč in Istria. He arrived in Victoria in June 1853.[63] Mavorvitch married an Irish woman, Mary Phelan, in St Mary's Catholic Church in Castlemaine on 16 October 1859 and they had nine children. In the same church, Giovanni Ivanussich became godparent to one of his sons, Peter, while Martin Pavilach was godparent to another son, Denis.[64] One of Peter Mavorvitch's mining claims known by a Croatian name was Marcovitch's (Mavorvitch's) Tunnel Alluvial which was registered in 1871. His mining partner was Mark Busanich. At the time Mavorvitch was living in a bark house.[65] Peter Mavorvitch died in the Castlemaine Hospital on 15 June 1913 and by the time of his death, he had lived in the Yandoit area for over 50 years.[66]

Antonio Pavich's mine in the Yandoit area. Antonio is on the right side

An early Croatian arrival to Victoria, who arrived in 1852, was Bartholomew Mercovich (Bartul Mirković) who was from Trpanj on the Pelješac Peninsula.[67] He primarily worked as a miner, although he was also a storekeeper and publican on the goldfields. He travelled around Victoria in search of gold, with his family accompanying him. He usually mined in areas where other Croatian pioneers were concentrated. Mercovich was in Steiglitz from 1857 to 1860, Redcastle in 1861 and

Bartholomew Mercovich with his family

Woods Point from 1863 to 1867, where he was the proprietor of the All Nations Hotel. In 1869 he was in Graytown, and in Redcastle again in 1870, where he registered the Marcovitch's (Mercovich's) Quartz claim. He was back in Graytown from 1871 to 1873, Costerfield from 1874 to 1880, and finally Carlton from 1882 until his death on 13 August 1886. He was survived by 11 of his children who were between two and 27 years of age.[68]

Connections between mining communities

At least 59 per cent of Croatian miners had documented connections with other Croatians in Victoria. As we have seen, a striking feature of their lives was their mobility: they travelled to various goldfields and associated with other Croatians. The highest number of documented connections for Croatian communities on the Victorian goldfields was in the 1860s, especially between 1860 and 1866. From the first gold rushes in Victoria up until 1859, no Croatian presence on the goldfields was documented in mining records. However, from naturalisation papers, death and marriage certificates, it is known that Croatians were mining on the goldfields during this entire period.

There were at least 11 Croatians who lived in a number of different Croatian gold mining communities in Victoria between 1860 and 1882.[69] For example, Nicolo Anticevich mined with other Croatians in Epsom, Woods Point and Crooked River. Similarly, Peter Cussianovich mined in Epsom, Yandoit and Crooked River. From 1860 to 1863, there was a concentration of Croatians at Epsom and another at Redcastle. Croatians from both of these communities subsequently moved to Woods Point where, from 1863 to 1866, they maintained a Croatian community. Others moved to Crooked River in 1864 and 1865 to form a community. With the Crooked River quartz rush peaking in 1865, Croatians registered or transferred over 203 quartz and alluvial claims in the Crooked River mining district. Peter Albich worked on 27 of these mining claims.[70] The overwhelming majority of Crooked River Croatians did not work for large mining companies, preferring to work for themselves. After spending some time on the Woods Point and Crooked River goldfields, a number of Croatians returned to the Redcastle and Costerfield goldfields where, between 1867 and 1874, there were over 60 quartz claims in which Croatians mined.[71]

Of all of the goldfields where there was a strong Croatian presence, the Redcastle–Costerfield and Crooked River goldfields boasted the highest percentage of Croatians. The total goldfield population fluctuated substantially, as the example of Redcastle highlights. In March 1864 there were 485 miners, and within 15 months, the total had decreased to 40. During the same period the population of Costerfield decreased from 658 to 150.[72] There was considerable Croatian activity in Redcastle–Costerfield in the early 1860s. Unfortunately, very few mining records exist for the region from this period of peak activity, but we do know many Croatians were still registering new mines there in the 1870s when the population was in rapid decline. There were also Croatian mining settlements in Wedderburn, Inglewood, Maryborough, Daylesford, Yandoit, Buckland, Ballarat and Bendigo.

Many friendships arose between miners from different Croatian mining communities. The Croatian communities of Daylesford and Wedderburn kept in contact with one another – Thomas Rossi from Zadar had Croatian friends in both these communities. Similarly, in 1855 Nicholas Siglich, who was mining in the Inglewood mining district, was the marriage witness to Joseph Marsich in Castlemaine.[73] As is to be expected, Croatian miners would also sometimes lose contact with one another when they moved to different goldfields, but inevitably they forged new ties and partnerships as they travelled.

In chapter 3 we saw that, before 1890, there were also communities of Croatian miners in Gulgong, Sofala and Grafton in New South Wales and Palmer River, Charters Towers and Mount Morgan in Queensland. Fortunato Alfredo Corsano (known as Alfred Carson), who was born on the island of Lošinj, was a miner on the

New South Wales goldfields in the areas of Grafton, Bathurst and West Wyalong. He married on 5 May 1874 in Grafton and had nine children.[74]

Some Croatians who left the Victorian goldfields later went to try their luck on the New South Wales, Queensland, Western Australian and New Zealand goldfields.[75] For example, John Muscardin, whom we met as a miner in the Dalmatia Gold Mining Company near McIntyre, later mined on various New South Wales goldfields, including Forbes, Ophir, Grenfell, Temora, Sofala, Gulgong and Lower Lewis Ponds near Orange. Muscardin, who was born in Mali Lošinj arrived in Melbourne in 1859. He died near Orange in 1913 and never married.[76]

In 1891, before the gold discoveries, the huge state of Western Australia had fewer than 50,000 people. In the next ten years, due to the gold rushes, the population of Western Australia almost quadrupled, with most of the new population coming from the eastern states.[77] After the discovery of gold in Western Australia in 1892, Croatians began to settle in the eastern goldfields of Western Australia, initiating a large-scale chain migration of Croatians to this region of Western Australia, where they worked as woodcutters, miners and labourers. Kalgoorlie, on these goldfields, boasted the famous Golden Mile, the richest 2.5 square kilometres of gold in the world. A number of Croatians with valuable gold mining experience moved to Western Australia from goldfields in the eastern states; for example, Vincent Vranjican (Vicko Vranjican), who was also known as Vincent Abbott, was a pioneer of the Murchison goldfields in Western Australia. He was born on the island of Hvar and was a gold miner in New Zealand before moving to the Palmer River goldfields in Queensland in the mid-1870s. At Palmer River he was successful, but contracted the tropical dengue fever. After recovering, he was engaged for several years in mining operations in the Adelong and the Grafton districts of New South Wales. In 1892 he moved to the Murchison district and discovered the Abbott's goldfield and other rich reefs in the district.

Vincent Abbott (Vicko Vranjican) a successful gold mining pioneer of the Murchison goldfields in Western Australia

According to *The Murchison Miner*, his mining lease was known as 'Mount Vranijan' [Vranjican]. Abbott was prosperous in his mining venues and retired a wealthy man.[78]

Impact of Croatians on the goldfields

Most miners during the Victorian gold rush had little or no success. The 1853 publication, *The Present State of Melbourne and the Gold Fields of Victoria*, estimated the success and failure of miners as follows: 25 per cent left the diggings having gained nothing, 10 per cent left having lost; 40 per cent left having gained a living or a little more, 25 per cent made over £50 and only 2.5 per cent made over £500. However, from 1852 the average return per head declined: in 1852 it was £390; in 1853, £240; in 1854, £148; in 1856, £157; in 1858, £93; and by 1861, it dropped to the low value of £87. For some miners the average earning dropped to subsistence level.[79] Many gold migrants were disillusioned by appalling living conditions, little success and the failure of their high expectations and ambitions. Others became addicted to the life of a miner and continued to mine, driven by the dream that one day they would strike it rich.

Mathew Hasdovaz (Mato Hazdovac), from Babino Polje on the island of Mljet, was a gold miner in Gulgong, which had the largest settlement of Croatian pioneer gold miners in New South Wales. Letters sent by Hasdovaz to his father and brother in Babino Polje reveal that, although he was a gold miner in Australia for many years, he was never lucky enough to strike it rich. He also lived in Victoria for ten years and South Australia for the same number. Hasdovaz died in Gulgong in 1898.[80]

Gold had stimulated Australia's economy. In Victoria for example, the enormous wealth resulting from the production of gold facilitated the rapid development of its cities and industries. With the huge increase in population and parallel demand for produce, agriculture and grazing prospered, and with the gold rush, transportation improved rapidly. Mining had brought many new arrivals, among them tradesmen whose skills were valuable in Australia and who were later employed in various farming and

Mathew Hasdovaz from the island of Mljet, a gold miner at Gulgong New South Wales in 1879

manufacturing industries. The gold mining industry became a vast market for timber, machinery and equipment. As the main port for the goldfields, Melbourne prospered and became the largest and richest coastal city. In 1853 the gold rush had made Melbourne one of the busiest ports in the world. Melbourne also became Australia's financial capital. In the late 1850s half of Australia's population lived in Victoria.[81]

As we have seen, Croatians had considerable impact on many goldfields by discovering gold, operating crushing plants and managing the main hotels in some gold mining towns. Because it was their usual practice to keep the amount of gold they found to themselves to avoid attracting the attention of other miners, it is extremely difficult to assess actual amounts of gold found by Croatian miners. From their business dealings and lifestyles, it would be reasonable to suggest that some Croatian miners, such as Stephen Paulussy, were highly successful. He owned one of the main crushing plants in Buckland and frequently employed others. In the 1880s he employed several men to build mining sluicing boxes, work on his mill, crush quartz and work on his mining claim. Paulussy also employed others in Buckland, including

Paulussy's mill next to the river in Buckland

his neighbours, in the building of his house. His house was completed in 1882; it was a well-built four-bedroom weatherboard cottage with a chimney made from stone.[82] Croatians also provided valuable jobs to the people in the McIntyre region. In 1879, the Dalmatia Gold Mining Company claim paid wages to a total of 33 men, who worked six shifts, day and night.[83]

Some Croatians developed mining expertise beneficial for the wider mining community. Matteo Gargurevich, who was a miner on the Victorian goldfields from the 1860s, patented apparatus for treating tailings for the recovery of gold or other minerals.[84] An example of a Croatian mine manager was Joseph Marich (Josip Marić), who managed the Victoria Junction Gold Mining Company, formed on 2 October 1890 in Taradale and was worth £12,000. A successful Croatian business associate, Peter Marich, who lived in George Street in Sydney, owned a quarter of the company. He later owned Palings music firm, the most prominent music warehouse in Sydney. After assessing the mine, Joseph Marich convinced Mr Allan of the music warehouse (Allan & Co. Pty Ltd) in Collins Street, the most prominent music firm in Melbourne, to buy shares in the proposed company.[85] According to the *Metcalfe Shire News*, Joseph Marich who died on 9 March 1892:

> was a very old resident of Taradale and district, and a most reliable man in mining matters. He would not permit his name to be used in connection with any mining venture unless its bona fides were as certain of success as anything in mining could be. He was reliable and honourable in all his mining transactions, and for this reason his counsel was sought far and wide. Syndicates of Melbourne capitalists frequently employed the deceased to travel to the adjacent colonies to watch their interests in mining ventures, and when his advice was accepted it generally turned out that by acting upon it was their advantage. He was the mining manager of the Victorian Junction Co. from its inception up to within a few weeks of his death.[86]

As we have seen, Croatians preferred to work for themselves rather than being labourers in large mining companies. However, at times they were forced to work for the large mining companies when they could not find enough gold to survive. Some Croatian miners, like Taddeo Gamulin, who was born in Jelsa on the island of Hvar in 1828, died or were injured in mining accidents.[87] Early in the morning on 13 February 1868, Gamulin had a terrible accident in the No. 1 South Bristol Reef mining claim in New Bendigo. While working at the bottom of the mine shaft, which was about 46 m deep, the winch broke and about 70 kilograms of quartz fell on to him. The impact fractured his skull and knocked him unconscious. A doctor's examination revealed that he had a massive wound over his left eyebrow, and parts of his skull were embedded deep into his brain. Taddeo Gamulin never regained consciousness and died on 17 February 1868. He had been mining for several years, but had only worked on this mining claim for a few weeks prior to the accident. Gamulin had been destitute when he had arrived to work on the claim.[88] Later that year Francis Papawitch died in Dunolly District Hospital from spinal injuries also caused in a mine accident.[89] In 1870 Francisco Gellussich (Franjo Jelušić) died from injuries caused by the accidental explosion of powder in a mining shaft in Grenfell in New South Wales, while in 1898, the Croatian pioneer, Francesco Vecerina (Franjo Večerina), was killed by a fall of earth in the cyanide works in Barmedman, New South Wales. In the early 1880s Vecerina was a miner on the Victorian goldfields.[90]

Many Croatians who arrived in Australia after 1890 were killed or injured in mining accidents while working for large mining companies in Boulder–Kalgoorlie and Broken Hill.

Mark Belanich was a miner in Yandoit from around 1870 until his death on 12 October 1883. Belanich married an Irish woman and they had three children. In 1870 Belanich and Mark Busanich registered an alluvial tunnel together in Yandoit. Mark Belanich incurred injuries that forced him to seek medical assistance in Castlemaine Hospital on two separate occasions. In 1872 he spent several days in hospital after an accident in which he fractured his arm. Similarly, he spent two weeks in hospital in 1880 after injuring his arms and ribs.[91]

On the goldfields the miners sometimes lived in improvised huts made from bark, although the huts did not fully protect them from the elements, especially in the cold winters of the Crooked River, Buckland, Woods Point and Walhalla goldfields. This temporary accommodation failed to protect Mr Nicholovich or Nicholas, who was born in Sclavonia, from a ferocious storm that raged on a Sunday in May 1865. During the storm Nicholovich was sleeping in his hut near the Jeff Davis Reef in Grant when a gigantic gumtree crashed down onto his hut killing him instantly. The next day his completely crushed body was found. Nicholovich had only just arrived at the Jeff Davis Reef from Woods Point and was about to commence work there.[92]

Work on the gold mines was often suspended for various reasons, including not finding payable gold, lack of funds, lack of water, lack of machinery, accidents, bush fires burning out the shaft support structure and excessive water in the deep mine shafts.[93] The work was laborious, uncertain and dangerous. As a result, some Croatians on the goldfields became publicans and storekeepers. These occupations were generally much more profitable than that of a miner. When they were convinced that their luck had run out or was not going to change, others moved to alternative forms of employment, such as farming, labouring or fishing. The next two chapters will describe how some former Croatian miners later became successful seamen, fishermen, publicans, vignerons and farmers.

CHAPTER 6

Pioneer Seamen
and Fishermen

Prior seafaring experience

The gold rushes in Australia from the 1850s greatly increased travel between Australia and Britain, with everyone in a hurry to seek their fortunes on the Australian goldfields. Liverpool became the principal starting point for the fast clipper sailing ships which carried immigrants and supplies, as well as Croatian seamen and passengers, to the Victorian and New South Wales goldfields, and wool back to Britain. Because they were designed for speed, the clippers had slender hulls and carried many sails, and with favourable winds, these fast ships could make the journey between Britain and Australia in less than 90 days. Conditions on the clippers were a substantial improvement over the immigrant ships that came to Australia before the gold rush.

The hysteria associated with the lure of gold on the Victorian goldfields resulted in whole crews deserting their ships. By June 1852, 50 ships abandoned by their crews were lying in Hobsons Bay. In the same year, over 290 ships arrived in the Port of Melbourne. Between 1852 and 1854, an average of 250 immigrants arrived daily in the Port of Melbourne.[1]

Many Croatians were seamen for periods of between two and ten years before coming to Australia. Some had served in the Austrian Navy and/or British merchant fleet. For example, James Zibilich was a navigator on the Croatian ship *Madre* from 1850 to 1854, which was captained by Captain Župa during this period. The *Madre* was a 673-ton merchant ship built in 1847 at Martinšćica, on the island of Cres. Zibilich came to Australia in approximately 1862.[2] When Croatian seamen came to Australia, some continued to work in this area while a number of them became fishermen. Some changed occupations once they had saved enough money to start a small business such as a hotel or grocer shop.

On occasions the voyage out to Australia could be dangerous. For example, the ship on which Matteo Benussi sailed on to Australia was involved in a collision near the equator. Benussi was brought up at sea and was a seaman in the merchant service of Austria. He sailed with an Austrian vessel to Istanbul in Turkey and the Black Sea, subsequently travelling with a cargo of linseed to Hull in England where he left the ship and became a seaman in the British merchant service. Benussi left London on 13 December 1853 on the ship *Mersey* and arrived in Melbourne four months later. During this voyage the *Mersey* collided with a French barque near the equator, and as a consequence, had to stop for repairs at the Cape of Good Hope. On arrival in Victoria until November of the following year, he was employed as a seaman in the coastal service between Victoria and the neighbouring colonies. Benussi then went to try his luck on the Victorian goldfields.[3]

Croatians travelled on ships between the colonies for business reasons. For example, Antonio Milatovich who was born in the Dubrovnik/Kotor district visited Port Fairy on a business trip in 1848. He had arrived in Sydney in 1843 on the *Persian* from London, and by 1850 was captain and agent of the 221-ton brig, *Portenia*. On 1 May 1850 he left Sydney on the *Portenia* for San Francisco, taking passengers who were proceeding to the Californian goldfields. Among the passengers was another named Milatovich. Antonio Milatovich carried supplies to build himself a hotel in San Francisco where he later became very wealthy.[4] By 1851 he was the proprietor of the Hotel de Ville in this city. By the late 1850s he had purchased over one million acres of land in Lower California in Mexico with the intent of settling it, his ownership of the land being recognised by the Mexican Government. Between 1859 and 1864, he paid for several expeditions to enable him to take possession of his land. However, the Mexican authorities in the state of Lower California prevented him from doing so. This was, in all probability, due to the rich gold and silver mines on his land as well as salt deposits. In an attempt to take possession of his land, Milatovich even went to Mexico City and spoke to the Mexican president. He later took the Mexican Government to court for damages for a sum of over half a million dollars and, although he never took possession of his lands in Mexico or was successful in his claim for compensation, he continued to prosper and became a successful landowner in San Francisco. He died in 1901 and was buried at the Calvary Catholic Cemetery in San Francisco.[5]

Croatian seamen visiting Australia

A number of Croatians visited Melbourne and other Australian ports while serving on ships, usually sailing under the Austrian flag. The brig, *Splendido*, under the Croatian captain, Ivan Visin, was in Melbourne four times between 1854 and 1858. The 311-ton brig imported cargoes of sugar, rice and rope from Asian ports, including Manila, Surabaja and Jakarta and typically docked in Melbourne for a couple of months on each visit, on which occasions members of Visin's Croatian crew deserted to seek their fortune on the Victorian goldfields. Ivan Visin's travels around the world started in Antwerpen, Belgium in 1852 and ended in Trieste in 1859. He was decorated by a flag of honour 'Merito navali' by the Austrian Emperor for his historic voyage around the world.[6] The 359-ton barque, *Lorenza*, under captain Karlo Poščić, arrived in Melbourne early in 1859 with a cargo of tea, silk and preserves from Macao. While in Melbourne, Poščić met fellow Croatians living there. In December 1860 the *Lorenza* suffered a shipwreck in the Dampier Strait near the Bismarck Archipelago in Papua New Guinea. Both the *Splendido* and *Lorenza* were built in Rijeka.[7]

In the 1880s several barques (*Ciro*, *Conte Oscar L*, *Gange*, *Gehon*, *Guisto*, *Metta* and *Triade Tarabochia*) with Croatian captains and crew members arrived in Port Melbourne. During this decade at least 11 Croatian barques visited other Australian ports. Careful examination of shipping arrival records revealed that, in the 1880s, Croatian barques were the eighth most frequent foreign group of vessels entering Melbourne, but only constituted about half of one per cent of the foreign vessels entering Melbourne. They were all importing goods to Melbourne but rarely leaving with exports. A few of these barques, including the *Ciro*, *Conte Oscar L* and *Guisto*, transported sugar to Melbourne from Asia for the Victorian Sugar Company, while the barques, *Triade Tarabochia* and *Gehon*, imported wood from Europe and the United States. All these barques were owned by Croatians and the majority were built in Mali Lošinj and Rijeka. For example, the *Ciro* was owned by Giuseppe Martinolich (Josip Martinolić). Between 1853 and 1884, the main shipbuilding centres in the Austro-Hungarian Empire were Rijeka where 383 ships were built, Mali Lošinj where 247 ships were built and Trieste where 150 ships were built. The Croatian barques that visited Australia in the 1880s were between 500 and 1250 tons and were usually wooden or made of iron. They typically took from four to five months to sail from either Europe or the United States to Australia.[8]

On occasions Croatian crew left these ships and settled in Australia. For example in 1882, Frank Cucel left the barque *Metta*; in 1883 Pietro Cibich, Ivan Grbić, George Mersuglia, Natale Radonich and Giovanni Rerecich deserted the *Ciro* at Port Melbourne, while Andrew Radoslovich and Luke Scoglier left the *Triade Tarabochia* in 1886. Radoslovich had served as a sailor on the *Triade Tarabochia* for a few years before settling in Victoria. Croatian seamen also jumped ship in Newcastle, Adelaide and Sydney.[9]

Due to the expert seamanship of their Croatian captains, these ships managed to sail through foreign seas far from Croatia. It was not always smooth sailing and they sometimes suffered damage from gales. The 627-ton barque *Metta*, captained by G. Stangher (Josip Stanger) from Volosko, arrived in Melbourne on 17 August 1882. Her cargo consisted primarily of cigarettes, tobacco, furniture, wood, machinery and tools. She had left Boston four months earlier and along the way lost her foresail and foretopsails, yards and several sails. As a result, the *Metta* spent four days in Duke's Dock, Yarra Bank for an overhaul. She then spent some time in Newcastle, Adelaide and Port Wakefield before proceeding to London.[10] The 583-ton barque *Ciro* under Marco Martinolich (Marko Martinolić) encountered storms on two trips made to

Melbourne in 1883. On the first she encountered a cyclone in which she lost her foresail and two of her topsails, but she still managed to bring her cargo of 645 tons of sugar safely to Melbourne. On the return trip from Surabaja to Melbourne, the *Ciro* encountered two gales, losing the topgallant yard and upper topsail yard in the first; in the second, the ship sustained damage to some of the bulwark planking.[11] The barques sometimes sailed in pairs to provide assistance to each other in bad weather and protection against pirates. For example, the barques, *Guisto* and *Conte Oscar L*, sailed together from Surabaja via Jakarta and arrived in Melbourne in March 1885 with cargoes of sugar and kapok.[12]

Some Croatian barques sailed to Australia on more than one occasion, suggesting that Australia was a regular trade destination for Croatian seamen. For example, between 1880 and 1886, the 829-ton barque *Triade Tarabochia*, made at least three trips to Australia. She visited Adelaide in 1880 and 1882, and Melbourne in 1886. On her second trip to Adelaide she was accompanied by another Croatian barque, *Genitori Tarabochia*.[13] The 1000-ton *Armida* left Mali Lošinj in 1881 and travelled around Europe, Australia, South Africa, Asia, South America and North America. Under Captain Callisto Cosulich this ship visited Adelaide in 1884 and Melbourne in 1890–1891.[14]

Before 1890 ships with Croatian captains and crew had visited all of the states, most frequently the cities of Newcastle, Melbourne, Adelaide and Sydney. They usually docked in Newcastle when trading with Asia. In 1887 the 1250-ton barque, *Ljubirod*, with Croatian captain Stjepan Bjelovučić and Croatian crew, sailed from London to Adelaide. They stopped in Adelaide and Newcastle before running into a reef 65 kilometres from Thursday Island. The crew was rescued and one of them, Simon Anicich (Šimun Aničić), from Lovranska Draga settled in Newcastle. He was married twice in Australia and worked as a labourer in the smelter in Newcastle. Anicich died in Newcastle on 4 May 1944 and was survived by two sons.[15]

Simon Anicich

Other Croatian vessels were wrecked in Australian waters. The best known of these shipwrecks was the 857-ton barque *Stefano* that was wrecked off the north-west coast of Western Australia on 27 October 1875 after hitting a reef near Point Cloates. The crew consisted of 16 Croatians and an English cabin boy.[16] Ten of the Croatian crew managed to reach the shore alive, but within three months, all but two (Miho Baccich and Giovanni Jurich) had died from hunger or exposure. They managed to survive in the harsh environment for a further three months with the assistance of Aborigines before they were rescued by a pearler in April 1876. During Baccich and Jurich's time living with the Aborigines they learnt their language and many of their customs and ceremonies.

The survivors were taken to Fremantle where a Croatian, Vicko Vuković, who was born on the island of Šipan, gave them assistance and took them into his home. Vuković, who had changed his name to John Vincent, had settled in Western Australia in about 1858 and had an Irish wife and five children. Vincent was captain of the 67-ton *Rosette* and transported Baccich and Jurich to the wrecksite of the *Stefano* to give a government reward to the Aborigines for saving them. He was also their interpreter during an inquiry into the wreck of the *Stefano*. In August 1876 Baccich and Jurich departed for Croatia. A few years later in 1879, Vincent himself was drowned when the *Rosette* was wrecked off Rosemary Island in the Dampier Archipelago.[17]

Miho Baccich and Giovanni Jurich, survivors from the Stefano *shipwreck. The photograph was taken in Fremantle in 1876*

John Vincent (Vicko Vuković) an early Croatian settler in Western Australia with his wife

The wreck of the barque *Gange*

The 1071-ton iron barque *Gange*, transporting a cargo of iron rails, cement, sulphur and bolts from London to Melbourne, was stranded at Port Lonsdale reef on the night of 23 July 1887.[18] The wreck caused much excitement. To enable its reporters to be at the scene, *The Argus* newspaper chartered a special train which left Melbourne shortly after 6 am and travelled to Queenscliff. Numerous spectators came from Geelong, Queenscliff and Melbourne to see the wreck.

Spectators in front of the wrecked barque Gange

The *Gange* had been waiting for a pilot clear of the Heads and the crew burned rockets to attract attention. At the time there was a south-westerly squall accompanied by rain and a strong ebb tide running out against rough seas. Port Phillip Heads is extremely dangerous in such conditions – 44 vessels were lost outside the Heads between 1839 and 1900.[19] The Croatian captain, Frank Ivancich (Franjo Ivančić), told *The Argus* he had:

> sighted the Point Lonsdale light at 6 pm, and now stood in there for a harbour pilot, and burnt rockets for a pilot to come off. A schooner was then descried shaping for the entrance, and I stood over towards Point Nepean, thinking that she was going to lead me in. A boat was put off from the schooner, but it could not reach us, and a line thrown from the ship was not taken by those in the boat ... a south-west squall of unusual force struck the ship, and carried away the foresail sheet, the lower topsail and the trysail.

The barque Gange *during the storm*

Apart from the squall damaging the sails and rigging, a number of the crew members on board the *Gange* were injured. Martino Matesich was wounded on the hand while cutting away some gear on the deck. Another seaman was struck on the head by the block from the starboard fore-sheet. According to Captain Frank Ivancich the:

> ... vessel was gradually drifting on the shore, and about 11 o'clock she shook badly from end to end, indicating that she had taken ground. In the next second the seas were breaking clean over her, and the cabin, being rendered untenable through the inrush of water, we went forward and prepared to launch the boats when an opportunity occurred. My wife is with me this trip, and I was very anxious for her safety. She was assisted forward to the forecastle ... The ship was drawing from 19 ft. [5.79 m] to 19 ft. 6 in. [5.94 m] of water, and is aground in the forefoot, pointing with her stern directly towards the Point Lonsdale Lighthouse. The chief officer, John Hreglich [Ivan Hreljić], stated that 'the vessel got beyond control, and grounded with such violence that the men at the wheel were thrown down ...' The waves came over the stern and passed the length of the ship, clearing away all before them and carrying everything out of the chart-house.

The crew of the *Gange* fired rockets, muskets and burned blue lights to attract the attention of the lighthouse and around 1 am the Queenscliff lifeboat reached them, although, because of the rough seas, the crew of the lifeboat had to wait until daylight before they could attempt the rescue, even though the *Gange* was taking in water. The Queenscliff lifeboat remained anchored near the vessel all night, and at first light the seamen threw out ropes and they were fastened. Due to the rough weather, they could only jump off the *Gange* into the lifeboat when a wave lifted the lifeboat.

According to *The Argus*, the Croatians all boarded the lifeboat calmly: 'The strangers, after all they had passed through, behaved with as much firmness as British seamen. There was no scrambling among them for the chance to leave the doomed vessel. One after another filled the vacant place on the ladder and watched his time to jump without betraying excitement or disorder'.[20] All those on board were saved, including the Croatian captain, Frank Ivancich, his wife Nilla, 15 Croatian crew members and three other crew members.[21] They were taken to Portsea for a medical examination, and after obtaining a clean bill of health, they were taken to Melbourne. After a couple of days the captain and his crew used a fishing boat to board the barque and retrieved some of their belongings and ship's stores. The wreck and cargo were sold by auction for £165. The barque broke up about a week later.[22] The *Gange* had been built in Mali Lošinj by Nikola Martinolić in 1885 and was owned by Eredi Tarabochia from Mali Lošinj. The *Gange* was the first iron merchant vessel built in Croatia and this had only been the vessel's second voyage.[23]

The Queenscliff lifeboat crew were regarded as heroes. They received praise from the Governor of Victoria, Henry Loch, and a reward that totalled £69 in recognition of their services and bravery. A banquet was also held in their honour at Adman's Grand Hotel in Queenscliff.[24]

The wreck can be attributed to a misunderstanding between the signals from the pilot schooner and the *Gange*, and sail troubles. The sinking of the *Glaneuse* and the *Gange* in less than a year attracted criticism of the Pilot Service. Both vessels had foreign captains who claimed they had searched for a pilot without locating one, although it would appear that the pilot service did not venture far enough to sea. A Pilot Board inquiry exonerated the pilots from all blame, but as a result of the inquiry, improvements were made to pilot procedure at the Heads. The wreck of the *Gange* also brought the Lifeboat Service into prominence, and a jetty was built at Point Lonsdale in 1890 to accommodate a second lifeboat.[25]

Warships

Numerous other merchant vessels and Austrian warships with Croatian captains and/or crew visited Australia for various reasons. For example in 1858, the Austrian frigate, *Novara*, visited Sydney on a scientific expedition. This frigate had been built in the Croatian port city of Pula, which was the main naval base in the Austro-Hungarian Empire. During the voyage, the majority of the 345 seamen on board this ship were Croatian. Similarly, in the 1890s the Austrian warship *Saida* with Croatian crew members visited Australia three times on scientific expeditions.[26] International exhibitions also attracted Austrian vessels with Croatian crews to Australia. The *Helgoland* came for the Sydney International Exhibition of 1879, while the steamship *Polluce* came for the Melbourne International Exhibition of 1880. The *Polluce*, under captain G. Ragusin, embarked from Trieste on 9 July 1880 with 2300 packages (400 tons) for the Austrian Exhibit at the Melbourne International Exhibition. Along the way she also picked up goods in Asia. The *Polluce* arrived in Melbourne on 8 September 1880 and subsequently anchored in Port Melbourne railway pier where her cargo was unloaded. Included amongst the crew and passengers were Croatians.[27] Chapter 7 describes how Croatian wines were displayed at Australian international exhibitions.

Croatian seamen also deserted Austrian warships visiting Australia. Typically rewards of £3 were offered for their capture by the commanders of the Austrian warships or by Austro-Hungarian Consuls. The evidence that some deserters were Croatian comes from the published deserters' notices where it was stated that they spoke and/or wrote 'Croatian, Croatish, Croatic, Croati, Sclavonian or Slavonic'. They also spoke Italian and German and some knew a little English. Vinko Franziskovic was among the Croatian seamen who deserted the Austro-Hungarian warship, *Albatros*. His deserter's notice stated:

Deserter from the H.I. and B. Austro-Hungarian warship *Albatros*. 1st December, 1896. Vinko Franziskovic, born at Tusak [Sušak], Croatia, about 26 years of age, 5 feet 8 inches [173 cm] high, dark-brown hair, oblong face, oblong nose. Speaks Croatish, Italian, and a little English. Franziskovic has an uncle, who resides at 245, George Street, Sydney. A reward of £3 will be paid if the deserter could be returned to the *Albatros* on Friday, the 11th, the date of sailing from Sydney.[28]

Croatian pioneer fishermen

As we have seen, many of the Croatian pioneers were seamen and fishermen prior to arrival in Australia, the main settlement of Croatian fishermen in Victoria becoming Portarlington. They mixed with much smaller groups of Croatian fishermen from Geelong, Port Fairy, Sandringham and Tarraville. There were also other Croatian fishermen in Melbourne, Paynesville, Hastings, Lakes Entrance, Port Albert and Dromana. In the Melbourne area, Croatian fishermen chiefly lived in Williamstown. Over a third of the Croatian fishermen in Victoria lived in more than one fishing community. For example, Natale Vuscovich fished from Geelong, Port Fairy and Portarlington.[29]

In the nineteenth century Croatian fishermen were not confined to Victoria; there were also Croatian fishermen in Port Lincoln, Port Augusta and Sydney. For example in the 1870s, Croatian fishermen at Coffin Bay near Port Lincoln had an oyster fishing boat called *Dalmatia*. Christopher Dabovich, who was born in Kostanjica in Kotor and arrived in Adelaide in about 1855, was appointed Inspector of Oyster

Christopher Dabovich with his family

Fisheries in South Australia in the 1870s and held the position till he retired in 1904. He supervised the oyster dredging – closing and opening the oyster beds to dredging where appropriate – to prevent destruction of oyster stocks. Dabovich had moved to Port Lincoln in the early 1860s and gained oyster fishing experience before being appointed Inspector of Oyster Fisheries.[30] The brothers Nicholas and Peter Park, from Dubrovnik, had an oyster farm at Little River near Grafton.[31]

The first Croatian fishing community in Australia was situated in Geelong where Croatians were fishing from the early 1850s. By the 1870s Croatians were also fishing in Portarlington, Port Fairy, Melbourne, Sydney and Port Lincoln. Most Croatian pioneer fishermen in Victoria ended up in Portarlington, which remained one of the major fishing ports in the Port Phillip Bay until the Second World War, although a number of Croatian fishermen from Portarlington moved to other ports because of better work opportunities. The Gippsland Lakes Croatian fishermen predominantly arrived in Australia in the 1880s, settling there because the area offered new markets as a result of an increase in population and better transport links. A permanent entrance was cut through the coastal dunes to allow better shipping access to Gippsland Lakes towns, including Paynesville and Lakes Entrance.

The types of fish, fishing methods and fishing boats varied in different regions of Australia. In Port Phillip Bay, whiting, snapper, flathead, Australian salmon and flounder were caught from double-ended sailing boats (sharp at both bow and stern) using fishing nets. The fishermen in ocean waters such as Port Fairy primarily fished for barracouta using line fishing, whereby a series of lines were trolled from 'couta sailing boats with square sterns. They also caught crayfish (lobster) using craypots in rocky waters. The lengths of double-ended and 'coata fishing boats varied between 7 and 9 m.

The ethnic background of the fishing community in Portarlington changed over time. In 1861 nearly all the fishermen in Portarlington were Chinese. In 1870 Croatian fishermen from Geelong started to settle in Portarlington, their main reason being its closer proximity to popular fishing grounds. The Portarlington jetty was also extended in 1870 to ensure a sufficient depth of water for their fishing boats. By the 1880s Croatians were the largest group of fishermen in Portarlington and constituted around 39 per cent of the fishermen. A decade or so later most of the fishermen in Portarlington were still non-British immigrants, of whom the majority were Croatians. In the early 1890s at least a third of the fishermen in Sandringham were also Croatian. Documented evidence confirms that Croatian fishermen in Victoria associated with other Croatian fishermen, and with over 75 per cent of Croatian fishermen maintaining close links with other Croatian fishermen, they were a very close-knit community. They lived together and shared fishing boats. For example, John Lekovich fished and lived with Mati Botica in Williamstown, and later he fished and lived with Gregory Pavletich in Portarlington. Marriage records indicate that over a third of the Croatian pioneer fishermen in Victoria had a Croatian fisherman as a marriage witness. Some Croatian pioneer fishermen like Dominick Lussich mixed with

John Lekovich in his 8-m double-ended boat
with a box of fish he had caught. His father-in-law
was the Croatian pioneer Gregory Pavletich

Croatians who arrived in Australia 50 years later. Established Croatian fishermen often allowed new Croatian arrivals to work with them on their fishing boats.[32]

A Croatian fisherman from the Portarlington fishing community was Joseph Zagabria (Josip Zagabrija) who was born in Plomin and arrived in Australia in 1888. Like the other Portarlington Croatian fishermen, he had numerous contacts with other Croatians. For example, when he married Morah McMahon in St Thomas' Roman Catholic Church in Drysdale in 1892, the marriage witnesses were the Croatian, Vincent Margitich, and Gregory Pavletich's wife. Zagabria had four children, of whom three had godparents who were either Croatian or had Croatian connections.[33]

Life for these fishermen was extremely difficult. They rose early, and their work involved considerable strenuous exertion and danger. In about 1905, Joseph Zagabria had a serious accident

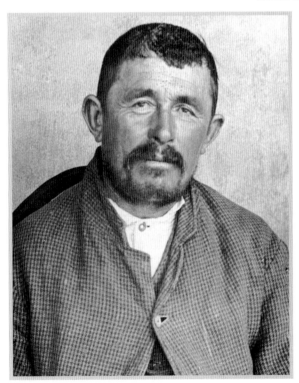

Joseph Zagabria

when a mast fell on his head while fishing. As a result, a metal plate was inserted into his skull. After this accident he was never the same, he refused to work, and did not worry if his children did not attend school regularly. Zagabria was subsequently admitted to Kew Asylum where he died on 10 January 1908.[34]

In the early 1890s five Croatian fishermen lived at Moor Street, Sandringham. From 1888 to 1890 Luke Scoglier from Split was one of them. He married Jane Tyrell in St Finbar's Catholic Church, Brighton, in 1888. The witnesses to the marriage were fellow Croatian Mathew Kazia, and Annie Coloper, the daughter of the Croatian fisherman, Stephen Coloper (Stjepan Kaloper). Scoglier had previously also fished from Portarlington before finally settling in Tarraville.[35] Mathew Kazia later had a wine saloon in Fremantle and was known for the assistance he gave to new Croatian arrivals. Apart from free meals, he helped Croatians find work and even helped some Croatians to select land in Spearwood, Western Australia.[36]

Andrew Radoslovich fished in Port Fairy for over half a century. He normally line-fished from a 8-m 'couta boat. Radoslovich died on 20 July 1958, and in his obituary in *The Port Fairy Gazette*, it was stated that he: 'was a professional fisherman in Port Fairy for many years, and he followed his calling in the days of sail when it was beset with all kinds of hazards. He often recalled the days when his boat was becalmed and he had to row for some miles'.[37]

Port Fairy fishermen and their sons at the Port Fairy wharf in about 1898.
In the back row on the left side are Andrew Radoslovich and his son

Croatian fishermen participated in boat regattas, on occasions, winning races. For example on 20 April 1908, the Portarlington Regatta was held and was the major tourist attraction in the Portarlington district during the Easter holidays. For the double-ended boat race with standing sails, Gregory Pavletich's 8-m *Nellie*, came first and he received a first prize of £2. Croatian fishermen sometimes named their fishing boats after their children, for example, Gregory Pavletich's *Nellie* and Natale Vuscovich's *Patrick*.[38] Croatian fishermen also made record fish and shark catches; for example, in 1877 Natale Vuscovich caught 225 fine barracouta in just over two hours in Port Fairy.[39]

Most Croatian fishermen enjoyed the independence of being self-employed. However, this independence came at a price – they had to spend their own money on fishing boats and gear. Portarlington fishermen were a case in point, largely owning their boats and dinghies. In 1903 an average fishing boat with associated fishing nets in Portarlington cost £46.

Before the Second World War Victorian fishermen (including Croatian immigrant fishermen) were generally poor, since the consumption of fish by Victorians in Melbourne was small by comparison with other cities in the world. The fish auctioned at markets in Melbourne incurred agent, selling and freight costs. There were also the costs of the fishermen's boats and nets, and their maintenance. The boats had to be registered and licenses were required for the fishermen's nets. To make ends meet, the Portarlington fishermen supplemented their incomes by farming and labouring, while some of the Croatian fishermen in Williamstown also worked as wharf labourers. A number of Croatian fishermen also owned pleasure boats, which they occasionally hired out to tourists to supplement their income. John Markovich or Markoveh (Ivan Marković), who was born in Malinska on the island of Krk, was a Lakes Entrance fisherman who also owned some small boats which he hired to tourists.[40] The type of accommodation these fishermen had also suggests that they were on low incomes. For example, Croatian fishermen in Portarlington and Port Albert occasionally lived in tents.[41] The Croatian fisherman, Dominic Tarabochia (Dominik Tarabokija), who was born on the island of Susak, lived on his boat for several years in Portarlington.[42]

By the late 1890s Croatian fishermen represented the majority of the Portarlington fishermen. They helped form the Portarlington Fishermen's Protection Society and worked to remove the injustices fishermen suffered at the hands of the fish auctioneers at the Melbourne Fish Market. The problem for the fishermen was that the auctioneers were sending their fish off by rail before sale, which resulted in their being denied a fair price for their fish. In January 1898 the local fishermen held a meeting to tackle this problem and, according to *The Bellarine Herald*:

> Mr G. Pavletich moved that this meeting form itself into a society to be called the
> Portarlington Fishermen's Protection Society. By this means they would have

John Markovich's wedding day in 1895

some standing and be enabled to look after their own interests. Mr H. Allen moved that Messrs D. Lussick, G. Pavletich, Chas Richards (secretary), be appointed [to] a committee to arrange all details in connection with the matter, and that the secretary write to all fishing centres in the bay inviting their co-operation in the matter.[43]

Croatian fishermen continued to work towards improving their working conditions. Gregory Pavletich represented the Portarlington fishermen in a meeting in 1901 with the Minister of Public Works in an attempt to have the Portarlington breakwater extended to give the fishermen's boats a safe anchorage in all weather.[44] Croatian fishermen also signed petitions to improve their working conditions; for example, in 1919 Andrew Radoslovich was

Dominic Tarabochia

one of the Port Fairy fishermen who signed a petition sent to the council complaining about the poor condition of the Port Fairy boat-slip which had been blocked by siltage. They demanded that the necessary improvements be made immediately to enable them to use the facility to clean their boats.[45]

Before 1900 Croatian fishermen had also established fishing communities in the United States and Canada. For example, there were over 220 Croatian fishermen in San Francisco between 1860 and 1900. Those fishermen also played an active role in fishermen's associations. August Splivalo was president of the Fishermen's Association of San Francisco in 1870; Anton Francovich was president of the San Francisco Fishermen's Protective Association on three occasions and Anton Mengola was president twice between 1877 and 1885. Croatian fishermen were also prominent in the oyster fishing industry in Plaquemines parish, south of New Orleans on the Mississippi Delta, where they numbered 100 fishermen in 1860 and 400 fishermen in 1893.[46]

Croatian fishermen were sometimes discriminated against by the other fishermen in Australia. For example, during the First World War some of the competing fishermen in Portarlington made allegations against the Croatian fishermen regarding their loyalties. They had no supporting evidence for these allegations, but it appeared that they were attempting to eliminate some of the competition. In 1917 letters were sent to the Department of Defence which stated that the Croatian fishermen in Portarlington had very good boats and were monopolising the fishing trade. It was alleged that they had behaved suspiciously in the preceding year. However, the representative from the Department of Defence concluded that they were 'men of good character and repute and I am unable to get any evidence regarding their suspicious movements. On the contrary these men attend to their work strictly and do not give anyone cause to complain about their conduct or movements'.[47]

Croatian fishermen were both versatile and highly resourceful in repairing their own and others' boats. Natale Vuscovich repaired yachts in Port Fairy and maintained his own boat in Portarlington. Croatian pioneers were also boatbuilders in Australia. Nicholas Matulick (Nikola Matulić) from Omiš worked as a boatbuilder in South Australia for many years. He married Elizabeth Huggins in Adelaide in 1853 and they had seven children who lived past childhood. Matulick initially worked as a boatbuilder and vigneron in Adelaide for several years, subsequently moving to Goolwa and Mannum to construct paddle steamers. Matulick died in Woodville, Adelaide, on 5 November 1899.[48] Joseph Vidulich (Josip Vidulić) who was born in Mali Lošinj on the island of Lošinj arrived in Queensland in 1873. He married Katherine O'Rourke in Townsville in 1878. Although Vidulich was initially a seaman in Townsville, by 1886 he was a timber merchant and contractor in that town and later a boatbuilder and timber merchant in Mackay. By the turn of the century Vidulich owned a sawmill also in Mackay – Joseph Vidulich & Co.'s Pioneer Saw Mill. In 1919 he died in Blackall where he was a furniture dealer.[49]

Joseph Vidulich's shipbuilder advertisement

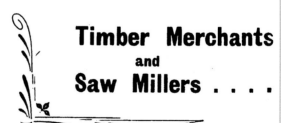
Joseph Vidulich and Co.'s sawmill advertisement

Croatian fishermen from Victoria such as Jerome Lussick, Mathew Kazia, Joseph Katnich, Joseph Marian, Andrew Rocke and Antone Rerecich, later went to live in Western Australia where they joined the Fremantle Croatian fishing community. Andrew Rocke (Andrija Roki) who was born on the island of Vis was a fisherman with other Croatians in Port Lincoln in the late 1860s. After a brief interlude in Melbourne, he moved to Hastings for a couple of decades before joining the Croatian fishermen in Fremantle.[50]

Jerome Lussick's sailing boat The Luksic *in Western Australia. The boat was used to transport fish in ice quickly from Carnarvon to Fremantle*

Croatian pioneer seamen

The Croatian seafaring men in Melbourne were mainly sailors, many of whom were captains and crew members of schooners that traded between Melbourne, Geelong, Gippsland and other colonies. Croatian seamen in Melbourne were mostly concentrated in South Melbourne, while other Croatian seamen in Victoria lived in Geelong, Port Albert and Paynesville. As we have seen, Croatian mariners in Echuca worked on the river boats of the Murray River.

Andrea Franktovich was captain of the 142-ton wooden schooner *Jane* which he purchased in December 1855. In four trips to Melbourne he imported 596 tons of coal from Newcastle and 150 tons of copper ore from Port Wakefield. The *Jane* was built in 1840 and had a length of 23 m.[51] After selling the *Jane* in September 1857 Franktovich returned to gold mining. Schooners owned by Croatian seamen in Australia were typically from 26 to 142 tons.

A South Melbourne-based Croatian seaman was Joseph Catarinich who arrived in Victoria in 1870 on the *Wimmera* from Calcutta. He captained schooners that traded between Melbourne and Gippsland Lakes, between Melbourne and Devonport, Burnie and Wynyard Tasmania. From the 1967 publication, *Story of Gippsland Shipping*, we learn that: 'During the early 1870s the schooner *Wellington* was a regular trader to Sale. She was commanded by Captain Catarnick [Catarinich], a well-known skipper of that period. He was later in charge of the *Jane Moorehead* and *Warrigal*, trading to Wynyard in Tasmania'.[52] Catarinich sometimes employed Croatian seamen on his vessels. For example, Mate Matich worked as a seamen on two occasions on board the 90-ton ketch, *Warrigal*, between 1909 and 1912.[53]

Captain Joseph Catarinich

Nicholas Gelletich (Nikola Jeletić) born in Rijeka was a fisherman and seaman who lived in Paynesville for more than half a century. According to *Every Week* newspaper, his cousin or brother, Captain John Gelletich, drowned at Lakes Entrance in 1889. John Gelletich was captain of the 49-ton schooner, *Abstainer*, which traded between Bairnsdale and Melbourne.[54] On 24 June 1889, the *Abstainer* was being towed from Lakes Entrance by the steamer *Rose of Sharon* when rough seas were encountered and the tow rope was cast off with the vessel still in a dangerous position. The vessel drifted over towards the pier, where she was fastened, but the strong current and heavy swell broke the lines. Moreover, as a result of bumping the pier in the rough seas, the vessel had begun to leak. On board the *Abstainer* were the mate, seaman, cook and Captain Gelletich who tried to save the *Abstainer* and its contents, but to no avail – the water was rising in the vessel. The mate and seaman managed to jump off the vessel before she sank. The topmast fell and struck the cook who sank with the vessel. Captain Gelletich swam clear of the breakers and drifted out to sea. His brother, on board the steamer *Emu*, saw the ship sinking in the distance but reached the scene of the disaster too late. Both Captain Gelletich and the cook were drowned.[55]

In the nineteenth century Croatian seamen were also living and working in other ports of Australia. The majority of Croatian pioneers in South Australia were seamen and usually lived in Port Adelaide and Adelaide, although some lived in Port Augusta and Port Lincoln. A typical Croatian pioneer in South Australia was

Nicholas Gelletich with his wife and two sons

Antonio Angelinawich (Anđelinović) who was born on the island of Hvar. He arrived in Port Adelaide in 1855 and worked as a master mariner. Angelinawich married Eliza Fitzgerald in 1858 and they had nine children. He died at his residence in Ship Street, Port Adelaide in 1915. Peter Host from Rijeka was also a seaman in South Australia. He arrived in Port Augusta in 1879 as part of the crew on the barque *Excelsior*. For the next four years Host worked on South Australian coastal

vessels. He was part of the crew on the barque *Goolwa*
that sailed to London, but he deserted it on its return
to Port Adelaide in 1884. Host then worked on other
South Australian coastal vessels. He married an
English woman in 1885 and they had 12 children.
Host subsequently worked as a roper in the mines of
Broken Hill for eight years and Kalgoorlie/Boulder
over ten years before returning to Adelaide. One of
his daughters Eva married a Croatian, Mate Klaric,
from the island of Vis in Boulder in 1908. Peter Host
died in Adelaide in 1933. According to his
descendants Peter Host served on a ship in South
Australia together with another Croatian pioneer
Ivan Zubrinich who was later a labourer in Port Pirie.
Interestingly, one of Ivan Zubrinich's granddaughters
married one of Peter Host's grandsons.[56] The
Croatian settlers in New South Wales, like their
South Australian counterparts, were generally seamen

Peter Host in Adelaide in the 1880s

Peter Host with his wife and nine of their children in Boulder in 1903

Peter Host's daughter Eva's and Mate Klaric's wedding in Boulder in 1908.
From left to right are: Daisy Host, Sam Klaric, Peter Host, Eva Host (bride), Mate Klaric (groom),
Vincent Klaric, Andy, Galena Maud Host. Sam and Vincent were Mate Klaric's brothers,
while Andy was a cousin.

and almost all of them lived in Sydney, although a few lived in Newcastle. In Queensland there was a concentration of Croatian seamen in Townsville. Croatian seamen also lived in Fremantle and Albany in Western Australia and Hobart in Tasmania.

Croatians in Argentina were highly successful shipowners. Nikola Mihanovich (Mihanović) who was born in Doli on the Pelješac Peninsula, arrived in South America in 1867. In the late 1870s he formed the Mihanovich, Cosulich y Zuanich shipping company with another two Croatians in Buenos Aires. By 1909 the Argentine Navigation Company (Nicholas Mihanovich) Limited (of which Mihanovich was a majority shareholder) owned 290 boats with a total tonnage of 84,960 tons. Mihanovich employed many Croatians and helped finance others to establish businesses. Many of his boats celebrated Croatian towns or regions with names such as *Croatia, Dalmata, Dalmacia, Doli, Spalato* (Split), *Sebenico* (Šibenik),

PIONEER SEAMEN AND FISHERMEN

Ragusa (Dubrovnik), *Curzola* (Korčula), *Fiume* (Rijeka), *Pola* (Pula), *Zara* (Zadar), *Stagno* (Ston) and *Narenta* (Neretva). Croatians also named their oyster fishing boats in Louisiana, and fishing boats in San Pedro in California and Fremantle in Western Australia, after Croatian towns or regions. In 1892 Mihanovich bought 800 square kilometres of land in the province of Chaco in Argentina, which he called *Kolonija Dalmacija*, and at his own expense, assisted Croatians to migrate there.[57]

Rescues and storms

In the nineteenth century fishermen and seamen in Australia had a dangerous life. Croatians accepted the life and behaved in an exemplary fashion, often saving lives. Croatian fishermen were involved in the rescue of drowning people from sinking boats. They also assisted in the location of the bodies of drowned persons. Croatian fishermen displayed outstanding bravery and they ferried passengers through storms at times when others refused to go to sea. Occasionally they were caught in very ferocious storms, but their skills and experience meant they were able to survive them. Croatian fishermen were also members of lifeboat crews. Earlier in this chapter we also saw how Croatian seamen acted bravely when involved in shipwrecks in Australian waters.

The following examples demonstrate that the acts of bravery committed by Croatian fishermen were not just isolated incidents, but suggest they had a sense of duty to help others in their community. John Lussich, for example, saved at least six people from drowning in the Geelong area, on 8 November 1885 saving the lives of two men. After a morning of fishing in the boat *Elsie*, six men went for a sail in Corio Bay in the Geelong area. On the return trip to Hutton's wharf, one of them accidentally moved the tiller which caused the mainsail to move suddenly and overturn the boat. The boat quickly filled with water and capsized about a kilometre from the wharf on the Western Beach. John Lussich who was on the wharf noticed the accident and immediately jumped into his boat where he was joined by another two volunteers. They quickly rowed out and managed to save Thomas Armstrong and Patrick Deegan, but the other four men drowned. Had it not been for Lussich's actions there would have been no survivors.[58] In November 1896 Natale Vuscovich saved the life of a young Melbourne boy who fell into deep water off the Portarlington pier. Vuscovich, who was 65 years old at the time, jumped into the water to save the six-year-old James Scott who would have drowned had it not been for Vuscovich's quick actions and bravery.[59]

When fierce storms struck, fishermen occasionally had to deal with a situation whereby their boats would sometimes break from their moorings. To avoid damage the boats had to be secured quickly. On 26 July 1898, Portarlington was hit by one of the worst storms in years, accompanied by gale-force winds and heavy showers. During the gale the mooring lines of the boats at the pier broke and the fishermen had to struggle to prevent their boats from being smashed to pieces. Nevertheless, Gregory Pavletich's *Sparrow* crashed into the *Caroline*, resulting in several broken planks on the latter. Although these boats were under control, there was now concern for a couple of fishing boats engaged in netting to the north-east of St George's buoy. One of these boats was manned by Joseph Zagabria and his assistant, and had last been seen around noon apparently hauling their nets, but disappeared when the storm erupted. The worst was expected and it was assumed that they were lost to the sea. However, at about 3 pm in the afternoon, a reassuring word was received that the boats had been seen making their way towards St Leonards for shelter.[60]

In 1906 Gladys Davis, the daughter of the Attorney-General of Victoria, the Hon. J. M. Davis, drowned near Portarlington. As she returned from a fishing trip, an unexpected gust of wind struck the boat she was in and threw all its occupants into the water. Gladys Davis was unable to swim and drowned even though numerous attempts were made to save her. The local Portarlington fishermen freely gave their own time and their boats to help find her missing body and were later commended for the way they generously assisted in the search for the body. Special thanks were made to several fishermen, including John Margitich and Gregory Pavletich.[61]

Croatian fishermen themselves drowned during storms. On 5 September 1867, two Croatian fishermen, Vincent Florio and Spiro Lazzarovich, were returning from fishing when a squall hit and their boat started to take on water near Geelong. After a couple of hours clinging to the half-sunken boat, Florio bravely decided to swim to shore to get help for Lazzarovich who could not swim. Florio managed to swim to shore, but Lazzarovich drowned before help could be dispatched.[62] Other Croatians were accidentally drowned elsewhere in Australia. In 1887 Nicholas Millowick who had lived in South Australia since the 1850s, drowned in the Blue Lake, Mount Gambier. In 1895 Simeon Lukene (Lukin) from the island of Zlarin was accidentally drowned at Waterfall Bay near Woy Woy, New South Wales.[63]

CHAPTER 7

Pioneers with Hotels, Wineries and Farms

The hotels and stores operated by Croatian pioneers on the goldfields were often tents or makeshift huts. Croatian pioneers were also involved in the 'sly grog' trade on the goldfields. Later they had hotels in Melbourne, Adelaide, Sydney and other towns. Croatian pioneers also had wineries and pursued careers in farming.

Antonio Radovick, 'Father of Korumburra'

The most successful Croatian pioneer in Victoria was Antonio Radovick (Antun Radović) who was dubbed the 'Father of Korumburra'. In times past Korumburra was the centre of an active coal mining district; today Korumburra has a population of about 2739 and is an important dairy and farming district, servicing many of the smaller towns and diary farms in the area. Radovick was born in Potomje on the Pelješac Peninsula in approximately 1838 and arrived in Victoria 1862.[1] He married an Irish woman, Elizabeth Gill, on 11 November 1872 in St Ignatius Catholic Church, Richmond. They subsequently had six children. In 1874 Radovick managed the Railway Hotel in Prahran, and from 1875 to 1891 he owned the Exford Hotel on Russell Street, Melbourne. His relative, Steffano Radovick, arrived in Melbourne in 1884 and was immediately employed in the hotel.[2]

Antonio Radovick contributed significantly to the development and transformation of Korumburra into a prosperous town. In 1888 he purchased land there when the first allotments were sold in the town. At the time the land was dense forest, and after it had been cleared, he built the first house in Korumburra on it.[3] Within a year he had built Radovick's Korumburra Hotel, a fine two-storey wooden hotel with 50 rooms.

KORUMBURRA HOTEL,

A. RADOVICK

DESIRES to intimate that he has just completed and opened the above Handsome and Commodious Hotel at Korumburra, containing Fifty Rooms, fitted up with Every Modern Convenience, and Visitors may rely on receiving every attention and the Best Accommodation.

——BATHS. BILLIARD TABLE. FIRST-CLASS STABLING.——

Ales, Wines and Spirits of only the Best Brands Kept.

A. RADOVICK, Proprietor.

Radovick's Korumburra Hotel advertisement

The construction of the hotel is an extraordinary story of Antonio Radovick's enterprising skill and determination to succeed. Naturally, a hotel required a license, and a condition of his being granted a license was that he had to complete the hotel by the next Licensing Court sitting which would take place in December 1889. Osborne and Sons were granted the contract to build the hotel in June 1889. At enormous expense (between £500 and £600), the materials for the hotel were carted from Drouin, 44 kilometres away, which was the nearest railway station – and the muddy roads from the station to Korumburra were almost impassable in winter. A complete sawmill plant had to be transported from Drouin, including a six-ton boiler that was towed through the mud. The bricks were made locally and a portion of the timber was obtained from trees in what is now the principal street of Korumburra.[4]

After a few months, construction was progressing slowly and it seemed that the contractors would not finish the hotel in time for the licensing board meeting. Antonio Radovick then assumed responsibility for building the hotel. He arranged for all available bullock teams to cart building materials for the hotel and employed many additional men. Carpenters and painters worked day and night. Such was the flurry of activity that, several days before the hotel was completed, *The Great Southern Advocate* reported: 'The building has now somewhat the appearance of a beehive, in fact there seems to be a tradesman for every plank of weatherboard or pine to be placed in position'. The hotel was completed in time and the license was granted. It had a spacious bar, billiard room, dining room, bar parlour, private parlour, commercial room, 36 double and single rooms all luxuriously furnished.[5] On 26 February 1890, over 250 guests, including Mr F. C. Mason, MLA, Mr Stirling

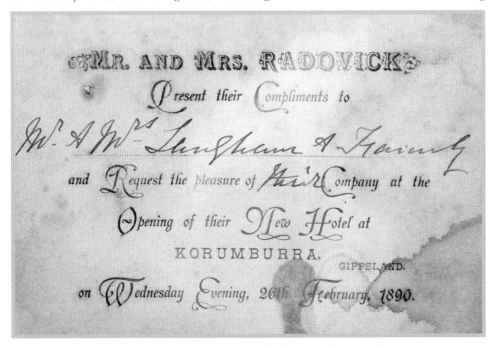

An invitation to the opening of Radovick's Korumburra Hotel

(assistant Government Geologist) and other mining officials, attended a ball commemorating the opening of Radovick's Korumburra Hotel. To mark the occasion, the hotel had been thoroughly decorated and a marquee was erected adjoining the main building where dinner was served.[6] Initially Steffano Radovick managed the hotel until Antonio Radovick settled permanently in Korumburra.[7]

The hotel became the central public meeting place where much of the future town was planned. Almost every society and sporting group in Korumburra had their meetings there. The first Catholic services were held on the steps of his hotel. Radovick also owned the adjacent buildings from which the National Bank of Australasia, post office, first police station and the town's newspaper operated. Radovick had the first sale yards in Korumburra behind his hotel.[8] In the early days of Korumburra he paid for deputations sent to Melbourne on public matters, and he also had banquets in his hotel to promote the town's interests.[9] Some of the non-sporting societies which had their meetings in Radovick's Korumburra Hotel included the Miners' Association, Coal Creek Colliery Accident Relief Fund, Mechanics' Institute, Korumburra Progress Association, Korumburra Agricultural and Pastoral Society, Korumburra Butter Factory, Cottage Hospital collection, Melbourne Hospital collection, Manchester Unity, United Ancient Order of Druids, Australian Natives' Association and Order of St Andrews.[10]

Radovick was a great patron of sport in Korumburra and donated generous prizes and trophies at various sporting events. He was the president of the Korumburra Cricket team and Korumburra Athletic Club, vice-president of the Great Southern Football Association, and judge for the Korumburra Athletic Club. The cricket team was known as the 'Radovick's Boarders' and 'Radovick's Trophy' was awarded for the best football player in the team during a season.[11] He allowed Radovick's paddock to be used for cricket, football, athletics, horse racing and wood chopping. Radovick's paddock was also used as the district showground.[12]

Radovick gave land and/or funds for the Mechanics' Institute, for the school and the Catholic Church. In 1890 for example, when Korumburra residents attempted to obtain land from the Lands Department to build their Mechanics' Institute he immediately donated £10 10s towards the building. Radovick was on the Mechanics' Institute building committee and allowed meetings to be held at his hotel. In relation to obtaining land for the Mechanics' Institute, he also organised a meeting in his hotel in Melbourne, where the Lands Office met a deputation from Korumburra. Radovick was also one of the three guarantors on the loan which financed the erection of the building. When completed, the Mechanics' Institute was used for many functions, including a school, courthouse and other public functions, but its location proved difficult on occasions – in winter it was almost inaccessible because of mud. In 1895 it was decided that the Mechanics' Institute required a site closer to the centre of town, and Radovick donated a piece of land 13 by 27.5 m in what is now Radovick Street, free of cost, for the erection of a new Mechanics' Institute. He also paid for the footpath to be made to the hall and provided a large lamp. In addition, Radovick lent the money necessary for the transfer of the building from the old site. Several years later he donated another 6 m of land at the back of the hall. The Mechanics' Institute could seat 300 people and also had a fine library and reading room.[13]

Radovick helped the coal miners in the district by allowing the Coal Creek Miners' Association, Coal Creek Colliery Accident Relief Fund and Miners' Accident Society to have their meetings in his hotel and donated funds to them. He helped negotiate a settlement in a dispute between miners and management, and represented miners in talks with parliamentarians. For example in October 1894, a meeting was held in Radovick's hotel to protest against the Railway Department limiting the amount of coal it used from the local mines. Radovick argued that, by buying Victorian coal, the government kept money in the colony. Since Victorian coal prices were competitive, the government had no excuse for limiting the amount of Victorian coal they purchased. Radovick, four other influential Korumburra citizens and two mine officials were selected to represent the miners in talks with parliamentarians. They met a deputation which included the Minister of Railways, the Minister for Mines (Hon. H. Williams), the member for Ballarat West (Hon. R. Vale), the Government Whip (Mr G. Turner) and the former Minister of Education (Hon. R. Baker). They lobbied the parliamentarians to force the Railway Department to lift the limits on the amount of Victorian coal purchased.[14]

Antonio Radovick's hotel and his adjacent buildings in the mid-1890s. The sign on the hotel reads Radovick's Korumburra Hotel. There is a geological survey party in front of the hotel

Antonio Radovick holding a stick with other important Korumburra townsmen.
The dense forest can be seen in the background

According to *The Great Southern Advocate*, Antonio Radovick:

was a well-known figure in public, and though he never tried for a seat in the shire council, he was a power behind the throne. He was gazetted the first Government representative on the Korumburra Waterworks Trust, but through a mistake made in his first name, there had to be a fresh notification. Mr Turner, the then member for West Gippsland, claimed as a right that he should nominate the Government representative and the notification had to be gazetted afresh. Mr Radovick was informed and he declined therefore to act on the trust.[15]

Radovick later pursued a career in dairy farming; he also became well known as a breeder of Shorthorn cattle and other prize stock.[16] Radovick died on 11 December 1903 and, as we have seen, one of the main streets in Korumburra is named in his honour.

A cricket team of pioneer settlers from the Korumburra district in 1897.
Antonio Radovick is seated on the left side

Antonio Radovick had documented contacts with at least another 11 Croatian pioneers in Australia. However, the real figure is probably much higher since, at one stage, he had a hotel in the centre of Melbourne. In 1882 Radovick signed a register for the Austrian Consulate's Census (mentioned earlier) on behalf of eight Croatian pioneers living in Melbourne, Portarlington and Geelong.[17] The following year, Radovick was gold mining at 30 Mile Creek, Crooked River where, as we have seen, there was a large concentration of Croatians.[18] His very close Croatian friend was Jacob Stiglich who also came to Korumburra in the early days. Stiglich was appointed to the position of overman (overseer in colliery) in the early operation of the Outtrim coal mine. He died on 5 August 1904 and was survived by ten children, the oldest of whom was 19. His infant son was only a week old at the time of his death.[19]

Hotels in gold mining towns

Until 1854 there was a total ban on liquor on the goldfields. To quench the thirst of the eager miners, 'grog shops' started up everywhere. Liquor was illegally carted to the goldfields day and night. The granting of hotel licenses in 1854 and the sale of blocks of land helped to normalise life on the goldfields. However, new rushes and fluctuating populations on the goldfields allowed sly grog shops to continue trading illegally for many years.[20]

The majority of Croatian pioneers who became publicans in Victoria had initially been miners on the goldfields. After saving up some funds they would start with a small hotel, then expand and develop their business into a respectable hotel. The hotels were not their only source of income as they also continued to be involved in mining. Croatians who owned hotels in the gold mining towns maintained contact with other Croatian pioneers in the community, normally locating their hotels in areas where there was a concentration of Croatian settlers. Thus it would seem reasonable to assume that Croatians were among the patrons in their hotels.

In 1861 after a few years of successful mining with a party of Croatian gold miners at the Slavonian mine in Redcastle, Antonio Geronevitch acquired a license for his All Nations Hotel. According to *The McIvor Times*, he had purchased a house and renovated it stylishly into a tasteful hotel, which was the third hotel to be built in Redcastle. The three new hotels signalled the town's new-found prosperity due to the gold rush.[21] However, a decade later it was noted by *The McIvor Times* that the only visible sign of progress to the Redcastle township for several years was the painting of Geronevitch's hotel and that a couple of small stores had been built. Antonio Geronevitch died in Redcastle on 16 May 1880.[22]

In some areas Croatian pioneers who had bought hotels would remain on the goldfields after the gold rush had subsided and most of their patrons had left the area. Having invested the majority of their funds into their hotels, they were then not able to sell them for a reasonable price. Examples of Croatian publicans who remained on the goldfields include Antonio Geronevitch, Frank Golden and Mattio Marassovich. In each of these three cases there had been a Croatian community in the mining town previously.

When Frank Golden from Starigrad on the island of Hvar died in his Costerfield Family Hotel on 22 August 1887, work on the principal gold and antimony mines in the Costerfield area had ceased. His weatherboard hotel with nine rooms, an iron roof, with paper and canvas partitions was by then run down.[23] The first license for the Costerfield Family Hotel was held by Frederick Field, one of the discoverers of gold in Costerfield.[24] Frank Golden had previously owned the All Nations Hotel at Heathcote and in the 1870s, the North Costerfield Hotel. In 1879 Golden purchased the Costerfield Family Hotel which he managed until his death. He was survived by ten of his 14 children. From the early 1860s, in addition to managing his hotel, he was a shareholder in several gold and antimony mines in the area. Two of his Croatian mining partners were Joseph Ploncich and Niccola Mitrovich.[25]

In Woods Point Croatian pioneers managed four hotels.[26] Three of these hotels operated between 1863 and 1866 during the period where there were at least 16 Croatians in Woods Point. Three of these Croatian publicans subsequently left Woods Point and went to search for gold in other areas where Croatian communities were located. Nicolo Anticevich (Nikola Antičević) from Dalmatia, who was a hotel keeper in Woods Point in 1863, moved his hotel business the following year at the start of a new gold rush to the Crooked River mining district where there was already a settlement of Croatian miners.[27] In 1864 Antonio Anticevich's Hotel was situated about five kilometres from the Dargo Inn. A couple of years later he managed the Mail Rest Hotel on Grant Road, the main road from Stratford to Grant.[28] It was strategically placed to cater for the miners and suppliers going to the Crooked River goldfields. Apart from his hotel business and mining, Anticevich was also involved in farming at Dargo.[29] Paulo Arnerich purchased land on Bridge Street, Woods Point in March 1864 where he was working as a miner. By August 1864 Arnerich had almost completed his Miners' Hotel in Woods Point. In 1866 however, he moved to New Zealand during the Westland gold rush.[30] Both Arnerich and Anticevich had lived in Epsom, where there was a Croatian mining community, before moving to Woods Point.[31]

Another successful Croatian publican was Frank Entra (Franjo Kentra) who was born in Gruž, which is now an outer part of Dubrovnik, on 28 June 1826.[32] In his early life he was a seafaring man and arrived in Victoria in 1856 on a French ship from Mauritius. Entra first mined in Stanley. Subsequently, from 1862 to 1880, he was a miner at Clear Creek, Swift Creek, Muddy Creek, Murphy's Gully and Murphy's Flat in the Yackandandah Junction area. He had various mining bank claims and bank sluicing claims where he constructed water races and dams.[33] Entra married an English woman, Sarah Sheilds, in Yackandandah on 29 March 1864. At Yackandandah Junction he was also storekeeper and publican.

MINERS' HOTEL.

Paulo Arnerich

BEGS to inform the inhabitants of Wood's Point that the above hotel is nearly completed, and that by a combination of comfort and moderate charges he hopes to merit a large share of public patronage.

Miners' Hotel newspaper advertisement with Arnerich's surname

Frank Entra

Frank Entra with his wife

On 7 April 1880, Frank Entra's home at Yackandandah Junction was burnt to the ground. All of the contents were completely destroyed, including a considerable amount of cash in notes, jewellery and silver. When the fire started he was working on his mining claim and his wife was in Melbourne. Entra returned in the evening to find his house totally engulfed by flames. He managed to save only his favourite parrot which had been in a cage hanging under the verandah, but while doing so, he was almost burnt by the fierce flames. Entra had insured his home with the Norwich Union for a sum of £250 and he would have been in a desperate situation without it.[34] Entra took full advantage of the insurance money and bought the Waterloo Hotel in September 1880.[35] The Waterloo Hotel, located on High Street opposite the post office, was the most popular hotel in Yackandandah. It was a large timber building with a verandah and was originally granted its liquor license in 1854. Previously the hotels in Yackandandah had been operating illegally.

In the 1890s Entra advertised his Waterloo Hotel in *The Yackandandah Times*. Most Croatian publicans on the goldfields advertised on the front pages of the local papers implying they had prosperous establishments. Entra stated that his hotel provided:

> Every accommodation for visitors and families. A first-class cuisine guaranteed. Only the best brands of ales, wines and spirits kept. First-class sample room bath, &c. Superior Alcock's billiard table. Commodious stables and loose boxes.[36]

Business must have been booming at that time because Frank Entra purchased four prime allotments of land on High Street, Yackandandah. From September 1895 he leased out his hotel and moved into his villa on High Street next to the post office where he lived in his retirement. He died on 1 May 1904. The hotel operated under many proprietors until it was burnt down in 1915. The Waterloo Hotel was never rebuilt and now the Memorial Gardens are located where it used to stand.[37]

WATERLOO HOTEL,

(OPPOSITE THE POST OFFICE.)

HIGH STREET, YACKANDANDAH.

———

OLD ESTABLISHED COMMERCIAL HOUSE.

———

Frank Entra - Proprietor.

———

EVERY ACCOMMODATION FOR VISITORS AND FAMILIES.

Newspaper advertisement for the Waterloo Hotel with Entra's surname

Croatians were also storekeepers on the goldfields and in regional Victoria and New South Wales. Although almost no written evidence exists of what they sold in their stores, it might be expected that they sold food and mining supplies. On the Victorian goldfields Croatians were storekeepers in Buckland, Ballarat, Heathcote, Hepburn, Stawell and Woods Point. They were also storekeepers in other parts of Australia. Giralomo Miloslavich, who was born in Dubrovnik, was a storekeeper in Normanton in Queensland in the 1880s and a storekeeper near Parramatta in New South Wales in the 1890s. Peter Park, who was born in Dubrovnik, was a miner on the Araluen goldfields in New South Wales, and then in 1870 he moved to Grafton in New South Wales where he later became a storekeeper.[38]

Many Croatian storekeepers on the goldfields were licensed victuallers and sold alcohol. Others were involved in the sly grog trade and used their stores as fronts to conceal the illegal sale of alcohol. This is known because some Croatians were charged with selling liquor without a license. Antonio Geronevitch, for example, was twice fined for selling liquor without a license. In the first case in 1869, his wife sold a glass of beer to the revenue inspector for 6p when the licensee of the All Nations Hotel was not present. This resulted in a fine of £5. In January 1871 Geronevitch was again fined for selling spirits without a license. Throughout that year he applied several times for a publican's license which was finally granted on 23 December 1871.[39] Similarly, in 1888 Antonio Yackovitze from Dalmatia was charged with carrying liquor for the purpose of sale in Wandiligong. He had borrowed a cart and was selling vegetables and other goods. An undercover policeman bought some bacon from him, before he convinced Yackovitze to sell him some wine. Antonio Yackovitze was fined £2, with £1 10s court costs. The horse, cart, wine and other contents of the cart were confiscated by the crown.[40]

The All Nations Hotels managed by Croatian pioneers (Frank Golden, Antonio Geronevitch and Bartholomew Mercovich) reflect the diverse backgrounds and nationalities of the miners on the goldfields. The name 'All Nations Hotel' also implies that Croatian pioneers associated and did business with miners of different nationalities. The Austro-Hungarian empire was a multicultural empire comprising several nations, so Croatians were used to dealing with people of other nationalities and cultures. Perhaps Croatian pioneers even supported the idea of a multicultural Australia before multiculturalism, as such, was invented. In the late 1860s, Frank Golden managed the All Nations Hotel at Caledonia Gully, Heathcote. It was about half a kilometre north of Croatian Louis Spallatrino's mining claims.[41] As we have noted, for almost two decades Antonio Geronevitch managed the All Nations Hotel in Redcastle. In the mid-1860s Bartholomew Mercovich was the proprietor of the All Nations Hotel in the Woods Point mining district. According to *The Mountaineer*, he had about 30 boarders in the hotel and the business was prosperous. Near his hotel, another Croatian, Charles Radovich, was working on the A1 West All Nations Quartz Mining Company.[42]

Bartholomew Mercovich

Metropolitan hotels

There were several Croatian pioneers who managed hotels in Melbourne. There is written evidence that all the Croatian publicans in Melbourne associated with other Croatians in Melbourne, and as before, it would be reasonable to suggest that Croatians were among the patrons in their hotels. These publicans moved around and

Joseph Pasquan

managed many hotels in Melbourne, indicating that initially some did not own the hotels. A typical example was Joseph Pasquan (Josip Paškvan) who was born in Rijeka on 17 March 1855. For a decade from about 1873, he was employed by Fern Bros of Liverpool in a seafaring occupation. In this capacity Pasquan was involved in trading to Australia, the United States, Canada and South Africa. He came to Australia to join his relative Martin Pasquan. Upon his arrival in Melbourne in 1883, Joseph Pasquan was employed in a tobacconist business followed by a hairdressing business on Bourke Street. Subsequently, he became the proprietor of the Park View Hotel, Parkville. He then managed seven hotels within Melbourne, including the Terminus Hotel at 97 King Street (1891–1895); Morning Star Hotel, Prahran; Langham Hotel, 250 Burwood Road, Hawthorn (1897–1899); Retreat Hotel on Sydney Road, Brunswick (1901); Royal George Hotel, 257 Chapel Street, Prahran (1907–1908); and Parade Hotel, 180 Wellington Parade, East Melbourne from 1911 until his death on 11 August 1935.[43]

Between 1902 and 1904 Pasquan managed the Commercial Hotel in Wangaratta. The hotel was one of the finest in Victoria outside Melbourne and the best in the north-eastern district.[44] *The Cyclopedia of Victoria* described the hotel as follows:

> The hotel … contains forty-three rooms, including a spacious billiard-room, and attached to the hotel is one of the finest halls outside of Melbourne, having seating accommodation for over 1000 people, and all the necessary appliances, dressing-rooms, etc. There is also a large banqueting hall, with accommodation for upwards of 400 guests, Mr Pasquan finding no difficulty in catering for that number at one time, the cooking, etc., being done on the premises. The hotel

Newspaper advertisement for the Commercial Hotel with Pasquan's surname

bedrooms are large, lofty, and comfortably furnished, the large ones opening on to a magnificent balcony 270 feet [82.3 m] in length and 15 feet [4.6 m] in width, from which a charming view of the surrounding district may be obtained.[45]

In country Victoria he also managed the Railway Hotel in Warragul in 1910 and 1911.

Martin Pasquan (Martin Paškvan), a relative of Joseph, was born in Calin near Rijeka and disembarked in Melbourne in June 1865 from the ship, *Queen of the North*. In 1872 Pasquan had a restaurant at 244 Elizabeth Street, Melbourne. He was the proprietor of the Station Hotel, Hopkins Street, Footscray from 1873 to 1877.[46] The Station Hotel still exists today and is diagonally opposite the Croatian Hall. In March 1875 Martin Pasquan was also building a new house with a view to leasing it out as a public house. *The Williamstown Chronicle* noted that: 'The most prominent of the new buildings in course of erection at Footscray is the large two-storied brick house, in Hopkins Street, near the new railway bridge. This is being built by Mr Pasquin proprietor of the Station Hotel ... when complete will be amongst the best houses in Footscray'.[47]

In 1878 Pasquan managed the Hotel de Roma in Victoria Parade, Fitzroy. For the next few years he managed the Albion Hotel at 15 Therry Street, Melbourne. In 1882 and 1883 Pasquan ran the Macs Hotel at 158 Smith Street, Collingwood. During the following four years Pasquan had a restaurant, dining rooms, wine cellar and tobacconist at 148 Little Collins Street. In 1887 he also had dining rooms at Normanby Road, South Melbourne, and in the following year Pasquan maintained dining rooms – Pasquan's Hotel – at 60 Bourke Street. He died on 19 November 1888.[48] After Martin Pasquan's death Joseph married his widow. Martin was a keen lawn bowler and received a gold medal from Fitzroy Bowling Club bearing the engraving: 'Presented to Martin Pasquin, 1878'. He proudly hung the medal from his gold hunting lever watch. Interestingly, this medal, watch and other jewellery were twice stolen from his home. In both cases they were retrieved by the police who apprehended the thieves. In the first case the stolen items were valued at £200 suggesting Pasquan's career as a publican was lucrative.[49]

Another Melbourne publican was Antonio Fornarich (Ante Fornarić) who was born on 9 January 1847 on the island of Cres. He arrived in Australia in about 1874. Four years later he married a widow in Melbourne, worked as a seaman and lived in Yarraville. By 1882 Fornarich was manager of the Steam Hammer Hotel at 19 Ireland Street, West Melbourne, where he died on 24 January 1883. He left behind three sons, the oldest aged five.[50]

Croatians were also publicans in the other capital cities of Australia. Matteo Marincovich, from Bol on the island of Brač, ran the Royal Pyrmont Bridge Hotel at 21 Wharf Street in Sydney from about 1878 to until 1886. A number of Croatians in Adelaide and Port Adelaide were publicans and wine merchants. For example, Dominick Leonard who was born in Sutivan on the island of Brač and arrived in

Adelaide in 1864 managed several hotels in Adelaide from 1889 to 1912. From the 1880s John Burich (Ivan Burić), from the island of Vis, was a publican who managed the Duke of Wellington Hotel in Payneham, Adelaide. Jerome Lussick ran the Brookton Hotel at Spencer's Brook, near Northam, Western Australia. Croatian pioneers were also licensed victuallers and wine merchants in Sydney, Perth, Melbourne and Birdwood, South Australia; for example, Natale Starcevich was a wine merchant in Sydney and Ignazio Descovich from Rijeka who settled in Australia in 1854 was a wine merchant in Birdwood.[51]

Croatians in the United States were also publicans or saloon keepers. For example, Nikola Barovich (Barović) was a successful saloon keeper in Nevada and California. He was born in Janjina on the Pelješac Peninsula and arrived in San Francisco in 1850. A few years later Barovich opened a store in San Francisco and a business in the mining camp in Sonara. From 1856 to 1860 he had saloons in San Francisco. In 1864 Barovich moved to Nevada because of the silver boom and established a saloon in Austin. When the silver boom subsided, he moved to San Jose, California, where in 1882 he opened the Dalmatia Hotel.[52]

Banquets, balls and dances

In the pioneering days, hotels were the primary social and entertaining venues. In mining towns, hotels were usually established before community halls were built. Banquets, balls and dances were held in hotels managed by Croatians. Radovick's Korumburra Hotel was used for various celebrations, including banquets for important events in Korumburra, parliamentarians' visits, farewells, Coal Commissioners' visits and Coal Creek Proprietary banquets.[53] On 17 February 1891, for example, Antonio Radovick gave a banquet in his hotel to commemorate the arrival of the first train at Korumburra. Among the 70 guests were members of parliament, the shire president, a government geologist, railway contractors and Douglas Buzolich (JP), the son of another Croatian pioneer.[54] The Radovick family were unusually generous and organised concerts in Korumburra.[55]

As a tribute to Antonio Radovick's contribution to the development of Korumburra, the town's residents held banquets in his honour. They held a celebratory banquet for him on 27 July 1891 for promoting the advancement of Korumburra. This banquet was attended by Korumburra residents, members of parliament and other guests from Melbourne.[56] The residents of Korumburra hosted another testimonial banquet on 20 February 1894. Several additional tables had to be brought into the hotel's large dining room which was filled to capacity. Among the guests were the president of the Miners' Association, president of the shire, chairman of the directors of the Coal Creek Proprietary Co. and various inspectors. In a letter they presented to Antonio Radovick they wrote:

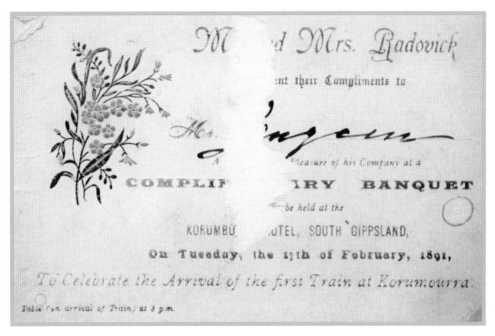

An invitation to a banquet at Radovick's hotel celebrating the arrival of the first train to Korumburra

On behalf of the residents and miners of Korumburra, we, the undersigned, desire to give expression to the esteem in which you are held as a man and citizen.

That you are a good citizen is evidenced by the enthusiastic interest you take in every movement for the welfare of those you live amongst, and that you are what is popularly termed 'a good fellow' can be denied by no one who has enjoyed your hospitality or had the privilege of witnessing your open-handed generosity.

Those of us who are sportsmen recognise that in you sport has its best patron; and the miners, whose interests you have always studied, feel themselves deeply indebted to you for the encouragement you have always given to the coal mining industry in the district.

Hoping that you may long be spared to reside among us and witness the spread of the town in whose growth we are all interested.[57]

On 4 August 1861, as part of an election campaign, a free evening ball and dinner was held at Antonio Geronevitch's Redcastle All Nations Hotel. Over 80 people sat down to dinner at the hotel and dancing continued until six in the morning. Geronevitch was complimented by the *McIvor News* on the way he managed his hotel and entertained the guests during the ball.[58] Balls and dances were regularly held on Boxing Day at Frank Golden's North Costerfield Hotel and the Costerfield Family Hotel in the 1870s and 1880s.[59] According to *The Ovens and Murray Advertiser*, Frank Entra courteously received the musicians and other guests at a concert and ball that was held in his hotel at the Yackandandah Junction in 1879.[60]

Along with drinking and gambling, billiards was another important social activity in hotels and Croatian publicans had billiard tables in their hotels. In the 1890s for example, Antonio Radovick held billiard tournaments in his hotel. Croatians also put on billiard tournaments in Port Fairy, Yackandandah, Redcastle and Costerfield.[61]

Trojano Darveniza's Excelsior Vineyard

The majority of the wineries run by Croatian pioneers in Australia were small, although the winery run by Trojano Darveniza (Trojan Drvenica) was an exception. He was born in Trnovica on 20 August 1838 and arrived in Victoria in 1860.[62] Darveniza subsequently moved to the New Zealand goldfields to try his luck during the Otago gold rush. He had some success and became one of the proprietors in the Deep Lead, a mining claim on the West Coast.

By 1869 Trojano Darveniza returned to Victoria where he acquired a farm where he planted grains and vines. Two years later he established the Excelsior Vineyard at Mooroopna.[63] By 1896 his vineyard covered about 100 acres. According to *The Weekly Times* the main varieties of wines cultivated at his vineyard included: 'Red, Hermitage, Carbinet, brown Muscat, Mataro and Malbec, white Riesling, Chasselas, Pedro and Hermitage'.[64]

Darveniza had an in-depth knowledge of wine culture and his vineyard was one of the largest in the area. In the 1890s, to complement his own expertise, he organised for Henry Fortin, a wine expert from Bordeaux, to work in his cellars. Fortin had been involved for many years in the wine industry in France before moving to London to manage an extensive wine cellar. He then made his way to Australia where Darveniza persuaded him to manage the Excelsior cellar. Employing Fortin was a progressive step that helped Darveniza ensure the success of his wines. In 1892 Fortin married a daughter of the Croatian pioneer, Thomas Milovitch.

By 1896 Trojano Darveniza had 273,000 litres of wine in his cellars and was exporting overseas.[65] Darveniza's fine wines were famous worldwide and he achieved great success with his wines in European exhibitions. He was elected a member of the Grand Jury of France and was awarded prizes in Bordeaux, Marseilles, Milan, Brussels and many other European cities. By 1898 he had been awarded over 300 prizes of which nine were champions, 24 specials, 16 gold, five silver and five bronze medals. Interestingly, Darveniza's Excelsior Vineyard trademark resembles the coat of arms of the Commonwealth of Australia.[66]

Darveniza was the president and treasurer of the Mooroopna and Shepparton District Winegrowers' Association which was formed in 1897 at his winery. Many of their meetings were held at his cellars. To deal with the excess grapes harvested by Trojano Darveniza and his colleagues, the Goulburn Valley Wine and Distillery Company was formed in the same year. Darveniza was the director, and comprehensive cellars and a distillery were built on Toolamba Road, Mooroopna. He

Distribution of Croatian speakers in Melbourne and Geelong as a percentage of the total population of the areas in 1996

Based on Census Collection District Boundaries 1996 Edition
Source: 1996 Census of Population & Housing
© Commonwealth of Australia, 1999

Per cent

7.3 or more
2.6 – 7.3
1.1 – 2.6
0.1 – 1.1
Less than 0.1

Highways

Coastline

Kilometres

0   30

*Croatian language and history teaching books produced
by the Croatian community in Australia*

Croatian Summer School of Language and Culture in Sydney in 1987

Croatian Summer School of Language and Culture in Brisbane in 1989

Geelong-based Croatian folkloric group LADO performing a unique traditional dance. Since the 1970s LADO has captivated audiences throughout Australia and Europe. The photograph was taken in 1995 when LADO performed for the Croatian President at the National Tennis Centre in Melbourne in front of over 10,000 spectators. This was the first visit of a Croatian president to Australia.

Sydney-based Croatian folkloric group Koleda (Christmas carol) in 1983 from their fourth record album produced in Australia

*Croatia soccer team, later Melbourne Croatia and now Melbourne Knights, celebrating after winning the
1971 Inter City Cup. In 1971 they won the Ampol Cup, Inter City Cup and State League Cup*

*Melbourne Knights soccer team formerly Melbourne Croatia celebrating after winning the
1994–95 National Soccer League grand finals*

Croatian Catholics in the Corpus Christi procession in Brisbane in 1972

Croatian children exiting Holy Family Catholic Church in Geelong after celebrating Easter Mass in Croatian in the early 1980s

The first Croatian 'Embassy' in Australia that was opened in 1977

Croatian community rally at Melbourne's City Square calling for the Australian Government to recognise Croatia in 1991

Croatian community rally on the steps of Parliament House in Canberra in 1991 where over 30,000 people called for the Australian Government to recognise Croatia

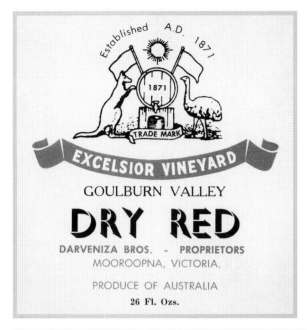

Trojano Darveniza established the Excelsior Vineyard in Mooroopna in 1871, a vineyard which produced
fine wines famous worldwide. On the wine labels are examples of the many medals that his wines
won throughout Europe

encouraged farmers to plant vines in the area, also offering them advice on the planting and testing of their vines.[67]

There was an outbreak of phylloxera disease in the Mooroopna district in the late 1890s, which first appeared in Toolamba at Burge's vineyard and potentially threatened surrounding properties. Trojano Darveniza went to inspect the state of the vineyard and dug out some vines to examine their roots. Darveniza was so afraid of taking the phylloxera disease with him and possibly infecting other vines that he stripped off all his clothes and apparently walked home naked. Later he replanted his vineyard with phylloxera-resistant stock. In the late 1890s, at a vine growers' conferences in Melbourne, Darveniza became an advocate for planting phylloxera-resistant vines in all vineyards in the colony. Another important advocate for planting phylloxera-resistant vines was a fellow Croatian, Romeo Bragato, who visited Darveniza's Excelsior vineyard on 13 May 1899 where he explained to the Mooroopna and Shepparton District Winegrowers' Association that the only way to eradicate phylloxera was to destroy the infected vines and plant phylloxera-resistant vines.[68]

The Excelsior Vineyard in 1922

Trojano Darveniza remained a bachelor all his life, although he brought out two of his brothers and their families to Mooroopna. Among Trojano Darveniza's Croatian pioneer friends are Seraphin Bersica, Thomas Milovitch and Emilios Rossely. Thomas Milovitch made him executor of his estate. Trojano Darveniza died in Mooroopna on 5 October 1927.[69] The vineyard was passed down to his nephews and then on to his great nephews who allowed the vineyard to fall into a state of disrepair. In Mooroopna where the ruins of the Excelsior Vineyard remain, the street is named Excelsior Avenue.

Apart from the arrival of two of his brothers and their families, Trojano Darveniza was also responsible for the chain migration of other Croatians to Victoria after 1890, migration which also included Croatian women, and continued to the late 1920s. Some of these later immigrants had links with the Croatian community in Mildura which differed from Croatian pioneer communities in Australia in four general aspects: these immigrants all came after 1920; the majority of the Croatians came from the Međimurje district north of the Croatian capital, Zagreb, which is inland away from the Croatian coastline; most married Croatian women who were an integral part of their community; and they formed clubs. One Croatian assisted by the Darveniza family was Ivan Rončević, who held important positions within the Mildura Croatian community, such as president and secretary of the Matija Gubec Club in Mildura which was established in 1937.[70]

Trojano Darveniza owner of Excelsior Vineyard which produced fine wines famous worldwide

The Darvenizas and friends in 1896.
In the second row the fourth person from the left is Trojano Darveniza and his brother John is the last person in the same row. John's son is the second person in the third row, while John's wife and three daughters are in the bottom row on right side of the photograph. On the left side of the top row is Thomas Milovitch and to his right is Peter Darveniza who later married Ane Milkovitch.

Other Croatian pioneers with wineries

In the nineteenth century Victoria was Australia's leading wine producer. In 1888–90 Victoria produced 7.1 million litres of wine compared with 3.1 million litres in New South Wales and just over two million litres in South Australia. However Victoria quickly lost its edge due principally to the phylloxera disease infecting the vines. On 31 December 1877 the dreaded phylloxera was found in Geelong. The government subsequently spent huge sums of money having vines destroyed and the soil sterilised. However, in the 1880s and 1890s, the phylloxera disease spread and ruined vines throughout the colony. Other reasons for the decline in Victoria's wine production include economic factors (the 1890s depression) and the fact that the Australian-born population did not consume as much wine as their European-born parents or grandparents.[71]

Almost all the wineries owned by Croatian pioneers in Victoria covered fewer than two acres, typically producing fewer than 1000 litres of wine per year. The majority of these wineries were worked by single or married Croatians without descendants. The main concentration of these wineries was in the Wedderburn area, where wine was primarily produced for their own consumption. However, when the opportunity arose, they also managed to sell some. As we have seen, sometimes they were fined for selling wine without a license. Almost all the Croatian pioneers who had wineries in Victoria had previously been miners. For example, Peter Vranzigan from Dalmatia was a miner and vigneron at Moonlight.[72] Croatian pioneers in Victoria also had wineries in Mooroopna, Maryborough, Avenel and Wandiligong.

Joseph Marian

There were also Croatian wineries in Young and Coolac in New South Wales and Armadale in Western Australia.

Many Croatian pioneers who settled in Australia had experience working in wineries in Croatia and sometimes this experience helped them find employment in vineyards. For example, Thomas Milovitch who worked in his father's vineyard in Sutivan on the island of Brač was a vigneron and wine seller in Mooroopna and also the manager of the Tabilk vineyard. Antonio Yackovitze, who was born in Dalmatia, planted and worked in Blummer's vineyard in Wandiligong in the 1860s, subsequently establishing his own vineyard and managing his wine shop in Wandiligong.[73]

Joseph Marian (Josip Marijan) who was born in Pitve on the island of Hvar, worked in Melbourne in the fishing industry from 1865 to 1897 and then in Fremantle for four years before settling in Armadale, Western Australia. There he planted a vineyard, and in 1905, he produced his first supply of wine – about 4550 litres. The winery was called the 'Slavonian' vineyard named after the Slavonia region in Croatia. His nephew, Ante Marian, came from Croatia to assist him with the winery and subsequently became his partner. The Slavonian vineyard's wine production increased steadily, and in the 1913 season produced about 36,400 litres. The following year Joseph Marian died.[74] Other Croatian vignerons in Western Australia had previously been fishermen in Australia.

The Slavonian vineyard cellar in Armadale, Western Australia

Romeo Bragato, who was an expert on viticulture, played an important role in the development of the wine industry in Australia and New Zealand. He was born in Mali Lošinj on the island of Lošinj on 26 February 1859. Bragato completed a three-year diploma at the prestigious Viticultural School of Conegliano, near Venice. After graduation he was employed by the Provincial Association of Agriculture of Istria for one year and for the following three years he was manager of Jerolimić brothers' cellars and vineyard. On 19 September 1888, after having been in Victoria for only a few days, Bragato submitted a report to the Royal Commission on Vegetable Products in Victoria, proposing the establishment of an experimental station combined with a School of Oenology and Viticulture which emphasised both the theoretical and practical aspects of the industry. According to Bragato, the school would produce 'intelligent viticulturists and wine makers' and some of the functions of the school would be to: study vines in the colony to make useful classifications and selections; investigate which varieties of vines and wine-making methods were best suited in each district; study methods of pruning and cultivation, study parasites and fungi attacking the vines (especially phylloxera), and the means for their destruction; and distribute their viticultural knowledge through reports, conferences and practical demonstrations.[75]

Victorian Government Viticulturist Romeo Bragato

Bragato was subsequently appointed the Victorian Government Viticulturist. Several years later he played a prominent role in the establishment of Rutherglen Viticultural College, the first viticultural college in Australia, and designed the cellars and gave lectures in viticulture. On 31 March 1897 the Rutherglen Viticultural College was officially opened by the Governor of Victoria, Lord Thomas Brassey. The main college building (comprising a lecture room, offices and accommodation for 36 students) and cellars were completed, but work on the laboratory, still and other minor buildings continued for another year. The elaborate cellars, capable of holding about 182,000 litres of wine, were a substantial brick structure with a bluestone floor and special provision for drainage. The cellars were ventilated to keep them at an even temperature throughout the year. Attached to the college were 1000 acres of land. In April 1898 *The Australian Vigneron and Fruit-Growers' Journal* stated: 'The whole of the work so far carried out at the college has been conducted under the personal supervision of Signor R. Bragato, who is practically the originator of the college and takes great pride in the institution'. At the time there were 30 acres under vines and the cellars contained 45,500 litres of wine. In 1890s there were over 350 vignerons in a

Judging wines at the Exhibition Cellars for the Royal Agricultural Show in 1900.
Romeo Bragato is on the front right side of the photograph

Rutherglen Viticultural College cellars designed by Romeo Bragato (left side in 1898 and right side in 2000)

56-kilometre radius of Rutherglen which made it the ideal location for a viticultural college. The establishment of the college, in addition to the land, cost a considerable amount well in excess of £7000.[76]

In the late 1890s, during Victoria's devastating phylloxera outbreak, Bragato submitted a report to the Secretary of Agriculture and gave lectures on methods to combat phylloxera. He was appointed as a phylloxera expert for a special phylloxera conference arranged by the governments of the vine-growing colonies. Bragato complained about the Victorian Government's indecision over importing American phylloxera-resistant vines and strongly advocated improved quarantine procedures and better methods to destroy infected vines. It seems that Bragato's recommendations on how to eradicate phylloxera were not fully supported by the government.[77]

In 1902 Bragato moved to New Zealand where he was appointed the first government viticulturist in New Zealand. He had previously toured New Zealand in 1895, seconded from the Victorian Government, to report on the suitability of different districts for growing vines and was well received there. In 1903 Bragato established a viticultural research station at Te Kauwhata. His positive identification of phylloxera in New Zealand led to the *Phylloxera Act* which ensured that all infected vines were destroyed. Several years later Bragato lost control of the research station as his superiors in the Department of Agriculture did not support his enthusiasm for the wine industry. He subsequently retired and migrated to Canada.[78]

Bragato made a number of substantial contributions to the wine industry in both Australia and New Zealand. In the former he helped to establish the Rutherglen Viticultural College in Victoria. He encouraged the Governments of Victoria and New Zealand to promote and distribute phylloxera-resistant vines and established the viticultural research station at Te Kauwhata. His *Report on the Prospects of Viticulture in New Zealand* published in 1895 encouraged the development of the industry in that country and resulted in a surge in planting. Furthermore, he wrote a handbook, *Viticulture in New Zealand* which was published in 1906. In New Zealand, unlike the situation in Australia, Romeo Bragato's contribution to the wine industry has not gone unnoticed. In 2003 the New Zealand Grape Growers' Council organised the ninth annual Romeo Bragato Conference named in his honour. There have also been Romeo Bragato Wine Awards in New Zealand.[79]

Croatian wines at Australian international exhibitions

At the first Australian international exhibition, the Sydney International Exhibition of 1879, a variety of Croatian wines, brandies and liqueurs were displayed among the Austrian exhibits. These alcoholic drinks came from Zagreb, Zadar and the island of Vis. They all received various awards at the exhibition, including honourable mentions, highly commended and order of merit certificates. For example, Luca Millicich from Zadar was awarded a first degree of merit special for his cherry liqueur. The names of the Croatian alcoholic drinks were also labelled in Croatian. The plum brandy was listed as rakia (rakija), wine as vino, sour cherry brandy was listed as visiyenac (višnjevača), cherry liqueur was listed as Maraschino (Maraskino), and the plum liqueur was listed as slibowitz (šljivovica). This was probably the first time Croatian alcoholic drinks had been promoted in Australia. Franz Pokorny's cherry brandy and liqueurs from Zagreb received various awards at the exhibition, including three first degrees of merit, two commended awards and one highly commended award.[80]

At the Centennial International Exhibition of 1888 in Melbourne, also under the umbrella of Austrian exhibits, were a number of exhibits from Croatia, including 'Croatic [Croatian] native costumes' and articles of the housing industry from Zagreb, 'Maraschino Excelsior' fine liqueurs from Zadar and machine-manufactured paper (letter, book, drawing, lithographic, cigarette and so on) from Rijeka. This is another early example of where Croatian products were promoted in Australia. Trojano Darveniza also displayed wines from his Excelsior vineyard at the exhibition.[81]

Croatian pioneers involved in farming

In the 1860s the Victorian and New South Wales Governments passed laws designed to provide opportunities for small selectors, other than squatters, to own land. This allowed selectors to move on to small parcels of land to establish farms, provided they paid the land off within the first three years.[82]

The average size of farms owned by Croatian pioneers in Victoria was 131 acres; only a few had farms larger than 500 acres. The size of Croatian farms in areas where Croatian farmers were concentrated, such as in Yandoit, was generally under 50 acres. Typically, Croatian miners with families kept cows and chickens to help feed their family. Similarly, single miners who remained on the goldfields for many years often kept several chickens next to their miner's hut to help support themselves. Croatian pioneers were also fruit growers and market gardeners on the outskirts of Melbourne.

One of the earlier Croatian farmers in Victoria was Simone Adam (Šimun Adam) from the island of Zlarin. While he was a storekeeper on the goldfields, he selected 377 acres of land near Glenlyon in 1857. Over time Simone Adam fenced and cleared his land for pasture and cultivation.[83] Several years after Adam had established his farm, Thomas Rossi, from Zadar, who was also a storekeeper on the goldfields, selected an adjacent property. A typical mining farmer was Peter Mavorvitch who, by 1866, had a garden under miner's rights in Yandoit Creek. In 1872 he selected about nine acres of land in the parish of Sandon, six acres of which he cleared and cultivated. After having been on this land for a few years, Mavorvitch later purchased various other properties in the Yandoit area and pursued farming in addition to mining.[84]

Born in Volosko in 1832, Joseph Postich (Josip Postić) became a prosperous farmer in Victoria. After disembarking from the ship *Constance* in Melbourne in September 1849, Postich first lived at Colac, but during the gold rush he moved to the Ballarat goldfields. He married an Irish woman, Alice Atkinson, in Geelong in 1852 and went on to have eight children. After his marriage Postich returned to Ballarat and lived there at the time of the Eureka Stockade, but it is unknown if he was involved. He also mined at Yandoit, Amherst and Maryborough. As a miner, Joseph Postich had some success which enabled him to purchase farming land in the Maryborough district. In 1873 he settled in West Charlton and subsequently purchased over 569 acres.[85] His sons, Thomas and Francis Postich, were also successful farmers, each having a larger farm than their father.[86] With the Postich family owning some of the best sheep grazing and cropping land in the district, theirs

Joseph Postich with his wife

became a household name in the Charlton district. In addition to barley, wheat, straw and grass, they grew a selection of fruit trees and grapevines. Thomas Postich also managed a general store and two shops in Charlton. In his general store he sold groceries, crockery, drapery, oats, bran and hay chaff. The Postichs also owned a race horse, Ploughboy, which won races in the district in the 1890s. Joseph Postich's sons later moved permanently to Miles, Queensland.[87]

Joseph Postich remained on the land until about 1910 when he moved to Charlton because of his wife's ill health. He died in Charlton on 14 September 1918 and was buried in the Catholic section of the Charlton Cemetery. *The East Charlton Tribute* noted 'the respect in which the deceased [Joseph Postich] was held was shown by the large cortege, which consisted of over 40 vehicles'.[88]

Of the dairy farms owned by Croatian pioneers, Antonio Radovick's farm in Korumburra in Gippsland was the most successful. He owned the Stephenhurst homestead, where he lived, and the adjoining Astolate homestead, about 2.5 kilometres from Korumburra railway station. The 324-acre Stephenhurst property was a model dairying or grazing farm on which was erected one of the finest houses in South Gippsland. The weatherboard house contained six large rooms, bathroom, kitchen etc. Stephenhurst had splendid milking sheds, dairy and all out-buildings necessary for the working of a well-kept dairy farm. The 307-acre Astolate property had a seven-roomed weatherboard house and all necessary out-buildings. Both properties had very fertile soil, were securely fenced and divided into numerous paddocks. They were well watered with underground tanks, springs, the Foster River and a creek which ran through both properties. The livestock on Radovick's properties were of very high quality and included many pure breed cattle and sheep.[89]

Another farmer in Gippsland was Natale Radonich (Božo Radonić) who was born in Vitaljina, south of Dubrovnik, in 1856. He deserted the barque *Ciro* in Melbourne, together with four other Croatians in 1883. Radonich married Emily Vickers on 24 February 1892 and they had ten children. Radonich selected land for his farm which he called 'Federal Farm', in Budgeree near Boolarra in the Gippsland district. Radonich and family later moved to a farm on Main Road, Dandenong near

Melbourne where he farmed from at least 1910 to 1912. Subsequently, they moved to 26 Davey Avenue, Oakleigh, where they lived until the house was destroyed by fire in about 1926 in which they lost everything. After this terrible event the Radonich family then lived in various suburbs of Melbourne, including Oakleigh, Malvern and Burnley. Natale Radonich died on 24 June 1934. His son Albert fought for Australia in the First World War.[90]

Many Croatians farmed successfully throughout Australia. Nicholas Jasprizza (Nikola Jasprica), who was born in Janjina on the Pelješac Peninsula and arrived in Australia in 1860, became a highly successful cherry orchardist. After mining at Lambing Flat and Three Mile diggings in New South Wales, he planted fruit trees and vines near Young. After some initial setbacks he acquired over 900 acres, where, as well as an orchard and vineyard, he had over 600 sheep and 20 cattle. In about 1876 he started growing cherries and conducted grafting experiments to improve his crop. According to *The Burrangong Chronicle*, by 1893 he had an extremely successful cherry orchard in Young with

Natale Radonich's wedding day in 1892

Natale Radonich with his family

Albert Radonich in World War I AIF uniform

100 acres under cherries, consisting of 7000 full-grown cherry trees and 3000 young trees. He also had 5000 cherry trees at the nursery stage and a 60-acre vineyard. In 1883 Baldo and Antony Cunich (Kunić), also from Janjina, joined him. Baldo Cunich married Nicholas Jasprizza's daughter. They were later joined by another brother, Andrew Cunich.[91] With some initial assistance from Jasprizza, the Cunichs subsequently had their own highly successful cherry orchards.

On 8 May 1901 Nicholas Jasprizza was murdered by a shot fired through one of the windows of his house. The government offered a £100 reward – increased by the family to £300 – for information leading to a conviction, but the crime was never solved. He left over 3000 acres and shops in Young to his children. His sons managed the orchard after his death. According to *The Country Journal*, in 1923 the Jasprizza brothers and Baldo Cunich had the largest cherry orchards in the world – Baldo Cunich had over 20,000 cherry trees in his orchard.[92] Other Croatians also

Nicholas Jasprizza a pioneer in the cherry industry in Australia

Baldo Cunich in the centre with his son Leo and wife Annie Elizabeth (nee Jasprizza) on his right

Andrew Cunich with his prize-winning horse, Baldo's elder daughter and his sister-in-law

Andrew Cunich's 'Cherry Grove' packing shed

Baldo Cunich holding a box of his fine cherries

Antony Cunich

settled in the Young district, and up to the 1930s, new Croatian arrivals were still coming to work at the Cunich's cherry farm and Darveniza's winery.[93]

Croatians in California also had very successful orchards. Mark Rabasa (Rabaza) from Janjina on the Pelješac Peninsula settled in California's Pajaro Valley in the 1870s where he began cultivating apple orchards, and through his persistence, made it into a highly profitable industry. Rabasa was joined by other Croatians who also established orchards. Croatians pioneered new ways of growing, packing, shipping and spraying apples. They also were highly successful in growing grapes, plums and other fruits.[94]

Belfast Oyster Room and Fruit Shop.
(Opposite the Post office, Bank st, Belfast.)

NATALE VUSCOVIH

BEGS respectfully to inform the inhabitants of Belfast and neighbourhood, that he has opened the above shop, where he will always keep a supply of Fresh Oysters and the best Fruit in season, and trusts by civility to customers to merit a share of patronage.

Stewed oysters every Wednesday and Saturday evening.

Charges will always be found very moderate.

N. VUSCOVIH,
Fruiterer and Confectioner,
(Corner of Sackville and Cox streets),

BEGS to inform the residents of Belfast that he has opened the well-known corner shop, and will always keep a supply of fresh Fruit, &c.

☞ Fresh Fish, Oysters. &c., on safe. Prices for everything moderate.

NEW FRUIT SHOP,
Sackville Street.

NATALE VUSCOVIH

BEGS to inform the public of Belfast and vicinity, that he has opened the shop in Sackville-street (formerly occupied by J. Howard), as a General Fruit and Greengrocer's Shop.

Fresh oysters twice a week.

BELL RINGING
AND
BILL POSTING.
N. VUSCOVIH

RESPECTFULLY announces that he is prepared o undertake the POSTING OF BILLS for Auctioneers, Business People, and Theatrical Agents, and to RING THE BELL and act as CRIER for Sales, Entertainments, &c.

Prices very moderate, and all work honestly performed.

ADDRESS—Cox Street, Belfast

Billiards!   Billiards!!
N. VUSCOVIH

RESPECTFULLY intimates to the public that he has removed his BILLIARD ROOMS to that centrally situated premises in Sackville-street, formerly occupied by Mr J. Gallin, next door to Clyde House.

First-class Tables.   Comfortably seated rooms, with every convenience.

CHARGES MODERATE.

FARMERS' INN,
SACKVILLE-ST., BELFAST.

N. VUSCOVIH

BEGS respectfully to inform the residents of Belfast and the country district, that he has taken that old-established hotel, known as the FARMERS' INN, formerly occupied by Mr. Wall. The whole premises have been thoroughly renovated, altered, and improved, and may now be classed as a respectable hostelry.

There are two BILLIARD ROOMS, in which are first-class tables.

Buggies and Horses.

☞ In order to accommodate the pubic, N. Vuscovih has always on hire first-class comfortable Buggies, Carryall, and American Waggons, with fast stepping and quiet horses

CHARGES MODERATE.

Large yard and stables for the accommodation of farmers and others.

Newspaper advertisements showing the diverse range of businesses Natale Vuscovich ran in Port Fairy in the 1870s and 1880s

CHAPTER 8

Pioneer Business Enterprise

Many Croatian pioneers had more than one occupation. The main occupations of the Croatian settlers in Victoria in descending order were gold mining, labouring, seafaring, catering (as publicans, restaurateurs, fruiterers and storekeepers), farming, fishing, wine growing and carpentry. By following the lives of ten Croatian pioneers we can see how interesting and diverse their careers and lives were. Often very resourceful in their quest to succeed in their new homes, many made contributions to Australian society, culture and industry.

Antonio Buzolich

One Croatian pioneer who had many occupations as well as contacts with other Croatians, was Antonio Buzolich (Ante Buzolić) who was born in Milna on the island of Brač in approximately 1831. He came from Liverpool on the ship *Stamboul* and arrived in New South Wales in December 1855, from where he moved to Victoria in the same year.[1] Buzolich married a Scottish woman, Janet Bell, in Ballarat on 14 November 1856. Their marriage witness was a fellow Croatian, Dominico Francovich. Antonio and Janet Buzolich had ten children. After a short period as a gold miner in Ballarat, he moved in 1858 to Melbourne where he lived in Collingwood. Records indicate that, during the 1860s, he lived at 108 Moray Street, South Melbourne, and from 1871 to 1875 he resided at 119 Dorcas Street, South Melbourne. During this time he worked as a shipwright. From 1876 to 1880 Buzolich managed the Prince Maximilian Hotel on Commercial Road, Prahran.[2]

In 1878 Antonio Buzolich became a shareholder with nine other Croatians in gold mining claims and companies located near McIntyre in central Victoria. John Buzolich and Fiovaranti Buzolich were among his Croatian partners in these claims. Antonio Buzolich had a twelfth share and was one of the five directors in both the Dalmatia Gold Mining Company and the Maximilian Gold Mining Company. He played an active role in these companies and chaired company meetings in Melbourne. As the only Croatian director, he looked after the interests of his

Croatian mining partners.[3] In 1881 Buzolich began managing the North Star Hotel on Nicholson Street, North Carlton, where he worked and resided until his death on 24 January 1886.[4] From 1882 the Buzolich family was also involved in the Buzolich Patent Damp Resisting and Anti-Fouling Paint Company Limited, whose factory was also located on Nicholson Street, but in Brunswick. After a few years however, the company experienced financial problems.[5]

In 1883 Antonio Buzolich and Co. opened a hat shop at 164 Bourke Street. The following year his son Douglas took over the business, which later expanded and became very successful. Over the next 60 years the D. Buzolich Pty Ltd hat shops were

Buzolich's hat bag logo

located at various prime locations in Melbourne including Bourke, Flinders, Swanston, Elizabeth, Little Collins and Queen Streets. The advertisement for Buzolich's hat shop indicates that, in 1941, the Buzolich family owned five city stores.[6] His sons and descendants continued to run the hat business for many decades after his death. Eventually the Buzolich family sold their hat business as a result of a gradual shift in fashion. City Hatters, located in the basement on the corner of Flinders and Swanston Street (next to Flinders Street Station) is a Melbourne icon and currently carries the largest collection of hats in Victoria. This shop used to be managed by the Buzolich family.

In 1888 Douglas Buzolich was appointed a Justice of the Peace (JP) and was probably the first JP of Croatian descent in Australia. He was also vice-president of the Royal Victorian Association of Honorary Justices, president of the Commercial Travellers' Association of Victoria and deputy coroner of the city of Melbourne. Douglas Buzolich kept in touch with other Croatian pioneers; for example, in 1878 he

Advertisement for Buzolich's hat shop

acquired a share in the Archduke Maximilian Dalmatian Reef quartz claim from the Croatian pioneer, John Grandi, and in 1891 he attended Antonio Radovick's banquet in Korumburra. Douglas Buzolich was the testifier at the naturalisation ceremonies of the Croatian migrants, Matthew Beovich and Luka Tomasevich. Three of his sons and a Buzolich nephew served in the AIF in the First World War.[7]

Three of Antonio Buzolich's grandsons in AIF uniform taken at the Broadmeadows Camp in 1914

Natale Vuscovich

Another Croatian pioneer involved in several different businesses was Natale Vuscovich (Božo Vušković), who was born in Supetar on the island of Brač on 6 September 1831. He arrived in Victoria on 7 July 1862 from England on the ship *Planter*.[8] Vuscovich married a German widow on 24 January 1863 in St Mary's Catholic Church, Geelong. They had at least one child, Patrick.[9] Initially Vuscovich was a sailor in Geelong, subsequently moving to Belfast (Port Fairy). From 1872 Vuscovich ran the Belfast Oyster Room and Fruit Shop in Bank Street which served stewed oysters every Wednesday and Saturday evenings.[10] The following year he sold the business and opened a general fruit and greengrocer's shop in Sackville Street, which also served fresh oysters twice a week.[11]

N. VUSCOVIH,
Fruiterer and Confectioner,
(Corner of Sackville and Cox streets),

BEGS to inform the residents of Belfast that he has opened the well-known corner shop, and will always keep a supply of fresh Fruit, &c.

☞ Fresh Fish, Oysters. &c., on sale. Prices for everything moderate.

Newspaper advertisement with Vuscovich's surname

Natale Vuscovich was a seafaring man, and while living in Port Fairy, according to *The Banner of Belfast*, he purchased a 'very fine boat [in Portland in 1875], which he intends to use in fishing operations in and around the bay. The boat is built of blackwood, and copper fastened. She is more roomy and larger than any other sailing boat on the river, and no doubt in a contest she would not have much of a stern with the yachts'.[12] In December 1875 Vuscovich completed painting the yacht *Ariel* as a part of her overhaul for the boating season.[13] In the 1870s Vuscovich sometimes sent cases of crayfish and fish caught by him to be sold in Melbourne. He was a superb fisherman and made record catches of barracouta in the waters near Port Fairy.[14]

In 1875 Vuscovich established what today would be considered an unusual business enterprise – a bell-ringing and bill-posting business whereby he undertook the posting of bills for auctioneers, business people and theatrical agents and rang the bell for entertainments.[15] In 1878 Vuscovich ran a fruit and confectionery store on the corner of Sackville and Cox Streets. The store also sold fresh fish and oysters.[16] Late in 1879 Vuscovich went to considerable effort and expense to open billiard rooms in Sackville Street. He had first-class billiard tables, decorated walls and comfortably seated rooms.[17] His presence there was brief, as in 1881, he transferred his business to the Farmers' Inn, also on Sackville Street, where he kept two first-class billiard rooms and sold alcohol. According to *The Belfast Gazette*, he had thoroughly renovated the hotel so it could 'be classed as a respectable hostelry'.[18] In 1881 Vuscovich also ran a buggy hiring business. He had 'on hire first-class comfortable Buggies, Carryall, and American Wagons with fast stepping and quiet horses'.[19] Vuscovich was a generous man and supported the Port Fairy community. For example, in September 1879 Vuscovich and a Mr Whatman initiated a fund to help the Burley family whose son had died suddenly. They collected £14 17s, which paid for the funeral and grave, the balance being given to Mrs Burley. A couple of months later Vuscovich donated 10s to the Nicoll Family Fund.[20]

By 1886 Vuscovich had moved to join the Croatian community in Portarlington where he became a fisherman. Records show that, within a few years, he had become a billiard room proprietor. When Vuscovich first moved to Portarlington, and before his house was built he lived in a tent.[21] In November 1896 he saved a six-year-old boy from drowning in Portarlington. The following month he prepared for the holidays by repainting and repairing his boat, *Patrick*.[22] On 8 April 1900, Vuscovich suffered an unfortunate accident. Turning his coach around on the footbridge near the Grand Hotel, his toe got caught which caused him to fall heavily, resulting in a number of his teeth being knocked out, and his nose and cheek being badly grazed and broken.[23] Vuscovich died on 27 March 1906 in the care of the Catholic nuns in the Convent of the Little Sisters of the Poor in Melbourne. A few weeks earlier, he had been living in the home of the Croatian pioneer, Victor Lusic, at Clarendon Street, South Melbourne.[24] During his life Vuscovich had many Croatian friends, including John Lussich, Gregory Pavletich, Andrew Radoslovich, Nicholas Torchie and Joseph Zagabria.

Natale Vuscovich was renowned for his ability as a storyteller and it was common in Portarlington for Vuscovich to have attracted a large audience who were enthralled by tales of the excitement and adventures of his youth. Like many early Croatian pioneers in Australia, he was illiterate. But a story told by him was published in the local newspaper, *The Bellarine Herald*, on 20 March 1897 and is given in full in appendix 2. The story includes details of how Vuscovich was forced, at knife point, into a vault on the island of Malta to steal jewellery from a corpse. He was also placed in a barrel and thrown off a ship because the superstitious crew believed they would perish unless they got rid of him.[25]

Fortunato Poschich

Fortunato Poschich (Srećko Poščić) had various occupations: coach proprietor, seaman and greengrocer. He was born in Rijeka in approximately 1833. Fortunato Poschich, together with Raymond Poschich (these two may have been related but records do not confirm this), had deserted the ship *Europa* in Sydney in 1853 after which they both made their way across to the Victorian goldfields.[26] In 1865 he was a coach proprietor in Steiglitz. Fortunato Poschich married an Irish widow in Geelong in 1865.[27] Although the widow had given birth to five children in her previous marriage, only two were surviving when she married for the second time. Fortunato and Sarah Poschich had another five children. In the 1860s Poschich owned shares in various mining companies such as the Albion Quartz Mining Company in Steiglitz and the Webster Street Freehold Gold Mining Company in Ballarat West.[28]

After his marriage Poschich lived on Victoria Terrace, Geelong and was working as a mariner on his own schooner. By 1872 he was the captain of the 26-ton wooden schooner, *James and Amelia*. Life was hard for seamen like Poschich, and on 3 September 1872, while pushing his vessel away from another ship from which he had been receiving cargo, his foot became entangled in the ship's mooring rope. As a result, his foot was almost completely severed at the ankle joint. Poschich was rushed to hospital where an amputation was performed. After this he needed crutches to walk. Several years later, Poschich spent over two months in Geelong Hospital due to problems with his stump. Incredibly, in 1894 he almost lost his other leg. While chopping a tree, Poschich missed the timber and accidentally hit himself in the boot, almost completely severing one of his toes. Due to the severity of the injury he was again taken to hospital.[29]

After his first accident Poschich purchased a grocery shop and general store which prospered. By 1879 he had acquired 'a neat cottage of five rooms, with stables and wood-house opposite Ladies' Baths, Western Beach' which he advertised to let in *The Geelong Advertiser*. At the time he was living in another home in Mercer Street. Also in the 1880s he advertised his grocery business in Mercer Street for sale or for lease in *The Geelong Advertiser*. In 1889 a number of Poschich's properties, including two weatherboard cottages (which already had good tenants), stables, coach house and outbuildings between Beach Street (off Western Beach) and Mercer Place were auctioned. In 1890 Poschich bought a cottage and land situated in Hawkes' Lane off Mercer Street. He died in Geelong Hospital on 23 November 1896.[30]

TO LET, grocery and general store, doing good business; rent moderate. Apply, F. Poschich, Mercer-street.

FOR SALE, Grocer's shop, with cottage at rear. Apply— F. POSCHICH, Mercer-street.

HOUSE TO LET.—A Neat Cottage of five rooms, with stable and wood-house, opposite Ladies' Baths, Western Beach. Apply to F. Poschich, Mercer-street.

Newspaper advertisements with Poschich's surname

Mattio Orlovich

Mattio Orlovich (Mate Orlović) was a Croatian pioneer who worked at several occupations in the Gulgong mining district of New South Wales – gold miner, mine manager and director, paymaster and gold receiver, publican, storekeeper, butcher shop proprietor and gardener. He was born on the island of Šolta in approximately 1837 and arrived in Australia in the 1860s.

Orlovich married Catherine Gates on 21 March 1872 in Mudgee. Between 1873 and 1886 they had six children. At the time of his marriage he was a publican and a butcher, as well as owning gold mines in the Gulgong mining district. Between 1872 and 1874, Orlovich managed the Paddock Hotel in Gulgong; in 1874 he sold his store, butcher's shop and

Retiring from Business.

THE undersigned, being about to retire from business, a good opportunity is now afforded to any one desirous of investing his money profitably in a STORE, BUTCHER'S SHOP and PUBLIC HOUSE, all doing a good business.

Apply on the Premises, Perseverance Lead, on Mr. Richard Rouse's ground, to
MATTIO ORLOVICH.

Newspaper business advertisement with Orlovich's surname

hotel at Gulgong.[31] Orlovich also was an agent for Richard Rouse, a wealthy and influential landowner in the area who later became a parliamentarian, and received applications for mining claims on Rouse's property.[32]

During this period there were at least 22 Croatian pioneers on the Gulgong goldfields. Another Croatian who had gold mines on Rouse's property was Michael Bogden (Bogdan), who was the witness at George Sabadine's burial in Gulgong.[33] Bogden was also present when Croatian Joseph Sabadine sold Peter Woolitch a restaurant business in Mayne Street, Home Rule.[34] In 1875 Paul Silovich was one of Orlovich's partners in a gold mining claim on the Perseverance Lead, Gulgong.[35] Another of Orlovich's Croatian friends was Luka Voinich who was born in Dubrovnik in 1838. Voinich arrived in Australia in 1864, residing in New South Wales for 33 years and Queensland for 25 years. In 1909 Voinich was a miner at Black Ridge near Clermont in Queensland. He never married and died near Clermont in 1922.[36]

Luka Voinich, a miner in New South Wales and Queensland

In the mid-1870s Orlovich obtained two puddling machines to wash dirt on the Gulgong goldfields. According to *The Gulgong Evening Argus*, 'Mr Orlovich some time since at a cost of nearly £500, erected two splendid puddling machines with every necessary appliance, and one diamond washing machine; also without exception the finest dam in the district, which when full would cover over six acres and contain water from one to twelve feet deep [0.3 to 3.7 m]'.[37] Sometimes these puddling machines were booked several weeks ahead.[38]

In 1875 he ran another Paddock Hotel on the Perseverance Lead. A year later and until 1880, Orlovich ran the Club House Hotel in Mitchell Creek, Wellington and, between 1883 and 1885, the Sportsman's Arms Hotel in Gulgong. At this time the Sportsman's Arms Hotel was one of the leading hotels in Gulgong[39]

The Sportsman's Arms Hotel in Gulgong, which Mattio Orlovich managed between 1883 and 1885

Orlovich was a generous person who donated to various causes in Gulgong, including the hospital, fire brigade and cemetery. As a practising Catholic, he donated funds for the erection of a new Catholic church in Gulgong. However, he did not restrict his charity to the Catholic Church, he also donated funds towards the erection of churches of other denominations in Gulgong, including the Church of England, Episcopalian and Presbyterian.[40]

Orlovich possessed a great deal of mining expertise and was manager and director of many mines in the Gulgong mining district, some of which included the Enterprise Gold Mining Company, Kaiser Gold and Copper Mining Company, Rouse's Paddock Gold Mining Company and White Horse Gold Mining Company.[41] In 1881 he explained details of his invention for separating copper from gold to the district mining registrar. An explanation of the process was later published in the *NSW Department of Mines Annual Report*. This invention greatly reduced the labour required for this activity.[42] In the 1880s Orlovich was instrumental in the revival of the mining industry in the Gulgong district. In 1883, after failing to arouse interest in the potential of Gulgong as a gold mining area in Sydney, he travelled to Melbourne where he persuaded Victorian capitalists, Brigham and Marshall, to fund the establishment of several gold mines in the Gulgong district. Orlovich was made general manager of these mines which employed many miners in the district. He was also employed as a general mines paymaster and gold receiver.[43] Mining activity in this district declined rapidly from late 1885 and did not recover, due largely to severe drought and not enough water for mining. Most of the mining companies became insolvent and mine workers lost their jobs. Orlovich was subsequently a gardener in the Canobolas district from the late 1890s until he died in Orange Hospital on 28 November 1908.[44]

Mattio Marassovich

Mattio Marassovich (Mate Marasović), born in the town of Vis on the island of Vis in about 1829, was a Croatian pioneer who settled in the Victorian gold mining town of Woods Point. He disembarked in Victoria on 28 September 1853 from the ship *Australia* arriving from London. By 1858 he was a miner in Ararat, and in Ballarat by 1860.[45] Marassovich married a Scottish woman, Mary Youl, and they had three daughters and a son. He also mined for gold in Heathcote.[46] By 1866 Marassovich had moved to Woods Point, initially to join a community of Croatian miners, where he pursued various occupations over the next two decades – chef, tobacconist and storekeeper. He finally became the owner and proprietor of Marassovich's Commercial Hotel, the main hotel in Woods Point. During this time he maintained a keen interest in mining and was involved in a few of the larger mining companies in the area. He held shares in the All Nations, New Morning Star and Victor's Quartz mining companies.[47] In 1866 Marassovich was the chef at the Imperial Bible Christian Church on Scott Street, close to the property owned by the Croatian, Paulo Arnerich.[48] In 1897 Marassovich placed an advertisement in *The Gippsland Miners' Standard* for Marassovich's Commercial Hotel at Woods Point, in which the hotel was described as ideal accommodation for tourists and visitors with all the best brands of wines, beers and spirits for sale, and providing good stabling accommodation for horses.[49] Marassovich always pursued a keen interest in public affairs, and at one stage, he was mayor of the old Woods Point borough. Furthermore, as the proprietor of Marassovich's Commercial Hotel, he was one of the most prominent people in Woods Point. According to *The Gippsland Miners' Standard*, Mattio Marassovich was known for 'an impulsive kindness of heart which won him many friends, by whom his memory will be treasured'. He died on 8 August 1897.[50]

— MARASSOVICH'S —
COMMERCIAL HOTEL,
WOODSPOINT.

THIS is the place for Tourists, and Visitors in search of Health and Scenery, to stay at.

BEST ACCOMODATION PROVIDED, AND APPOINTMENTS PERFECT.

WINES, ALES, AND SPIRITS OF THE BEST BRANDS ALWAYS ON HAND.

GOOD STABLING ACCOMMODATION.

Marassovich's Commercial Hotel advertisement

According to Marassovich's descendants, he would proudly sit his grandson, Noel, on the hotel bar and feed him pickled figs from a barrel that they assumed to be imported from the island of Vis.[51] The Marassovich surname has died out in Australia because his son, Matthew, who married very late in life had no children. Matthew Marassovich fought for Australia in the First World War where he attained the rank of captain.

Two letters were sent to Mattio Marassovich from the island of Vis in 1897, one from a brother Giuseppe (Josip) Marasović and another from a sister Ana Mandacovich (Mandaković). The letters to Mattio were written mainly in Italian as this was the official language of administrative and legal bodies along coastal Croatia at that time. Even so, they contained sentences written in Croatian, Croatian words and the letters ć, č, š and ž not found in Italian, and Croatian surnames were dispersed throughout the letters.[52] When referring to God in his letter, Giuseppe Marasović preferred Croatian – 'Bog mi vas živio [May God give you long life]'. Appendix 2 gives an English translation of the letter sent to Mattio Marassovich from his brother Giuseppe. The letter has a brief outline of Giuseppe's life, including the economic hardships, family financial burdens and their paternal inheritance. He also mentions a battle between Italy and Austria off the Croatian island of Vis. Giuseppe stated that he had witnessed the battle, but he did not support any side (possibly because he was of Croatian background). The famous battle took place in July 1866 and in it Austria was victorious. In the letter to Mattio Marassovich from his sister Ana Mandaković dated 20 June 1897, she wrote that her daughter, Maddalena, had requested that Mattio Marassovich or his son be the best man at her wedding by proxy. Ana Mandaković wrote: 'Dear brother, I only remember you when I was about ten years old and you returned with your battalion dressed in yellow. Now I am already 56 and am prematurely old thanks to all the hardship I have endured'. She also explained that there was a disease attacking the vines on the island of Vis. They had sprayed the vines with vitriol to try to eradicate the disease.[53]

Kosmos

Another fascinating life was that of Croatian gold miner Kosmos (Kuzma) from Rijeka who was mining in Victoria in 1856, whose surname is unknown, but it seems certain that he was neither of the two Croatian pioneers called Cosmo who came to Victoria later: they were Cosmo Antich from Bakar and Cosmo Dragovitch from Dalmatia. Kosmos was good friends with the Polish patriot, Seweryn Korzelinski.[54] Even though they were good friends, Kosmos was quite mysterious and never mentioned anything of his past or personal affairs to Korzelinski. When asked about his nationality, he always replied: 'I am cosmopolitan', a reply which perhaps explains his name! Korzelinski described Kosmos as a walking encyclopedia who knew several European languages. However, his intelligence was somewhat difficult to gauge from his appearance since Kosmos had long dark hair and dressed in a scruffy manner. He wore a hat covered with holes, and over his old mining clothing he always wore a blanket. Korzelinski claimed that it was his dark eyes which expressed his intelligence. Although Korzelinski was unable to find out much about Kosmos, he did believe that he was very wealthy – Kosmos once returned £100 that someone sent him, which was the amount the average miner earned in eight months.

In March 1856, a week before Korzelinski left Australia permanently, he solved the mystery of Kosmos's past. One of Korzelinski's friends had met a Polish man a few weeks earlier who was making beer next to the highway in Castlemaine and who employed a Croatian assistant, Giuseppe B, from Dalmatia. Giuseppe B, who was Kosmos's friend, had previously been captain of the ship, *The Son of Giuseppe B*, which was owned by Kosmos's father. He stated that Kosmos's father was an extremely wealthy man – one of the wealthiest men in Rijeka – and owned a fleet of ships on the Adriatic. Remarkably, the reference to Rijeka was omitted in the English translation of Seweryn Korzelinski's published diary. Kosmos had been given the best education money could buy. However, he lost his father's favour after having a romantic affair in Paris. Consequently, Kosmos left to try his luck on the Victorian goldfields. Around the time of Korzelinski's departure for Europe, Kosmos was busy equipping a ship to sail on a voyage of discovery to the South Pole. The Croatian, Giuseppe B, was to be the captain of this expedition and the ship was due to leave Melbourne on 27 March 1856. Giuseppe B was doubtful of the success of the proposed expedition as the British would not allow Kosmos to sail under the British flag. If, on the other hand, he tried to hoist the flag of another country on any newly discovered lands, the British warships would use their cannons to blow him out of the water, perhaps an explanation for Kosmos's claim for being 'cosmopolitan'. Nothing else is known about Kosmos or his expedition.[55]

John Terdich

John Terdich (Ivan Terdić), was born in Lovran on 30 October 1841. His occupations in Australia include seaman, captain, fisherman, wharf and railway labourer, bullock driver, steward, cook, hotel keeper and restaurateur.[56] Terdich arrived in Melbourne in 1866, where he worked on the railways for five years. For the next several years Terdich worked as a seaman, steward and cook on 13 different ships trading between Melbourne, Victorian coastal towns, other Australian colonies, New Zealand and Pacific islands, although for a period he was a fisherman on his own fishing boat and also did carpentry. He married an English woman, Charlotte Pascoe, on 6 April 1878. The marriage witness was the fellow Croatian, Martin Pasquan, who had married Charlotte's sister. John and Charlotte Terdich had five sons and five daughters.

John Terdich with his family

In 1878 Terdich was the hotel keeper of the Grosvenor Hotel in Grosvenor Street, Collingwood. The following year he managed the Burke and Wills Hotel at 89 Victoria Street, Abbotsford, and in 1880 he purchased the Railway Dining Rooms on Little Collins Street, between King and Spencer Streets where he lived with his family for the next 12 years and where he was the restaurateur. The building itself was quite spacious, accommodating a restaurant, guest rooms and John and Charlotte Terdich's family which included six of their children. It had a double shop frontage of two-storey brick construction. The advertisement on the upper story declared: 'Tardy's [John Terdich was also known as John Tardy] Railway Dining Rooms, Convenient for Early Trains, Accommodation for Families, Meals 6 Pence'. From 1884 to 1885 Martin Pasquan had dining rooms, a wine cellar and tobacconist business in the same street, a couple of buildings away.[57] Terdich was also friends with other Croatian pioneers, including Joseph Pasquan, Frank Cucel, Anton Margitich, and Luka Margitich. From 1892 to 1894 Terdich lived at 64 Falconer Street, North Fitzroy, again running a dining room. From 1895 until his death on 8 September 1923, he lived in his home, Rose Villa, at 107 Falconer Street, North Fitzroy.[58] In early 1902 Joseph Pasquan also lived in Falconer Street.

In 1916, during the First World War, a letter addressed to a Melbourne police detective and signed a 'resident of Wellington Parade' (East Melbourne) attempted to cast suspicion over Joseph Pasquan's and John Terdich's activities. At the time Joseph Pasquan managed the Parade Hotel at 180 Wellington Parade. An intelligence inquiry subsequently found that Joseph Pasquan and John Terdich were not guilty of any suspicious activity.[59] The anonymous letter containing the false allegations was possibly written by a person jealous of the success these two Croatians had achieved, rather than someone who genuinely suspected them of being enemy aliens.

John Terdich's descendants have made distinguished contributions to Australian society. His son, Arthur, won the second Australian Grand Prix at Phillip Island in 1929. Another son, Albert, was also a driver in the same Grand Prix. Arthur Terdich's contribution to Australian motor sport will be fully detailed in chapter 9. In 1911 John Terdich's sons, Alexander and Arthur, established the Terdich Bros Furniture, Mantelpiece and Fly Door Manufacturers business which they registered as a company in 1926. Alexander Terdich became the managing director of the company, whose business, as its name suggests, was the manufacturer of flydoors, dining-room and bedroom suites. Over the years their factory was located in Clifton Hill, Collingwood and North Fitzroy.[60] John Terdich also worked at his sons' factory as a cabinet maker. Alfred Terdich served in France in the AIF during the First World War. John Terdich's grandson, Bruce Terdich, died from illness while serving with the Royal Australian Air Force (RAAF) during the Second World War and in 1983, a granddaughter, Maud Frances Terdich, was awarded the Order of Australia in recognition for service to charity and industry.[61]

John Sersic

Another interesting Croatian pioneer was John Sersic (Ivan Seršić) who received letters written in Croatian from his sister Catte Bobuš, in Rijeka. In a letter dated 13 June 1900, John Sersic was informed of his family's wellbeing and the tragic loss of his mother and father who had died two years earlier. His sister wrote,

> We are very happy that you remembered to write us a letter, but you could have written more often when our father and mother were still alive. Your letter would have made them very happy ... I know that we cannot help each other because we have our own responsibilities but through letters we can communicate and write to each other. Stay with God, dear brother, I remain your sister until death. Catte Bobuš. With God's assistance, I pray for a reply. God be with you.[62]

John Sersic was born in Rijeka on 18 December 1855. After leaving Croatia he lived in England for a few years and arrived in Sydney in 1875. Sersic was a seaman and spent a great deal of time building boats and fishnets. He moved

John Sersic with his wife

to Melbourne where he purchased a fish shop; he was also a professional fisherman working out of Sandringham. Between 1887 and 1901 Sersic lived at various addresses in West Melbourne, during which time he was mostly a seaman. John Sersic married Lily Mahoney whose parents had come from Ireland on 23 November 1892. The ceremony was held at St Francis Catholic Church in Melbourne. They subsequently had four children, two sons and two daughters. In 1895 Sersic worked as a fisherman and lived at Moor Street, Sandringham where fellow Croatian fishermen Nicholas Budinich, Stephen Coloper, Mathew Kazia and Luke Scoglier had lived a few years earlier.[63] According to his descendants, he then worked on the wharves in Sydney with Billy Hughes who later became the Australian Prime Minister.[64] From 1913 to at least 1940, John Sersic lived at 24 Edgar Street, Kingsville. He was employed at McIlwriath and Coy for about 20 years on the wharves in

Melbourne. He died on 20 December 1943 and there are no descendants with the Sersic surname.[65]

John Sersic's son-in-law was Mate Matich (Mate Matić) who was born in Vačani near Šibenik. Matich had lived in the United States for about five years before coming to Australia in 1909. After his arrival in Melbourne, Matich found employment with the Croatian pioneer, Captain Joseph Catarinich, who owned a 90-ton ketch, the *Warrigal*. He subsequently found employment at the Mount Lyell Chemical and Manure Works located at Whitehall Street, Yarraville. In July 1914 Matich received a letter at work which requested him to report to the Austrian Consul at 173 Collins Street, Melbourne on 1 August 1914 for active service in Serbia. If he failed to do so, the Consul stated, he was liable for up to 15 years imprisonment.[66] Matich never went to the Austrian Consul. He courted and married John Sersic's eldest daughter, Dorothea, who was born in Melbourne. They had one son.

During the First World War a fellow worker employed at the Mount Lyell Chemical and Manure Works initiated a petition demanding that the company sack Mate Matich since he had been born in a country occupied by Austria. The majority of Matich's fellow workers signed the petition and he lost his job. Matich subsequently developed an abscess in one lung which almost killed him. When he was finally discharged from hospital, Matich had to find other means of supporting his family. He

Mate Matich with his wife, son and friends next to his Model T Ford truck. Mate Matich is on the left side. His father-in-law was the Croatian pioneer John Sersic

was granted a second-hand dealer's license and traded in sacks, bags, wooden butter-boxes, and scrap iron, an occupation which gave him just enough money to provide his family with the bare necessities. When the war was over Matich could not return to work at the Mount Lyell Chemical and Manure Works so he struggled on as a second-hand dealer. Matich's situation gradually improved until, in 1929, he was hit by the Depression. He was friends with fellow Croatians Joseph Catarinich, Vincent Despot and Vice Karadole (Karadole). We know of this latter connection since he received a letter from Vice Karadole who lived with the Darveniza brothers in Mooroopna. He also maintained correspondence with relatives in Skradin and Bjelovar Croatia. In July 1936, Mate Matich had the first of many heart attacks until one finally claimed his life on 30 July 1964 in Footscray.[67] His son has no living male heirs; when he dies the Matich surname will die out with him.

George Bathols

Another Croatian pioneer with multiple occupations was George Bathols (Jure Vidulić) who was born in Mali Lošinj on the island of Lošinj on 24 May 1841. He arrived in Melbourne in 1865 and prior to his arrival, changed his surname from Vidulić to Bathols. George Bathols lived for seven years in South Australia and the

George Bathols (Vidulić) with his family. George Bathols is the third seated person from the left side

George Bathols carved the decorated stone chest for a competition for the
Melbourne International Exhibition of 1880

remainder of his life in Victoria. He married Mary Ann Jury on 6 March 1872 and
they had 11 children. One daughter, Lussina Adelaide, was named after the
birthplaces of her parents, Lussin being the Italian spelling of the island of Lošinj,
George Bathols's birthplace, and Adelaide being his wife's birthplace. From 1873 to
1927 George Bathols lived at 1 Bell Street, Footscray.

In Melbourne Bathols primarily worked as a carpenter, although he held various
positions as a labourer, grocer and stonemason.[68] Bathols appears to have been a
talented craftsman: he once made a small bluestone chest (about 15 by 10 cm) with
hinges, which was carved from a solid bluestone block, for a competition arranged
prior to the Melbourne International Exhibition of 1880. A valuable prize was offered
to the first person to carve a chest from a single stone. The chest had to be hollow,
have a hinged lid, moveable handle and had to be finished before the exhibition. No
chests were ready in time for the exhibition, so the prize was not awarded. George
Bathols eventually finished the stone chest in 1881. Unfortunately, the handle was
broken by a family member in the 1930s. During the First World War, his son
Nicholas Bathols served with the 3rd Light Horse Field Ambulance. George Bathols
died on 13 August 1927. In 1996 there were over 200 of Bathols's descendants living
all over Australia.[69]

Nicholas Bathols in AIF uniform

Prospero Stanich

Many Croatians brought valuable skills with them to Australia. Prospero Stanich (Stanić), who was born on the island of Hvar in 1839, was an ear and eye specialist. He also treated nose and throat diseases. Stanich studied and trained under professors at university and hospital clinics in Vienna and in Halle, Germany.[70] By 1873 he had established his practice in Sydney and in 1881 he was practising at 153 Collins Street, Melbourne.

According to *The Nepean Times*, before Stanich's departure from Melbourne, the Mayors of the municipalities of Fitzroy, South Melbourne, Collingwood, North Melbourne, Brighton and Richmond gave signed testimonials presented under the seals of these councils thanking him for his skilful treatment of poor people with ear diseases. In addition, he was given the metal seal stamp of the City of Fitzroy in recognition of his valuable work. Stanich also had a number of well-known people from Australian and New

The ear and eye specialist Prospero Stanich in 1887

Zealand society among his patients, including Lord Augustus Loftus (Government House, Sydney), Robert Graham (ex-Premier of New Zealand), Mayor of Brunswick, Mayor of Alexandra and opera singers. According to records held in Hvar, he treated

Queen Victoria in London in about 1886 and in recognition, Queen Victoria gave him a labelled model of the ear. Prospero Stanich's specialised skills were highly valued. The words 'by appointment to his Excellency the ex-Governor of New South Wales' or 'Under Vice Regal Appointment' were attached to his name. In Sydney in 1894 he married Edith Bell Newton, who was 30 years his junior. From 1882 to until his death on 23 February 1915, Stanich usually resided in Sydney. He maintained ties with other Croatians in Australia, including the owners of 'Dalmatinska Gostiona' boarding house/hotel in Sydney. His brother, Ante Stanich, also came to Australia, but later returned to Croatia.[71]

Mr. P. Stanich, Aurist.

PUPIL to Professor Jas. Gruber, Chief of Imperial Royal University Ward for Diseases of the Ear, and Physician of Ear Diseases at General Hospital at Vienna. To Dr. Adams Politzer, Imperial Royal Professor of the Vienna University for Diseases of the Ear, and Chief of the Ward at the General Hospital for Diseases of the Ear. To Professor Dr. Schwartze, Director of the Royal University Clinic for Diseases of the Ear, and Privy Councillor of Medicine. Halle, Germany, and by appointment to his Excellency the ex-Governor of New South Wales.

Consulting Rooms—At Stanich Lodge, Mt. Pleasant, Penrith, and on Monday at 149, King-street, Sydney.

Newspaper advertisement for Prospero Stanich's aurist (ear specialist) business

Stanić in Melbourne

CHAPTER 9

Beyond Pioneers
1891–1945

The important contribution which some of the descendants of Croatian pioneers have made to Australian society occupies the beginning of this chapter, the main focus being a summary of the history of Croatians who settled in Australia between 1891 and 1945. The chief regions where these Croatians settled and formed communities is highlighted. During this period the number of Croatian-born in Australia increased dramatically, especially the number of Croatian-born women. Unlike Croatian pioneers, these settlers were better organised and established many Croatian clubs in Australia which supported tamburica orchestras, social and cultural activities. Also relevant to Croatians in Australia at this time is a discussion of the discrimination suffered by these Croatians, and the internment of Croatian-born as enemy aliens during the First World War.

Descendants' contributions to Australian society

A number of descendants of the Croatian pioneers have achieved great success in sport, public life, medicine, journalism and academia. As we have seen, Arthur Terdich (Terdić) was well known in motor sport, winning the second Australian Grand Prix at Phillip Island in 1929; Ray Gabelich (Gabelić) was a legendary footballer; Douglas Buzolich (Buzolić) was a renowned magistrate and Justice of the Peace who held many other important positions; and John Tripovich (Tripović) was a distinguished politician in the Victorian branch of the Australian Labor Party. Archbishop Matthew Beovich (Beović) was the Catholic Archbishop of Adelaide for over three decades; Dr John Catarinich (Katarinić) was Director of Mental Hygiene in Victoria and Inspector of the Inebriates' Institute of Victoria; and Leonard Radic (Radić) is a well-known theatre critic, playwright and journalist.[1]

On 18 March 1929 the second Australian Grand Prix motor race was held at Cowes, Phillip Island. Over 2000 visitors travelled to the island on special ferries and trains; hundreds of cars were also ferried to the island. The race had a 200-mile (322 kilometres) course which consisted of 31 laps, with many turns that tested the drivers' skills. Halfway through the race, Arthur Terdich, driving a Bugatti type T37A, took the lead and held it until the finish, only stopping once to change a wheel, unlike most of the other drivers who had to stop several times, either for mechanical problems or for refuelling. On the 29th lap, his closest rival was forced to stop, leaving the way open for an easy victory. Terdich won the second Australian Grand Prix in 3 hours, 14 minutes 22.2 seconds. The runner-up was also a Bugatti and

Arthur Terdich's racing car No. 19 crossing the finish line in the 1929 Australian Grand Prix

came in over 15 minutes later; a Lombard came third. Terdich's supercharged Bugatti averaged 99 km/h over the rough track used for the race, at times achieving speeds in excess of 130 km/h. Terdich's prize was a £100 trophy.[2]

The previous year, Arthur Terdich, whose brother Albert was also a driver in both these races, had come first in his class, but had failed to win the race overall due to engine trouble. Arthur Terdich was co-founder of the Light Car Club of Victoria in 1924 which later became the Light Car Club of Australia. He was organiser and administrator of many motor races. Terdich also served as a council member of the RACV from 1927 to 1970.[3]

1929 Australian Grand Prix cocktail cabinet trophy, the plaque on the cabinet has the shape of Phillip Island

Ray Gabelich, grandson of Croatian pioneer Rerecich, was one of Collingwood's best players in the 1958 Australian Rules football grand final win over Melbourne. He won the Copeland Trophy as Collingwood's best and fairest player in 1960 and the Simpson Medal for Western Australia's best player in the state's carnival win the following year. Gabelich returned to Victoria and captained Collingwood in the 1964 grand final. He resigned the captaincy midway through 1965 because of an injury, but was still an effective contributor and played his last game in the 1966 grand final.[4] There were several other descendants of Croatian pioneers who retained their Croatian surnames and played Australian Rules football in the Victorian Football League (VFL). However, the majority of well-known Australian Rules football players in the Australian Football League (AFL) of Croatian descent are second- and third-generation Croatians who came from Western Australia.[5]

On many occasions, descendants of Croatian pioneers were also very successful all-round sportsmen. For example, Dr John Catarinich was bowls Champion of Champions in 1924 and played football for South Melbourne Football Club. He also played cricket, tennis and golf.[6] On the goldfields many descendants of the original pioneers also played sport. In the Redcastle district, where there was a community of Croatians, Bartholomew Mercovich's sons were active in cricket and football clubs.[7]

Douglas Buzolich, one of the best known JP magistrates appointed to the Commission of Peace in Victoria before the First World War, also owned the successful D. Buzolich Pty Ltd hat shops in Melbourne. According to the Victorian Premier, the Hon. W. Watt, Buzolich was 'a gentleman of the highest character and of first-class qualifications for the position herein [with the State of New South Wales Commission]. I have always considered him one of the best of the Honorary Magistrates of Victoria'. Buzolich was a founding member of the Royal Victorian Association of Honorary Justices which was established in 1910, and he was the vice-president of the association from its inception until his death in 1916. Buzolich was a deputy coroner of the city of Melbourne as well as being involved in the management of many clubs and hospitals.

The First Council and Officers of the Honorary Justices' Association. Douglas Buzolich is the second person on the left side in the front row

Buzolich had other civic responsibilities: he was secretary of the Citizens' Committee which arranged the decorations and festivities in Melbourne in honour of the royal visit for the opening of the Commonwealth Parliament and Federation in 1901. The Duke and Duchess of York, who later became King George V and Queen Mary, were among the many people who thanked him for the exceptional job he had done. He was also thanked by the government and presented with a fitting memento by the Citizens' Committee in the Town Hall.[8]

John Tripovich was prominent in the Victorian branch of the Australian Labor Party and was the state secretary for the Australian Labor Party from 1955 to 1961.

John Tripovich at the Preston Railway Station in 1926 while he was a railway employee before entering politics. John Tripovich is on the left side in the back row

During the time of 'the split' (when the DLP [Democratic Labor Party] was formed), immense demands were placed on him. In 1960 he was elected to the upper house of the Victorian Parliament. He was Labor Deputy Leader of the Victorian Legislative Council for six years. Tripovich held the seat of Doutta Galla from August 1960 to until his death in August 1976. In 1970 he became Labor Deputy Leader in the Legislative Council, a position he held until March 1976.[9]

Kaye Darveniza, MLC, is currently a Labor representative in the upper house of the Victorian Parliament for the Melbourne West Province. Her sister Gail Gago, MLC, is currently a Labor representative in the upper house of the South Australian Parliament. Both were nurses and held leading nursing union positions prior to entering state politics in 1999 and 2002, respectively. Other descendants of the Darveniza pioneers are successful academics and neurologists.[10]

In Victoria most of the successful Croatian descendants lived in Melbourne and received a good education. However, there were also descendants in regional Victoria who became successful farmers and storekeepers. Like their pioneer forebears, successful Croatian descendants all maintained ties with other Croatians in Australia. In terms of their success and contribution to Australian society, encouragement by their Croatian migrant fathers to better themselves may have been one of the influencing factors in their success. Croatian pioneers valued highly the education of their children. They signed petitions to improve schools in districts throughout Victoria, including Yandoit, Barongarook, and Korumburra.[11]

Not surprisingly, the children of Croatian pioneers had much better opportunities than their fathers, due to the advantage of a better knowledge of English and usually, a better education. Their occupations were much more diverse than their Croatian-born fathers. For example, Matteo Gargurevich's seven children worked in a variety of professions. Henry and John were clerks; Louise was a music teacher, pianist and later a florist. Philomena worked as a costumier and dressmaker. Fanny was a machinist, while Catherine and Maria worked at home.[12] Similarly, Matthew Beovich's children had occupations that differed from his occupation of fruiterer, largely due to their better education. As we have seen, his son Matthew became a priest, later archbishop, Vera became a nun and Francis became a school teacher. Bartholomew Mercovich's sons also were employed in various occupations different from their father's. In some instances the sons of Croatian pioneers occasionally worked together in family businesses, sometimes their fathers with them. Examples of these family businesses include Terdich Bros Pty Ltd, furniture manufacturers and Buzolich hat shops.

Descendants of Croatians who arrived in Australia between 1891 and the First World War were also successful in Australian society. For example, Fred Franich's son, Ivan, and grandson, Roger, both became magistrates.[13] Interestingly, Fred Franich himself was more of a 'physical' type; he had enormous strength and was involved in wrestling and strongman exhibitions. In 1908 Fred Franich and Webster were billed in a vaudeville show as 'Franich and Webster, The Australian Sandows, Sensational

Three of Bartholomew Mercovich's sons in different uniforms – Sergeant Bartholomew Mercovich in AIF uniform, Constable Francis Mercovich in Victorian Police uniform and John Mercovich in a seaman's uniform

Strong Men, Art Poseurs and Heavy-weight Balancers'. They were named after Eugene Sandow, a famous European bodybuilder at the time. On Saturday 18 January 1908, they were the first performers for the night at the Victoria Theatre, Newcastle.[14]

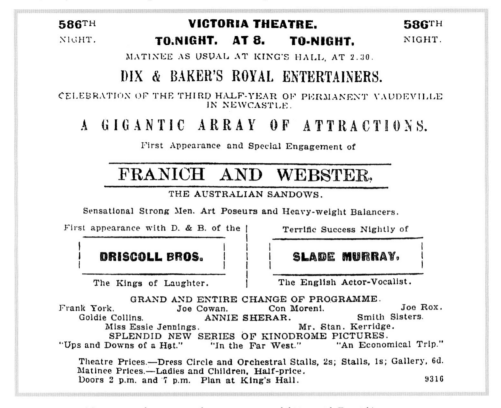

Newspaper advertisement for a strongman exhibition with Franich's surname

According to the *Newcastle Morning Herald* of 20 January 1908:

> The splendid physique of Franich was brought into wonderful relief by his exhibition of muscular posing. Every muscle was defined distinctly as he went through a series of violent exercises. Gradually turning, Franich conveyed to view the excessive power of the muscles of his neck. These muscles are abnormally developed, the neck being ordinarily 18 inches [45.7 cm], and 25 inches [63.5 cm] expanded. His chest is normal 44.5 inches [113 cm]. He contracted to 37 inches [94 cm], and, expanding, brought the chest to 47.5 inches [121 cm] … Franich asserted his strength by lifting a 200 pound [91 kilogram] bar-bell above his head, dropping it into the bend of the arms. Lying down, the big bell was placed upon the soles of his feet, and with a 13 stone [83 kg] man sitting on each end he balanced the implement and the men together. The various acts were loudly applauded.[15]

Fred Franich pulling a rope in a pose

Fred Franich flexing his muscles in a pose

Descendants who fought for Australia

The First World War was a major turning point in Australian history. A total of about 59,342 soldiers of the Australian Imperial Force died and 168,000 were wounded during this war. On the Western Front in France, the Anzacs suffered the highest casualty rate among the Allied forces. During three years of trench warfare, nearly two out of three Anzacs on the Western Front were killed or wounded. The AIF lost 8500 men at Gallipoli.

The Croatian pioneers of Australia had 78 descendants who still retained their Croatian surnames and fought for Australia during the First World War. Of these, 15 were killed in action and another four died of wounds in France, Belgium and Gallipoli. They are commemorated at the Canberra War Memorial and on various war memorials in Australia and Europe. There were also other Australians of Croatian descent without Croatian surnames who fought for Australia during this war.[16] The

 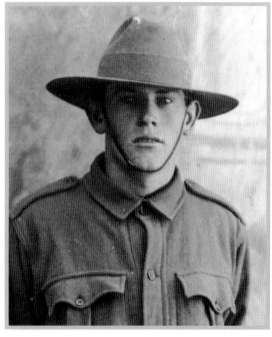

Private Matthew Cunich in AIF uniform, he was killed in action on the Western Front

Private Victor Lusic in AIF uniform, he was killed in action in Gallipoli

majority of these servicemen were privates, but there were also captains, corporals, lieutenants and sergeants amongst them. Some of those who managed to survive returned home wounded.

A number of Croatian pioneer families had up to four descendants with Croatian surnames who fought for Australia during the First World War. For example, Antonio Pavich had four grandsons who fought for Australia. One of these, Private Antonio Pavich was killed in action in France on 11 August 1918. Descendants of Croatian

Antonio Pavich's grandson Antonio Pavich in AIF uniform, he was killed in action in France

pioneers were proud to serve their country and, like other Australian servicemen, some were married in their uniform.

Children of Croatian fishermen and seamen served in the Australian Navy during this war. Charles Radoslovich, whose father was a fisherman, enlisted in the Australian Navy. He later changed his surname to Piller as he thought the Croatian surname would work against him since Australia was at war with Austria, which at the time was occupying Croatia. However, the surname Radoslovich is displayed on the war memorial in Port Fairy.[17]

A larger number of descendants with Croatian surnames served in the Australian Armed Forces during the Second World War. Some families of Croatian descent, for example, the Buzolichs, had members who were killed in both world wars.[18] Croatian descendants in Australia proved themselves to be patriotic and displayed great

Private Percival Dominick on his wedding day in July 1919 in his AIF uniform

Antonio Pavich's grandsons Antonio Pavich (left side) and Nick Pavich (right side) in AIF uniform

bravery during the wars. Private Leslie Starcevich of the 2/43rd Australian Infantry Battalion, who is of Croatian descent, received the Victoria Cross Medal for exceptional bravery in the face of the enemy in North Borneo during the Second World War. The Victoria Cross is the Commonwealth's highest military decoration and has been won by fewer than 100 Australians. His battalion was ordered to capture Beaufort from the Japanese. On 28 June 1945 Starcevich single-handedly charged and captured four Japanese machine-gun posts, killing 12 enemy Japanese. This helped speed up relief to an isolated and surrounded group of his battalion.[19]

Enemy aliens and internment

With the outbreak of the First World War, many Croatian-born who were living in Australia and had not been naturalised were interned as enemy aliens. The Australian authorities technically considered them enemy Austrian subjects, even though the Australian Government, through intelligence reports, knew these Croatians were loyal to the Allied cause and were opposed to the Austro-Hungarian regime. At this time, several hundred Croatian-born, primarily from Western Australia, were interned in the Holdsworthy Concentration Camp in Liverpool, New South Wales, together with Germans and Austrians. In total 6890 persons were interned in Australia during the First World War and the overwhelming majority of these were Germans.[20] Only a few Croatian-born from Victoria were interned in Liverpool and, interestingly, prior to their internment, they were unemployed or destitute, due to their having been sacked from their jobs and denied employment opportunities because they were considered aliens. In 1919 most of the Croatians interned at Liverpool were deported to Croatia on board the ship, *Frankfurt*.[21]

Stefano Kazia who was interned in Liverpool, New South Wales, during the First World War and deported in 1919

During the process of internment by the Australian authorities, the Croatians had the humiliating experience of being assigned a registration number, photographed and finger-printed like criminals. Their personal details and descriptions were recorded. A number of Croatians from New Zealand and Asia were also interned at Liverpool. During the First World War Australia was not the only country to intern Croatians, they were also interned in Canada, South Africa and New Zealand, although some were released on parole during the war. In New Zealand others were conscripted to work for the Home Service as labourers often under poor working conditions.[22]

Even though the Croatians and Germans were interned in the same camps, they did not mix. According to Anthony Splivalo, a Croatian who was interned at Rottnest Island Internment Camp in Western Australia and later at Holdsworthy: 'The Germans and the so-called Austro-Hungarians, ninety-nine percent of whom where Dalmatians, formed two separate little worlds in the enclosure. Even the tents they occupied were grouped in two separate sections. The language barrier kept them apart as nothing else did. The

Dalmatians spoke no German, and hardly enough English to greet their German fellow exiles comfortably'. At Liverpool, 'The commandant had special warning signs hung at regular intervals on the inside of the barbed wall. These were in two languages, German and Croatian'. The Croatian sign read 'Ne Budite Blizu Ograde!' [Do Not Be Near The Fence!].[23]

Those Croatian-born who were not interned during the First World War were registered as aliens and released on parole, whereby they were compelled to report to the police, usually on a weekly basis. They also required permission to move to another place of residence. Most Croatian pioneers from Victoria were not interned during the First World War since they were usually naturalised and beyond military age. Most had Australian or British-born wives and had lived in Australia as law-abiding citizens for over 25 years (some for over 50 years). Croatians who had settled in Victoria in the decade prior to the First World War were rarely interned as there were so few of them and hence they posed no real 'threat'.

Nevertheless, those Croatians in Victoria who were not interned suffered discrimination from other Australians who were swept up with patriotism and the anger accompanying Australian deaths in Europe. False allegations were made against Croatian publicans in Melbourne and Croatian fishermen in Portarlington, allegations sometimes being made by business competitors. In one case, a Croatian's former girlfriend made false allegations about him after their relationship ended. The allegations were usually made anonymously and they varied from alleged suspicious behaviour, alleged threatening language and alleged firearms or ammunition possession. All the allegations against Croatians in Victoria were investigated by the police and proved false.[24]

In Victoria a number of Croatians lost their jobs due to discrimination against enemy aliens. As we have seen, Mate Matich's co-workers signed a petition that demanded the company sack him. In Kalgoorlie in Western Australia, where there was a significant concentration of Croatians working in the gold mines, the discrimination against Croatians was much more severe. Most lost their jobs, and many Australian-born wives and children of interned Croatians were on the verge of starvation. The Australian Government made a pitiful provision for the support of the wives and children of Croatians who surrendered for voluntary internment. Few Croatians opted for voluntary internment as the allowance was not enough for their families to survive on the goldfields. The Catholic Archbishop of Perth called it the 'starvation allowance' when he was lobbying the military authorities on behalf of the Croatians.[25]

While some Croatian-born Australians were being interned by the Australian authorities, others were training with the Australian Armed Forces. Several Croatian-born managed to enlist into the AIF and served alongside other Australians in Europe.[26] Since Croatian-born were technically enemy aliens, the Australian Government subsequently stopped them from joining the AIF. In a later compromise, the government allowed the formation of a special, predominantly Croatian, contingent which was to fight on the Allied side at the front in Salonika. However, because of the Australian Government's indecision, this contingent was not formed until 1917. In a letter dated January 1916 from the Point Cook prisoners of war depot to the Intelligence Section of the 3rd Military District it was stated that: 'G. Salacan, Prisoner of War No. 617, wishes to be released to join a Battalion of Croatians, to fight on the side of the Allies. Salacan states that he is a native of Dalmacia, a district of Croata [Croatia], formerly a part of the Austro-Hungarian Empire'.[27] His comment

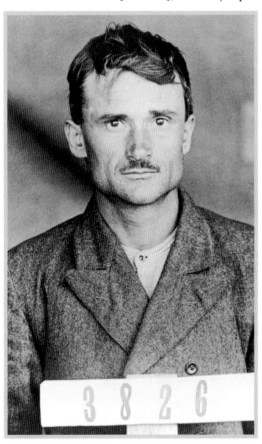

George Salacan who served in the Croatian contingent sent from Australia to Europe to fight on the Allied side during the First World War

regarding Croatia was interesting as the Austro-Hungarian Empire had not collapsed at that stage. Internees were allowed to join this special Croatian contingent, but after being interned for a few years, the enthusiasm for joining had subsided for most of the Croatian internees. In 1917, some Croatian internees also managed to enlist in the AIF. During the First World War, the Croatian Slavonic Society in Boulder, Western Australia, encouraged Croatians to volunteer for the Croatian contingent, which, during the course of the war, became known as the Yugoslav contingent. The Croatian Slavonic Society collected funds for the Allied war effort and established the Croatian Slavonic Society Trust Fund. The president of the society, George Stella, was an informer working for various Australian intelligence services. However, he was not impartial, since his false statements helped intern Croatians who were not members of his society and were not pro-Russian and pan-Slavonic, a position he considered to be in opposition to that of the Allies.[28] During the First World War the Russian consulate gave Russian citizenship papers to many Croatian-born in Australia in an attempt to prevent their internment.

In all, about 63 Croatians together with several Czechs and Slovaks, joined the Croatian contingent.[29] After Australian military training, they were dressed in Australian army uniforms and departed on a troopship alongside Australians for Europe. When they reached the front in Salonika they were ordered to change their Australian uniforms for Serbian ones. After the war some tried to get assisted passage back to Australia, but despite being trained by Australians and travelling to Europe to fight for Australia, they were not allowed to return on the navy ships with other

Australians. Some of the Croatian contingent later managed to return to Australia by paying their own way.

In March 1917, the 3rd Military District Brigadier-General's assessment after interviewing a potential Croatian-born recruit in Victoria was that he 'with his fellow countrymen, might enlist, but may prefer the Australian Army as he would get better pay'. It seems reasonable to suggest that many more Croatians would have enlisted had they been offered the same pay as Australian soldiers or had they been allowed to serve in the AIF.[30]

Interwar Croatians and strikes

Between 1891 and the First World War the main concentration of Croatians in Western Australia was in the Boulder–Kalgoorlie area where they were woodcutters on the woodlines (providing timber for the mines), miners and labourers. Because of the employment opportunities provided by the discovery of gold in Western Australia in 1892, they were attracted to the Kalgoorlie goldfields. Many Croatians were injured in mining accidents and on the woodlines; in mining accidents in Kalgoorlie and Broken Hill some even lost their lives.

Many Croatians later moved from the Western Australian goldfields to the Swan Valley and Perth districts. Croatians also settled in Spearwood, Osborne Park and Swan Valley districts where they were market gardeners. Other Croatians were woodcutters in the south-west of Western Australia providing timber for railway sleepers. Before the First World War a Croatian fishing community was established in Fremantle.

In 1913 Croatians formed the Croatian Slavonic Society of Western Australia in Boulder. Their club premises became an important social and cultural centre for Croatians in Australia. The society had a Croatian tamburica orchestra (string orchestra), singing group, athletics club and a small library. Croatians later also formed tamburica orchestras in Broken Hill and Queensland. Another club, the Croatian Bowling Club Jedinstvo (Unity) established in the Swan Valley in Western Australia in 1931 is still active today.

After the First World War Croatians settled in Western Australia's Swan Valley in large numbers, bringing their strong wine culture into the district. Croatians in this area became known for their wineries. Today, almost half of the 20 or so wineries in the Swan Valley are run by descendants of these Croatian settlers. Two examples of well-known wineries in the Swan Valley with Croatian connections include Kosovich's Westfield Wines which was established in 1922, and Talijancich Wines. John Kosovich received an Order of Australia in 1995 for his contribution to the wine industry.[31] Croatian settlers also run highly prosperous wineries elsewhere in the world, the most notable of these include the Grgich Hills Cellar in California, Babich Wines and Nobilo Wines in New Zealand.

Boulder-based Croatian tamburica orchestra in Boulder, Western Australia in the 1910s

Broken Hill-based Croatian tamburica orchestra in Broken Hill, New South Wales in 1929

Croatians also continued to settle in Broken Hill where there was an established Croatian community. By 1929 there were 300 Croatians in Broken Hill, although many of the Broken Hill Croatians later moved to market-gardening areas of Sydney. In 1928 Croatian immigrants in Broken Hill formed the Borbeni Radnički Pokret (Militant Workers' Movement). A few years later the headquarters of this organisation were moved to Sydney and its name was changed to Savez jugoslavenskih iseljenika u Australiji (Federation of Yugoslav Immigrants in Australia). Between 1928 and 1948, this left-wing organisation dominated the political life of Croatians in Australia and actively supported the socialist movement. In the interwar period, the main concentrations of Croatians in the Sydney area were at Warriewood, Leppington, Cabramatta, Blacktown and Dee Why where they were primarily market gardeners. In Warriewood their principal market garden crop was tomatoes which were grown in greenhouses.

Northern Queensland Croatians worked as cane cutters in the Cairns, Innisfail, Tully and Mossman districts. In the 1920s, a Croatian Club linked to the Croatian Peasant Party was formed in South Johnstone. Other Croatians concentrated in Dimbulah and Mareeba where they worked in the tobacco industry.[32] In the interwar period the main concentration of Croatians in Victoria was in Melbourne and Mildura, while in South Australia, they were mainly located in the Riverina district. The Mildura and Riverina Croatians worked in the fruit-growing industry.

The majority of Croatians who settled in Australia between 1890 and the Second World War came from the Croatian coastline and coastal hinterland, especially from the part of Dalmatia between Dubrovnik and Split. Areas which experienced higher migration from Croatia to Australia between 1890 and 1940 include the Makaraska district, Vrgorac district and the island of Korčula. In the late 1920s Croatian migration from the inland region of Međimurje began, and between 1890 and 1940, people from this area constituted about 5.5 per cent of the Croatian migration to Australia. These Croatians mainly settled in Mildura, Melbourne and the Riverina in South Australia.[33] In 1937 Croatians formed the Matija Gubec Club in Mildura and a couple of years later they built club premises which still exist today, but under the new name of Međimurski Club. The Mildura Croatian community worked in the fruit-growing industry, initially as labourers, but they subsequently purchased their own farms.

During this period, the number of Croatian-born women in Australia increased, but they were still greatly outnumbered by Croatian-born males. Not all the Croatians who migrated to Australia remained in Australia permanently; over half who came to Australia between 1924 and 1944 returned to Croatia, and during the Depression years when there were limited employment opportunities, more Croatians departed Australia than arrived. Naturalisation records indicate that many Croatians who came to Australia between 1890 and 1940 worked for several years before returning to Croatia to get married. Most returned to Australia after some time in Croatia and

The opening of the Matija Gubec Club hall in Mildura in 1939

later sent for their wives and children. In the interwar period, 60 per cent of Croatians in Australia lived in Western Australia – largely because of work opportunities and also due to factors associated with patterns of chain migration. The remainder in descending order lived in New South Wales, Queensland, Victoria and South Australia.[34] The number of Croatians increased dramatically from the 1920s. Chain migration attracted more Croatians to areas where Croatian settlements had already been established. Most found work as unskilled labourers, often moving as work opportunities presented themselves, and many lived in more than one Croatian community in Australia. Croatian-born men often lived in boarding houses run by other Croatians. During the interwar period almost half of the married Croatian-born men in Australia at the time of their naturalisation still had wives in Croatia, while 20 per cent had their Croatian-born wife in Australia.[35] Between 1891 and the Second World War at least 550 Croatians settled in Victoria, mainly in Melbourne and Mildura.[36]

Croatian migrants were involved in union movements, and poor working conditions convinced some to become socialists or communists. They participated in strikes in the mines at Broken Hill, on the woodlines of Western Australia and in cane-cutters strikes in Queensland. Even before the interwar period, Croatians were participating in strikes in Australia; for example, the first major strike on the woodlines of Western Australia which occurred in July 1908 was carried out by Croatian woodcutters and carters who downed tools for better pay. A year later they took further strike action as the demands the government had agreed to in 1908 had not been implemented.[37]

A number of Croatians who arrived in the interwar period were socialists or communists, anti-monarchists who had been influenced by the Russian Revolution and who consequently supported the idea of a Communist Yugoslavia. Most of the ethnic Croatian community leaders were socialists. By the 1930s, therefore, the committees running the Croatian clubs also supported the concept of a Communist Yugoslavia. For example, the Napredak club established in Broken Hill in 1936 was biased towards Communist Yugoslavia. The *Napredak* newspaper was banned from 1940 to 1942 for its Communist propaganda. At this time there were no Croatian priests within the Croatian communities in Australia to counter the effects of these socialists.

During the Second World War, most Australian Croatians actively supported the communist forces under Tito. They collected over £100,000 which was sent to help rebuild Yugoslavia. Croatian community leaders in Australia who supported Communist Yugoslavia convinced almost 1000 Croatians to be voluntarily repatriated from Australia to Yugoslavia in 1948 and 1949 on the ships *Partizanka* (Partisan) and *Radnik* (Worker). However, within several years most had returned to Australia disillusioned with the Communist Yugoslavia they had previously supported. These ships also repatriated Croatians from New Zealand, and North and South America. The Soviet-Yugoslav dispute which erupted in 1948 split the pro-Yugoslav Croatian community in Australia and dramatically reduced community interaction and activities.[38]

There was a history of continued discrimination against Croatians in Kalgoorlie and other gold mining towns in Western Australia. As described previously, several hundred Croatians (many from Kalgoorlie) were interned during the First World War – as 'Austrian subjects' they were labelled enemy aliens. Other Croatians were sacked during this time, especially in the Kalgoorlie mines, because of the 'enemy alien' label. In 1916 the unions on the goldfields held strikes protesting against the employment of 'enemy aliens' in the mines. This resulted in a Royal Commission on the Employing of Enemy Aliens in Mines. To appease the unions, of the 138 miner workers investigated (133 were Croatian-born), 33 were prevented from working in the mines (and were interned) on dubious evidence from pro-Russian and pan-Slavonic Croatians. Croatians continued to suffer discrimination in Boulder–Kalgoorlie after the war. The worst example of discrimination was seen during the 1934 Kalgoorlie riots where Anglo–Australian rioters burnt and looted Croatian and Italian homes and businesses. Five hotels, two boarding houses, numerous shops and about 100 dwellings of foreigners were destroyed. The damage to property due to the riot was close to £100,000. Three Croatians who had served in the Australian Army during the war had their homes burnt and belongings stolen. The Croatian Slavonic Society which collected funds for the Australian war effort also had its building wrecked during the riots.

The 1934 Kalgoorlie riots began after an Italian barman struck a drunk Australian who attacked him for refusing to sell him alcohol. The Australian's skull was fractured on the kerb and he later died in Kalgoorlie Hospital. Incorrect rumours of Italian migrants stabbing the Australian to death resulted in a large group of about 1000 angry Anglo–Australians proceeding to riot against foreigners. In reality however, the

The Croatian Slavonic Society hall after the 1934 Kalgoorlie riots

cause of the riots went deeper. Ill feeling harboured by Anglo–Australians against foreigners, a hangover from the Depression where Australians blamed foreigners for unemployment and the loss of jobs, was still widespread. Anglo–Australians also accused foreign miners of paying kick-backs for better jobs or jobs in the mines. After the Kalgoorlie riots Anglo–Australian miners demanded that the mining companies sack all non-British miners. Instead of their being sacked, a basic English test was introduced which had to be passed to gain employment in the mines. *The West Australian* newspaper organised a relief fund and raised almost £2000 from the public for foreigners who suffered during the riots in Kalgoorlie. About 65 per cent of the relief was given to Croatians and the remainder was given to Italians and other foreigners. After the devastation of the Kalgoorlie riots many Croatians moved to Swan Valley and Fremantle.[39]

Discrimination against Croatians was not confined to the goldfields. Croatians and Italians working as woodcutters in the sleeper industry in the south-west of Western Australia also suffered discrimination. The Forests Department discriminated against Italians and Croatians by restricting the employment of sandalwood cutters on crown land to natural born or naturalised British cutters. This limited the choice of work for many Croatians to hewing (this highly wasteful technique, which only utilised 30 per cent of the logs, consisted of cutting railway sleepers from logs by hand) on private land which resulted in highly exploitive work conditions. Later in an attempt to control hewing on private land, the Forests Department blamed Italian and Croatian hewers for over-cutting which caused a fall in prices and rising unemployment among Anglo–Australians. The prejudice thus aroused would further decrease Croatian woodcutters' prospects of gaining future employment.[40]

Clubs and community activities

Between the late 1920s and the beginning of the Second World War, over 22 Croatian clubs were formed in Australia. This period was one of significant expansion of community social, sporting and cultural activities. Croatian clubs purchased land and erected club buildings. Some clubs went through a number of name changes during this period. Eventually almost all the clubs became affiliated with the left-wing Yugoslav Immigrants' Association of Australia. However, most Croatians joined the clubs for social rather than political reasons.

Many of the clubs supported tamburica orchestras or folkloric groups that celebrated Croatian music and culture. A women's group or a women's section was also an important element of Croatian associations, as were sporting clubs which hosted *bocce* and soccer. Some clubs supported language schools and theatre groups. The club halls were also places where dances and wedding receptions were held.

In Western Australia there were Croatian clubs at Osborne Park, Spearwood, Fremantle, Swan Valley, Boulder, Wiluna, Lakewood, Gwalia, and Manjimup. In the Sydney region there were clubs in Sydney, Leppington, Warriewood, Cabramatta, Blacktown, and Brookvale–Dee Why. There was also a club at Broken Hill. In Victoria there were clubs in Melbourne and Mildura; in North Queensland, in Cairns, Dimbulah, South Johnstone, and Innisfail. The community activities of

Children's tamburica orchestra Zvijezda (Star) in Boulder City, Western Australia in 1936

pro-Yugoslav Croatians in Australia decreased dramatically after the war due to the voluntary repatriation of Croatians after the war and splits in the community caused by the Soviet–Yugoslav dispute that erupted in 1948. Many club premises and land were sold, with some of these assets used to merge and establish new clubs.

H.S.N.K. Zora (Croatian Sports Soccer Club Zora) at a picnic in Sydney in 1937

CHAPTER 10

Post-Second World War Settlement

Overview of Croatians in Australia today

Today three-quarters of the Croatian-born population in Australia live in Victoria and New South Wales, and in all states they are concentrated in urban areas. The Australian cities with the main concentrations of the Croatian-born population, in descending order are Melbourne, Sydney, Perth, Adelaide, Brisbane, Canberra, Geelong, Wollongong, Gold Coast, Newcastle and Hobart. In all states the majority of Croatians live in capital cities, although Queensland has 45 per cent living outside Brisbane.[1] There are also communities of Croatians in Mildura in Victoria working in the fruit-growing industry, in the Swan Valley in Western Australia working in the wine industry, and fishermen in Port Lincoln, South Australia. In North Queensland, Croatians work in the sugar cane and tobacco-growing industries. Table 3 shows the distribution of the Croatian-born population within Australia according to the 2001 Australian Census.

In the mid-1990s, a study by the Australian Croatian Community Services

State/Territory	Number/Percentage of total Croatian-born		Capital city	Number/Percentage of total Croatian-born	
Victoria	18,899	(36.4%)	Melbourne	16,059	(30.9%)
New South Wales	18,434	(35.5%)	Sydney	15,700	(30.3%)
Western Australia	5,190	(10.0%)	Perth	4,783	(9.2%)
Queensland	3,721	(7.2%)	Brisbane	2,056	(4.0%)
South Australia	3,577	(6.9%)	Adelaide	3,074	(5.9%)
Australian Capital Territory	1,709	(3.3%)	Canberra	1,709	(3.3%)
Tasmania	298	(0.6%)	Hobart	215	(0.4%)
Northern Territory	81	(0.1%)	Darwin	60	(0.1%)
Australia	51,909	(100.0%)	—	43,656	(84.1%)

* This table does not include Croatians who were born in Bosnia-Herzegovina, Vojvodina, Kotor, Yugoslavia and Slovenia or stated they were born in Yugoslavia.

Table 3: Distribution of Croatian-born within Australia according to the 2001 Australian Census

(ACCS), funded by the Commonwealth Bureau of Immigration, Multicultural and Population Research (BIMPR), showed that the overwhelming majority of second-generation Croatians, in a sample aged between 14 and 25 with at least one Croatian parent, were involved in the Croatian community with social and sporting organisations and religious or cultural activities. The study also showed that nearly all the participants in the study had Croatian friends.[2]

According to the 2001 census, the most common occupations of the Croatian-born workforce were found among the categories of tradespersons and related workers, labourers and related workers, and intermediate production and transport workers. Croatian-born were twice as likely to have occupations in the tradespersons and related workers category than were all other overseas-born or Australian-born.

The second generation were three times more likely to speak English at home compared with their Croatian-born parents. The second generation had considerably better qualifications than their Croatian-born parents, especially in terms of higher education qualifications. There is a very high rate of Australian citizenship (91.7 per cent) amongst the Croatian-born population compared with other migrant groups (67.3 per cent).[3]

Post-Second World War Croatian settlers

Large numbers of Croatian settlers arrived after the Second World War and can be divided into the following categories: displaced persons, political immigrants, economic immigrants, family reunion migrants and refugees. These Croatians came from all parts of Croatia, including the coast, the interior and from Bosnia-Herzegovina and Vojvodina.[4]

Post-war Croatian immigrants came to Australia largely for economic and political reasons, hoping to create a brighter future for themselves and their families. That Australia was a free and democratic nation was of great significance for many fleeing the Yugoslav Communist regime of the time. For them Australia was a land of opportunity.

Three-quarters of Croatian-born living in Australia today arrived before 1981. Between 1947 and 1954 there were 170,700 displaced persons introduced into Australia under the Displaced Persons Scheme, whereby they were contracted to work for two years anywhere the government directed. Among these displaced persons were over 10,500 Croatians. They were Australia's fifth largest group of displaced persons, only the Polish, Latvian, Ukrainian and Hungarian migrants included more displaced arrivals than Croatians.[5]

The largest number of Croatians arrived in Australia in the 1960s and 1970s when Yugoslavia relaxed its migration restrictions to combat rising unemployment. Although they were officially considered economic migrants by the Australian authorities, many saw themselves as political migrants who were forced to leave

Croatian cultural and welfare association Jadran (Adriatic) at Australia Day celebrations in Sydney in 1958

because of discrimination against pro-independence Croatians in Yugoslavia. The number of Croatian arrivals in Australia decreased in the late 1970s and 1980s, but rose again in the 1990s (due to the war against Croatia), with the arrival of Croatian refugees from Croatia and Bosnia-Herzegovina.[6]

Most Croatian immigrants found employment in the fields of manufacturing and construction. In Victoria they contributed to many projects such as the Hume Weir, the West Gate Bridge, Melbourne's City Loop railway line and, more recently, the City Link road project. Many of their children now have undergraduate degrees and other tertiary qualifications, are fluent in Croatian and identify strongly with their Croatian background. The Croatian Students' Association, which was established in Melbourne in 1980, helps to promote Croatian culture among students and youth. The association has organised conferences and has published its own magazine *Klokan* (Kangaroo). There are also numerous university Croatian clubs in Australia, the most active being Melbourne University's Croatian club.[7]

Victoria has over 36.4 per cent of Australia's Croatian-born population, which is slightly greater than New South Wales. Eighty-five per cent of Croatian speakers in Victoria live in Melbourne. The highest proportion of these live in Melbourne's western suburbs: Keilor, St Albans, Avondale Heights, Sunshine, Altona, Footscray and Taylors Lakes. The local government area of Brimbank in Melbourne has the largest number of Croatians in Australia. This has been reflected in the election in 1999 of a Croatian-born mayor.[8] Many Croatians who originally settled in the

Klokan (*Kangaroo*) *magazine published in English
by the Croatian Students' Association in the 1990s*

inner suburbs have resettled in outer suburbs. For example, upwardly mobile Croatians from Footscray moved to Keilor where they built new houses. There are also concentrations of Croatians in Springvale, Dandenong, Berwick, Bundoora, Mill Park and Broadmeadows. In Melbourne there are Croatian social and sporting venues at Footscray, Sunshine, Campbellfield, Springvale and St Albans. The map of Croatian speakers in Melbourne and Geelong in the colour section of this book clearly shows high concentrations of Croatian speakers in Melbourne's western and south-eastern suburbs, and Geelong.[9] Like other Southern Europeans, Croatians place high importance on owning their own home. Almost 66 per cent of the Croatian-born population in Victoria own their own homes which is more than 24 per cent higher than the state average.

Croatians are the second largest ethnic group in Geelong. Most of them live in or near Bell Park, where they have built two social clubs, a Catholic centre and chaplaincy servicing its parishioners in Croatian. The Geelong Croatian priest also meets the pastoral needs of Croatians in Ballarat and Mildura. Croatians have also built the Croatian Sporting Centre, North Geelong Soccer Club. Two primary schools in Bell Park (Holy Family and Bell Park North) teach Croatian as part of their curriculum, since a significant number of their students are of Croatian descent. For example, 107 of the 250 students at Holy Family Primary School are from a Croatian background, and 110 of these learn Croatian. In Victoria there are also Croatian communities in Ballarat, Wodonga, Mildura and Morwell. Each Croatian community has social and sporting venues.

Croatian immigrants settled near the hostels where they were housed on arrival and close to their places of employment. From the 1950s they established Croatian clubs in these areas. For example, the Wodonga Croatian community was established near Bonegilla immigration reception and training centre, which was Australia's first and biggest post-war migrant reception centre. Between 1947 and 1971 it was the first home in Australia for about 300,000 migrants from many nations. Similarly, Croatian communities were also established near the Maribyrnong and Springvale hostels in Melbourne.[10]

In Sydney Croatians mainly live in Sydney's western suburbs of Fairfield, Liverpool and Blacktown. In Perth Croatians are concentrated in the local government areas of Cockburn and Fremantle to the south and Stirling, Wanneroo and Swan to the north. In Adelaide the largest concentration is in the local government area of Hindmarsh–Woodville, while in Brisbane they are located in the middle and south-eastern suburbs.

Croatian rally in Kings Park in Perth against the Yugoslav communist regime

Employment

Originally post-Second World War Croatian immigrants mainly found employment in factories, but many now work as tradesmen in the building and construction industry. They primarily worked in capital cities and industrial centres. In Melbourne, Croatians found employment in various types of factories, including car manufacturing, textile, rubber and plastics, metal fabrication and food processing. Croatians living in Footscray were employed in nearby factories as well as in the meat industry, and in Altona they often worked in the petrochemical industry. In the Springvale and Dandenong area Croatians worked in small factories and food processing plants. Ford car manufacturers in Broadmeadows and tyre manufacturers were other important employers.

Many Croatian men are now builders, carpenters, painters and bricklayers working in the housing industry. Other Croatian men are employed in highly paid building and construction jobs as labourers and tradespersons. In contrast, Croatian women are generally employed in low-paid factory and textile industry jobs. Some unskilled Croatian women work as seasonal farm labourers and fruit pickers. There are more Croatian-born males than females in Australia (52.3 per cent compared to 47.7 per cent).

In Geelong the main employer of Croatians is Ford, while other major employers are the Brintons carpet manufacturing factory, Alcoa and the Shell refinery. As in Melbourne, many are now employed in the housing industry. In the late 1950s, due to the high number of Croatians in Geelong, the Croatia soccer team moved from Melbourne to Geelong, where it remained until the early 1960s, when in response to an increase in the number of Croatians in Melbourne, it returned. The closure in the 1980s of International Harvester and other industries in Geelong caused a decrease in the percentage of Croatians migrating to Geelong compared to the rest of the state.

Croatia Geelong soccer team in 1959 when they were champions of the Victorian First Division – North

Because of better employment opportunities, most of Ballarat's Croatians have now moved to Melbourne and Geelong. Similarly, in the Myrtleford district there were Croatians working on tobacco farms, but most have now moved to larger towns and cities. In Mildura however, most Croatians still work in the fruit-growing industry in their wine and sultana grape vineyards and citrus orchards. There are also Croatian fruit growers in South Australia's Riverina region. Croatians in Morwell and the Latrobe Valley district in Gippsland work in the power stations and coal mines.

Many Croatians were employed in the construction of the Snowy Mountains

River Hydro-Electric Scheme. Croatian migrants worked in the Wollongong, Newcastle and Whyalla steel mills. In Canberra, like their compatriots in Victoria, they have been highly successful in the building and construction industry. The marble work in the National Library of Australia in Canberra was built by stone masons from the island of Brač.[11] As we have already observed, Croatians are prominent in the Swan Valley wine industry and in the sugar cane and tobacco industries in North Queensland. In Mount Gambier, Croatians worked as wood fellers and there are Croatian market gardeners in Perth. Post-war Croatians who have settled in the Australian outback are primarily opal miners at Coober Pedy, Mintabie and Andamooka in South Australia and Lightning Ridge in New South Wales.[12] Today, Croatians in Port Lincoln are highly successful fishermen involved in the lucrative tuna fishing and tuna farming industry. The wealthiest of Port Lincoln's tuna fishermen are Croatian-born Sam Sarin and Tony Santic (Šantić) who have amassed fortunes of $220 million and $150 million respectively.[13] Croatians are also fishing in Fremantle and in Nelson Bay, New South Wales. Boat-building is another area where Croatians have been successful, particularly in Adelaide and Fremantle where they have their own boat-building companies. Joe Glamočak's Adelaide Ship Construction International Pty Ltd (ASCI) is the most prominent of these boat-building companies.

Prior to Croatian independence, the percentage of Croatian professionals arriving in Australia was low, as most tertiary-educated migrants from Croatia settled in Western European countries and the United States. As a result, Croatian-born migrants are less likely to be employed as professionals compared to the general Australian population. In contrast to earlier Croatian arrivals, many of the Croatians who arrived after 1985 and refugees who arrived in the 1990s were professionals. However, the percentage of Croatian-born in Australia working as labourers is still twice that of the rest of the Australian population.

Community activities

Currently there are over 250 Croatian clubs and societies in Australia devoted to a huge spectrum of activities and interests – social, language, sporting (soccer, golf and bocce), folkloric, drama, literary, musical, arts, religious, women's, student's and senior citizen's clubs. As well as catering to specific interests, Croatian clubs provide a means of passing down Croatian culture and traditions to their descendants. Croatian folkloric groups, especially the Geelong-based LADO and Sydney-based Koleda, are well known for their performances at multicultural events. These folkloric dances date back centuries and reflect characteristic Croatian customs and traditions. In 2002, Geelong-based LADO celebrated its 30th anniversary, while Sydney-based Koleda celebrated its 35th anniversary. Currently, there are 24 Croatian folkloric groups in Australia. Among their other activities, the women's organisations raise money for

A Melbourne-based Croatian folkloric group at a Croatian community dance in Geelong in the late 1960s

Sydney-based Croatian folkloric group Mladi Frankopani (Young Frankopans) at the Cro Festival in 2000

local charities. For example, the Melbourne women's group, Katarina Zrinski, contributes annually to the Royal Children's Hospital Appeal.

In Melbourne in 2001, during the Australian Centenary of Federation celebration event, 'Our Nation on Parade', the Croatian community mounted an impressive float depicting the Church of St Mark in Zagreb. The float also carried a Croatian tamburica orchestra. Preceding the Croatian float were participants depicting the waves of Croatian migration to Australia – from the gold miners of the 1850s to the refugees of the 1990s. Folkloric dancers in Croatian costumes followed the float.

The Croatian-born population is ageing: 60 per cent of the Croatian-born population in Australia is over the age of 50 with the percentage of Croatian-born aged 55 to 64 years three times the Australian average for this age group. Croatian old age nursing homes already exist in Sydney, Adelaide, Perth and Canberra. Planning is underway to have one built in Melbourne in the near future. There are 11 Croatian senior citizen clubs in Victoria alone.[14]

The overwhelming majority of Croatian-born in Australia are Catholics. Since the 1950s Croatian priests have been coming to Australia to serve the Croatian communities in Croatian, and Croatian nuns have also been giving the Croatian community spiritual guidance and run Croatian language schools. Croatian nuns are based in Sydney, Canberra and Adelaide. Currently, there are 14 Croatian Catholic centres or parishes in Australia, with four of them located in Victoria. For four decades, the Croatian Catholic Church at Clifton Hill in Melbourne has been an important religious, social and cultural centre, largely due to Christianity having been an integral part of many aspects of Croatian culture for thirteen centuries. Croatians have built Catholic churches at Springvale and Sunshine. The Croatian priest at Springvale also provides services to Croatians in Gippsland. Apart from their church commitments, Croatian priests in Australia have taught Croatian language and given welfare assistance to the Croatian community. They have also published their own Catholic periodicals in Croatian. For example, in Geelong, Rev. Stjepan Gnječ published *Čovjek, Duša i Tijelo* (Man, Spirit and Body). New South Wales has three Croatian Catholic centres or parishes in Sydney (at Summer Hill, Blacktown and St Johns Park), a church in Wollongong and another in Newcastle. There are also Croatian Catholic centres in North Fremantle, Hobart, Brisbane, Canberra and Adelaide.

In the past, the Australian Catholic Church has been one of the few mainstream bodies sympathetic to Croatians. In 1955, on the tenth anniversary of the unjust imprisonment of Croatian Cardinal Alojzije Stepinac by the Yugoslav Communist authorities, a mass organised by the Croatian Catholic organisation, Križari, in conjunction with Archbishop Mannix was celebrated for about 3000 Catholics – largely Croatians – at Melbourne's St Patrick's Catholic Cathedral. During this service they prayed for Cardinal Stepinac's release. Similarly, in 1991 the Archbishop of Melbourne, Thomas Little, assisted by Croatian priests, celebrated a Pontifical Mass for Peace in Croatia and Slovenia in St Patrick's Cathedral. In 2001, in St Patrick's Cathedral, the Archbishop of Melbourne, Dr George Pell (now Cardinal Pell), celebrated a mass and unveiled a statue of the now Blessed Cardinal Alojzije Stepinac. Over 4000 Catholics, the overwhelming majority Croatians, attended the mass and dedication ceremony.

Blessing of both the Croatian and Australian flags on Easter day in 1952 by Archbishop Beovich
in Adelaide, and celebrations afterwards with the Croatian priest

Croatian procession in Fremantle in 1962. On the banner is written 'Our Lady of Sinj, Save the Croats'.
The 'Our Lady of Sinj' (Gospa Sinjska) shrine in Sinj is one of the most important Catholic religious shrines in Croatia

Croatians exiting a Catholic church in Melbourne after celebrating mass in Croatian with the Croatian priest

Croatians on the steps of Melbourne's St Patrick's Catholic Cathedral in 1955 on the tenth anniversary of the unjust imprisonment of Croatian Cardinal Stepinac by the Yugoslav Communist authorities. About 3000 Catholics had attended a mass praying for Cardinal Stepinac's release

Although Croatians are overwhelmingly Catholic, there is also a Croatian Islamic centre in Maidstone and Croatian Seventh Day Adventists meet in St Albans in Melbourne. Croatian Seventh Day Adventists also meet in Dundas in New South Wales and Eight Mile Plains in Brisbane.

Culture, language and the arts

Croatian identity in the diaspora is tied to its language and cultural traditions. Since the 1960s Croatian ethnic language schools have operated in Australia. Croatian language study was first introduced at Year 12 level in New South Wales in 1981 and in Victoria in 1984. It has been ranked as high as the seventh largest Year 12 language enrolment in Victoria. In 2000, there were 944 school students studying Croatian in Victoria.[15] Croatian language is an accredited subject at Australian universities. Throughout Australia there have been Croatian summer school camps where students of Croatian descent from around Australia learnt about Croatian language and

Croatian community participants in Australia Day celebrations in Sydney in 1980

culture.[16] According to the 2001 Australian Census, Croatian is the eleventh most widely spoken language other than English (69,851 Croatian speakers) in Australia. Croatian is ranked as the ninth most widely spoken language other than English in Victoria and Western Australia, while in regional Victoria it is ranked fourth. Croatian is the second most widely spoken language other than English in Canberra after Italian.[17]

The most widely read Croatian language newspaper in Australia is the Melbourne-based *Hrvatski Vjesnik* (Croatian Herald) which was established in 1983. The *Hrvatski Vjesnik* has an English language supplement, 'The New Generation'. The Sydney-based *Spremnost* (Readiness), begun in 1958, is still published today. *Nova Hrvatska* (New Croatia) is another major Croatian language newspaper in Australia. Throughout Australia in areas where Croatians have established communities there are numerous Croatian radio programs. There is also a Croatian program on the community television channel.

Croatian individuals have contributed to the arts in Australia. Perhaps the most famous is Charles Billich, the official artist of the Australian Grand Prix and Sydney Olympics.[18] The Australian Croatian community has had numerous arts exhibitions, the most successful being *New Beginnings* at the National Gallery of Victoria in

1992. At the Melbourne Immigration Museum in 1999, the Croatian community mounted an exhibition entitled *Croatian Settlement in Victoria, The Untold Story*. This exhibition documented aspects of the history of Croatian settlement in Victoria hitherto unknown, such as Croatian pioneers in Victoria in the 1850s. It was also the starting point of a large research project documenting the history of Croatian settlement in Australia.

Sport

The most obvious area where Croatians have contributed substantially to sport in Australia has been soccer. Croatians' love for soccer helps them bond, and bridges the gap between first and later generations. Since the 1950s the name Croatia has been associated with soccer clubs throughout Australia. The extremely successful Melbourne Knights Soccer Club (formerly Melbourne Croatia and Croatia), whose club grounds are in Sunshine, has been the pride of the Croatian community since 1953. Their greatest achievement was winning the National Soccer League (NSL) grand finals back to back in the 1994–95 and 1995–96 seasons. Sydney United (formerly Sydney Croatia) was the other Croatian community-backed soccer club in the National Soccer League. In the 1990s these two Croatian community-backed clubs were in seven of the ten National Soccer League grand finals. Throughout Australia there are another 37 Croatian soccer clubs. Over 50 international soccer players of Croatian background, nurtured through the ranks of Croatian soccer clubs in Australia, have represented Australia in international competition and/or have played for overseas clubs. The internationally renowned soccer player Mark Viduka is one of the Socceroos' most accomplished players. Glasgow Celtic acquired him for almost $8 million dollars and later he was transferred to Leeds United for over $17 million. Mark Bosnich previously played for Manchester United and Chelsea. Eddie Krnčević was Australia's first successful international soccer player in Continental Europe.[19]

Before Croatian independence, success in soccer was a way for Croatians to publicise the Croatian name and identity within the Australian community. Since the Second World War there have been over 50 soccer clubs in Australia with Croatian names.[20] In 1975 the Croatian Soccer Association of Australia held its first national tournament amongst Croatian soccer teams from all over Australia to select the best team for that year. Since then the tournament has been held annually at various Croatian soccer club venues across Australia. The Croatian soccer tournament was established to promote community ties.[21]

The large participation of migrants from Europe and their descendants in soccer in Australia has given soccer the 'wogball stereotype'. Consequently, soccer officials have required that ethnic names be banned in order to attract a wider audience and more financial support. In 1992 the Australian Soccer Federation banned ethnic names at all levels of soccer, although violence had been almost non-existent in the

Adelaide Croatia soccer team, the first post-Second World War Croatian soccer team in Australia in 1952, the year it was established

years preceding the ban. Some soccer officials unjustifiably claimed that soccer violence was solely associated with ethnic hatreds. In 2004 the Australian Soccer Association introduced many club requirements and high club fees, forcing the Croatian community-backed Melbourne Knights and Sydney United to exit the National Soccer League.

Notwithstanding their love of soccer, Croatians in Australia are passionate about other sports. Individuals of Croatian descent have excelled in Australian Rules football, Rugby, basketball, weight lifting, boxing and canoeing. For example, Glen and Allen Jakovich, Peter Sumich and Ray Gabelich are well-known names in Australian Rules football, Max Krilich captained the Australian Rugby League team in 1982, and Andrew Vlahov represented Australia in basketball for many years. Andrew Bogut and Frank Drmić have also played for the Australian national basketball team in international competitions. Dean Lukin won a gold medal in weight lifting at the 1984 Los Angeles Olympics.[22] Croatian Australians have also participated in seemingly Anglocentric sports such as surf lifesaving and lawn bowls. They were active in surf lifesaving on Sydney's northern beaches (Warriewood, North Narrabeen and Manly), while in Western Australia they have been very successful in lawn bowls.[23] In 2003 the racehorse, Makybe Diva, belonging to Croatian-born tuna fisherman Tony Santic, won the Melbourne Cup, with the horse and jockey dressed in the colours of the Croatian flag and the Southern Cross.[24]

Many Croatian clubs in Australia have *bocce* courts and some have formed

Croatia ten pin bowling team who won the Geelong championship in 1962

Croatian *bocce* clubs which compete in the Bocce Federation of Australia competition.[25] There are several Croatian golf clubs throughout Australia which hold regular golf tournaments, golf being so popular among Croatian Australians that some Croatian golf clubs have long waiting lists for new members.[26] There are also Croatian fishing clubs throughout Australia.

Halls and sporting venues

In Australia, apart from building churches, the Croatian community has spent a considerable amount of time and money building Croatian community halls and sporting venues, normally referred to as 'Croatian clubs'. As we have seen, these venues have helped to ease Croatian migrant isolation due to the language barrier. The clubs were also venues where new Croatian arrivals could seek advice on obtaining temporary accommodation, work, interpreting and translating services. The names of all the Croatian halls and sporting venues in Australia are listed in appendix 3. Included amongst the Melbourne Croatian community halls are the Croatian Australian Association hall in Footscray, the Istra Social Club in Campbellfield and Croatian Catholic Centre halls in Springvale and Sunshine. The Melbourne Knights Soccer Club has premises in Sunshine and the St Albans Saints Soccer Club has its premises in St Albans.

Geelong supports the Australian Croatian National Hall Kardinal Stepinac in Bell Park, the Croatian Community Centre of Geelong Inc. and the Australian Croatian Sporting Centre, North Geelong Soccer Club. The Međimurski Club and Croatian Sporting Club Zagreb are located in the Mildura district, while in regional Victoria, there are also the Croatian club, Dr Ante Starčević, in Wodonga, a Croatian club in Traralgon/Morwell, and the Croatian club, Stjepan Radić, in Ballarat.

Tasmania has only 298 Croatian-born residents. Nevertheless, the Croatian community is active. Hobart has a Croatian church, Croatian club and soccer team, while Launceston has a Croatian social and sporting club. In South Australia the main Croatian club is in Ridleyton, a suburb of Adelaide and there is also a social and sporting club at Gepps Cross. In regional South Australia there are Croatian clubs at Mt Gambier, Whyalla, Port Lincoln and Coober Pedy. Croatians also meet in a hall in the Riverland.

Croatians attending the Marian procession in Adelaide in the early 1950s

In Western Australia the main Croatian club is in North Fremantle. Perth has a Croatian club in Gwelup and there are also Croatian clubs in the Swan Valley, Spearwood and Caversham. Croatians also meet in Carnarvon. In Queensland there are Croatian halls and/or sporting venues at Rocklea in Brisbane, on the Gold Coast, in Cairns and Dimbulah. As in Victoria, there are numerous Croatian clubs in New South Wales. In Sydney there are Croatian clubs in the suburbs of Punchbowl, Edensor Park, St Johns Park, St Marys, Terrey Hills, Blacktown and Liverpool. Regional New South Wales has Croatian clubs in Wollongong and Newcastle, while Canberra has Croatian clubs in Deakin and O'Connor.

*Croatian group in Fremantle in the 'Year of Refugees' concert which was organised by the
Good Neighbour Council in 1960*

Croatian Cardinal Stepinac Day commemorations in the King Tomislav Croatian Club in Sydney in 1985

Croatian national day celebrations in the Croatian club in Deakin, Canberra, in 1969

Prominent Croatian Australians

Croatian Australians have made significant contributions to many aspects of Australian society. To highlight their diverse occupations and the contributions they have made to Australian society, a number of successful Croatian Australians will be described. Senator Natasha Stott Despoja is the former leader of the Australian Democrats. She is the youngest woman to enter the Australian Parliament and was appointed to the Senate in 1995. Senator Stott Despoja's portfolios have included higher education, status of women, science and biotechnology, and treasury. She is particularly popular with younger voters. Her father, Mario Dešpoja, opened the first Croatian 'Embassy' in Canberra in the late 1970s to bring to public attention Croatia's right to independence and to highlight that Croatians were a distinct ethnic group and not Yugoslav.[27]

Ljiljanna Ravlich, Member for East Metropolitan Region, is the first Croatian-born woman elected to the Legislative Council of Western Australia. Ravlich was born in Split and migrated to Australia with her family in 1963 at the age of five. She is Labor's spokesperson for public sector management, higher education, employment and training.[28] Jaye Radisich is another Labor parliamentarian of Croatian descent in Western Australia. She is the Member for Swan Hills in the Legislative Assembly of Western Australia.[29]

Robert Vojaković, who was born in Zagreb, received an Order of Australia Member award (AM) for his service to community health, particularly through his work with the Asbestos Disease Society in Western Australia. He highlighted and advanced the cause of people (particularly the Wittenoom victims) suffering from asbestos-related diseases such as malignant mesothelioma. Vojaković was instrumental in developing processes whereby compensation has now been obtained for more than 600 sufferers and their families.[30]

Ralph Sarich, whose parents came from Croatia, received an Order of Australia Officer award (AO) for his service to engineering. He developed the orbital engine and orbital combustion process that is based on a redesign of the two-stroke engine using direct gasoline injection. It is believed the Orbital Combustion Process Technology applied to two-stoke engines in commercial production will result in huge fuel savings. Sarich has amassed a fortune of $779 million and is the fourteenth richest man in Australia. He made his fortune by selling his share of the Orbital Engine Corporation and subsequently investing the profit in real estate.[31]

Numerous other Croatian Australians have been awarded an Order of Australia Medal for their contributions to various industries including: transport (Slavko (Jim) Bošnjak), wine (John Kosovich), and chicken meat (Lennard Brajkovich). Ljerka Drapač, Milan Karamarko, Vinko Romanik, Frank Hesman, Vanda Podravac, Michael Furjanić, Nedjelko Marunčić, Dr Tomislav Gavranić and Dr Norman Marinovich are all recipients of Order of Australia medals for their services to the Croatian community and/or other migrants. Dragana Brkljaca was awarded the Centenary Medal for service to the Croatian community.

Croatian descendants have also been prominent in the arts. For example, Eric Bana is a well-known actor who was awarded the Australian Film Institute (AFI) best actor award in 2000 for his performance in *Chopper* (2000). He recently starred in the Hollywood movies, *Black Hawk Down* (2001), *The Hulk* (2003) and *Troy* (2004).[32] Director Robert Luketic's debut feature film, *Legally Blonde* (2001), was number one at the box office in the week it opened in the United States and made $40 million in the first three days of its release.[33] Simone Young is an international musical conductor. She received the Young Australian of the Year award in 1986 and an Order of Australia Member award (AM). Gregory Yurisich was an opera and concert singer for the Australian Opera.

There have been Mayors of Croatian descent in Sunshine and Brimbank in Victoria, and Kalgoorlie and Spearwood in Western Australia. Similarly, there have been numerous academics of Croatian descent who have taught at Australian universities. Second- and third-generation Croatian Australians are continuing to make their mark in Australian society.

*Melbourne's Croatian ethnic school picnic and sports competition's winning team
Clifton Hill in 1984*

Victorian School of Languages Croatian language high school students and teachers from Geelong attending the exhibition,
Croatian Settlement in Victoria, The Untold Story, *at the Immigration Museum in Melbourne in 1999*

Croatian community float and participants in the Blue Gum Festival in Hobart (left side in 1970 and right side in 1972)

Croatian community float at the Centenary of Federation celebrations in Melbourne in 2001

Canberra-based folkloric group Croatia performing at the National Multicultural Festival in Canberra in 2001

Adelaide-based Croatian folkloric group Lenek and the Croatian community float at the Fringe Festival opening parade in Adelaide in 2002

Geelong-based Croatian women's charity society Klanjateljice Presvetom Srcu Isusovom (Worshippers of the Sacred Heart of Jesus) in 1977

Croatian Catholics in an Ascension Day procession in Salisbury, Brisbane

Sydney-based Croatian folkloric group Jadran (Adriatic) with the former Prime Minister Bob Hawke at the old Parliament House in Canberra in 1985

Opening of the Cardinal Stepinac village residential aged care facility in Sydney by the Prime Minister John Howard in 1999. It was established and built by the Croatian community in Sydney.

Croatian rally in Melbourne against the Yugoslav communist regime in 1978

Croatian rally in Melbourne in the 1990s calling for Australia to recognise Croatia

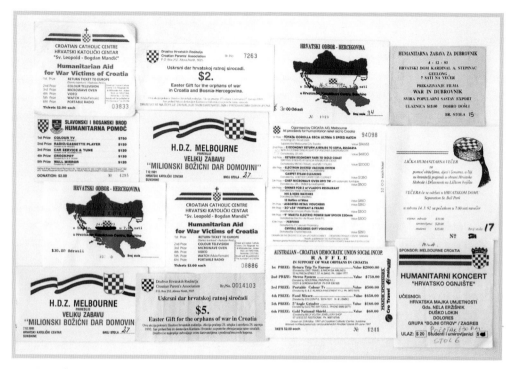

Examples of Croatian community dance and raffle tickets used to collect funds for humanitarian aid for Croatia in the 1990s, during the war of aggression against Croatia

Brisbane-based folkloric group Croatia at the Brisbane Expo in 1988

Sydney Croatia soccer team on tour in Indonesia in 1983 together with an Indonesian team

*Students learning Croatian on Croatian Day at Holy Family primary school in Geelong where Croatian is
taught as part of the curriculum and where 43 per cent of the students are of Croatian descent*

Negative stereotypes attached to Croatians

The Yugoslav Communist regime invested considerable effort to blacken the Croatian name in order to discredit Croatians' right to self-determination. Some Croatians in the diaspora who were seen as a political threat to the Yugoslav Communist regime were assassinated by Yugoslav secret service agents (UDBA).[34] From the 1960s Yugoslav diplomats and agents in Australia perpetuated the myth that Croatian terrorists were operating in Australia. They manipulated the media and leftist politicians to sensationalise the Croatian terrorist threat; for example, left-wing Labor parliamentarian, Dr Jim Cairns, who was closely tied to the Yugoslav Settlers' Association, continually accused Croatians of terrorist activities in Australia and slandered the Croatian community in parliament without producing evidence. The Australian Communist party also published and distributed anti-Croatian propaganda.[35]

Yugoslav diplomats and the media blamed so called 'Croatian terrorists' for a series of bombings in Australia in the 1960s and early 1970s (the Yugoslav Consulate bombings and Yugoslav travel agency bombings). These bombings resulted in property damage but no loss of life. However, Croatians never claimed responsibility nor were arrested for the bombings. Even though there was no evidence to prove Croatian involvement, the media continually portrayed images of Croatians as terrorists. To escape the relentless negative stereotyping of all Croatians as terrorists by the media, some Croatians in Australia began to identify themselves as Yugoslavs while others disassociated themselves from other Croatians.[36]

The Whitlam Labor Government subsequently falsely accused Croatians of terrorist activities in Australia for political gain, claiming that the previous Liberal Government had protected and helped Croatian terrorists. These accusations were accompanied by a slanderous media frenzy against Croatians in Australia. In 1973, a couple of days before the visit of the Prime Minister of Yugoslavia to Australia, Attorney-General Senator Lionel Murphy along with Commonwealth Police raided the offices of ASIO claiming they were looking for hidden files on Croatian terrorists. In fact, the Labor Government was showing its support for the Yugoslav regime and reinforcing its control over ASIO.[37]

The following month Senator Murphy organised raids on the private homes of Croatians in Victoria and New South Wales who, he claimed, were suspected of terrorist activities. The Croatians' civil rights were violated as the police had not produced warrants in many of the raids. No evidence was found to support Murphy's claims of Croatian terrorist activities in Australia.[38] In 1973, under pressure from the opposition and the public, a Senate Select Committee on Civil Rights of Migrant Australians was established which subsequently found that infringement of civil rights had occurred and that the Croatians had been discriminated against by Murphy and members of the police force.[39]

Croatians demonstrating in Geelong against communism in 1953. The sign reads 'Croatia country of Cardinal Stepinac'. This demonstration was also attended by Hungarians, Poles and other migrant groups against communism

Yugoslav agents helped frame six Croatians in Australia, known as the 'Croatian Six', who were arrested in 1979 and falsely accused of plotting terrorist activities. After a lengthy trial in 1981, they were found guilty on alleged unsigned verbal confessions and statements from a Yugoslav secret service agent, Vico Virkez, who was known to the police. They were each sentenced to 15 years imprisonment. In July 1989, *The Australian* published articles detailing how the 'Croatian Six' were framed by the Yugoslav secret service. By this time however, all the Croatians had been released. *The Australian*, through an ASIO source, also revealed that high-ranking public servants in the Department of Foreign Affairs, the Department of the Prime Minister and the Department of Defence were informants/agents for the Yugoslav secret service. In 1991 the ABC's *Four Corners* television program broadcast a special report in which they interviewed the Yugoslav agent who had framed the 'Croatian Six' and presented further evidence confirming they had been framed.[40]

On 27 November 1988 Joseph Tokić, a 16-year-old student, was shot in the neck by a Yugoslav consulate official while participating in a peaceful demonstration outside the Yugoslav consulate in Sydney. Tokić was among 1500 protesters calling for Croatian independence from Yugoslavia. The Australian Government subsequently ordered the Yugoslav consulate to be closed, and several Yugoslav diplomatic staff with their families were expelled.[41] The shooting showed the Yugoslav Communist regime in a negative light in the Australian media.

The negative stereotyping of Croatians as terrorists, raids on the Croatian community in Australia and lack of public sympathy caused many Croatians to become withdrawn and distrustful of the Australian media, police and government, which resulted in a slowdown in assimilation, making it extremely difficult during that time for Croatians to be accepted in the wider Australian community.

Struggle for national recognition

Since the Second World War, the Croatian community in Australia had struggled to be recognised as an ethnic entity separate from Yugoslavs, and for the Croatian language to be recognised as a separate language. Prior to the 1980s, Croatians did not have access to the Australian Government-funded, ethno-specific migrant services provided to other ethnic groups. Croatians usually boycotted the government-sponsored Yugoslav migrant services as they believed that the government should provide separate services for the large Croatian community in Australia. As a result, Croatians generally went without government assistance and formed their own networks which ultimately disadvantaged the community by isolating it from mainstream Australian society.

By the 1980s when the government gave partial recognition to Croatians as a separate ethnic group, Croatians were still not receiving their government funding entitlements. For example, many government departments used the Australian Census as a guide when allocating funding to individual migrant groups. Prior to 1996 however, the census did not record Croatians as a separate group, making funding almost impossible to access.

Croatians also campaigned for the Croatian language to be recognised by the government. Croatians believed that the Serbo-Croatian language curriculum was politically oriented, forcing the Croatian community to establish its own Croatian language schools and even publish its own teaching materials.[42] The Croatian Studies Foundation was also formed to promote the study of Croatian language and literature. In 1983 Croatian was introduced at tertiary level at Macquarie University, signifying acceptance of the Croatian language by the Australian authorities.

From the 1950s until Croatian independence in 1992, the Croatian community in Australia organised demonstrations against the Yugoslav Communist regime. These demonstrations signified Croatians' desire for Croatia's secession from Yugoslavia and hence acknowledgment of their own history, language and culture.

Croatian Australians opened a Croatian 'Embassy' in Canberra in 1977 in an attempt to direct public attention to Croatia's right to self-determination and the rights of Croatians in Australia to be recognised separately from those of Yugoslavs.

The first Croatian 'Embassy' in Canberra in the late 1970s established to promote the Croatian independence cause

The charge d'affaires (ambassador's deputy) of the Croatian embassy, Mario Dešpoja, who had the support of the Croatian community, insisted that the government treat Croatians in Australia as a separate ethnic group. The Croatian embassy affair from 1977 to 1979 gave positive media exposure to Croatians in Australia and the Croatian independence cause. The Croatian embassy was an embarrassment for Yugoslavia. Even though the embassy was eventually made illegal by special government legislation (the *Diplomatic and Consular Mission Act*), it brought public attention to Croatian issues and forced the government to acknowledge Croatians as a separate ethnic group.

Descendants of Croatian migrants in Australia also lobbied to attract public attention to Croatia's right to self-determination. Along with many other organisations and groups, the Croatian Students' Association was involved in fundraising, lobbying and media awareness. They sent letters to Australian parliamentarians, organised lectures and attended demonstrations. In 1991 and 1992 after Croatians voted for independence, the Croatian community held rallies across Australia calling for the Australian Government to recognise Croatia. In Victoria the rallies were typically held on the steps of the Victorian Parliament. In 1991 the Croatian

Croatian community marching through the streets of Sydney in 1991 calling for the Australian Government to recognise Croatia

community also held a candlelight vigil for peace in Croatia at the Melbourne City Square. On 31 August 1991, a rally was held on the steps of Parliament House in Canberra where over 30,000 people called for the Australian Government to recognise Croatia.[43]

Croatian community at the Croatian club in Deakin preparing to walk to Parliament House in Canberra to call for the Australian Government to recognise Croatia. Over 30,000 people attended this rally in 1991 which is the largest number of Croatians gathered at a single event in Australia

A forum, 'Croatian Democracy and Independence', organised by the Croatian community in Victoria was held at the Southern Cross Hotel in Melbourne in 1991. The forum was used to inform several guest parliamentarians and the Australian media of the situation in Croatia and to promote recognition of Croatia. Many Australian parliamentarians became members of the Parliamentarians for Croatia and Slovenia group which promoted the recognition of these countries.

During the early 1990s the Croatian community throughout Australia sent humanitarian aid to Croatian war victims in Croatia and Bosnia-Herzegovina. In addition to donations and raffles, various dances and discos were held by the Croatian community to raise money for humanitarian aid. In 1991 and 1992 the Croatian community organised and supported the sale of the pop song, 'Stop the War in Croatia' which reached number seven on the Australian national charts where it remained for seven consecutive weeks. It reached number two in the New South Wales charts. The proceeds from the sale of this tape raised over $120,000, which was donated to a hospital in Zagreb to purchase medical equipment to help victims of the war. A walkathon at Albert Park Lake in Melbourne raised over $30,000 for Croatian war orphans. From 1991 to 1994, the Australian Croatian Youth Organisation in Sydney collected over $250,000, subsequently used to sponsor 106 Croatian war invalids and children. Their main fund-raising activity was an annual three-day Cro-Aid open-air concert and festival.

Croatian celebration

After a long struggle and a war to defend its borders, Croatian independence was recognised on 15 January 1992. In the same year Croatia became a member of the United Nations. This recent establishment of Croatia as a sovereign state was an important turning point in Croatian history, and the Croatian community in Australia participated in the global celebrations marking the beginning of a new future for Croatia and Croatians worldwide. After the Australian Government recognised Croatia, the Croatian community throughout Australia gathered on the steps of the various state parliament buildings to thank Australia for recognition. Since independence a number of Australian Croatians have returned to Croatia to help rebuild the country, and now several Australian Croatians who live in Croatia are employed by Croatia's Ministry of Foreign Affairs. A few of these have become Croatian Consuls. Other Australian Croatians work in Croatia's Ministries of Immigration and Finance and the Hrvatska Matica Iseljenika (Croatian Heritage Foundation). Australian Croatians who live in Croatia have formed the Croatian Australian Association (Hrvatsko-australsko društvo) and the Croatian National Cricket Team, 'Zagreb Cricket Club'.

Since Croatia's independence, Australia and Croatia have begun to develop ties. To strengthen relations, Croatian Consulates were opened in Melbourne, Perth and Sydney, and the Croatian President visited Australia in 1995. The opening of a Croatian Embassy in Canberra and an Australian Embassy in Zagreb signifies that these two countries intend to strengthen their relationship. Interestingly, the Croatian Embassy in Canberra was built through donations from the Croatian community in Australia.

The community recognises with pride the descendants of the Australian Croatian-born population who have been successful in public life – the soccer star Mark Viduka, Senator Natasha Stott Despoja, Archbishop Matthew Beovich and inventor/businessman Ralph Sarich. The large Croatian community in Australia is now well established and looks forward to a bright future in multicultural Australia.

Future prospects for the Croatian community

The establishment of a Croatian independent state has brought full recognition to the Croatian community in Australia. In addition to Croatian embassies and consulates established by the Croatian Government with the assistance of Australian Croatians, various other Croatian institutions have been formed by Australian Croatians, for example, the Croatian Community Credit Union Ltd and Australian Croatian Chamber of Commerce. Apart from providing competitive interest rates and lower fees than banks, the Croatian Community Credit Union injects money back into the Croatian community. For example, half of each loan applicant's establishment fee can be donated to an Australian Croatian community organisation of the applicant's choice. The credit union also sponsors various Croatian community projects. The Australian Croatian Chamber of Commerce promotes bilateral trade between Croatia and Australia. To date their main achievement has been the production of a guide to Croatian businesses in Australia.

In Western Australia the Croatian Cultural Week is held annually and concurrently with the Fremantle Festival. During the week of the festival the Australian public is provided with opportunities to view Croatian films, exhibitions, theatre and folkloric performances in various venues throughout Fremantle. The Croatian city of Korčula and Fremantle are now officially sister cities as are Split and Cockburn. In addition, the Croatian Food, Wine and Tourism Festival has been held in capital cities of Australia to promote Croatian food and wine.

Since Croatian independence, there has been some complacency in participation in Croatian community activities which can be partly attributed to an ageing population. Many previously active Croatians are exhausted after lobbying for Croatian independence and collecting humanitarian aid during the recent war and have left others to continue running the Croatian clubs and organisations. Nevertheless, descendants of Croatian migrants are now taking up more prominent positions in Croatian clubs. For example, the board of Melbourne Knights (formerly Melbourne Croatia) now mainly comprises young second-generation Croatian Australians.

With well-established Croatian clubs and Croatian Catholic centres throughout Australia and second-generation Croatian Australians taking a more active role in club activities the future remains bright for the Croatian community in Australia.

Table of Croatian Pioneers in Australia

Appendix 1 lists all the known Croatian pioneers in Australia, their birthplace, year of arrival, and place of residence and occupation in Australia until 1890. When a Croatian pioneer was known to maintain contacts with other Croatians in Australia but the town or region of birth was unknown a probable birthplace was obtained from the *Leksik Prezimena Socijalističke Republike Hrvatske* (1976) which lists all the towns in Croatia where each surname is found. These probable birthplaces are placed in brackets in the table and are limited to coastal Croatia since the overwhelming majority of Croatian pioneers in Australia came from the Croatian coastal regions and islands. However, it should be noted that many of these Croatian surnames are also common in inland regions of Croatia. Croatian pioneers from the Kotor district were also included in the table since in the nineteenth century Croatians constituted over 70 per cent of Kotor's population and Kotor was part of Croatia until the Second World War.

Name	Croatian version	Birthplace	Arrival	Residence	State	Occupation
Abbott (Vranizan) Vincent	Vranjican Vicko	Island of Hvar – Starigrad	1875	Murchinson	WA	Miner
Aceglav Nicholas	Jaceglav Nikola	Kotor	1877	Sydney	NSW	Fishmonger
Adam Simone	Adam Šimun	Island of Zlarin	1854	Hepburn	VIC	Farmer
Albich Laurentz	Albić Lovre	Island of Lošinj	1855	Tabulum	NSW	
Albich Peter	Albić Petar	Island of Lošinj	1864	Crooked River	VIC	Miner
Alic Alfred	Alić Alfred	(Pag, Žirje, Zadar, Rijeka)		Port Pirie	SA	Seaman
Andricevic Franc	Andričević Franjo	(Pelješac, Split, Krk, Rijeka)	1888	Sydney	NSW	
Angelinawich Antonio	Anđelinović Ante	Island of Hvar	1855	Port Adelaide	SA	Seaman
Anich Marco	Anić Marko	Dubrovnik	1882	Melbourne	VIC	Seaman
Anicich Simon	Aničić Šimun	Lovranska Draga	1887	Newcastle	NSW	Labourer
Anticevich Antonio	Antičević Ante	(Pelješac, Brač, Lastovo)	1880	Kingsborough	QLD	Miner
Anticevich Mato	Antičević Mato	Dalmatia	1888	Merredin	WA	Woodcutter
Anticevich Nicholas	Antičević Nikola	Pelješac	1880	Sydney	NSW	Fishmonger
Anticevich Nicolo	Antičević Nikola	Dalmatia	1861	Woods Point	VIC	Publican
Antich Cosmo	Antić Kuzma	Bakar – Mirca	1857	Crooked River	VIC	Miner
Antivich Nicolo	—— Nikola		1863		VIC	

Name	Croatian version	Birthplace	Arrival	Residence	State	Occupation
Antoch Antonia	—— Ante		1866	Melbourne	VIC	Seaman
Antoncich Dominico	Antončić Dominik	Island of Lošinj – Mali Lošinj	1875	Point Cloates	WA	Seaman
Antoncish G	Antončić	(Island of Lošinj)	1889	Sydney	NSW	
Antoniwich John	Antunović Ivan	Pelješac – Janjina	1874	Echuca	VIC	Miner
Antonowich Antonio	Antunović Ante	Makarska	1855	Bendigo	VIC	Miner
Antonowich Antonio	Antunović Ante	(Makarska, Pelješac, Korčula)	1881	Melbourne	VIC	Patient
Arnerich Frank	Arnerić Franjo	Island of Brač	1876	Melbourne	VIC	Miner
Arnerich Paulo	Arnerić Pavao	Island of Brač	1860	Woods Point	VIC	Miner
Augustinvich Michele	Agustinović Miho	Pelješac – Trpanj	1866	Buckland	VIC	Miner
Aviani Nicolo	Aviani Nikola	Island of Brač – Milna	1882	Melbourne	VIC	Miner
B Giuseppe	—— Josip	Dalmatia	1856	Castlemaine	VIC	Brewer
Babare Matteo	Babare Mate	Island of Hvar – Starigrad	1885	Sydney	NSW	Carpenter
Babarovich Antonio	Babarović Ante	Island of Brač – Milna	1866	Sydney	NSW	Labourer
Bacchich John	Bačić Ivan	(Zadar, Rab, Split, Opatija)	1883	Melbourne	VIC	
Baccich Miho	Bačić Miho	Dubrovnik	1875	Point Cloates	WA	Seaman
Baillich Matteo	—— Mate		1875	Wedderburn	VIC	Miner
Baladinivinsh Nicolo	—— Nikola		1854	Melbourne	VIC	Labourer
Barbalich Mattio	Barbalić Mate	Rijeka	1886	Sydney	NSW	Seaman
Barbaric Stephen	Barbarić Stjepan	(Hvar, Split, Crikvenica, Zaostrog)	1872	Died at sea	NSW	
Baric-Ravich Peter	Barić Petar	(Zadar, Split, Rijeka, Iž)	1885	Sydney	NSW	Boarding house keeper
Barry Peter	—— Petar	Island of Lošinj	1878	Newcastle	NSW	Seaman
Basica Stijepan	Bašica Stjepan	Island of Mljet – Babino Polje	1879	Gulgong	NSW	Miner
Bassich Antonio	Bašić Ante	(Split, Zadar, Pašman)	1857	Crooked River	VIC	Miner
Bathols George	Vidulić Jure	Island of Lošinj – Mali Lošinj	1865	Melbourne	VIC	Carpenter
Bautovich Joseph	Bautović Josip	Dubrovnik	1865	Swan Hill	VIC	Labourer
Beban Steffano	Beban Stjepan	Island of Zlarin	1859	Woods Point	VIC	Miner
Belanich Mark	Belanić Marko	Island of Lošinj – Veli Lošinj	1853	Yandoit	VIC	Miner
Belin	Belin	Island of Mljet – Prožura	1879	Gulgong	NSW	Miner
Bendich Anthony	—— Ante	Rijeka	1879		QLD	
Bennis John	Benić Ivan	Makarska	1858	Melbourne	VIC	Seaman
Benovitch Mark	—— Marko	Rijeka	1863	Melbourne	VIC	
Benussi Christopher	Benussi Kristo	Rovinj	1856	Creswick	VIC	Miner
Benussi Matteo	Benussi Mate	Rovinj	1854	Daylesford	VIC	Baker
Beovich Mark	Beović Marko	Island of Brač – Supetar		Melbourne	VIC	
Beovich Matthew	Beović Mate	Island of Brač – Supetar	1884	Melbourne	VIC	Grocer
Berber Ivan	Berber Ivan	Lisac	1882	McIntyre	VIC	Miner
Bercich Vincenzo	Berčić Vicko	Rijeka	1855	Stawell	VIC	Storekeeper
Beriza Stephen	Berica Stjepan	(Island of Hvar)	1877	McIntyre	VIC	Miner
Bernecich Frank	Bernečić Franjo	(Opatija)	1889	Sydney	NSW	Labourer
Bersica Seraphin	Beršić Serafin	Island of Hvar – Jelsa	1855	Mooroopna	VIC	Vigneron
Bersich A	Beršić	(Vodnjan, Pula)	1856		VIC	
Bilic Ivan	Bilić Ivan	Pelješac – Oskorušno	1890	Sydney	NSW	
Bilic Martino	Bilić Martin	(Šibenik, Trogir, Split, Pelješac)	1888	Sydney	NSW	
Billich Ignatio	Bilić Ignatije	Trogir	1854	Wedderburn	VIC	Miner

Name	Croatian version	Birthplace	Arrival	Residence	State	Occupation
Billich Jacob	Bilić Jakob	Dalmatia	1870	Sydney	NSW	Seaman
Billich John	Bilić Ivan	(Šibenik, Trogir, Split, Pelješac)	1888	Sydney	NSW	Labourer
Bircovitch Giavonni	—— Ivan		1871	Heathcote	VIC	Miner
Bisculch Nicholas	—— Nikola		1889		VIC	
Blasevich Franc	Blasević Franjo	(Poreč, Vabriga, Rijeka)	1888	Sydney	NSW	
Blessich Antonio	Blešić Ante	Rovinj	1872	Melbourne	VIC	Seaman
Blossage Gaspar	—— Gašpar	Rijeka	1857	Huntly	VIC	Miner
Bogden Michael	Bogdan Miho	Dubrovnik	1873	Gulgong	NSW	Miner
Bogerstich Lawrence	—— Lovre	Dalmatia	1866	Kiandra	NSW	Miner
Bogovich Antonio	Bogović Ante	(Krk, Zadar)	1858	Yandoit	VIC	Miner
Bogovich Paolo	Bogović Pavao	(Krk, Zadar)	1888	Melbourne	VIC	Labourer
Boljan Antonio	Boljan Ante	(Šibenik)	1887	Melbourne	VIC	
Bolmarcich Mattio	Bolmarčić Mate	Island of Cres	1882	Melbourne	VIC	Labourer
Bonacich Henry	Bonačić Henrik	Island of Brač	1860	Bendigo	VIC	Miner
Bonacich Nicholas	Bonačić Nikola	Island of Brač – Milna	1858	Port Adelaide	SA	Seaman
Bonnitch Nicolas	—— Nikola	Dubrovnik	1856	Hobart	TAS	Seaman
Borac Daimo	Borac	(Rijeka)	1888	Sydney	NSW	
Borcech Gasper	Borčić Gašpar	Rijeka	1861	Murchison	VIC	Miner
Borcich John	Borčić Ivan	Rijeka – Draga	1861	Whroo	VIC	Miner
Bosanic Matthew	Bosanić Mate	(Pula)	1875	Gulgong	NSW	
Boscovich A	Bošković	(Brač, Split, Dubrovnik, Baćina)	1875	Wattle Flat	NSW	
Boscovich M	Bošković	(Brač, Split, Dubrovnik, Baćina)	1863		VIC	
Bosinna Antonio	Bosina Ante		1856	Melbourne	VIC	Fisherman
Bozovich Nichlis	Božović Nikola	(Korčula, Dubrovnik)	1890		VIC	
Bragato Joseph	Bragato Josip	Island of Lošinj – Mali Lošinj	1873	Nambour	QLD	Engineer
Bragato Romeo	Bragato	Island of Lošinj – Mali Lošinj	1888	Rutherglen	VIC	Vigneron
Bragulin Andrea	Bragulin Andrija	Topolo	1882	Melbourne	VIC	
Braicovich John	Brajković Ivan	Herceg Novi	1884	Sydney	NSW	Fishmonger
Brajevich Nicolo	Brajević Nikola	Konavle	1875	Point Cloates	WA	Seaman
Branie Joseph	Branić Josip	Rijeka	1877	Brisbane	QLD	Labourer
Breskovich M	Brešković	(Brač, Split, Dubrovnik)	1888	Melbourne	VIC	
Brown George	—— Jure	Pula	1884		NSW	Stoker
Brown John	—— Ivan	Zadar	1857	Lower Temora	NSW	Miner
Brsiza Steffano	Brzica Stjepan	Island of Mljet	1882	Buckland	VIC	Miner
Bucich Fortunato	Bučić Srećko	Rijeka	1875	Point Cloates	WA	Seaman
Budessa Luka	Budeša Luka	(Island of Olib)	1885	Sydney	NSW	Fishmonger
Budinich Antonio	Budinić Ante	Island of Lošinj	1852	Ballarat	VIC	Miner
Budinich Nicholas	Budinić Nikola	(Island of Lošinj)		Melbourne	VIC	Fisherman
Budmich Domingo	Budinić Dominik	(Island of Lošinj)	1886	Melbourne	VIC	Seaman
Bujacich D	Bujačić	(Island of Premuda)	1862		VIC	
Bujan Simon	Bujan Šimun	(Rijeka)	1872		NSW	Farmer
Bulic Jure	Bulić Jure	(Split, Zadar, Brač, Hvar)	1888	Sydney	NSW	Seaman
Bundara Antonio	Bundara Antun	Pelješac – Žuljana	1863	Portarlington	VIC	Fishmonger
Bundara John	Bundara Ivan	Pelješac – Žuljana	1860	Melbourne	VIC	Grocer
Buntilich Stefan	Buntjelić Stjepan	(Dubrovnik, Rijeka)	1888	Sydney	NSW	
Burazin Ivan	Burazin Ivan	Cista Velika Imotski	1890	Kamballie	WA	Miner

Name	Croatian version	Birthplace	Arrival	Residence	State	Occupation
Burich John	Burić Ivan	Island of Vis	1878	Adelaide	SA	Publican
Busanich Francisco	Busanić Franjo	(Island of Lošinj)	1856	Ballarat	VIC	
Busanich Mark	Busanić Marko	Island of Lošinj	1855	Yandoit	VIC	Miner
Bushick John	Bušić Ivan	(Imotski)	1861	Inglewood	VIC	Miner
Bussanich Matteo	Busanić Mate	(Island of Lošinj)	1860	Grenfell	NSW	Miner
Buzolich Antonio	Buzolić Ante	Island of Brač – Milna	1855	Melbourne	VIC	Publican
Buzolich Fioravanti	Buzolić Cvjetko	(Brač, Hvar, Split)	1878	McIntyre	VIC	Miner
Buzolich John	Buzolić Ivan	(Brač, Hvar, Split)	1877	McIntyre	VIC	Miner
Buzzi Nicola	—— Nikola	Rovinj		Port Pirie	SA	Miner
Caberic Mate	Čaberić Mate	Pelješac – Oskorušno	1857			
Caberica Damjanovic Nikola	Čaberica Damjanović Nikola	Pelješac – Ruskovići	1880	Townsville	QLD	Miner
Cabrich Nicolo	Čabrić Nikola	(Split)	1861	Epsom	VIC	
Cacich John	Kačić, Čačić Ivan	Dalmatia	1862	Melbourne	VIC	Miner
Cadic Oekr	Kadić	(Split)	1888		VIC	
Calafatovich Joseph	Kalafatović Josip	Pelješac	1879	Sydney	NSW	Labourer
Calafatovich Joseph	Kalafatović Josip	Pelješac – Janjina	1889	Echuca	VIC	Fishmonger
Candor Andreas	Candor Andrija	(Rijeka)	1882	Sandgate	QLD	Labourer
Carey Andrew	—— Andrija	Island of Krk	1886	Rockhampton	QLD	Labourer
Carles Dominick	—— Dominik	Island of Lošinj	1877		NSW	Bushman
Carson Fortunato	Corsano Srećko	Island of Lošinj	1867	Grafton	NSW	Miner
Carstellovich Gregorio	Krstulović Grgur	(Split)	1880	Sydney	NSW	Bushman
Carstilovich A	Krstulović	(Split)	1857	Ballarat	VIC	
Cartis Radin Terence Frank	—— Franjo	Island of Cres	1889	Launceston	TAS	Sail maker
Castel Sabaz Giovanni	Sabaz Ivan	Umag	1878	Port Adelaide	SA	Seaman
Catarinich Antonio	Katarinić Ante	Island of Krk – Malinska	1887	Melbourne	VIC	Seaman
Catarinich Joseph	Katarinić Josip	Island of Krk – Malinska	1870	Melbourne	VIC	Seaman
Cavarcevich Matthew	Kovačević Mate	(Hvar, Split, Dubrovnik)		Bundaberg	QLD	Farmer
Celovich Constantino	Čelović Konstatin	Kotor	1886	Wedderburn	VIC	Miner
Celovich Stefano	Čelović Stjepan	Kotor	1853	Wedderburn	VIC	Miner
Cerezin Stjepan	Ćerezin Stjepan	Pelješac – Viganj		Sydney	NSW	
Cettina Francis	Cettina Franjo	Rijeka	1883	North Botany	NSW	Labourer
Chernich Vincent	Cernić Vicko	Rijeka	1876	Sydney	NSW	Storekeeper
Chillivish Simon	—— Šimun		1854	Melbourne	VIC	Seaman
Chiorco Vincent	—— Vicko	Kotor – Perast	1859	Mount Morgan	QLD	Miner
Cibic Peter	Cibić Petar	Rijeka		Adelaide	SA	Labourer
Cibich Pietro	Cibić Petar	(Rijeka)	1883	Melbourne	VIC	Miner
Cibich Valentine	Cibić Valentin	Rijeka – Draga	1862		NSW	Miner
Cibilic John	Cibilić Ivan	(Pelješac)		Beaconsfield	QLD	Engine driver
Cietiovich (Catovich) Simeone	—— Šimun		1860		VIC	
Citanich Bartolomeo	Kitanić Bartul	(Split)	1868	Graytown	VIC	Miner
Civtorch Giuseppe	—— Josip	Island of Zlarin	1882	Melbourne	VIC	Miner
Claric Giov	Klarić Ivan	(Crikvenica, Split, Dubrovnik)	1888	Sydney	NSW	Labourer
Clarich Elia	Klarić Ilija	(Crikvenica, Split, Dubrovnik)	1884		VIC	

Name	Croatian version	Birthplace	Arrival	Residence	State	Occupation
Clech Thomas	—— Tomilsav	Rijeka	1877	Cawell	SA	Farmer
Colich John	Kolić Ivan	(Dubrovnik, Pula, Split)		Goulburn	NSW	
Coloper Stephen	Kaloper Stjepan	Island of Zlarin	1853	Portarlington	VIC	Fisherman
Comandich A	Komandić	(Rijeka)	1888		VIC	
Comandich Jacomina	Komandić	(Rijeka)	1888	Townsville	QLD	Domestic duties
Comandich John	Komandić Ivan	(Rijeka)	1888	Townsville	QLD	Seaman
Constatine John	—— Ivan	Rovinj	1876	Launceston	TAS	Labourer
Copenech Fran	—— Franjo		1889	Sydney	NSW	Seaman
Cossack Antonio	Kosić Ante	(Krk, Rijeka)	1858		VIC	Sail maker
Costa Carlo	Kosta Karlo	Dubrovnik	1875	Point Cloates	WA	Seaman
Cosulich Achille	Kozulić	(Lošinj, Rijeka)	1881	Sydney	NSW	
Covacevich Giovanni	Kovačević Ivan	(Hvar, Split, Dubrovnik)	1857	Castlemaine	VIC	
Covacevich Mitchell	Kovačević Miho	(Hvar, Split, Dubrovnik)	1862	Castlemaine	VIC	Miner
Covacevich Prospero	Kovačević Prospero	Dalmatia	1858	Port Adelaide	SA	Seaman
Covacevich Vincent	Kovačević Vicko	(Hvar, Split, Dubrovnik)	1854	Melbourne	VIC	
Covacich Peter	Kovačić Petar	(Omiš, Rijeka)	1885		VIC	
Craglitto Nicola	Craglietto Nikola	Island of Cres	1856	Waanyarra	VIC	Miner
Cravarovich Matteo	Kravarević Mate	Dubrovačka Rijeka – Mokošica	1866	Whroo	VIC	Miner
Crewechich	Krivičić	(Lošinj, Cres, Buzet)	1861	McIntyre	VIC	Miner
Cristicerich Vicenzo	Krstulović Vicko	Split	1863	Epsom	VIC	
Cristilovich Gregory	Krstulović Grgur	(Split)	1863	Costerfield	VIC	Miner
Crusich Anton	Krušić Anton	(Rijeka, Pula)	1887		VIC	Labourer
Cucel Frank	Kućel Franjo	Volosko	1882	Melbourne	VIC	Restaurateur
Cucel John	Kućel Ivan	Volosko	1887	Melbourne	VIC	Grocer
Cunich Antony	Kunić Ante	Pelješac – Janjina	1883	Parks	NSW	Farmer
Cunich Baldo	Kunić Baldo	Pelješac – Janjina	1883	Young	NSW	Farmer
Curajanovich	Kurjanović	(Dubrovnik)	1862		VIC	
Curliza Giovanni	Čurlica Ivan	Dubrovnik	1882	Wedderburn	VIC	Miner
Curlizza Jacob	Čurlica Jakob	Dubrovačka Rijeka – Mokošica	1867	Sydney	NSW	Labourer
Curtoric Saverio	Kurtović	Dubrovnik	1883	Sydney	NSW	Fisherman
Cussianovich Peter	Kusijanović Petar	Dubrovačka Rijeka – Mokošica	1862	Crooked River	VIC	Miner
Cutovich Nicholas	—— Nikola		1878	Inglewood	VIC	Labourer
Czar John	Car Ivan	Island of Lošinj – Mali Lošinj	1883	Port Adelaide	SA	Seaman
Dabawick Speer	Dabović Špiro	(Rijeka, Zadar, Kotor)	1864		VIC	Miner
Dabovich Christopher	Dabović Kristo	Kotor – Kostanjica	1855	Port Lincoln	SA	Seaman
Dabowick Antonio	Dabović Ante	(Rijeka, Zadar, Kotor)	1888	Melbourne	VIC	
Damianovich Demetred	Damjanović Demetrije	(Korčula, Split, Dubrovnik, Brač)	1861	Epsom	VIC	
Damianovich Paulo	Damjanović Pavao	(Korčula, Split, Dubrovnik, Brač)	1881		QLD	
Dan Joseph	Dan Josip	Rijeka	1862	Melbourne	VIC	Seaman
Dani James	Dani Jakov	Rijeka	1882	Melbourne	VIC	Labourer
Dapas Giorgio	Dapas Jure	Rovinj	1882		VIC	
Dapaz Giovanni	Dapas Ivan	Rovinj	1882	Melbourne	VIC	Restaurateur
Darveniza John	Drvenica Ivan	Trnovica	1889	Mooroopna	VIC	Vigneron
Darveniza Trojano	Drvenica Trojan	Trnovica	1860	Mooroopna	VIC	Vigneron
Davies Gregory (Grgo Davis)	—— Grgur	Makarska	1890	Brisbane	QLD	Waiter

Name	Croatian version	Birthplace	Arrival	Residence	State	Occupation
De Murska Ilma	Pukšec Ema	Ogulin	1875	Melbourne	VIC	Opera singer
Dediol Juricevic Tommaso	Dediol Juričević Tomo	Pelješac – Kučište	1875	Point Cloates	WA	Seaman
Dedo Stefano	Dedo Stjepan	(Dubrovnik)	1879	Sydney	NSW	Seaman
Delistovich Gregorio	Delistović Grgur	(Premuda, Lošinj, Cres)	1888	Sydney	NSW	
Delistovich Zomaria	Delistović Zvonimir	(Premuda, Lošinj, Cres)	1886	Comera	QLD	Seaman
Demerich Paul	—— Pavao		1879	Port Adelaide	SA	Seaman
Depolo Mathew	Depolo Mate	(Island of Korčula)	1865	Crooked River	VIC	Miner
Derrick John	Derić Ivan	(Rijeka)		Townsville	QLD	Seaman
Descovich Ignazio	Dešković, Desković Ignacije	Rijeka	1854	Birdwood	SA	Wine merchant
Devescove Mathew	Devescovi Mate	Rovinj	1867	Melbourne	VIC	Fisherman
Dicklich Nicholas	Diklić Nikola	Dubrovnik	1857	Maryborough	VIC	Miner
Dobrigh George	Dobrić Jure	Kotor	1854	Bendigo	VIC	Miner
Dobrilla Guiseppe	Dobrila Josip	(Rijeka, Pula, Poreč)	1859	Ballarat	VIC	
Dobrilla Martin	Dobrila Martin	Rijeka	1877	Port Adelaide	SA	Seaman
Domanish Domane	——		1887	Melbourne	VIC	
Dominick Charles	—— Dragutin/Karlo	Bakar	1877	Dapts	NSW	Carpenter
Dominick George	—— Jure	Dalmatia	1840	Coolac	NSW	Miner
Dominick Paul	Domančić Pavao	Pelješac – Stankovići	1874	Melbourne	VIC	Seaman
Dominkovic Giovanni	Dominković Ivan	(Dubrovnik)	1884		VIC	
Dorich Antonio	Dorić Ante	(Hreljin, Rijeka, Čiovo)	1886	Sydney	NSW	Labourer
D'Polle Louis	Depolo Alojzije	Rijeka	1883	Port Adelaide	SA	Seaman
Drageawich David	Dragović David	(Šibenik, Močići, Krk)	1854	Ballarat	VIC	Miner
Draggerzich Antonio	Dragović Ante	(Šibenik, Močići, Krk)	1859	Hepburn	VIC	Miner
Draghicevich Steffano	Dragičević Stjepan	(Brač, Hvar, Pelješac)	1862	Castlemaine	VIC	
Draghichivich Gerola	Dragičević Jerolim	(Brač, Hvar, Pelješac)	1859	Newstead	VIC	Miner
Dragietevich Vito	Dragičević Vid	(Brač, Hvar, Pelješac)	1858		VIC	
Dragon John	Dragon Ivan	Dalmatia	1877	Bendigo	VIC	Miner
Dragovich Antonio	Dragović Ante	(Šibenik, Močići, Krk)	1861	Epsom	VIC	
Dragovitch Cosmo	Dragović Kuzma	Dalmatia	1866	Inglewood	VIC	Miner
Dragovitch Johan	Dragović Ivan	(Šibenik, Močići, Krk)	1860	Inglewood	VIC	Miner
Drajecevich Antonio	Dragičević Ante	(Brač, Hvar, Pelješac)		Ballarat	VIC	
Draskovitch Peter	Drašković Petar	(Solin)	1854	Melbourne	VIC	Seaman
Dubricich (Dubrich) Christie	Dubričić Kristo	Kastav near Rijeka	1880	Adelaide	SA	Labourer
Ducich Peter	Dučić Petar	(Vitaljina, Split)	1860	Epsom	VIC	
Dudrick John	Dudrić Ivan		1863	Yandoit	VIC	Labourer
Duper Nicholas	Duper Nikola	Dalmatia	1884	Melbourne	VIC	Fishmonger
Elith Peter	Ilijić Petar	Island of Krk – Omišalj	1879	Cobar	NSW	Labourer
Entra Frank	Kentra Franjo	Dubrovnik – Gruž	1856	Yackandandah	VIC	Publican
Fabrio Antonio	Fabrio Ante	Island of Lošinj		Townsville	QLD	Seaman
Fabrio Luca	Fabrio Luka	Island of Hvar – Starigrad	1857	Moonlight	VIC	Miner
Fantella Luca	Fantella Luka	(Island of Lastovo)	1865	Crooked River	VIC	Miner
Ferentza Gregorio	Ferenca Grgur	Pelješac – Trpanj	1854	Stuart Mill	VIC	Farmer
Ferghina (Ferguson) Francesko	Fereghin Franjo	Rijeka	1877	Adelaide	SA	Stoker

Name	Croatian version	Birthplace	Arrival	Residence	State	Occupation
Ferrara Joseph	Ferrarra Josip	Rovinj	1847	Maryborough	VIC	Miner
Filess Antonio	Files Ante	(Labin)	1873	Sydney	NSW	Fisherman
Filiarich Peter	—— Petar	Herceg Novi	1882	Melbourne	VIC	Merchant
Filinich Gasper	Filinić Gašpar	(Island of Cres)	1841	Melbourne	VIC	Cook
Fillenih (Filinick) Giovanni	Filinić Ivan	(Island of Cres)	1880	Raglan	QLD	Labourer
Florio Girollamo	Florio Jerolim	Island of Brač – Bol	1851	Geelong	VIC	Seaman
Florio Matthew	Florio Mate	Island of Brač – Bol	1848	Geelong	VIC	Carter
Florio Vincent	Florio Vicko	Island of Brač – Bol	1858	Geelong	VIC	Fisherman
Fornarich Antonio	Fornarić Ante	Island of Cres	1874	Melbourne	VIC	Publican
Francini Joseph	Francin Josip	Island of Lošinj	1847	Amercrombie River	NSW	Farmer
Francis Frank	—— Franjo	Volosko	1878	Botany	NSW	Grocer
Francis John	—— Ivan	Rijeka	1876	Boggy Creek	VIC	Miner
Francovich Decio (Desi)	Franković	Island of Korčula	1871	Crooked River	VIC	Miner
Francovich Dominico	Franković Dominik	Dalmatia	1852	Bendigo	VIC	Miner
Franktovich Andrea	Franotović Andrija	Island of Korčula	1853	Redcastle	VIC	Miner
Freddotowich Anthony	Fredotović Ante	Island of Hvar	1872	Melbourne	VIC	Storekeeper
Gableish Nicholas	Gabelić Nikola	Island of Hvar – Vrboska	1879	Albany	WA	Farmer
Gamulin Taddeo	Gamulin Tadija	Island of Hvar – Jelsa	1862	St Arnaud	VIC	Miner
Gargurevich Matteo	Grgurević Mate	Dubrovačka Rijeka – Mokošica	1860	Melbourne	VIC	Miner
Gasparo John	Gašper Ivan	Island of Brač – Selca	1855	Melbourne	VIC	Labourer
Gazettick Stanislaus	—— Stanislav		1860	Inglewood	VIC	Miner
Gellencih Vincenzo	Jelenić Vicko	(Pašman, Pula, Rijeka)	1884	Sydney	NSW	Labourer
Gelletich John	Jeletić Ivan	Rijeka	1889	Lakes Entrance	VIC	Seaman
Gelletich Nicholas	Jeletić Nikola	Rijeka	1888	Paynesville	VIC	Fisherman
Gellussich Francisco	Jelušić Franjo	(Rijeka, Jelušići Rijeka)	1870	Grenfell	NSW	Miner
George Peter	—— Petar	Kaštel near Split	1854	Huntly	VIC	Miner
Gerberts Francis	Gerbec Franjo	Rijeka	1866	Eaglehawk	VIC	Carpenter
Gercovich Vincent	Jerković Vicko	Island of Hvar – Starigrad	1860	Ballarat	VIC	Miner
Germano Antonia	Germano Ante	Dalmatia	1854	Woods Point	VIC	Miner
Geronevitch Antonio	—— Ante	Dubrovnik	1853	Redcastle	VIC	Publican
Getgovitch Natali	—— Božo		1854	Melbourne	VIC	Seaman
Gevirosick Nicolo	—— Nikola		1859	Melbourne	VIC	Labourer
Giacich Nicholas	—— Nikola	(Lovran)	1887	Sydney	NSW	
Giaconi Antonio	Giaconi Ante	Island of Vis – Komiža	1890	Sydney	NSW	Boot maker
Giadrosich Joseph	Giadrosić Josip	(Island of Lošinj – Mali Lošinj)	1883		QLD	
Giadrowitch G			1854		VIC	
Giarcorich Marino	—— Marin		1859	Ballarat	VIC	
Giarcovich Tomaso	—— Tomislav		1854	Melbourne	VIC	Miner
Ginerovich Stefano	—— Stjepan		1873	Gulgong	NSW	
Gintvonich Lawrence	—— Lovre			Bundaberg	QLD	Farmer
Giovanelli Guissepe	Giovanelli Josip	Rovinj	1852	Grafton	NSW	
Giovanovich Besco	—— Boško		1864	Whipstick	VIC	
Giuranovich Nicolo	—— Nikola		1863		VIC	
Glaninich Lawrence	Glavinić Lovre	Dubrovačka Rijeka – Mokošica	1885	Sydney	NSW	

Name	Croatian version	Birthplace	Arrival	Residence	State	Occupation
Glavinovich Matee	Glavinović Mate	(Split, Dubrovnik, Brač)	1858		VIC	
Glinbich Francesco	Glinbić Franjo	(Lošinj, Rijeka)	1860	Inglewood	VIC	Miner
Gobbie John	Gobbi Ivan	Island of Korčula	1852	Raglan	VIC	Miner
Godena Nicholas	Godena Nikola	Rovinj	1856	Eganstown	VIC	Miner
Goick Giovanni	Goić Ivan	(Island of Brač)	1862	Ballarat	VIC	
Golden Frank	—— Franjo	Island of Hvar	1857	Costerfield	VIC	Miner
Goodrich Joseph	—— Josip	Dalmatia	1856	Melbourne	VIC	Publican
Gospodnetic Juraj	Gospodnetić Juraj	Island of Brač – Dol	1885			
Grandi John	Grandi Ivan	Dubrovnik	1853	Wedderburn	VIC	Miner
Grbic Ivan	Grbić Ivan	Pelješac – Kučište	1883	Melbourne	VIC	Seaman
Griercoorch A			1855	Ballarat	VIC	
Grummowitch			1861	Redcastle	VIC	
Grussich Mark	Grušić, Grubšić Marko	Island of Brač	1861	Geelong	VIC	Seaman
Guercovich Simene	—— Šimun		1861	Hepburn	VIC	
Guininovich Nicholas	—— Nikola		1871	Sydney	NSW	
Guircovich Andrea	Jurković Andrija	Opatija	1868	Wedderburn	VIC	Miner
Guircovich Giovanni	Jurković Ivan	Herceg Novi	1860	Inglewood	VIC	Miner
Guirich (Jackson) Giuseppe	—— Josip	Island of Lošinj – Mali Lošinj	1886	Stranthorpe	QLD	Labourer
Guovich Nicola	—— Nikola		1859	Melbourne	VIC	Labourer
Guratovich Matteo	Đuratović Mate	Dubrovnik	1874	Port Adelaide	SA	Seaman
Gurinch Paul	Jurinić Pavao	(Zadar, Pula, Split, Dubrovnik)	1885	Sydney	NSW	Labourer
Guschich Ellia	Guščić Ilija	Dalmatia	1874	Charlton	VIC	Farmer
Hanich Robert	Hanić Robert		1860	Inglewood	VIC	Miner
Harlovich Antonio	Harlović Ante	Dalmatia	1859	Georgetown	QLD	Miner
Harlovich John	Harlović Ivan	Pelješac	1878	Sydney	NSW	Seaman
Hasdovaz Mathew	Hazdovac Mato	Island of Mljet – Babino Polje	1868	Gulgong	NSW	Miner
Herzgovich Guro	Hercegović Đuro		1868	Buckland	VIC	Miner
Host Peter	Host Petar	Rijeka	1879	Adelaide	SA	Seaman
Ilich Francis	Illić Franjo	(Vis, Rab, Šibenik)			QLD	
Illich Stefano	Illić Stjepan	(Vis, Rab, Šibenik)	1882	Cairns	QLD	Seaman
Illik Nicola	Illić Nikola	(Vis, Rab, Šibenik)	1890	Sydney	NSW	Seaman
Illik Peter	Illić Petar	(Vis, Rab, Šibenik)	1890	Sydney	NSW	Seaman
Ivancovich Matthew	Ivanković Mate	Dubrovnik	1851	Ballarat	VIC	Miner
Ivannisseuch Tomaso	Ivanišević Tomislav	(Hvar, Dubrovnik, Zadar)	1861	Melbourne	VIC	
Ivanusic George	Ivanušić Jure	Brseč	1870	Melbourne	VIC	Miner
Ivanussich Giovanni	Ivanušić Ivan	Brseč	1854	Yandoit	VIC	Miner
Ivusic Antun	Ivušić Antun	Pelješac – Tomislavovac				
Jadrick James	Jadrić Jakov	Rijeka	1883	Hoskins Town	NSW	Carpenter
Jakovich Niklis (John Niklis)	Jaković Nikola	Kraljevica	1888	Melbourne	VIC	
Jancovich Luka	Janković Luka	(Brač, Split, Rijeka)	1861		VIC	
Jannack Mark	Janić Marko	(Rijeka, Split)	1877	Melbourne	VIC	Labourer
Jaranich John	—— Ivan			Thursday Island	QLD	Diver
Jasich James	Jašić Jakov	(Island of Brač)	1886	Townsville	QLD	Miner

Name	Croatian version	Birthplace	Arrival	Residence	State	Occupation
Jaspriza Giovanni	Jasprica Ivan	Pelješac – Janjina	1865	Crooked River	VIC	Miner
Jasprizza Nicholas	Jasprica Nikola	Pelješac – Janjina		West Maitland	NSW	
Jasprizza Nicholas	Jasprica Nikola	Pelješac – Janjina	1860	Young	NSW	Farmer
Jassich Pietro	Jakšić Petar	Island of Brač	1861	Costerfield	VIC	Miner
Jehilička Emanual	Jehlička Emanuel	Island of Cres	1886	Melbourne	VIC	Carpenter
Jeuras Thomas	Juras Tomislav	Kotor	1855	Fiery Creek	VIC	Miner
Jocovich Tomaos	Joković Tomislav	(Korčula, Split)	1852	Melbourne	VIC	
Joseph James	—— Jakov	Dalmatia	1878	Sydney	NSW	Confectioner
Jugovic Dragutin	Jugović Dragutin	Island of Brač – Bol	1890			
Juratowitch Nicholas	Đuratović Nikola	Dubrovnik	1860	Singleton	NSW	Mail contractor
Jurich Giovanni	Jurić Ivan	Pelješac – Oskorušno	1875	Point Cloates	WA	Seaman
Jurick Frank	Jurić Franjo	(Vranjić, Krpanj, Žirje)	1889	Cairns	QLD	Miner
Jurjevic Ivan	Jurjević Ivan	Island of Brač – Sutivan	1862			
Jurjevic Roko	Jurjević Roko	Island of Brač – Sutivan	1866			
Jurrinovic Luke	Jurinović Luka	(Vis, Rijeka)		Wellington	NSW	
Justice Ferdinand	Justić Ferdo	Kraljevica	1869	Port Adelaide	SA	Labourer
Justice Polito	Justić	Kraljevica	1873	Young	NSW	Labourer
Jutronic Lovre	Jutronić Lovre	Island of Brač – Sutivan	1880			
Juvic Giovanni	—— Ivan		1888		VIC	
Jvancich Mathew	Ivančić Mate	Island of Olib – Olib	1883	Sydney	NSW	Fishmonger
Kadic Matin Peter	Kadić Petar	(Split, Dubrovnik, Omiš)	1888	Sydney	NSW	
Katnich Joseph	Katnić Josip	Hrvatskoj Primorje – Crikvenica	1878	Melbourne	VIC	Fisherman
Kazia Mathew	Kazija Mate	Island of Zlarin	1888	Melbourne	VIC	Fisherman
Kilwick G		Dubrovnik	1882	Newcastle	NSW	Seaman
King (Zar) Charles	Zar Dragutin/Karlo	Rijeka	1874	Cunnamulla	QLD	Carpenter
Kisselich Jacob	Kiselić Jakob	(Rijeka)	1882	Melbourne	VIC	Labourer
Kisselich John	Kiselić Ivan	Rijeka – Draga	1884	Sydney	NSW	Labourer
Knesevich Marco	Knežević Marko	(Rijeka, Split, Dubrovnik)	1863		VIC	
Kosmos		Rijeka	1856	Alma	VIC	Miner
Kovacevic Giov	Kovačević Ivan	(Hvar, Split, Dubrovnik)	1888	Sydney	NSW	Labourer
Kovacevich Ivan	Kovačević Ivan	Pelješac	1889		WA	Labourer
Kozmo Andrea	Kosmi Andrija	Island of Vis	1889		WA	Labourer
Krmpotic Dominic	Krmpotić Dominik	Krivi Put	1890	Melbourne	VIC	Miner
Krmpotich Frank	Krmpotić Franjo	Veljun Primorski	1886	Meekatharra	WA	Miner
Kucan John	Kučan Ivan	(Hreljin, Rijeka)	1889		QLD	
Kuchan Matthew	Kučan Mate	Hreljin	1889	Melbourne	VIC	Labourer
Kuis Micel	Kuiš Mićel	Island of Brač – Bol	1883			
Kulisich Baldus	Kulišić Baldo	(Dubrovnik, Split)	1888		VIC	
Kuscovich G			1887		VIC	Labourer
Laich Nicholas	Laić Nikola	Dalmatia	1878	Port Adelaide	SA	Seaman
Lasich Nicholas	Lasić Nikola	Dubrovnik	1859	Dargo	VIC	Miner
Lavierri Giovanni	Daveri Ivan	Island of Brač – Milna	1882	Geelong	VIC	Fisherman
Lazarawitch	Lazarević	(Vodavada, Dubrovnik, Šipan)	1861	McIntyre	VIC	Miner
Lazarich Antonie	Lazarić Ante	(Opatija, Mošćenica, Cres, Rijeka)	1868	Sydney	NSW	Seaman
Lazarovich Vincent	Lazarević Vicko	(Vodavada, Dubrovnik, Šipan)	1864	McIntyre	VIC	Miner

Name	Croatian version	Birthplace	Arrival	Residence	State	Occupation
Lazzarovich Spiro	Lazarević Špiro	(Vodavada, Dubrovnik, Šipan)	1857	Geelong	VIC	Fisherman
Leonard Dominick	—— Dominik	Island of Brač – Sutivan	1864	Adelaide	SA	Publican
Lettich Antonio	Letić Ante	(Island of Lošinj – Veli Lošinj)	1867	Sydney	NSW	
Lettich Gaspard	Letić Gašpar	(Island of Lošinj – Veli Lošinj)	1879	Port Douglas	QLD	Miner
Lettich Joseph	Letić Josip	(Island of Lošinj – Veli Lošinj)	1856	Darmarch	QLD	Miner
Lettich Mark	Letić Marko	Island of Lošinj – Veli Lošinj		Sydney	NSW	
Lewis John	—— Ivan	Rijeka	1884	Sydney	NSW	Seaman
Lissen Nicholas	—— Nikola	Island of Vis	1863	Mount Morgan	QLD	Miner
Lobrovich Antonio	Lobrović Ante	Majkovi	1877	Sydney	NSW	Seaman
Lobrovich John	Lobrović Ivan	Majkovi	1886	Sydney	NSW	Seaman
Lovrinovich Giovanni	Lovrinović Ivan	Dubrovnik	1875	Point Cloates	WA	Seaman
Lucas James	—— Jakov	Island of Hvar – Starigrad	1889	Sydney	NSW	Publican
Lucas John	Lukšić Ivan	Island of Brač – Sutivan	1881	Sydney	NSW	Fishmonger
Luchinovich George	—— Jure	Dalmatia	1856	Avenel	VIC	Miner
Luchinovich George	—— Jure	Dalmatia	1858	Avenel	VIC	Miner
Lucich George	Lučić Jure	Kotor	1885	Walhalla	VIC	Miner
Lucich Jacomer	Lučić Jakov	(Dubrovnik, Hvar, Rijeka, Brač)	1889	Sydney	NSW	
Lucich Joseph	Lučić Josip	Opatija	1862	Melbourne	VIC	Seaman
Luckvitch A			1888		VIC	
Lujo Pietro	Lujo Petar	Dubrovnik	1889	Boulder	WA	Miner
Lukene Simeon	Lukin Šimun	Island of Zlarin		Gosford	NSW	
Lupis Antoni	Lupis Ante	(Pelješac, Dubrovnik, Krk)	1884	Broadwater	NSW	Labourer
Lupis Antonio	Lupis Ante	(Pelješac, Dubrovnik, Krk)	1888	Sydney	NSW	Labourer
Lupis Antonio	Lupis Ante	(Pelješac, Dubrovnik, Krk)	1888	Sydney	NSW	
Lupis John	Lupis Ivan	(Pelješac, Dubrovnik, Krk)	1887	Sydney	NSW	Seaman
Lupis Matteo	Lupis Mate	(Pelješac, Dubrovnik, Krk)	1888	Sydney	NSW	Labourer
Lusetich Francis	Lusetić Franjo	(Pula, Rijeka)	1856	Melbourne	VIC	Labourer
Lusic Victor	Lukšić Viktor	Island of Brač – Milna	1888	Melbourne	VIC	Grocer
Lussich Dominick	Lukšić Dominik	Island of Brač – Sutivan	1856	Portarlington	VIC	Fisherman
Lussich John	Lukšić Ivan	Island of Brač – Sutivan	1853	Portarlington	VIC	Fisherman
Lussich John	Lukšić Ivan	Island of Brač – Sutivan	1854	Geelong	VIC	Fisherman
Lussich Natale	Lukšić Božo	Island of Brač – Sutivan	1857	Portarlington	VIC	Miner
Lussich Slavich John	Lukšić Slavić Ivan	Island of Brač	1881	Portarlington	VIC	Fisherman
Lussick Jerome	Lukšić Jerolim	Island of Brač – Sutivan	1890	Portarlington	VIC	Fisherman
Machiavelli Constantine	Machiavelli Konstantin	Island of Vis	1874	Stannifer	NSW	Miner
Macic John	Mačić Ivan	(Split)	1854	Ballarat	VIC	
Mackovitch	Mačković		1861	Redcastle	VIC	Miner
Malolich Giacomo	—— Jakov		1878	McIntyre	VIC	Miner
Mancich Joseph	Mančić Josip	(Hvar, Rijeka, Olib)	1869	Costerfield	VIC	Miner
Mandelick James	Mandelić Jakov	(Hvar, Olib, Rijeka)	1852	Bendigo	VIC	Publican
Mandeville Louis	—— Alojzije	Pelješac – Ponikve	1855	Wedderburn	VIC	Miner
Mandich James	Mandić Jakov	(Split, Omiš, Vranjic, Matulji)	1885	Sea	NSW	
Mandussich Adolf	Mandušić	(Pula, Omiš, Split)	1882	Melbourne	VIC	
Manuel George	—— Jure	Makarska	1866	Sydney	NSW	Coal lumper
Maraspin Antonio (Lewis)	Maraspin Ante	(Lošinj, Pula, Rovinj)	1858	Sydney	NSW	Labourer
Marassovich Mattio	Marasović Mate	Island of Vis	1853	Woods Point	VIC	Publican

Name	Croatian version	Birthplace	Arrival	Residence	State	Occupation
Marcovitch Joseph	Marković Josip	(Kućine, Rijeka, Brač, Zlarin)	1865	Crooked River	VIC	Miner
Marghetich Simeone	Margitić Šimun	Bakar	1885	Melbourne	VIC	Labourer
Margitich Anton	Margitić Anton	Bakar	1861	Melbourne	VIC	Cabdriver
Margitich George	Margitić Jure	Bakar	1865	Adelaide	SA	Labourer
Margitich John	Margitić Ivan	Bakar – Škrljevo	1883	Portarlington	VIC	Fisherman
Margitich Luka	Margitić Luka	Bakar	1861	Sydney	NSW	Cabdriver
Margitich Vincent	Margitić Vicko	Bakar		Portarlington	VIC	
Margudick Giovanni	Margitić Ivan	(Bakar)	1865	Costerfield	VIC	Miner
Marian Joseph	Marijan Josip	Island of Hvar – Pitve	1865	Melbourne	VIC	Vigneron
Marich	Marić	(Drvenik Mali, Dubrovnik, Čepikuće)	1885		VIC	
Marich (Mariette) Joseph	Marić Josip	(Drvenik Mali, Dubrovnik, Čepikuće)	1888	Taradale	VIC	Miner
Marich Peter	Marić Petar	Herceg Novi	1877	Sydney	NSW	Music warehouseman
Marich Pietro	Marić Petar	(Drvenik Mali, Dubrovnik, Čepikuće)	1886	Melbourne	VIC	
Maricic Anton	Maričić Anton	Novi Vinodolski		Cobar	NSW	
Marienovich Marko (Angelo Louis)	Marinović Marko	(Korčula, Baćina, Split, Dubrovnik)	1849	Sydney	NSW	
Marincovich Matteo	Marinković Mate	Island of Brač – Bol	1873	Sydney	NSW	Publican
Marini Nicolas	Marini Nikola	Island of Lopud	1858	Costerfield	VIC	Miner
Marinich Matthew	Marinić Mate	(Kastav near Rijeka)	1877	Bathurst	NSW	Publican
Marinich Paul	Marinić Pavao	(Rijeka, Lovran)	1858	Maryborough	VIC	Miner
Marinkovic Ivan	Marinković Ivan	Island of Brač – Bol	1885			
Marinkovic Simic Mate	Marinković Simić Mate	Island of Brač – Bol	1860			Miner
Marinovich A	Marinović	(Korčula, Baćina, Split, Dubrovnik)	1881	Sydney	NSW	
Marinovich Antonis	Marinović Ante	Island of Korčula	1841	Melbourne	VIC	Miner
Marinovich Marco	Marinović Marko	(Korčula, Baćina, Split, Dubrovnik)	1858		VIC	
Marinovich Michele	Marinović Miho	Pelješac – Trpanj	1859	Redcastle	VIC	Miner
Marinovich Spiro	Marinović Špiro	Island of Korčula – Blato	1881	Adelaide	SA	Publican
Marinovitch George	Marinović Jure	(Korčula, Baćina, Split, Dubrovnik)	1862	Redcastle	VIC	Miner
Marinzulis Govani (John Olsen)	Marinzulić Ivan	Island of Hvar – Hvar	1884	Mackay	QLD	Labourer
Marionowitch John	Marinović Ivan	(Korčula, Baćina, Split, Dubrovnik)	1860	Melbourne	VIC	Seaman
Mark Antonio	—— Ante	Dalmatia	1879	Port Augusta	SA	Fisherman
Markovich John	Marković Ivan	Island of Krk – Malinska	1886	Lakes Entrance	VIC	Fisherman
Markovitch Braddijo	Marković	Kotor	1863	Cue	WA	Miner
Marks John	—— Ivan		1888	Sydney	NSW	Labourer
Marohnic Gasper	Marohnić Gašpar	(Zlobin, Rijeka, Crikvenica)		Melbourne	VIC	Vigneron
Marotte John	Marotti Ivan	Rijeka	1885	Melbourne	VIC	Saw dust merchant
Marovich Alexander	Marović Aleksandar	Dalmatia	1884	Melbourne	VIC	Farmer
Marrissevich Antonio	Marišević Ante	(Split)	1859	Huntly	VIC	

Name	Croatian version	Birthplace	Arrival	Residence	State	Occupation
Marsanich Antonio	Maršanić Ante	(Rijeka)	1855	Melbourne	VIC	Farmer
Marsich Joseph	Maršić Ivan	Lovran	1856	Melbourne	VIC	Labourer
Marsich Joseph	Maršić Ivan	Dubrovnik	1882	Malmsbury	VIC	Importer
Martin John	—— Ivan	Island of Iž – Iž Mali	1877	Pyrmont	NSW	Engineer
Martinich George	Martinić Jure	(Brač, Bakar)		Port Adelaide	SA	Labourer
Marush Mateo	Maruš Mate	Plomin	1882	Portarlington	VIC	Fisherman
Marusic Giuseppe	Marušić Josip	(Marušić, Vinišće, Cres, Brst)	1863	Stawell	VIC	
Marwick Luke	—— Luka	Dalmatia	1856	Amherst	VIC	Miner
Massilina Peter	Massalin Petar	(Island of Lošinj)	1868		VIC	
Matcovic Andrea	Matković Andrija	(Hvar, Kućine, Lošinj, Dubrovnik)	1889	Sydney	NSW	
Matesic Pavel	Matešić Pavao	Kukuljanovo	1857	Hay	NSW	Publican
Matesich Andrew	Matešić Andrija	Rijeka	1887	Port Macquarie	NSW	Maintenance man
Mathovitch E	Matović	(Dubrovnik)		Walhalla	VIC	Miner
Matich (Martich) Peter	Matić, Martić Petar	(Korčula, Dubrovnik, Poreč, Pag)	1875	Port Augusta	SA	
Matich Nathaniel	Matić Božo	(Korčula, Dubrovnik, Poreč, Pag)	1884	Newcastle	NSW	Seaman
Matovich Giovanni	Matović Ivan	(Dubrovnik)		Cairns	QLD	Seaman
Mattich (Mallich) John	Matić Ivan	(Korčula, Dubrovnik, Poreč, Pag)	1874	Barcaldine	QLD	
Mattich Dominic	Matić Dominik	Dalmatia	1887	Portarlington	VIC	Fisherman
Matulich James	Matulić Jakov	Island of Brač – Dol	1878	Melbourne	VIC	Storekeeper
Matulich Nicola	Matulić Nikola	(Brač, Omiš, Dugi Otok, Molat)		Tingha	NSW	
Matulick Nicholas	Matulić Nikola	Omiš	1853	Mannum	SA	Boatbuilder
Maturlich Samuel	Matulić Samuel	(Brač, Omiš, Dugi Otok, Molat)		Sydney	NSW	
Mavorvitch Peter	Mavrović Petar	Brseč	1853	Yandoit	VIC	Miner
Mavrowick Fortunato	Mavrović Srekćo	Rijeka	1856	Melbourne	VIC	Carpenter
Maztarnich Marco	—— Marko		1863	Epsom	VIC	
McNish (Mackavich) James	—— Jakov	Dalmatia	1877	Melbourne	VIC	Miner
McSiersrich Natale	—— Božo		1861	Epsom	VIC	
Medich Nicholas	Medić Nikola	Šibenik	1880	Port Pirie	SA	Labourer
Melford (Martinwich) John	Martinović Ivan	Dalmatia	1854	Castlemaine	VIC	Cook
Mercovich Bartholomew	Mirković Bartul	Pelješac – Trpanj	1852	Melbourne	VIC	Publican
Mercovitch Antonio	Mirković Ante	Dubrovnik	1874	Casterton	VIC	Labourer
Mersuglia George	—— Jure	Kotor – Prčanj	1883	Bairnsdale	VIC	Seaman
Meslovic G			1888	Sydney	NSW	
Mesotich Giovanni	—— Ivan		1860		VIC	
Metrowich John	Mitrović Ivan	(Split, Dubrovnik, Biograd)	1860	Redcastle	VIC	Miner
Mialorick Charles	—— Dragutin/Karlo		1860	Inglewood	VIC	Miner
Miculicich F	Mikuličić	(Rijeka)	1863	Castlemaine	VIC	
Mijch Peter	Mijić Petar	(Island of Brač)	1873	Sydney	NSW	Miner
Mikulicich P	Mikuličić	(Rijeka)	1863		VIC	
Milach Frank	Milač Franjo		1884	Sydney	NSW	
Milatovich Antonio	Milatović Ante	Dubrovnik/Kotor	1843	Sydney	NSW	Seaman
Milderwick Nicolo	—— Nikola		1859	Melbourne	VIC	Labourer
Milford Stephen	—— Stjepan	Dubrovnik	1836	Sydney	NSW	

Name	Croatian version	Birthplace	Arrival	Residence	State	Occupation
Milkovic Louis	Milković Alojzije	(Dubrovnik, Rijeka)	1887	Ballarat	VIC	Bookkeeper
Millawich Frank	Milavić Franjo	(Split)	1877	Melbourne	VIC	
Miller Carlo	Miller Karlo	Island of Lošinj	1882	Melbourne	VIC	Miner
Miller Frank	Miller Franjo	Šibenik	1864	Melbourne	VIC	Farmer
Millich Bartholomew	Milić Bartul	Bakar	1888	Melbourne	VIC	Miner
Millovich Giovanni	Milović Ivan	(Pelješac, Šibenik, Dubrovnik)	1863		VIC	
Millowick Nicholas	Milović Nikola	(Pelješac, Šibenik, Dubrovnik)	1858	Glenburnie	SA	Labourer
Miloslavich Giralomo	Miloslavić Jerolim	Dubrovnik	1888	Normanton	QLD	Storekeeper
Miloslavich Vlaho	Miloslavić Vlaho	Dubrovnik	1877	Menzies	WA	Miner
Miloslavich Vlaho	Miloslavić Vlaho	Dubrovnik	1875	Point Cloates	WA	Seaman
Milovitch Dominic	Milović Dominik	Dalmatia	1854	Maryborough	VIC	Miner
Milovitch Thomas	Milović Tomilsav	Island of Brač – Sutivan	1857	Nagambie	VIC	Vigneron
Mirack Antonio	—— Ante	Rijeka	1884	Stuart Mill	VIC	Miner
Missetich John	Mišetić Ivan	(Brač, Split, Dubrovnik, Rijeka)	1860	Yandoit	VIC	Miner
Missitich Demetris	Mišetić Demetrije	(Brač, Split, Dubrovnik, Rijeka)	1860	Melbourne	VIC	Miner
Mitrovich Niccola	Mitrović Nikola	(Split, Dubrovnik, Biograd)	1858	Costerfield	VIC	Miner
Mladosevich Peter	Mladošević Petar	(Vitaljina)		Forbes	NSW	
Mladovich Giuseppe	Mladević Josip	Rijeka	1882	Melbourne	VIC	Farmer
Mlican (Petrasich) Vead	Petrašić Vid	Island of Vis	1882	Wedderburn	VIC	Miner
Mohoric Francis	Mohorić Franjo	(Rijeka, Cernik, Opatija)	1888	Sydney	NSW	
Monkivitch John	Monković Ivan	Dubrovnik	1861	Colac	VIC	Carter
Morgan John	Margan Franjo	Rijeka	1885	Ballarat	VIC	
Moriawitch Antonio	—— Ante		1858	Ballarat	VIC	Labourer
Mozzara Nicholas	Mozara Nikola	Dubrovnik	1872	Sydney	NSW	Storekeeper
Muscardin John	Muscardin Ivan	Island of Lošinj – Mali Lošinj	1859	McIntyre	VIC	Miner
Musich Nicholas	Mušić, Musić Nikola	(Korčula, Zaton, Rijeka, Pula)		Melbourne	VIC	Restaurateur
Nedevitch Joseph	—— Josip		1883	Maryborough	QLD	Labourer
Neil Martin	—— Martin	Dubrovnik	1878	Inverloch	VIC	Contractor
Nelson		Island of Vis	1889	Hobart	TAS	
Nelson Louis	—— Alojzije	Dubrovnik	1884	Diamond Creek	VIC	Miner
Nesetie John	—— Ivan		1866	Newcastle	NSW	Waterman
Nicholas Francis	—— Franjo	Dalmatia	1880	Walcha	NSW	Selector
Nicholovich Nicholas	—— Nikola	Sclavonia	1865	Woods Point	VIC	Miner
Nicolich Francis	Nikolić Franjo	Dalmatia	1862	Walhalla	VIC	Miner
Nicolich Ivan	Nikolić Ivan	Dalmatia	1866	Woods Point	VIC	Miner
Nicolich Matthew	Nikolić Mate	(Dalmatia)	1855		VIC	
Nobilo Antonio	Nobilo Ante	(Island of Korčula)	1885	Sydney	NSW	Oyster saloon keeper
Orlovich Mattio	Orlović Mate	Island of Šolta	1869	Gulgong	NSW	Storekeeper
Osoinak Martino	Osojnak Martin	Rijeka	1875	Point Cloates	WA	Seaman
Pachirwick S			1859	Melbourne	VIC	Labourer
Palmich Antoni	Palmić Ante	Bakar	1880		NSW	Miner
Palmich Gasparo	Plamić Gašparo	(Lovran, Rijeka)	1887	Sydney	NSW	Labourer
Pandrige Stephen	—— Stjepan	Dalmatia	1859	Buckland	VIC	Miner
Pandwick Pietro	—— Petar		1859	Melbourne	VIC	Labourer
Pannich Giovanni	Panić Josip		1888	Sydney	NSW	

Name	Croatian version	Birthplace	Arrival	Residence	State	Occupation
Paoletich Philip	Paoletić Filip	(Brioni, Pula, Poreč, Rovinj)		Mt Morgan	QLD	Labourer
Papawitch Francis	—— Franjo		1853	Dunolly	VIC	Miner
Park Nicholas	—— Nikola	Dubrovnik	1859	Grafton	NSW	Oysterer
Park Peter	—— Petar	Dubrovnik	1859	Grafton	NSW	Storekeeper
Pascoe Susan	—— Suzana	Dubrovnik	1886	Melbourne	VIC	Home duties
Pasetich T			1855	Melbourne	VIC	
Pasquan Christopher	Paškvan Kristo	(Rijeka)	1866	Daylesford	VIC	Miner
Pasquan Diodatta	Paškvan Božidar	(Rijeka)	1855		VIC	
Pasquan Joseph	Paškvan Josip	Rijeka	1883	Melbourne	VIC	Publican
Pasquan Martin	Paškvan Martin	Rijeka – Calin	1865	Melbourne	VIC	Publican
Passalick Antonio	Pašalić Ante	Island of Vis	1853	Yandoit	VIC	Miner
Paul John	Paul Ivan	Rijeka	1877	Drouin	VIC	Labourer
Paulovich Robert	Paulović Robert	(Rijeka)	1856	Melbourne	VIC	
Paulussy Nicholas	Pauluci Nikola	Dubrovnik	1860	Buckland	VIC	Storekeeper
Paulussy Stephen	Pauluci Stjepan	Dubrovnik	1859	Buckland	VIC	Miner
Pavcorich Micheli	—— Miho		1864		VIC	
Pavesich Matthew	Pavešić Mate	(Rijeka, Krasica, Kukuljanovo)		Townsville	QLD	Labourer
Pavich Antonio	Pavić Ante	Island of Zlarin	1854	Yandoit	VIC	Miner
Pavilach Martin	—— Martin	Dalmatia	1868	Yandoit	VIC	Miner
Pavisich Gregorio	Pavišić, Pavičić Grgur	Rijeka	1875	Point Cloates	WA	Seaman
Pavletich Antonio	Pavletić Ante	Bakar		Melbourne	VIC	Fishmonger
Pavletich Gregory	Pavletić Grgur	Bakar	1873	Portarlington	VIC	Fisherman
Pavletich John	Pavletić Ivan	Bakar	1862	Graytown	VIC	Miner
Pavletich Martin	Pavletić Martin	Rijeka	1885	Melbourne	VIC	Fishmonger
Pavletich Nicolo	Pavletić Nikola	(Krasica, Rijeka, Bakar)	1861		VIC	
Pavletich Paul	Pavletić Pavao	Bakar	1885	Mittagong	NSW	Labourer
Pavletich Thomas	Pavletić Tomislav	Bakar	1853	Castlemaine	VIC	Publican
Pavlicevic Nicholas	Pavličević Nikola	(Lastovo, Majkovi, Dubrovnik)	1870	Sofala	NSW	Miner
Pavlicevich Steffano	Pavličević Stejpan	Dubrovnik	1882	Buckland	VIC	Miner
Pavlovich Andrew	Pavlović Andrija	(Ston, Dubrovnik, Rijeka, Cres)	1857	Port Adelaide	SA	
Pavlovich M	Pavlović	(Ston, Dubrovnik, Rijeka, Cres)	1890	Broken Hill	NSW	Miner
Pavolivich Louis (Luca)	—— Luka		1888	Broken Hill	NSW	Miner
Pepovitch Stefano	Pepović Stjepan			Bendigo	VIC	Patient
Perancich Giuseppi	Perančić Josip	Island of Lošinj – Mali Lošinj	1875	Point Cloates	WA	Seaman
Percovich Matteo	Perković Mate	(Šibenik, Ljubač, Klis, Pula)	1869	Mudgee	NSW	Miner
Percy John	—— Ivan	Rijeka	1874	Brisbane	QLD	Carpenter
Pergolis Venier	Pergolis	Rovinj		Sydney	NSW	
Perich Matteo	Perić Mate	(Split, Rijeka, Pula, Dubrovnik)	1867	Melbourne	VIC	Miner
Perie Giovanni	Peri Ivan	(Poreč, Pula, Rijeka)	1858	Araluen	NSW	
Perorish Guivani	Perović Ivan	(Zadar, Rijeka, Dubrovnik, Krk)	1854	Melbourne	VIC	Labourer
Perorish Nicolo	Perović Nikola	(Zadar, Rijeka, Dubrovnik, Krk)	1854	Melbourne	VIC	Labourer
Perovich Elia	Perović Ilija	(Zadar, Rijeka, Dubrovnik, Krk)	1860		VIC	
Perovich John	Perović Ivan	(Zadar, Rijeka, Dubrovnik, Krk)	1866	Buckland	VIC	Miner
Perrin Louis	Perin Alojzije	Dubrovnik	1852		NSW	Railway ganger
Perussick Antonio	Perušić Ante	Kotor	1887	Melbourne	VIC	Labourer

Name	Croatian version	Birthplace	Arrival	Residence	State	Occupation
Petcovich Mattio	Petković Mate	Dalmatia	1871		NSW	Labourer
Petcovich Theodore	Petković Teodor	Kotor – Risan	1862	Dunolly	VIC	Miner
Peters Antony	—— Ante	Dubrovnik	1877	Botany	NSW	Labourer
Petrasich Andrea	Petrašić Andrija	Island of Vis – Komiža	1884	Wedderburn	VIC	Miner
Petrasich Antonio	Petrašić Ante	Island of Vis – Komiža	1863	Wedderburn	VIC	Miner
Petrich Francis	Petrić Franjo	(Split, Hvar, Vis, Rijeka)	1862	Woods Point	VIC	Miner
Petrich Marino	Petrić Marin	Island of Hvar – Starigrad	1889	Sydney	NSW	Broom maker
Petrich Martin	Petrić Martin	Island of Hvar – Grablje	1877	Dargo	VIC	Miner
Petrovich Peter	Petrović Petar	(Rijeka, Dubrovnik, Pula, Split)	1862		VIC	
Pezely John	Pezelj Ivan	Rijeka	1884	Port Adelaide	SA	Seaman
Phillips John	Filips Ivan	Rijeka	1865	Melbourne	VIC	Miner
Phillips Joseph	Filips Josip	Rijeka	1855	Melbourne	VIC	Miner
Picevach Phillip	—— Filip		1862	Epsom	VIC	
Picinich (Pigniech) Phillippo	Pičinić, Picinić Filip	(Susak, Lošinj)	1861		VIC	
Piglic Josip	Piglić Josip	(Opatija, Lovran, Pula)	1889	Sydney	NSW	
Plancich P	Plančić	(Hvar, Brač, Dubrovnik, Šibenik)	1889		VIC	
Planiech G			1861		VIC	
Ploncich Joseph	Plančić Joseph	(Hvar, Brač, Dubrovnik, Šibenik)	1867	Redcastle	VIC	Miner
Polianich Pavao	Poljanić Pavao	Pelješac – Potomje	1884	Sydney	NSW	
Pollich James	Polić Jakov	(Hreljin, Rijeka, Split, Zlobin)	1860	Inglewood	VIC	Miner
Polorineo James	Polovineo Jakov	Kotor – Perast	1878	Dunolly	VIC	Miner
Popovich Vincent	Popović Vicko	Dalmatia		Omeo	VIC	Miner
Poschich Fortunato	Poščić Srećko	Rijeka – Bregi	1853	Geelong	VIC	Grocer
Poschich Raymond	Poščić Rajmund	Volosko	1853	Inglewood	VIC	Miner
Postich Joseph	Postić Josip	Volosko	1849	Charlton	VIC	Farmer
povich Vicenzo	—— Vicko	Island of Hvar	1882	Melbourne	VIC	Miner
Proleta Nicholas	Proleta Nikola	Dubrave	1878	Port Adelaide	SA	Seaman
Prolich Gregory	Prolić Grgur		1860	Inglewood	VIC	Miner
Purich Marc	Purić Marko	(Krk, Split, Cres, Pula)	1867	Sydney	NSW	
Radic Vido	Radić Vid	(Čiovo, Vrsine, Split, Brač)	1889	Sydney	NSW	
Radich John	Radić Ivan	Dalmatia	1882	Melbourne	VIC	Fishmonger
Radich Peter	Radić Petar	Dalmatia		Melbourne	VIC	Labourer
Radich Thomas	Radić Tomo	Island of Brač – Bol	1875	Sydney	NSW	Labourer
Radinovich	Radinović	(Split, Rijeka)	1862	Redcastle	VIC	Miner
Radish George	Radiš Jure	(Dubrovnik, Gromača, Mrčevo)	1856	Melbourne	VIC	
Radonich Natale	Radonić Božo	Vitaljina	1883	Budgeree	VIC	Farmer
Radoslarnich Antonio	Radoslavić Ante	(Island of Lošinj)	1854	Maryborough	VIC	Seaman
Radoslavich Antonio	Radoslović Ante	Island of Unije	1862	Rushworth	VIC	Miner
Radoslovich Andrew	Radoslović Andrija	Island of Lošinj	1886	Port Fairy	VIC	Fisherman
Radoslovich Joseph	Radoslović Josip	Island of Lošinj		Port Pirie	SA	Labourer
Radovich Charles	Radović Dragutin/ Karlo	(Pelješac, Labin, Čilipi, Dubrovnik)	1860	Woods Point	VIC	Miner
Radovich Mark	Radović Marko	(Pelješac, Labin, Čilipi, Dubrovnik)		Orange	NSW	
Radovich Paolo	Radović Pavao	Pelješac – Potomje	1875	Point Cloates	WA	Seaman

Name	Croatian version	Birthplace	Arrival	Residence	State	Occupation
Radovich Vincent	Radović Vicko	(Pelješac, Labin, Čilipi, Dubrovnik)	1873	Sofala	NSW	Miner
Radovick Antonio	Radović Ante	Pelješac – Potomje	1862	Korumburra	VIC	Publican
Radovick Steffano	Radović Stjepan	Pelješac – Potomje	1884	Melbourne	VIC	Publican
Radovitch Thomas	Radović Tomislav	(Pelješac, Labin, Čilipi, Dubrovnik)		Crooked River	VIC	Miner
Raicevich Matteo	Rajčević Mate	(Zadar, Dubrovnik, Brač, Makarska)	1861	Epsom	VIC	
Raicovich Nicolla	Rajković Nikola	Dubrovnik	1874	Kalgoorlie	WA	Miner
Rascevitch Matteo	Raščević Mate		1862		VIC	
Rerecich Antone	Rerečić Ante	Island of Lošinj – Veli Lošinj	1886	Melbourne	VIC	Fisherman
Rerecich Giovanni	Rerečić Ivan	(Unije, Lošinj)	1883		VIC	Seaman
Rerecich Marco	Rerečić Marko	Island of Lošinj – Veli Lošinj		Port Pirie	SA	Labourer
Restar Jozo	Reštar Jozo	Kotor	1880	Innisfail	QLD	Seaman
Rich Antoni	—— Ante	Dalmatia	1878	Grafton	NSW	Seaman
Rismondo George	Rismondo Jure	Rovinj	1851	Melbourne	VIC	Restaurateur
Roberts Massline William	Masalin Vilim	Plomin	1864	Melbourne	VIC	Labourer
Rocco Giacomo	Rocco Jakov	Rovinj			NSW	
Rocke Andrew	Roki Andrija	Island of Vis	1869	Hastings	VIC	Fisherman
Roderick Frederick	Kos Jerolim	Island of Krk – Baška	1881	Walpa	VIC	Farmer
Roger John	—— Ivan	Split	1859	Port Adelaide	SA	Publican
Rosich Anton	Rošić, Rosić Anton	Rijeka	1882	Sydney	NSW	Seaman
Rosmanich Romeo	Rozmanić	Kostrena	1878	Melbourne	VIC	Grocer
Rossely Emilios	—— Emil	Dubrovnik	1879	Youanmite	VIC	Carpenter
Rossi Tomaso	Rossi Tomislav	Zadar	1852	Wedderburn	VIC	Farmer
Rossich Frederick	Rosić, Rošić Franjo	Island of Premuda	1881	Sydney	NSW	Fishmonger
Rossovich Martin	Rosović Martin	Mošćenica	1875	Paynesville	VIC	Fisherman
Rozenie Matthew	—— Mate	Dalmatia	1884	Sydney	NSW	Seaman
Rubesa (Rubbissir) Ludoviko	Rubeša Lodovico	Rijeka	1882	Sydney	NSW	Seaman
Rusich Antonio	Rusić, Rušić Ante	(Split, Pula, Zadar, Rijeka)	1870	Redcastle	VIC	Miner
Rusich George	Rusić, Rušić Jure	(Split, Pula, Zadar, Rijeka)	1885	Melbourne	VIC	Seaman
Ruzicka Joseph	Ružička Josip	(Rijeka, Split)	1875		NSW	Miner
Sabadina Joseph	Šabadin Josip	Dubrovnik	1882	Townsville	QLD	Labourer
Sabadina Nicholas	Šabadin Nikola	Dubrovnik	1859	Charters Towers	QLD	Miner
Sabadine George	Šabadin Jure	Dubrovnik	1862	Gulgong	NSW	Horse dealer
Sades Andrea	—— Andrija	Island of Lošinj	1882	Maryborough	VIC	
Sambralo George	Sambrajilo, Sambrailo Jure	(Island of Korčula, Dubrovnik)	1875		VIC	
Sarich Giovanni	Šarić Ivan	(Split, Tučepi, Šibenik, Pakoštane)	1861	Epsom	VIC	
Sarich Matte	Šarić Mate	Dalmatia	1880	Cairns	QLD	Miner
Sarinich Lorenzo	Sarinić Lovre	(Rijeka, Split)	1866	Sydney	NSW	Seaman
Sbisa Christoforo	Sbisa Kristo	Rovinj	1885	Sydney	NSW	Merchant
Scoglier (Skoljar) Luka	—— Luka	Split	1886	Tarraville	VIC	Fisherman
Scokenich Pietro	Skoknić Petar	Pelješac – Boljenovići	1882	Wedderburn	VIC	Farmer

Name	Croatian version	Birthplace	Arrival	Residence	State	Occupation
Scopenage Antonio	Scopinich, Skopinić Ante	(Island of Lošinj, Rijeka)	1858	Geelong	VIC	Fisherman
Scopinich Gaspar	Scopinich Gašpar	Island of Lošinj	1860	Bendigo	VIC	Miner
Seftrovich Thomas	—— Tomislav		1861	Inglewood	VIC	
Sellovich Luke	Šilović Luka	(Rijeka)	1855	Ballarat	VIC	Miner
Senara John	Sonjara Ivan	(Trogir)	1890	Wedderburn	VIC	
Senjara Lucas	Sonjara Luka	Trogir	1857	Wedderburn	VIC	Miner
Sentch Nikola	Doričić Pavao	Kostrena	1864			
Sepich Matthew	Šepić, Sepić Mate	Rijeka	1882	Brisbane	QLD	Oyster saloon keeper
Serovich Samuel	Šerović Samuel	Dalmatia	1885	St Johns Park	NSW	Farmer
Sersic John	Seršić Ivan	Rijeka	1875	Melbourne	VIC	Fisherman
Sersich Georgio	Seršić Jure	(Rijeka)	1857	Gulgong	NSW	Miner
Serventi Ante	Serventi Ante	Island of Brač – Bol	1890			
Seville Julius	Ševelj Julijan	Dalmatia	1879	Ballarat	VIC	Labourer
Sharowitch (Sarovich) Christopher	Šarović Kristo	(Dubrovnik, Ugljan)	1864	Melbourne	VIC	Seaman
Siercovich Allesandro	Siercovich Aleksandar	Island of Lošinj – Mali Lošinj	1861		VIC	
Sierech Giovanni	—— Ivan		1862		VIC	
Sievcorich Stefano	—— Stjepan		1861	Epsom	VIC	
Siglich Nicholas	Štiglić Nikola	(Praputnjak, Krasica, Rijeka, Bakar)	1855	Inglewood	VIC	Miner
Silovich Paul	Šilović Pavao	(Rijeka, Split)	1875	Gulgong	NSW	Miner
Simotich Felice	Simotich Srećko	Opatija	1887	Sydney	NSW	Cook
Sincovich Stefano	Sinković Stjepan	(Labin, Pelješac, Rijeka)	1861	Bendigo	VIC	Miner
Singer Bela	Singer	Vukovar	1885	Sydney	NSW	Merchant
Sinnet Thomas	—— Tomislav		1881	Sydney	NSW	Seaman
Sinranovich Nicola	—— Nikola		1875	Gulgong	NSW	
Sirovich Andrea	Sirović Andrija	(Bakar)	1856		VIC	
Sirovich S	Sirović	(Bakar)	1856		VIC	
Sitanich Nicholas	Cvitanić Nikola	Island of Brač – Bol	1874	Palmer River	QLD	Miner
Skalica Tomo	Skalica Tomo	Slavonski Brod	1853	Sydney	NSW	Miner
Skorlic Matteo	Škorlić Mate	Island of Iž – Iž Veli	1887	Sydney	NSW	
Slabich Ant	Slabić Ante	(Pelješac, Klis)	1888	Sydney	NSW	
Slabich Anton	Slabić Antun	Pelješac – Nakovanj	1882	Boulder	WA	Fireman
Slabich Giov	Slabić Ivan	(Pelješac, Klis)	1888	Sydney	NSW	
Slocovich Bogden	Sloković Bogdan	Slavonia	1861	Redcastle	VIC	Miner
Smith (Sepich) Henry	Šepić, Sepić Henrik	Rijeka	1874	Sydney	NSW	Seaman
Smokvina Vicko	Smokvina Vicko	Rijeka	1884	Sydney	NSW	Labourer
Spadier Stephen	Špadijer Stjepan	(Dubrovnik – Gruda)	1876	Melbourne	VIC	Carpenter
Spallatrino Louis	Spalatin Alojzije	Split	1856	Redcastle	VIC	Miner
Sparocrich N	Sparožić	(Krk, Rijeka)	1881	Sydney	NSW	
Sparozvich Nicolo	Sparožić Nikola	Island of Krk – Omišalj	1880	Maryborough	QLD	Boatman
Sponza George	Sponza Jure	(Rovinj)	1887	Townsville	QLD	Seaman
Sponza Giovanni	Sponza Ivan	Rovinj	1877	Port Adelaide	SA	Seaman
Sponza Marko	Sponza Marko	(Rovinj)	1885	Townsville	QLD	Seaman
Stagatich (Slagatich) Tom	—— Tomislav	Dalmatia	1877	Boulder	WA	Labourer

Name	Croatian version	Birthplace	Arrival	Residence	State	Occupation
Stanich C	Stanić	(Omiš, Lovka, Zvečanje, Rijeka)	1890	Broken Hill	NSW	Miner
Stanich Prospero	Stanić Prosper	Island of Hvar – Hvar	1873	Sydney	NSW	Ear/eye doctor
Stanwich Peter	—— Petar		1868	Sydney	NSW	Seaman
Star Joseph	—— Josip	Zadar	1863		NSW	Seaman
Starcevich Natale	Starčević Božo	Kraljevica	1852	Sydney	NSW	Wine merchant
Starnich Antonio	—— Ante		1889	Sydney	NSW	
Stepparich Martin	—— Martin		1887	Sydney	NSW	Labourer
Sticpewich Nicolas	—— Nikola		1861	Newcastle	NSW	Labourer
Stiglich Francesco	Štiglić Franjo	(Praputnjak, Krasica, Rijeka, Bakar)	1887	Sydney	NSW	Labourer
Stiglich Jacob	Štiglić Jakob	(Praputnjak, Krasica, Rijeka, Bakar)	1879	Korumburra	VIC	Miner
Stiglich Martino	Štiglić Martin	(Praputnjak, Krasica, Rijeka, Bakar)	1861	Epsom	VIC	
Stipicich Giovanni	Stipičić Ivan	(Island of Brač)	1860	Crooked River	VIC	Miner
Stipicich Nicholas	Stipičić Nikola	Island of Brač	1874	Buckland	VIC	Miner
Stippitch John	Stipić Ivan	(Gradac, Podhum, Split, Drvenik Mali)	1858	Cookstown	QLD	Miner
Stippitch Nicholas	Stipić Nikola	(Gradac, Podhum, Split, Drvenik Mali)	1873	Cookstown	QLD	Miner
Stooks John	Stuk Ivan	Rijeka	1871		NSW	Quarryman
Stuparich Giuseppe	Stuparić Josip	(Lošinj, Pula, Opatija, Vis)	1863	Epsom	VIC	
Sucocovich Matteo	Uskoković Mate	Dubrovnik	1865	Port Lincoln	SA	Seaman
Suhar Luca	Suhor Luka	(Pelješac – Nakovanj)	1888	Sydney	NSW	
Suhor Antun	Suhor Antun	Pelješac – Nakovanj	1886			
Sulich Andria	Sulić Andrija	Makarska		Townsville	QLD	Seaman
Susanich James	Suzanić Jakov	(Rijeka, Pula, Opatija)	1883	Gulgong	NSW	Horse dealer
Svilaric Mateo	Svilarić Mate	Čepikuće	1886	Mulgabbie	WA	Miner
Svitanovih Antonio	Cvitanović Ante	Zadar	1856	St Arnaud	VIC	Miner
Tadich Nicholas	Tadić Nikola	Island of Vis	1852	Melbourne	VIC	Farmer
Tadich Samuel	Tadić Samuel	Island of Vis	1885	Melbourne	VIC	Miner
Tarabochia Antonio	Tarabokija Ante	(Susak, Lošinj – Mali Lošinj)	1877	Sydney	NSW	Labourer
Tarabochia Dominic	Tarabokija Dominik	Island of Susak	1890	Portarlington	VIC	Fisherman
Terdich John	Terdić Ivan	Lovran	1866	Melbourne	VIC	Restaurateur
Ticiak Louis	Tičak, Tićak Alojzije	(Jablanac, Zadar, Rijeka, Crikvenica)	1870	Sydney	NSW	Farmer
Tintor John	Tintor Ivan	Bakar	1866	Melbourne	VIC	Seaman
Todorovich Lazar	Todorović Lazar	Dalmatia	1864	Crooked River	VIC	Miner
Tomanovich Pietro	Tomanović Petar	Kotor	1860	Epsom	VIC	Miner
Tomasevich Luka	Tomašević Luka	Baćina	1884	Melbourne	VIC	Farmer
Tomich Mattes	Tomić Mate	Dalmatia		Port Pirie	SA	Labourer
Toncovick Cosmo	Tonković Kuzma	(Dubrovnik, Rijeka, Makarska)	1857	Geelong	VIC	
Topic L	Topić	(Makarska, Split, Kućine, Dubrovnik)	1887		VIC	
Topic Louis	Topić Alojzije	(Makarska, Split, Kućine, Dubrovnik)	1876	Brisbane	QLD	Farmer
Torchie Nicholas	Trče Nikola	Pelješac – Hodilje	1875	Portarlington	VIC	Fisherman

Name	Croatian version	Birthplace	Arrival	Residence	State	Occupation
Tripovich Matthew	Tripović Mate	Kotor – Tivat	1851	Colac	VIC	Labourer
Trobog Baldosa	Trobok Baldo	(Pelješac – Prizdrina)	1866	Wedderburn	VIC	Miner
Trumbich Giovanni	Trumić Ivan	(Split)	1884		VIC	
Tuckton John	Tuchton Ivan	Rijeka	1857	Clunes	VIC	Miner
Tussup Spirodine	Tušup Špiro	Dalmatia	1860	Huntly	VIC	Farmer
Tverdeich Andrew	Tvrdeić Andrija	(Island of Korčula)		Sydney	NSW	
Urdessich Pietro	—— Petar		1863		VIC	
Usanorich Diodato	—— Božidar	Kotor	1882		VIC	
Vagliarn Antony	—— Ante	Bakar	1882	Wedderburn	VIC	Miner
Vancasich John	—— Ivan		1853	Maryborough	VIC	Miner
Vasavich Pasquale Giacomo	—— Jakov		1863		VIC	
Vecerina Francesco	Večerina Franjo	Rijeka – Draga	1882	Barmedman	NSW	Miner
Vedelitch Domenico	Vidulić Dominik	(Lošinj, Rijeka, Pridvorje Konavle)	1859	Mount Blackwood	VIC	
Veleich Nicolo	Velečić Nikola	Island of Cres	1859	Buninyong	VIC	Miner
Venticich Peter	Vantačić Petar	Island of Krk – Malinska	1880	Melbourne	VIC	Farmer
Veolich Peter	Violić Petar	Dalmatia	1870		NSW	Seaman
Verabona Antonio	Verabona Ante	Rijeka	1882	Wedderburn	VIC	Miner
Veselich Stephano	Veselić Stjepan	(Pridvorje Konavle, Rijeka, Trogir)	1860		NSW	Miner
Vicevich Matthew	Vičević, Vićević Mate	Rijeka	1888	Somerset	TAS	Saw miller
Vichevich Alexander	Vičević Aleksandar	Rijeka	1880	Sydney	NSW	Painter
Vichie (Vichi) Nichols	—— Nikola		1885	Sydney	NSW	Miner
Vidacovich Spiro	Vidaković Špiro	(Kožino, Ugljan, Biograd, Split)	1890	Avenel	VIC	Labourer
Vidas Pavle	Vidas Pavle	Hreljin	1889	Lilydale	VIC	Labourer
Vidisich Giovanni	—— Ivan	Island of Olib	1882	Melbourne	VIC	Proprietor
Vidotto Giovanni	Vidotto Ivan	Rovinj		Australia		
Vidulech Felice	Vidulić Srećko	(Island of Lošinj)	1874	Brooklyn	NSW	Labourer
Vidulich Antonio	Vidulić Ante	Island of Lošinj – Mali Lošinj		Melbourne	VIC	Labourer
Vidulich Joseph	Vidulić Josip	Island of Lošinj – Mali Lošinj	1873	Townsville	QLD	Seaman
Vidulich Joseph	Vidulić Josip	Island of Lošinj – Mali Lošinj	1889	Townsville	QLD	
Viehovich (Vncetich) Antony	—— Ante		1875	Wattle Flat	NSW	
Vigelic Bald	—— Baldo		1888	Sydney	NSW	Seaman
Vincent John	Vuković Vicko	Island of Šipan	1858	Fremantle	WA	Seaman
Violich Rocco	Violić Roko	Pelješac – Potomje	1884	Sydney	NSW	
Viscestorick Giovani	—— Ivan		1860	Inglewood	VIC	Miner
Viscovitch Pasco	Visković, Višković Paško	(Hvar, Labin, Tučepi, Makarska)	1857	Bendigo	VIC	Miner
Viscowitch Paul	Visković, Višković Pavao	(Hvar, Labin, Tučepi, Makarska)	1864	Sydney	NSW	
Viskovich Vincent	Visković, Višković Vicko	(Hvar, Labin, Tučepi, Makarska)		Sydney	NSW	
Vizkovich Vincent	Vicković Vicko	(Split)	1887	Townsville	QLD	Seaman
Vizles Spero	—— Špiro	Kotor	1882	Sydney	NSW	Labourer
Vizulin Antonio	Viculin Ante	(Split, Zlarin)	1863	Gulgong	NSW	Miner
Vlach Francis	Vlach, Vlak Franjo	(Pula, Rijeka)	1856	Port Adelaide	SA	Seaman

Name	Croatian version	Birthplace	Arrival	Residence	State	Occupation
Vodanovich Gerald	Vodanović	Island of Vis	1885	Sydney	NSW	Fishmonger
Vodanovich Lena	Vodanović	Island of Vis	1885	Sydney	NSW	
Voinich Luke	Vojinić Luka	Dubrovnik	1864	Clermont	QLD	Miner
Vokick Mateo	Vokić Mate	(Dubrovnik)	1858	Melbourne	VIC	
Volich John	Volić Ivan	Kotor	1864	Wedderburn	VIC	Labourer
Vonvich Matthew	—— Mate			Sydney	NSW	
Voscovich John	Vušković Ivan	(Brač, Split)	1885	Sydney	NSW	
Vragulin Andrea	Bragulin Andrija	Topolo	1886	Sydney	NSW	Glass blower
Vranat Peter	Vranac Petar	Dubrovnik	1883	Adelaide	SA	Seaman
Vranca Pietro	—— Petar	Island of Hvar – Starigrad	1882	Moonlight	VIC	
Vranik (Vranick) Joseph	Vranić Josip	(Rijeka, Poreč)	1880	Sydney	NSW	Engine driver
Vranzigan Peter	Vranjican Petar	Dalmatia	1868	Moonlight	VIC	Miner
Vucelich	Vucelić	(Dubrovnik)	1873	Melbourne	VIC	
Vucetih Antonio	Vučetić Ante	Island of Hvar – Starigrad	1882	Wedderburn	VIC	Miner
Vucotich Stefano	Vučetić Stjepan	(Hvar, Dubrovnik, Pula, Korčula)	1861	Epsom	VIC	
Vukasinovich Baldassare	Vukašinović Baldo	Dubrovnik – Gruž	1875	Point Cloates	WA	Seaman
Vukasovich John	Vukasović Ivan	Kotor	1854	Maryborough	VIC	Miner
Vukelich Frank	Vukelić Franjo	(Senj, Rijeka, Crikvenica, Bakar)	1882	Sydney	NSW	
Vulisich Nicolo	—— Nikola	Dubrovnik	1882	Maryborough	VIC	Miner
Vulovich Diodato	Vulović Božidar	Kotor – Dobrota	1875	Point Cloates	WA	Seaman
Vuoolich Stevano	Vulić Stjepan	(Island of Brač, Split)	1874		QLD	
Vuscovich Bartholomeu	Vušković Bartul	(Island of Brač, Split)		Sydney	NSW	
Vuscovich Matteo	Vušković Mate	Island of Brač – Sutivan	1886	Sydney	NSW	Fishmonger
Vuscovich Natale	Vušković Božo	Island of Brač – Supetar	1862	Portarlington	VIC	Fisherman
Waldren Charles	—— Dragutin/Karlo	Rijeka	1888	Melbourne	VIC	Seaman
White Thomas	—— Tomislav	Rijeka	1880	Melbourne	VIC	Carpenter
Williams Marco	—— Marko	Island of Korčula	1882	Melbourne	VIC	Carpenter
Wolfe Antonio	Vuković Ante	Dubrovnik	1852	Tumbarumba	NSW	Miner
Woolitch (Woolich) Peter	Vulić Petar	(Brač, Split)	1875	Gulgong	NSW	
Yackovitze Antonio	—— Ante	Dalmatia	1857	Wandiligong	VIC	Vigneron
Yannich (Yanich) Vincent	Janić Vicko	(Rijeka, Split)	1870	Sydney	NSW	Fishmonger
Yannich Luke	Janić Luka	Dalmatia	1877	Omeo	VIC	Miner
Yerko Giov	Jerko Ivan		1888	Sydney	NSW	
Yerko Paolo	Jerko Pavao		1888	Sydney	NSW	
Zagabria Jacob	Zagabrija Jakob	(Plomin)		Sydney	NSW	
Zagabria Joseph	Zagabrija Josip	Plomin	1888	Portarlington	VIC	Fisherman
Zagabria Rocco	Zagabrija Roko	(Plomin)		Korumburra	VIC	
Zan Clara	Zaninović Klara	Island of Hvar – Starigrad	1889	Melbourne	VIC	Domestic duties
Zan Manda	Zaninović Manda	Island of Hvar – Starigrad	1889	Melbourne	VIC	Singer
Zan Marino	Zaninović Marin	Island of Hvar – Starigrad	1889	Melbourne	VIC	Broom maker
Zan Ursula	Zaninović Uršula	Island of Hvar – Starigrad	1889	Melbourne	VIC	
Zan Vincent	Zaninović Vicko	Island of Hvar – Starigrad	1889	Melbourne	VIC	Broom maker
Zan Vincent	Zaninović Vicko	Island of Hvar – Starigrad	1889	Melbourne	VIC	Broom maker
Zanchi Vincent	Zanki Vicko	Island of Vis – Komiža	1890	Moruya	NSW	Fisherman
Zanetic Antonio	Zanetić Ante	(Dubrovnik, Pula, Korčula)		Mossman	QLD	Seaman
Zanetovich Matteo	Zanetović Mato	Kotor	1875	Point Cloates	WA	Seaman

Name	Croatian version	Birthplace	Arrival	Residence	State	Occupation
Zani Joseph	Zani Josip	(Pula, Rijeka, Vrsar)	1874		NSW	Contractor
Zaninovich George	Zaninović Jure	Island of Hvar – Starigrad	1861	Majorca	VIC	Miner
Zaninovich Mary Elizabeth	Zaninović Marija	Island of Hvar – Starigrad	1889	Melbourne	VIC	
Zarich Vincent	Zarić Vicko	Island of Hvar – Starigrad	1857	Moonlight	VIC	Miner
Zenovitch (Zanovich) George	—— Jure		1861	Hill End	NSW	Miner
Zibilich James	Cibilić Jakov	Pelješac – Duba	1862	Buckland	VIC	Miner
Zilic Grigorio	Zilić, Cilić Jure	(Dubrovnik)	1890	Sydney	NSW	Grocer
Zivurich Nicholas	—— Nikola		1857		VIC	
Zourich Andrew	Zurić, Curić Andrija	(Dubrovnik, Vis, Split, Šibenik)	1879	Wedderburn	VIC	
Zubrinich John	Žubrinić Ivan	Senj – Otočac	1880	Port Adelaide	SA	Labourer
Zuilanovich Giovanni	—— Ivan		1862	Epsom	VIC	
Zurach Vincent	Curać Vicko	Pelješac – Viganj	1890	Melbourne	VIC	Seaman
Zurich Joseph	Zurić, Curić Josip	(Dubrovnik, Vis, Split, Šibenik)		Wedderburn	VIC	
Zustovich Antonio	Zustović Ante	(Labin, Pula, Rijeka)	1876	Melbourne	VIC	Seaman
Zuzulich Martin	Cuculić Martin	(Kukuljanovo, Rijeka, Škrljevo)	1882	Sydney	NSW	Seaman
Zuzulich Thomas	Cuculić Tomislav	Kukuljanovo, Škrljevo	1883	Melbourne	VIC	Cook
Zvitanovich Giovanni	Cvitanović Ivan	(Iž, Igrane, Podaca, Brač)	1860	Ararat	VIC	
Zvitanovich Nikola	Cvitanović Nikola	Island of Korčula – Trstenik	1885		VIC	Fisherman
Zvitarovich Antonio	Cvitanović Ante	(Iž, Igrane, Podaca, Brač)	1868	Avoca	VIC	Miner

Croatian Pioneer Letters

A story told by Natale Vuscovich that was published in the local newspaper *The Bellarine Herald* on 20 March 1897 is detailed as follows:

As there was no sign of the steamers arriving, the time was whiled away in telling yarns. The one told by 'Christmas' was the most thrilling, and I now give it as told by himself – and, no doubt, it will be equally interesting to the readers of *The Bellarine Herald*. He said: 'I was born in St Peter, Austria [Supetar on the island of Brač], in 1837 [actually born on 6 September 1831]. When I was 18 years old I decided to follow the sea-faring life, and shipped aboard a brigantine called Marie Diano, which was bound to Troon [in Scotland] for a cargo of coal. During the trip nothing out of the way occurred. We loaded with coal, and then shaped our course to the island of Malta. We arrive there safely, and lay alongside the pier for several days, and then we received orders to proceed to a port in Sicily. Shortly before the vessel sailed the first mate called me up, and said, "Christmas, go ashore and go to my house, and ask my wife for my clean clothes." I set out on my errand, found the house, received the parcel, and made my way back to the pier. Imagine my dismay to find that I had no means of reaching the vessel, which was anchored some distance off, and on the point of sailing. None of the Maltese boatmen would consent to row me to the ship unless I paid them in advance. This I was unable to do, as all my money, etc., was on board the brigantine. It was now late in the evening, and, finding all efforts to get board unavailing, I turned my steps toward the town. I came across a coffee shop, where there was a big stone seat. No one was about, and I put the parcel down so as to make a pillow. I lay down, and was soon fast asleep. About half-past two next morning I was awakened by three men shaking me. One of them said, "You thief; what are you doing here?" I was very frightened, and told them of the plight I was in. The one who appeared to be the head man of the party said, "Come with us, you blackguard," and took hold of me by one arm and one shoulder, and, holding me at arm's length, kept kicking me on the back of the legs to make me walk faster. They took me along a lonely road for about two miles, when we came to a big stone wall. Getting closer to the wall, one of the men crouched down close to it, and another one seized me and put me on his back. The man on whose back I was standing gave a heave, and I found myself lying on the other side. They quickly followed, and, on my looking around, I found myself along a number of tombstones, and at once concluded we were in the cemetery. I was then taken to a certain grave, which was reality a vault. One of the men produced some tools, and quickly scraped the cement out of the joints and removed one of the slabs. He then seized me by the neck and produced a big knife, which he placed on my throat, and said, "Look down; there is where the lady is buried with all her jewellery. Go down and get it, or else I'll kill you." I was half dead with fright, and replied, "If I go down I'll die, and if I stay here you'll kill me; so it is all the same." Without more ado they put a rope round me and lowered me into the vault. I was afraid to look at the corpse, and, in a kind of dazed state, I felt for the jewels and got a number of rings, chains and earrings, and then stepped back from the corpse. One of the rings was a beauty, being set with a number of diamonds. Seeing this one, and thinking of my destitute state, I decided to keep it for myself, and quickly placed it in my mouth, and then shook the rope as a signal to be pulled up. I could not speak, and when once more above the ground I was searched, for I was quite helpless. They evidently knew of the beautiful ring, for, on not discovering it in my pockets, the leader questioned me, and, as my speech seemed thick, one of them seized me by the chin, and, forcing my mouth open, put his fingers in and brought forth the ring. They then covered the vault and put fresh cement in the joints so as to hide any clue to it having been tampered with. We then made "tracks" for the wall; but they had to carry me, for I was almost in a state of collapse. They put me over the wall, and before leaving me on the roadway the leader said, "Do you know us?", "No," replied I. "We do not care if you do know us," said he, "we did not steal anything – it was you." He then tripped me, and I fell close to the wall, where I remained and slept until about nine o'clock. On looking about me I did not know where I was, so decided to walk straight ahead. I met an old woman, and asked her the way to the pier. She directed me to keep straight on and I would not go wrong. On arriving in the town of Malta I was very weak, and made my way to the coffee shop where I had slept a portion of the night, and asked the keeper to give me some breakfast, which he did. After having a good feed I went to the pier, and found the Marie Diano had left the harbour during the night. This placed me in a very awkward position, for here I was a stranger in a strange land, without money or friends. I considered my position from all points, and finally decided to lay my case before the Austrian Consul. I accordingly waited on him, and he listened patiently to my story, and then gave me a sovereign, telling me to call on him every day while I was there, and he would try and secure for me a berth in some ship. Next morning I presented myself at the Consulate, and was informed that a yacht would sail for Sicily next morning at eight o'clock, and that I could go by it. At the hour appointed I went to the pier where the boat was lying and interviewed the captain, who told me they would sail in about half-an-hour, and decided to remain on board. Before we started a member of the clergy came on board, thus making a total of five persons on board the vessel. When we had been out about six or seven hours a stiff breeze came up. The clergyman was very frightened, and called on the captain to shorten sail. On hearing this request I used "one swear word," which evidently did not please the reverend gentleman, so he told the captain I was a very bad boy, and if he did not get rid of me all would perish. He kept this tale so much that the captain, being superstitious, believed him, and while I was leaving against the mast he sent two sailors to seize me. One grabbed me by the arms, and the other by the legs, and the skipper brought up a big barrel, into which I was put. Before the top was put on they asked me to forgive them, and kissed me, laying all the blame of their act on the reverend gentleman. I replied, "God forgive you; I forgive you. I do nothing wrong; no steal, no murder, no nothing. I go to Heaven after this". They then put a lid on the cask, and, after making a very small hole as a ventilator, dropped it overboard. I must have become unconscious, for I do not know, even now, the length of my residence in the barrel. When I came to my sense I found the cask so still that the conclusion dawned on me that I was on the land. I said, "Oh, my God! where am I," and then made efforts to try and get out of my prison, but without success. Fortunately I had my large clasp-knife with me, and, taking the small hole as a starting point, I determined to try and cut my way out of the barrel. After a lot of hard work I made the hole larger, and got a better supply of fresh air, which was very beneficial to me. I kept cutting my way, and soon had the satisfaction of seeing trees close by, and the knowledge of being on the land gave me fresh hopes. I still kept cutting the top of my prison, and presently saw a donkey grazing close by. I continued cutting the lid, and also kept my eye on the donkey. The day was very warm, and I saw the donkey coming closer and closer to my prison. At last he got close up and started to rub his body against the cask, at the same time going around it. I could now put my hand through the hole I had made. I got hold of his tail and put my clasp-knife in the hair of his tail, twisting it round and round until I reached the butt of the tail. I then hung on for dear life, and Mr Donkey started to kick at the cask, and at last he knocked several staves out, and thus I partly was free. I would not let go of his tail, and last he set off at a good pace, dragging the cask and myself behind him. He went about several hundred yards, and then stopped. I then got out of the cask, and, glad to be free, I sat down to consider. I decided to get on the donkey, for these animals always make for their homes at sunset. I caught him and quietened him considerably, and then mounted him – with my back to his head and my face to his tail. I let him go his own way, and after travelling about a mile I heard a man shouting, and, on looking round, I noticed a peasant pointing a gun at me, at the same time demanding in loud tones what I was doing with his donkey, terming me a thief and a blackguard. I told him of my adventures, but he was doubtful as to their truthfulness, and made me accompanying him to the shore. On seeing the barrel he was convinced, and then took me to his house, where I was well cared for, my host doing all in his power to make me comfortable. He told me that I could get to the port where the Marie Diano was lying on payment of five dollars to the boatman. On my telling him that I had no money, he said, "I have only two dollars, which you may have. Give them to the boatman, and tell him that he will get the other three from the captain of the ship." I heartily thanked him for his kindness and advice, and eventually I reached the ship. I saw the yacht from which I had been cast adrift lying in the harbour. My captain, on seeing me back again, gave orders for me to be placed in irons for desertion, but I loudly protested, and requested him to listen to my story, to which he agreed. After hearing my tale he asked me to point out the yacht, which I did. He made me accompany him to it, and we interviewed the captain and sailors, who supported my story as far as they were concerned. I may say that the men on the yacht were greatly surprised at seeing me again – in fact they took me for a ghost. The captain made inquiries as to the whereabouts of the clergyman, and was informed that he was in a monastery. Summonses were issued against the four persons, but the captain and sailors turned what is called "Queen's evidence," and the clergyman was committed for trial. However, before the trial came off the owner of Marie Diano made a sail for England, refusing to keep the ship waiting until the trial came off, so I never heard how the reverend gentleman fared.'[1]

Even though Natale Vuscovich's story may be exaggerated it gives one an idea of the kind of story he was famous for.

Two letters were sent to Mattio Marassovich from the island of Vis in 1897. Here is an English translation of the letter sent to Mattio Marassovich from his brother Giuseppe (Josip) Marasović.

18 July, 1897

Beloved Brother,

Woods Point
Australia Melbourne

Some days ago, my nephew Father Gregorio Pečarević sent me your letter from Vis, your letter posted last April. Oh! How surprised I was to see it, and happy. But reading it I became sad. I say surprised and happy, yes, because your news arrived unexpectedly. Happy because I still have a brother in the world, the other two having been buried as also our parents. Thank God. May they rest in peace.

I was saddened in reading that Mr Michele Tadin had erroneously informed you that my son was in those parts of the world and had not wanted to come and visit you.

But you must know that I have no children; I have never had any descendants.

Father Gregorio possibly explained to you our existence and the dispersal of our family. Here is a brief story of my life after your departure. I think it is fifty years since I saw you or heard from you, therefore I thought you among the dead. After you left, I went to study at Supetar on the island of Brač under the guidance of our uncle Father Giuseppe Tomić and I stayed there for 3 years and attended 3 normal classes and then sat for examinations at Split. After that I studied on the island of Vis for 2 years – the first 2 'matriculation' years with Father Simeone Stanić Bardella and I presented for examination at Split. Then I had to terminate my studies because of the hardship the island of Vis was undergoing due to the destruction of the farmlands by a fungi pest. Hence there were no means for everyday survival. I could not go to sea because of my physical indisposition so I had to learn the art of blacksmithing at my brother-in-law's place . . . Giorgio Tramontara Moro. After doing this for one year I went on with the now deceased Uncle Antonio Tomašević Schiopetter, married a second time to aunty Anetta, – it was with him that I worked and continued to get experience at Kaštela near Split where I stayed for 8 years; that is 5 years with him and 3 years after his death with aunty Anetta until 1860 when the revenue collection offices were opened in Vis. So I started to work with my brother-in-law. At that time all my earnings were consumed by the family, that is my parents, 3 sisters and an aunt, there were seven of us. I could not extricate myself from these commitments until the death of the old people and the marriage of the young ones. For Cate's wedding I gave her 250 florins, I gave Gele 100 and 39 to Ana and so my meagre financial situation. Also I had to pay certain debts of my deceased father – this consisted of about 200 florins and for all this I received not even a thankyou from anyone.

In 1865 people came to work in Alexandria on behalf of the French Agricultural and Industrial Society of Egypt. This society had to build dams and canals to clean the city. I went there and stayed for eight months as a blacksmith at the naval place and then because the company went broke I had to come home with a small bundle of 80 pounds sterling. When I came home I married the daughter of the deceased Vice Bučić Kuzmetto Caffettiere who lived near our place.

As she was sterile I have no heirs. Two months after the wedding there was a battle at Vis between Italy and Austria which I witnessed. As soon as the war finished I went to work at the Suez canal there I stayed for 3 years and brought home the sum of 350 pounds sterling. I am writing to tell you that I have not wasted my time. But what is the use?

I had dysentery in Egypt for 5 years which destroyed my strength and my body. So much so that the doctors forbade me my craft. Therefore to live honestly I got a job at the maritime lighthouse where 22 years have already passed. The stipend is miserable. That is 450 florins annually but we survive on it and soon I hope to be on a pension because of my eyesight is diminishing day by day.

This is a precis of my life of 58 years. Ah, if only I had known your whereabouts I would have come to embrace you. But now? It is too late because my body is decaying. Imagine being near death's door three times, three times confession and communion for the dead and I have even made a will due to the dysentery. I fear that life is short.

I now pass on to more important news. I wish to inform you of your paternal inheritance. It exists only in half of the large home in the quarter of Kut where our deceased grandmother and grandfather lived. This division occurred after their death. The house where we used to live was inherited by uncle Giovanni.

Uncle Michele was entitled to the one near the church of San Spilice. Aunty Anetta was entitled to the eastern half of the large house and our father to the western half. Last year the large house was valued at 800 florins.

Nothing remains of the farmlands after the death of our parents because the vines had not been tended … the house was threatened with collapse because it had been let go.

Last year because of necessity and under the advice of Father Gregorio and all of my sisters I had it restored. I had it raised a metre, I changed the door frames, I replaced all the wood and the roof. It nearly resembled a villa and could house two families. It comprised 1 kitchen, 2 rooms and a dining room per floor. I spent 1700 florins of my meagre finances to do all the renovations.

I am the future beneficiary of aunty Anetta as I have to maintain the property until her death. The restoration is complete, that is of all the house for the above sum.

I am now asking for your release (by letter or affidavit) of all your rights to your paternal inheritance which may consist of about 100 florins. That is only the paternal will that made his half to be available to his sons and the other half was to be equally divided amongst all his children – boys and girls. However, as I have restored all the house I thought it should be mine. So could you arrange who should look after your rights – your opinion will be my guide to put our affairs in order. Whatever your decision is it will be fine as far as I am concerned.

Let's pass on to giving my regards:

After so many years of silence and near oblivion permit me to embrace you and kiss you as a brother. With much jubilation I wholeheartedly embrace your son Matteo Noella. I bow and kiss the hands of your daughters Mrs Mari Giovanna and Miss Barbara. I warmly shake your son-in-laws hand. Caressing your children, I kiss everyone and kiss them again. It goes without saying that my consort Nina joins me in embracing you and says she remembers you well! Goodbye my dearest brother and descendants!

Bog mi vas živio. [May God give you long life]

Your affectionate brother

Beppo

If you should want to write, here is my address

Giuseppe [Josip] Marasović

Austria

Dalmazia [Dalmatia]

Lizza [Vis][2]

Croatian Halls and Sporting Venues

Victoria

Croatian Australian Association	Melbourne (Footscray)
Istra Social Club	Melbourne (Campbellfield)
Melbourne Knights (Melbourne Croatia)	Melbourne (Sunshine)
Croatian Catholic Centre Sunshine Hall	Melbourne (Sunshine)
Croatian Catholic Centre Springvale Hall	Melbourne (Springvale)
St Albans Saints (Dinamo)	Melbourne (St Albans)
Australian Croatian National Hall – Kardinal Stepinac	Geelong (Bell Park)
Croatian Community Centre of Geelong Inc	Geelong (Corio)
Australian Croatian Sporting Centre North Geelong Soccer Club	Geelong (Lara)
Croatian Club Dr Ante Starčević	Wodonga
Croatian Sporting Club Zagreb Inc	Mildura (Irymple)
Međimurski Club Mildura Inc	Mildura
Croatian Club (Gippsland Croatian Association Limited)	Traralgon
Australian Croatian Association Stjepan Radić	Ballarat

New South Wales

Croatian Club Ltd	Sydney (Punchbowl)
King Tomislav Croatian Club Ltd (Sydney United/Sydney Croatia)	Sydney (Edensor Park)
Jadran Hajduk Croatian Club Ltd	Sydney (St Johns Park)
Croatian Culture Association Bosna St Marys Ltd	Sydney (St Marys)
Dalmacija Sydney Croatian Club Ltd	Sydney (Terrey Hills)
Istra Social and Sports Club Sydney Inc	Sydney (Liverpool)

Croatian Cultural & Educational Association
  (Braća Radić Blacktown Ltd)   Sydney (Blacktown)
Croatian Catholic Centre Blacktown Hall   Sydney (Blacktown)
Croatian Community Centre   Wollongong
Croatian Wickham Sports Club Co-Op   Newcastle (Wickham)

Australian Capital Territory

Croatia Deakin Soccer Club   Canberra (Deakin)
Australian Croatian Club Ltd O'Connor   Canberra (O'Connor)

Western Australia

WA Croatian Community Centre   North Fremantle
Croatian House (Hrvatski Dom)   Perth (Gwelup)
Spearwood Dalmatinac Club Inc   Spearwood
Croatian Bowling Club Jedinstvo Inc   Swan Valley
Croatian Club Caversham Inc   Caversham

Queensland

Croatian Community Centre Qld   Brisbane (Rocklea)
Croatian Sports Centre – Gold Coast Inc   Gold Coast
Croatian Community Centre   Dimbulah
Croatian Club Cairns   Cairns

South Australia

The Croatian Club Adelaide Inc   Adelaide (Ridleyton)
Raiders Soccer Club Inc   Adelaide (Gepps Cross)
Australian-Croatian Community Club
  Eugen Kvaternik Mount Gambier Inc   Mt Gambier
Croatia Whyalla West Soccer and Social Club Inc Whyalla
Croatian Sporting Club of Port Lincoln Inc   Port Lincoln
Croatian Welfare and Sport Club Coober Pedy Coober Pedy

Tasmania

Australian Croatian Club   Hobart (Glenorchy)
Croatia Social and Sporting Club Invermay   Invermay

Acknowledgments

It has been a long and laborious, but satisfying journey researching and writing this book on the history of Croatians in Australia. However, I must sincerely thank all the people who have helped me along on this journey.

A special acknowledgement is due to Dr Vesna Drapač (senior lecturer in the History Department at the University of Adelaide) for the initial editorial comments and guidance. I would like to wholeheartedly thank my brother Dr Ivan Šutalo for his help with some of the preliminary research and my wife Ana Šutalo for photographically reproducing many of the original pioneer photographs over the years. Another special note of thanks is in order to Neven Smoje for his useful comments and help. I would also like to thank Dr James Jupp for writing the foreword to the book, Maria Zmijarević for her proof-reading assistance, and Nikola Rašić and Mate Bašić for the summary translation.

I am indebted to the following people/organisations for giving me access to photographs for the book: Marin Alagich, Andrew Allen, Richard Anicich, Bruce Bathols, Neale Bathols, Jim Beovich, Tomislav Beram, Charles Billich, Marijan Bošnjak, Braća Radić Sydney, Ivan Brajdić, Karl Bratković, Jakov Brdar, Steve Brdar, Višnja Brdar, Beverly Brighton, Debbie Brighton, Luka Budak, Buzolich family, Sheila Canny, Cardinal Stepinac Village, Vincent Chernich, Croatian Cartographic Society, Vera Crvenković, Graeme Cucel, Joan Culvenor, Agnes Cummins, Peter Cunich, Ivo Dabelić, Elsie Day, Daylesford and District Historical Society, Sofia Denis, Mario Despoja, Patrick Dominick, Angela Doros, Dr Vesna Drapač, East Gippsland Historical Society, Essendon Historical Society, Branko Filipi, Zdenka Filipi, Roger Franich, Michael Furjanić, Geelong Historical Record Centre, Rev. Stjepan Gnječ, Tom Grgich, Josip Grgurić, Frank Grivec, Mona Hammond, Steve Horvat, Kaye Host, Hrvatska Matica Iseljenika, Hrvatska Zora Melbourne, Tom Irga, Damir Ivka, Jure Jakovljević, Reg James, Donald Jasprizza, Margaret Jones, Slavka Jureta, Sue Kelly, Koleda Sydney, Korumburra Shire Historical Society, Rev. Mato Križanac, Zlata Krpan, LADO Geelong, Miljenko Lapaine, Ivan Lekovich, Linđo Sydney, Fabian Lovoković, John Lussick, Mary Macak, Nedjelko Marunčić, Mat Matich,

Loretta Meagher, Vin Mercovich, Mladi Frankopani Sydney, Mladi Hrvati Melbourne, Moharich family, Deborah Murray, Maureen O'Kelly, Old Court House, Orlovich family, Otago Settlers Museum, Dianne Parker, Robyn Parsons, Bernard Pavletich, Betty Pedretti, Katica Perinac, Ann Piller, Vanda Podravac, Leonard Radic, Rosalie Raftis, Margery Richardson, Brian Roderick, Pam Roderick, Mrs D. Rush, Neven Smoje, Dinko Stanić, Tomislav Starčević, Stawell Historical Society, Vesna Strika, Emilija Šutalo, Arnold Terdich, Dražen Tutić, Mr J. Vidovich, Vincent family, Bill Vojtek, Bruce Watt, Young Historical Society, Zagreb Wollongong, Leon Zann and Maria Zann.

I would also like to express my gratitude to all the people whom I interviewed and corresponded with. Also, all the people in libraries (especially the State libraries of Victoria, New South Wales, South Australia and Western Australia), Australian Archives, Public Records Office of Victoria, historical societies, Australian Bureau of Statistics and elsewhere who gave me assistance.

Lastly, I would like to thank the staff at Wakefield Press for editorial and administrative support.

Dr Ilija Šutalo

Notes

Chapter 1

1   Prior to the First World War, Croatians were also known as Dalmatians and Sclavonians. Yugoslavs was also spelt Jugoslavs or Jugo-slavs. 'Slavs' was a term commonly used for Croatians in Australia and some Croatians from Istria were known as Istrians.

2   2001 Australian Census Statistics, Australian Bureau of Statistics.
C. Price, 'The Ethnic Character of the Australian Population', p. 82.

3   In the 2001 Australian Census 15 per cent of Croatian speakers born in former Yugoslavia were born in republics other than Croatia or stated they were born in Yugoslavia. It should be noted that in the 2001 census some Croatians may have put South Slavic nfd, Serbian or Bosnian as the language spoken at home, especially in mixed marriages. According to the 2001 census 14,606 people stated they spoke South Slavic nfd.

4   It is expected that the number of Croatian-born in the Yugoslav-born category would be higher, as there are other Croatian-born who are not Catholic, classify themselves as Yugoslav-born and do not speak Croatian at home. The figure also does not include Croatians in the Bosnia-Herzegovina-born category who stated they spoke South Slavic nfd or English at home.

5   This figure does not include ethnic Serbians born in Croatia who said they were born in Yugoslavia, and does not include ethnic Italians born in Croatia who said they were born in Italy in the Australian Census.

6   In 1999 a third of the Giuliano-Dalmati clubs and associations in Australia had Croatian-born presidents.
G. Cresciani (ed.) *Giuliano-Dalmati in Australia: Contributi E Testimonianze Per Una Storia*, pp. 215–16, 227–31.
Personal communication with Alessandro Gardini on 11 July 2003 who is doing a PhD on Giuliano-Dalmati in Australia.

7   D. Stefanovic, 'Serbs', pp. 674–81.

8   In 1986 the Croatian language spoken at home category was first included in the Australian Census. Croatian speakers born in former Yugoslavia have been steadily increasing from 30,964 in 1986, 38,710 in 1991 and 43,811 in 1996 and then levelled off to 43,392 in 2001 as many more Croatians identify themselves as Croatian speakers rather than so called Yugoslav, Serbo-Croatian or South Slavic nfd speakers.

9   E. Kunz, *Displaced Persons: Calwell's New Australians*, pp. 43, 123.

10   *The McIvor News*, 7 Sept. 1860, p. 2; 8 Mar. 1861, p. 2; 31 May 1861, p. 2.
The McIvor Times, 14 Sept. 1893, p. 2.

11   By the 1870s, Croatian language newspapers and Croatian language schools gained more prominence in Dalmatia and Istria.

12   *NAA: A401/1, Catarinich, Catarinich Record of Aliens 6th Military District. NAA: A456/2, W3/29/170.*

13   Possible reasons for giving the false information about their age was that they generally wanted to impress their younger wife or perhaps their employers.

14   The Croatian alphabet is as follows:
A B C Č Ć D Dž Đ E F G H I J K L Lj M N Nj O P R S Š T U V Z Ž
a b c č ć d dž đ e f g h i j k l lj m n nj o p r s š t u v z ž

Croatian	English or Italisation
C	Z
Č	C, CK, TCH
Ć	C, CH, TCH
Đ	G, J
I	E
J	G, Y
K	C, Q, X
LJ	LY
Š	S, SS, SH
V	F
Ž	Z

Croatian surnames usually had two versions, the Croatian version and another version to make life easier under Venetian (Italian) and Austro-Hungarian rule. Many Croatian surnames were Italianised since the official language of administrative and legal bodies in Dalmatia and Istria was Italian. The Italian alphabet has no J or K so the Croatian surnames were modified accordingly. For example, J became G, K became C, and C became Z. Some examples of surnames where the C was replaced by Z include: Curać became Zurach, Cibilić became Zibilich, Ferenca became Ferentza, Drvenica became Darveniza. In the nineteenth century the church records in Croatia were sometimes in Latin or Italian, so the surnames are recorded in the Italianised version. Many Croatian pioneers' surnames ended in 'ić', which refers to 'son of'. For example, Marković is derived from son of Marko, in Croatian grammar Markov means Marko's.

P. Šimunović, *Hrvatska Prezimena – Podrijetlo, Značenje, Rasprostranjenost.*
A. Eterovich, *Croatian and Dalmatian Coats of Arms.*
15   *Iseljeništvo Pavla Vidasa.*
16   J. White, *The History of the Shire of Korumburra.*
K. Bowden, *The Early Days of Korumburra.*
17   T. Leavitt and W. Lilburn, *The Jubilee History of Victoria and Melbourne,* p. 40.
W. Bayley, *Rich Earth, History of Young New South Wales,* pp. 127, 225.
18   J. Flett, *The History of Gold Discovery in Victoria,* p. 155.
19   N. Smoje, 'Croatians in Western Australia 1858–1920'.
N. Smoje, 'Shipwrecked on the North-West Coast: The Ordeal of the Survivors of the "Stefano"', 1978, pp. 35–47.
N. Smoje, 'Early Croatian Settlement in Western Australia', pp. 338–9.
M. Alagich, 'Early Croatian Settlement in Eastern Australia', pp. 335–7.
20   M. Stenning, *Croatian and Slav Pioneers, New South Wales 1800's–1940's.*
M. Stenning, *Croatian and Slav Pioneers of South Australia and Victoria.*
M. Stenning, *Croatian and Slav Pioneers of Australia.*
M. Tkalcevic, *Croats in Australia: An Information and Resource Guide.*
M. Tkalčević, *Hrvati u Australiji.*
M. Tkalčević, *Povijest Hrvata u Australiji.*
21   C. Price, *Southern Europeans in Australia.*
C. Price, *The Method and Statistics of Southern Europeans in Australia,* pp. 2–3, 16.
22   K. Derado and I. Čizmić, *Iseljenici Otoka Brača.*
N. Vekarić, *Pelješki Rodovi (A–K).*
N. Vekarić, *Pelješki Rodovi (L–Z).*
S. Vekarić and N. Vekarić, *Tri Stoljeća Pelješkog Brodarstva.*
23   T. Jelić, *Gradišćanski Hrvati u Austriji.*

S. Božić, *Kroaten in Wien, Immigranten und Integration im Zusammenhang mehrschichtiger ethnischer Beziehugen.*

S. Krpan, *Hrvati u Keci.*

S. Krpan, *Hrvati u Rekašu Kraj Temišvara.*

Tjedan Moliških Hrvata.

Tjedan Hrvata iz Slovačke.

D. Pavličević, *Moravski Hrvati – Povijest – Život – Kultura.*

R. Jarabek, *Moravsti Charvati: Dejiny a Lidova Kultura.*

J. Lončarević, *Hrvati u Mađarskoj i Trianonski Ugovor.*

I. Lokos, *Hrvatsko-Mađarske Književne Veze, Rasprave i Članci.*

Ž. Mandić, *Povijesna Antroponimija Bunjevačkih Hrvata u Madžarskoj.*

24 J. Clissa, *The Fountain and the Squeezebox (La Fontana e L'Organetto/Funda aš Orginet).*

25 A. Eterovich, *Croatian Pioneers in America 1685–1900.*

A. Eterovich, *Croatians in California, 1849–1999.*

A. Eterovich and J. Simich, *General Index to Croatian Pioneers in California, 1849–1999.*

G. Prpic, *The Croatian Immigrants in America.*

A. Rasporich, *For a Better Life A History of the Croatians in Canada*, pp. 10–28.

26 L. Antić, *Hrvati u Južnoj Americi do Godine 1914*, pp. 10–11, 118–25, 197, 206–7, 244–50.

M. Martinic, *Voyagers to the Strait of Magellan Yugoslav (Croatian) Immigration to Southern Chile.*

M. Martinić, *Hrvati u Magallanesu Na Krajnjem Jugu Čilea.*

27 A. Trlin, *Now Respected, Once Despised Yugoslavs in New Zealand.*

T. Mursalo, *In Search of a Better Life: A Story of Croatian Settlers in Southern Africa*, pp. 42, 56–66.

28 Not all of the Croatian settlers to the United States before 1890 were from coastal Croatia. By the 1880s Croatians from inland Croatia had begun to settle in Pittsburgh, Chicago and Cleveland. During this period of Croatian emigration, non-Croatians (particularly Hungarians) migrated to Croatia.

L. Antić, *Hrvati u Južnoj Americi do Godine 1914*, pp. 31, 297, 309.

I. Čizmić, I. Miletić, and G. Prpić, *From the Adriatic to Lake Erie: A History of Croatians in Greater Cleveland*, p. 6.

S. Gaži, *Croatian Immigration to Allegheny County, 1882–1914*, pp. 24–7.

29 J. Lakatoš, *Narodna Statistika.*

M. Lorković, *Narod i Zemlja Hrvata.*

I. Čizmić, 'Emigration from Croatia, 1880–1914', pp. 143–67.

V. Mikačić, 'Overseas Migration of the Yugoslav Population in the Period between the Two World Wars', pp. 168–90.

30 During the Second World War many Croatians were left in foreign lands as prisoners of war or enforced labourers. Large numbers of people from territories occupied by Italy left when the territories were annexed into former Yugoslavia.

I. Nejašmić, 'Iseljavanje iz Hrvatske u Evropske i Prekomorske Zemlje od Sredine 19. Stoljeće do 1981. Godine – Pokušaj kvantifikacije', p. 517.

31 According to the 1991 Yugoslav Census, there were 285,216 Croatian citizens abroad, but the number was actually higher as many Croatians abroad did not participate in the census and Croatians from Bosnia-Herzegovina were not included. After the Second World War Australia became the main destination for migrants from some Croatian islands like Lastovo, Brač and Korčula. According to the 1991 Yugoslav Census, over 15 per cent of Lastovo's population lived in Australia.

I. Nejašmić, 'Hrvatski Građani na Radu u Inozemstvu: Razmatranje Popisnih Podataka 1971, 1981, i 1991,' pp. 139–56.

I. Nejašmić, 'Hrvatski Građani na Radu u Inozemstvu i Članovi Obitelji Koji s Njima Borave Prema Popisu 1991: Prikaz Prema Novom Teritorijalnom Ustrojstvu Jedinica Lokalne Samouprave', pp. 205–18.

K. Derado and I. Čizmić, *Iseljenici Otoka Brača*, pp. 11–12.

Z. Šeparović, *Od Sydneya Do San Francisa Dijaspora ili Rasutnost Mještana Blata na Korčuli Diljem Svijeta*, p. 23.

32 Boka Kotorska, 1871, Petrović, Rade, *Nacionalno Pitanje u Dalmaciji u XIX Stoljeću.*

J. Pečarić, 'Hrvati Boke Kotorske od 1918. Godine do Danas', pp. 290–300.

J. Pečarić, 'Težak Položaj Hrvata u Boki Kotorskoj', pp. 311–17.

Hrvati u Sloveniji, pp. 162, 255, 400.

33 Boka Kotorska (Kotor) and parts of Vojvodina were part of Croatia until they were annexed in 1945 to Montenegro and Serbia respectively. The Srijem and Bačka regions of Vojvodina still have a high concentration of Croatians, even though 30,000 were expelled from Vojvodina during the recent war. According to the 1931 Yugoslav Census, Germans constituted 40.9 per cent of the Vojvodina population. They were all forced to leave at the end of the Second World War and Serbs were resettled into their homes. In the 1990s many ethnic Hungarians were also forced to leave Vojvodina by the Serbian population.

A. Sekulić, *Bački Bunjevci i Šokci*.

Glasnik Foruma Hrvatskih Manjina, pp. 27–33.

Chapter 2

1 J. Donohoe, *The Forgotten Australians: the Non Anglo or Celtic Convicts and Exiles*, p. 52.
Castle Hill Catholic Church, baptism records.

2 Letter dated 9 March 1999 from Patrick Dominick, descendant of George Dominick.
New South Wales marriage certificate.
New South Wales death certificate.

3 This research is an ongoing project and as more Croatian pioneers are discovered they will be added to this number.

4 Price's estimates also do not show that in 1918 there were several hundred Croatians interned in Liverpool, New South Wales, many of whom were repatriated as aliens the following year.
C. Price, *Southern Europeans in Australia*, pp. 11, 22.
C. Price, *The Method and Statistics of Southern Europeans in Australia*, pp. 103, 108, 111.

5 Victorian Census statistics, 1881.

6 In the 1881 Victorian Census there were 323 Austrian-born in Victoria of which the 172 Croatians constituted 53 per cent. While in the register carried out by the Austrian Consulate of Austrian subjects in Victoria in 1882 Croatians constituted 71 per cent.
Akten des Ministeriums des Äußern, Administrative Registratur F8/169 Konsulate, Melbourne 1880–1918 (November 1882), Österreichisches Staatsarchiv (Austrian Archives) Haus-, Hof- Und Staatsarchiv.

7 Victorian marriage certificate.
Catholic parish records at Jelsa on the island of Hvar.
HAD, baptism records for Mokošica in Dubrovačka Rijeka.

8 L. Baldassar, *Visits Home, Migration Experiences between Italy and Australia*, p. 110.

9 N. Vekarić, *Pelješki Rodovi (A–K)*, pp. 133–5.
A. Jutronić, *Naselja i Porijeklo Stanovništva na Otoku Braču, Zbornik za Narodni Život i Običanje*, pp. 45, 84, 86.

10 E. Balch, *Our Slavic Fellow Citizens*, pp. 192–4.

11 HAZ, baptism records for Starigrad on the island of Hvar.

12 S. Vekarić and N. Vekarić, *Tri Stoljeća Pelješkog Brodarstva*, p. 108.
Naturalisation certificate.

13 HAD, baptism and marriage records for Orebić-Stankovići on the Pelješac Peninsula.
S. Vekarić and N. Vekarić, *Tri Stoljeća Pelješkog Brodarstva*, p. 130.

14 J. Tomasevich, *Peasants, Politics and Economic Change in Yugoslavia*.

15 Many Croatians in Dalmatia made a living from wine production. However, in the early 1890s the 'wine clause' trade agreement between Italy and Austro-Hungary allowed the importation of cheap wines from Italy at low duty into the Austro-Hungarian empire which decreased the sale price of wine in the Austro-Hungarian empire and severely affected Croatian vignerons. This was then followed by the phylloxera outbreak of the 1890s that devastated the wine industry in Croatia. This led to an increase in Croatian migration after 1890.
E. Balch, *Our Slavic Fellow Citizens*, pp. 161–3, 194–5.

16 J. Wilkinson, *Dalmatia and Montenegro*, pp. 6–7.

17 E. Balch, *Our Slavic Fellow Citizens*, p. 51.
18 I. Perić, *A History of the Croats*, pp. 137, 162–72, 177, 181–2.
19 E. Balch, *Our Slavic Fellow Citizens*, pp. 179–80, 194–5.
20 S. Korzelinski, *Opis Podrozy do Australii*, pp. 112–14.
21 PROV, VPRS 11448/P1 [Index to Inward Overseas Passengers from British Ports 1852–1923].
22 PROV, VPRS 945/P, Unit 7 [18/Release Books of Ships' Crew].
23 C. Price, *The Method and Statistics of Southern Europeans in Australia*, p. 47.

Chapter 3

1 *Victorian Census.*
   G. Serle, *The Golden Age*, p. 370.
   I. Wynd, *Geelong The Pivot*, pp. 38–9.
2 St Mary's Catholic Church, Geelong, baptism records.
3 A. Campbell, *Tourist Guide to Geelong and Southern Watering Places*.
   Bailliere's Victorian Gazetteer and Road Guide, 1879, p. 385.
4 The Croatians living in Portarlington in 1882 were Antonio Bundara, John Bundara, Stephen
   Coloper, John Lussich, Dominick Lussich, Natale Lussich, John Lussich Slavich, Matteo Marush,
   Gregory Pavletich and Nicholas Torchie.
   Akten des Ministeriums des Äußern, Administrative Registratur F8/169 Konsulate,
   Melbourne 1880–1918 (November 1882), Österreichisches Staatsarchiv (Austrian Archives)
   Haus-, Hof- Und Staatsarchiv.
   F. Maning and W. Bishop, *Maning and Bishop's Geelong and Western District Directory 1882–83*,
   pp. 141–3.
5 *The Geelong Advertiser*, 13 June 1892, p. 2.
   Shire of Bellarine, Riding of Paywit, rate books.
6 *The Geelong Advertiser*, 5 Jan. 1884, p. 3.
7 Shire of Bellarine, Riding of Paywit, rate books.
8 Naturalisation certificate.
9 Victorian death certificate.
   Sands and McDougall's Directory.
10 G. Davison, *The Rise and Fall of Marvellous Melbourne*, pp. 4–5, 14.
11 *Australians Historical Statistics*, pp. 29, 41.
   G. Davison, *The Rise and Fall of Marvellous Melbourne*.
12 HAR, baptism records for Kukuljanovo.
   Naturalisation certificate.
   Victorian marriage certificate.
13 *Sands and McDougall's Directory.*
14 *The Age*, 15 Aug. 1918, pp. 1, 10.
   Naturalisation certificate.
15 *The Southern Cross*, 10 Apr. 1980, p. 2.
16 HAR, baptism records for Bakar.
   Naturalisation certificate.
   Sands and Kenny's Commercial and General Melbourne Directory.
17 Naturalisation certificate.
   Catholic parish records, Rovinj.
18 Catholic parish records, Supetar on the island of Brač.
   Sands and McDougall's Directory.
19 *The Age*, 4 July 1933, p. 1.
   The Argus, 4 July 1933, p. 1.
20 *The Victoria Government Gazette*, 1882, pp. 1658, 1708, 1980, 3124.
21 Some Croatian fishmongers in Melbourne were Antonio Bundara, Stephen Coloper, Nicholas
   Duper, James Matulich, Nicholas Musich, Antonio Pavletich, Martin Pavletich, John Radich and
   John Sersic. From 1887 until the First World War there were always at least two Croatian
   fishmongers in Melbourne.

Sands and McDougall's Directory.

22 Conversation on 23 July 1995 with Leonard Radic, the grandson of John Radich.
Victorian marriage certificate.

23 The number of Melbourne householders renting increased from 54.5 per cent in 1881 to
65 per cent in 1901, due to the 1890s depression in Melbourne.
G. Davison, *The Rise and Fall of Marvellous Melbourne*, pp. 180–1, 187.
Sands and McDougall's Directory.

24 The surnames of the Croatian pioneers buried in Melbourne General Cemetery were Arnerich,
Blessich, Bundara, Buzolich, Catarinich, Filinich, Fornarich, Lucich, Lusetich, Lusic, Marghetic,
Marinovich, Marinowitch, Marsich, Mercovich, Missitich, Pasquan, Radich, Rusich, Scopenage,
Terdich and Zustovich.
Melbourne Cemetery records and tombstone inscriptions.

25 Bunjevci are Croatians who primarily came from the Bačka region in Vojvodina and southern
Hungary, while Banovci are Croatians who came from the former military frontier region of
Croatia.
Iseljeništvo Pavla Vidasa, pp. 18, 22–4.

26 In Yandoit there was also a concentration of Italians.

27 Parish of Yandoit, County of Talbot.
Parish of Sandon, County of Talbot.

28 St Mary's Catholic Church, Castlemaine, baptism records.
Sandon Cemetery records.
PROV, VPRS 795, Unit 1265 [2050].

29 Naturalisation certificate.

30 St Mary's Catholic Church, Castlemaine, baptism records.
Rate book, Shire of Mount Franklin – North Riding.
Parish of Yandoit, County of Talbot.

31 *The Mount Alexander Mail*, 8 Feb. 1894, p. 3.
Victorian death certificate.

32 *The Echo* (Newstead), 10 Feb. 1909, p. 2.

33 Korzelinski only states that Giuseppe B's surname begins with B.
S. Korzelinski, *Opis podrozy do Australii*, pp. 112–14.

34 C. Glass, *The Castlemaine Directory and Book of General Information Comprehending Glass's Model
Calendar for the two years 1862 and 1863*, p. 51.

35 *The Metcalfe Shire News*, 12 Mar. 1892, p. 4.

36 S. Korzelinski, *Opis podrozy do Australii*, p. 8.
S. Korzelinski, *Memoirs of Gold-Digging in Australia*, p. 110.

37 The Castlemaine district included Yandoit, Castlemaine, Taradale, Daylesford, Hepburn
and Eganstown.
Catholic parish records, Rovinj.
Victorian marriage certificate.
Victoria and its Metropolis Past and Present Vol. IIA. The Colony and its People in 1888, p. 240.
The Victoria Government Gazette, 1866, p. 744.
Letter dated 4 January 1994 from Daylesford and District Historical Society Incorporated
Records – written records.
The Geelong Advertiser, 17 Dec. 1896, p. 1.
The Daylesford Herald, 18 Dec. 1896, p. 2.

38 Township of Wedderburn, Parish of Wedderburn, County of Gladstone.
Parish of Wedderburn, County of Gladstone.

39 A cross-section of the Wedderburn community are: Stefano Celovich from Kotor, Giovanni
Curliza (Ivan Čurlica) from Dubrovnik, Antonio Vucetih (Ante Vucetić) from Starigrad on the
island of Hvar, Thomas Rossi from Zadar, Ignatio Billich from Trogir and Andrea Guircovich
from Opatija.

40 Naturalisation certificate.
PROV, VPRS 263 [Korong Division, Register of Claims]
Victorian death certificate.

Wedderburn Cemetery records.
PROV, VPRS 28/P3, Unit 278 [124/245].
41   Naturalisation certificate.
The St Arnaud Mercury, 5 June 1875, p. 2; 27 Apr. 1904, p. 2.
42   A. Strange, *Ballarat A Brief History*, p. 22.
43   HAZ, birth and marriage records for Starigrad on the island of Hvar.
The Ballarat Courier, 8 Aug. 1900, p. 5; 9 Aug. 1900, p. 5.
44   Victorian death certificate.
45   HAZ, birth records for Starigrad on the island of Hvar.
Maryborough and District Hospital Victoria, Index to Admissions 1855–1907.
PROV, VPRS 1645 [Registrar of Claims, Maryborough].
Victorian death certificate.
46   *The Pleasant Creek News*, 16 June 1875, p. 2.
Tombstone inscription, Stawell Cemetery.
47   Stawell Historical Society Incorporated, records.
The Pleasant Creek News, 6 Apr. 1872, p. 1 to 24 Nov. 1874, p. 1.
48   There were also Croatian miners in Ararat, Beaufort and Raglan.
The Pleasant Creek News, 19 Apr. 1875, p. 2; 16 June 1875, p. 2; 18 June 1875, p. 2.
Naturalisation certificate.
Parish of Beaufort, County of Ripon.
49   *Bailliere's Victorian Gazetter and Road Guide*, 1865, p. 328.
50   *The Bendigo Advertiser*, 23 Mar. 1853, p. 1; 25 Oct. 1875, pp. 1–2; 26 Oct. 1875, pp. 1–2; 27 Oct. 1875 pp. 2–3.
51   PROV, VPRS 24, Unit 296 [1021/Inquest to Deposition Files].
52   *The Victoria Government Gazette*, 1854, p. 1868; 1858, p. 504; 1860, p. 617; 1862, p. 2682.
Victorian birth certificate.
E. Sanders and J. Treauore, *Sandhurst, Castlemaine and Echuca Districts Directory for 1872–3*, pp. 31, 71.
Victorian death certificate.
53   Victorian marriage certificate.
The Bendigo Advertiser, 16 Aug. 1916, p. 1.
Victorian death certificate.
M. Shaw, *Our Goodly Heritage History of Huntly Shire*, p. 72.
54   *The Victoria Government Gazette*, 1860 to 1863.
55   Electoral roll, 1903.
Sands and McDougall's Directory.
56   Naturalisation certificate.
PROV, VPRS 3719 [Registrar of Mining Claims – Daylesford].
Victorian marriage certificate.
The Shepparton News, 16 Oct. 1916, p. 3.
57   Victorian marriage certificate.
Questionnaire completed on 16 September 1996 by Agnes Cummins, the grand-daughter of Emilios Rossely, and a letter from Agnes Cummins on 21 May 1994.
The Age, 2 Feb. 1928, p. 1.
The Argus, 6 Feb. 1928, p. 9.
58   Naturalisation certificate.
Swan Hill Hospital records.
Victorian birth certificate.
The Swan Hill Guardian, 1 Dec. 1930, p. 4.
59   G. Serle, *The Golden Age*, pp. 325–7.
60   *Henry Morgan's Diary*, (1852–1908), p. 36.
The Victoria Government Gazette, 1863, p. 1172.
Register of Claims in the Buckland Sub-Division, Beechworth District (Buckland Book, Burke Museum).
61   Tombstone inscription, Buckland Cemetery.

62 *The Victoria Government Gazette*, 1863, p. 2595.
    PROV, VPRS 1332, Unit 1 [Register of Claims, Crooked River].
    PROV, VPRS 1334 [Registration of Water Rights, Division of Crooked River, Gippsland].
    The Alpine Observer, 28 Apr. 1922, p. 2.
    Buckland Cemetery headstone inscription.
63 *The Victoria Government Gazette*, 1864, p. 2489; 1865 p. 2654; 1866, p. 2344.
64 Victorian death certificate.
65 G. Blainey, *The Rush That Never Ended*, pp. 72–3.
66 Registration of Claims in the Jamieson Jordan Sub-Division, Beechworth District (Goulburn Book, Burke Museum).
    Victorian death certificate.
67 *The Gippsland Times*, 14 Oct. 1864, p. 2.
68 Bundara's were referred to as Sclavonians which is another term for Croatians.
    PROV, VPRS 1332, Unit 1 [Register of Claims, Crooked River].
    PROV, VPRS 1334 [Registration of Water Rights, Division of Crooked River, Gippsland].
69 Naturalisation certificate.
    Registration of Claims in the Crooked River, Beechworth District (Omeo Book, Burke Museum).
    PROV, VPRS 1332, Unit 1 [Register of Claims, Crooked River]
    PROV, VPRS 570, [Shire of Avon rate books, North Riding]
    Victorian death certificate.
70 Naturalisation certificate.
    PROV, VPRS 1332, Unit 1 [Register of Claims, Crooked River].
    Victorian death certificate.
71 J. White, *The History of the Shire of Korumburra*.
    K. Bowden, *The Early Days of Korumburra*.
72 *The Sydney Morning Herald*, 4 Nov. 1935, p. 10; 5 Nov. 1935, pp. 9–10.
    Some Croatian fishmongers in Sydney were Nicholas Aceglav, Nicholas Anticevich, John Braicovich, Luka Budessa, Mathew Jvancich, John Lucas, John Pavletich, Gerald Vodanovich, Matteo Vuscovich and Vincent Yannich.
73 *The Sydney Morning Herald*, 9 May 1918, p. 5.
74 Naturalisation certificate.
    New South Wales marriage certificate.
75 Rookwood Cemetery records and tombstone inscriptions.
76 *The Bega District News*, 26 Oct. 1944, p. 2.
    The Sydney Morning Herald, 17 Oct. 1944, p. 5.
    Two letters from 1880 written in Croatian in the possession of Vincent Chernich, grandson of Vincent Chernich.
77 *The Singleton Argus*, 5 Sept. 1896, p. 5.
78 In the early 1890s Pavle Vidas worked in Broken Hill where there were about 150 Croatians.
    Iseljeništvo Pavla Vidasa, p. 24.
79 Peter Vranat's probate.
80 Questionnaire completed on 25 February 2003 by Jay Dubrich whose husband is the grandson of Christie Dubricich.
81 The first gold rush in Queensland began after gold was discovered in Gympie in 1867. Other goldfield discoveries include Charters Towers in 1872, Palmer River in 1873 and Mount Morgan in 1882. At Charters Towers and Mount Morgan the gold miners worked for companies in deep quartz mines. Nicholas Lissen, from the island of Vis, was a miner at Mount Morgan for many years.
82 *The Maryborough Chronicle*, 13 Apr. 1903, p. 2; 23 Aug. 1910, p. 2; 20 Feb. 1915, pp. 8–9.
83 *The Mercury* (Hobart), 25 Sept. 1913, p. 1.
    Tasmanian death certificate.
    Naturalisation certificate.
84 *The Albany Advertiser*, 13 Mar. 1935.
    M. Verschuer, *Echoes of the Past*, pp. 51–3.

N. Smoje, 'Croatians in Western Australia, 1858–1920'.
85 Naturalisation certificate.
86 *The Sydney Morning Herald*, 18 May 1914, p. 7.
    Naturalisation certificate.
    Victoria Police Gazette, 6 Apr. 1892, p. 315.
87 G. Serle, *The Golden Age*, p. 247.

Chapter 4

1 Andrew Radoslovich had numerous close connections with Croatians in Portarlington. He was the godparent to Gregory Pavletich's daughter, Augustina in 1889. His wife was godparent to Joseph Zagabria's son in 1895. Radoslovich also had friendships with Croatians in other parts of Australia. For example, in 1891 his marriage witnesses at St Francis Catholic Church in Melbourne were the Croatian, John Pavletich and Joseph Marsich's daughter, Mary.
2 Croatian settlers in North and South America, New Zealand and South Africa also often worked and maintained ties with other Croatian settlers.
3 Naturalisation certificate.
    PROV, VPRS 1332, Unit 1 and 2 [Register of Claims, Crooked River].
    PROV, VPRS 3611 [Register of Races, Crooked River].
4 In 1882 Cosmo Antich signed a register for the Austrian Consulate on behalf of the following Croatians, Marco Anich, Mark Belanich, Ignatio Billich, Nicholas Dicklich, Nicholas Godena, Giovanni Ivanussich, Giuseppe Mladovich, Vead Mlican, Peter Mavorvitch, Antonio Passalick, Martin Pavilach, Pietro Scokenich, Luca Senjara, Antonio Verabona, Pietro Vranca, John Vukasovich and Nicolo Vulisich.
    Akten des Ministeriums des Äußern, Administrative Registratur F8/169 Konsulate, Melbourne 1880–1918 (November 1882), Österreichisches Staatsarchiv (Austrian Archives) Haus-, Hof- Und Staatsarchiv.
5 Naturalisation certificate.
    Western Australian probate.
6 Tombstone inscription, Portarlington Cemetery.
    Naturalisation certificate.
7 *The McIvor News*, 31 May 1861, p. 2; 11 Oct. 1861, p. 3.
8 Victorian marriage certificate.
9 *The McIvor News*, 5 Sept. 1862, p. 3.
    The Victoria Government Gazette, 1863, p. 1252; 1865, p. 753.
10 St Mary's Catholic Church, Geelong, baptism records.
11 Victorian marriage certificate.
    St Thomas' Catholic Church, Drysdale, baptism records.
12 *The Bellarine Herald*, 21 May 1904, p. 2.
13 Gregory Pavletich's son Martin married John Lussich's step granddaughter.
    St Thomas' Catholic Church, Drysdale, baptism records.
14 HAR, baptism records for Bakar.
    Naturalisation certificate.
15 The godparents with Croatian connections of four of Gregory Pavletich's children were Andrew Radoslovich, Joseph Zagabria's wife and John Lussich's daughter.
    St Mary's Catholic Church, Geelong, baptism records.
    St Thomas' Catholic Church, Drysdale, baptism records.
    Victorian marriage certificate.
16 In 1882 the Croatian, Antonio Radovick, signed a register on Gregory Pavletich's behalf for the Austrian Consulate.
    Shire of Bellarine, Riding of Paywit, rate books.
17 *The Bellarine Herald*, 1 May 1908, p. 2; 8 May 1908, p. 2; 9 Oct. 1908, p. 2.
18 Victorian birth certificate.
19 *The Geelong Advertiser*, 16 Apr. 1929, p. 2.
20 *NAA: MP16/1, 1914/3/476.*

The Bellarine Herald, 27 Feb. 1904, p. 2.
21 Victorian marriage certificate.
22 Mark Belanich and Mary Mavorvitch were the godparents to Martin Pavilach in 1876, Peter and Mary Mavorvitch were the godparents to Robert Pavilach in 1878, while Antonio and Louisa Passalick were the godparents to Janet Pavilach in 1883. Mark Belanich's daughter was baptised at the same time as Robert Pavilach.
St Mary's Catholic Church, Geelong, baptism records.
St Mary's Catholic Church, Castlemaine, baptism records.
23 A. Eterovich, *Croatians in California, 1849–1999*, pp. 229–30.
24 Victorian death certificate.
25 Matteo Marincovich and Peter Mijch later moved to New South Wales. Marincovich then managed a hotel in Sydney.
Queensland death certificate.
New South Wales death certificate.
26 Tombstone inscription, Geelong Cemetery, Lussich plot.
27 *The Bellarine Herald*, 19 Jan. 1906, p. 2.
28 In the same cemetery on Trojano Darveniza's brother Mato's tombstone were also inscribed Croatian words. The inscription reads 'In Memory of Matheo Darveniza Born Dalmacia 1832 Died Mooroopna 1917 Mato Drvenica Roden na 17.XI.1832 Urmo na 2.XI.1917 R.I.P'.
Tombstone inscription, Mooroopna Cemetery.
29 Gulgong Cemetery records.
The Gulgong Guardian, 14 Aug. 1872.
30 Tombstone inscription, St Kilda Cemetery.
The Age, 15 Sept. 1892, p. 8; 16 Sept. 1892, p. 8.
Victorian death certificate.
31 Luka Margitich was instructed to send part of Anton's estate to their family in Croatia.
PROV, VPRS 28, Unit 635 [50/147].
32 Tombstone inscription, Buckland Cemetery.
Burwood Cemetery records.
33 On the shipping passenger list Stephen Paulussy was listed as S Pachirwick.
Victorian marriage certificate.
Tombstone inscription, Buckland Cemetery.
PROV, VPRS 11448/P1 [Index to Inward Overseas Passengers from British Ports 1852–1923].
34 Assuming a price of $410 per ounce of gold; $410 x 1916 = $785,560.
Reports of the Mining Surveyors and Registrars: Beechworth Mining District, Buckland Division.
Register of Claims in the Buckland Sub-Division, Beechworth District (Buckland Book, Burke Museum).
35 *Henry Morgan's Diary* (1852–1908), p. 165.
Reports of the Mining Surveyors and Registrars, 30 Sept. 1884, p. 40; 31 Dec. 1884, p. 36; 31 Mar. 1885, p. 15; 30 June 1886, p. 16.
36 Tombstone inscription, Buckland Cemetery.
The Alpine Observer, 29 Jan. 1909, p. 2.
37 Some of John Grandi's Croatian mining partners were Stephen Beriza, Antonio Buzolich, Fiovaranti Buzolich, John Buzolich, Vincent Lazarovich, Giacomo Malolich, John Miscardini, Theodore Petcovich and James Polorineo.
PROV, VPRS 1647 [Mining Registrations, Maryborough District, Korong Division, Register of Claims].
PROV, VPRS 567, Unit 1601 [Dalmazia Quartz Mining Company Limited].
PROV, VPRS 3671 [Wedderburn Division Mining Registrar, Register of Signature Book].
The Victoria Government Gazette, 1878, p. 1695.
Naturalisation certificate.
38 *The Inglewood Advertiser*, 23 Apr. 1907, p. 2.
The Wedderburn Express, 26 Apr. 1907, p. 2.
Victorian death certificate.
39 *Sands and McDougall's Directory*.

The Sydney Morning Herald, 25 Apr. 1904, pp. 1, 5, 10.

40 *Victoria Government Gazette*, 1889, p. 1494.

41 Naturalisation certificate.

42 Ellen, daughter of the Croatian pioneer, George Luchinovich, married the Croatian Spiro
Vidacovich (Špiro Vidaković) in St Michael's Roman Catholic Church, Nagambie in 1890.
The marriage witnesses were a fellow Croatian, Nichlis Bozovich, and Mary Luchinovich.

43 PROV, VPRS 28/P2, Unit 803 [102/936].
Boroondara Cemetery records.

44 PROV, VPRS 28/P3, Unit 733 [151/620].

45 PROV, VPRS 28/P2, Unit 462 [64/826].

46 Croatians who lived on George Street, Sydney include Nicholas Anticevich, Luka Budessa, Grgo
Buljan, Joseph Calafatovich, Antonio Dorich, Vinko Franziskovic, James Joseph, James Kosovich,
John Lupis, Peter Marich, Ivan Marinovich, Frederick Rossich, Ivan Stanicick (Stanich), Nagle
Stula, Ante Vella, Gerald and Lena Vodanovich, Mate Vujevic, Andri Vukasich, Mate Vukovic,
and Matteo Vuscovich.
Sand's Sydney, Suburban and Country Commercial Directory.

47 E. Balch, *Our Slavic Fellow Citizens*, pp. 161–3.

48 Letter to Mattio Marassovich from John Cvitanovich dated 21 September 1897.

49 A. Eterovich, *Croatian Pioneers in America 1685–1900*, pp. 162–3.
L. Antić, *Hrvati u Južnoj Americi do Godine 1914*, p. 50.
A. Trlin, *Now Respected, Once Despised Yugoslavs in New Zealand*, p. 173.
I. Čizmić, *History of the Croatian Fraternal Union of America 1894–1994*.
I. Smoljan, *Sto Godina Hrvatske Bratske Zajednice*.

50 *Zora*, 7 Mar. 1914, p. 1.
A. Trlin, *Now Respected, Once Despised Yugoslavs in New Zealand*, pp. 163–73.
L. Antić, *Hrvati u Južnoj Americi do Godine 1914*, pp. 53.
L. Antić, *Croats and America*, pp. 212–13.

51 Croatian pioneers from Croatian communities in Australia who migrated to New Zealand still
corresponded with Croatians in Australia. A number of Croatian settlers from New Zealand who
settled in Australia after 1905 also mixed with Croatian pioneers.

52 Croatian pioneers who were married in Victoria according to other rites, but still remained
Catholics include Vincenzo Bercich, Antonio Blessich, John Cacich, Stephen Coloper, Vincent
Florio, Antonio Fornarich, John Marotte, John Monkivitch, Martin Pasquan, Martin Pavilach,
Martin Pavletich, Martin Rossovich and Thomas Zuzulich.

53 *The Great Southern Advocate*, 17 Nov. 1904, p. 5.
The Bellarine Herald, 15 Feb. 1902, p. 2; 10 Jan. 1903, p. 2; 14 Feb. 1903, p. 2; 1 Aug. 1903, p. 2;
16 Apr. 1904, p. 2; 28 Jan. 1920, p. 2.

54 *The Southern Cross*, 10 Apr. 1980, p. 2.

55 *The Southern Cross*, 12 Apr. 1940, p. 7; 29 Oct. 1981, pp. 1, 3, 5–11.

56 *The News* (Adelaide), 13 Oct. 1954, p. 3.

57 Gabriele Goidanich's marriage witness in Ireland was Giovanni Goidanich.
Gabriele Goidanich's tombstone inscription, Old Church Cemetery, Cobh, County of Cork,
Ireland.
Marriage Certificate St Patrick's Cork, Ireland.
The Ararat Advertiser, 21 Aug. 1918, p. 2.

58 I. Wynd, *Churches of Geelong*.

59 St Mary's Catholic Church, Geelong, baptism records.

60 St Thomas's Catholic Church was built in Drysdale in 1855–1856.
St Thomas' Catholic Church, Drysdale, baptism records.
I. Wynd, *Balla-Wein a History of the Shire of Bellarine*, pp. 61, 81.

61 *The Bellarine Herald*, 5 Aug. 1899, p. 2.

62 J. Tough, *A Short History of St Francis' Church 1839–1979*, pp. 6–11.
Victorian marriage certificate.

63 Victorian death certificate.
The Bellarine Herald, 6 Apr. 1906, p. 2.

St Patrick's Catholic Church, Sydney, marriage records.
64 St Mary's Catholic Church, Castlemaine, baptism records.
Sandon Cemetery records.
65 *The Great Southern Advocate*, 1 Jan. 1892, p. 2; 5 Apr. 1894, pp. 2–3.
The Southern Mail, 27 Apr. 1895, p. 2.
66 *The Great Southern Advocate*, 2 May 1895, p. 3.
67 *The Great Southern Advocate*, 15 Oct. 1903, p. 5.
68 *The Great Southern Advocate*, 17 Dec. 1903, p. 5.
69 *The Alpine Observer*, 2 May 1968, pp. 3, 5.
70 Letter dated 19 July 1994 from the Tambo Shire Historical Society.
71 *The South West News Pictorial*, 31 Oct. 1962, p. 8.
72 St Joseph's Catholic Church, Townsville, baptism records.
73 *The Korumburra Times*, 19 Mar. 1894, p. 2.
74 *The McIvor Times*, 14 Mar. 1878, p. 3; 21 Mar. 1878, p. 3; 15 Apr. 1880, p. 3.
75 *The Great Southern Advocate*, 11 Aug. 1904, p. 3.
The Sydney Morning Herald, 13 Feb. 1885, p. 10; 14 Feb. 1885, p. 24.
76 *The Otago Daily Times*, 27 Aug. 1875.
77 *The Otago Daily Times*, 4 Sept. 1875.
Letter dated 10 June 1995 from Bernard Pavletich, the great-grandson of Thomas Pavletich.
78 *The Gulgong Evening Argus*, 8 July 1875, p. 3; 12 July 1875, p. 3.
79 C. Kiernan, *Calwell A Personal and Political Biography*, pp. 27–30.
80 Letter dated 23 May 1981 written by Archbishop Matthew Beovich to a Croatian relative, Dragan Beović.
Matthew Beovich's Diary, 22 June 1923.
81 *Katolička Crkva i Hrvati Izvan Domovine*, pp. 142, 195–8.
D. Bourke, *The History of the Catholic Church in Western Australia*, p. 256.
82 *Katolička Crkva i Hrvati Izvan Domovine*.
75th Anniversary 1894–1969 St. Nicholas R.C. Church, The First Croatian R.C. Parish in America.
83 Vincent Zan returned from the USA to Starigrad on the island of Hvar and married Ursula on 11 February 1873. Their children were Maria, Vincent, Clara, Marino and Manda.
HAZ, baptism and marriage records for Starigrad on the island of Hvar.
84 Interview on 6 December 1998 with David Canny the grandson of Manda (Zan) Canny and his mother Sheila.
85 *The Sydney Morning Herald*, 21 Aug. 1917, pp. 5–6.
Field of Mars Catholic Cemetery records.
86 PROV, VPRS 1650 [Registrar Book, Majorca].
The Sydney Morning Herald, 31 Aug. 1906, p. 6.
New South Wales death certificate.
87 N. Smoje, 'From Starigrad to Sydney, the Story of the Zaninovich Family', pp. 116–17.
A. Eterovich, *Croatian Pioneers in America 1685–1900*, pp. 47–50, 93, 162–3, 168–70.
The Slavonic Pioneers of California, pp. 44–5.
88 Lena and Gerald Vodanovich had eight children.
Naturalisation certificate.
89 Susan Pascoe does not have a Croatian surname, so it is probable she changed her surname or may have been a daughter of a diplomat who had lived in Dubrovnik.
Victorian marriage certificate.
90 *The Age*, 25 July 1887, p. 5.
The Argus, 25 July 1887, p. 5.
91 *The Age*, 9 Mar. 1876, p. 4; 10 Mar. 1876, p. 3; 17 Mar. 1876, p. 3; 21 Mar. 1876, p. 2; 23 Mar. 1876, pp. 2, 4.
The Argus, 12 Aug. 1875, p. 5; 17 Aug. 1875, p. 7; 20 Aug. 1875, p. 7; 23 Aug. 1875, p. 9; 26 Aug. 1875, p. 5; 30 Aug. 1875, p. 6; 31 Aug. 1875, pp. 5–6; 6 Sept. 1875, p. 5; 2 Feb. 1876, p. 8; 21 Feb. 1876, p. 8; 23 Feb. 1876, p. 8; 24 Feb. 1876, p. 8; 6 Mar. 1876, p. 8; 11 Mar. 1876, p. 8; 14 Mar. 1876, p. 8; 16 Mar. 1876, p. 8; 18 Mar. 1876, p. 8.
The Ballarat Courier, 9 Sept. 1875, p. 2; 11 Sept. 1875, p. 2.

The Bendigo Advertiser, 21 Oct. 1875, p. 2; 25 Oct. 1875, pp. 1–2; 26 Oct. 1875, pp. 1–2; 27 Oct. 1875, pp. 2–3.

The Geelong Advertiser, 14 Feb. 1876, pp. 2–3; 15 Feb. 1876, p. 2.

92 Ilma de Murska arrived in Sydney from San Francisco on 2 August 1875. A week later she was on stage at the Melbourne Town Hall. She married her accompanist, Alfred Anderson, in Sydney on 29 December 1875 knowing he was extremely ill. He died in Melbourne on 22 March 1876. In New Zealand she married her new accompanist, John Hill, on 15 May 1876.

93 *The Argus*, 10 Mar. 1876, p. 5.

94 *The Australasian Sketcher*, no. 32, vol. 8, 4 Sept. 1875, pp. 86–7, 89–93.

95 *The New Grove Dictionary of Music and Musicians*, p. 480.

96 W. Little, *Guide to Ballarat with Map and Illustrations*, pp. 13–14.

The Victoria Government Gazette, 1880, p. 241.

Notes of the Sydney International Exhibition of 1879, p. 292.

Official Record of the Sydney International Exhibition, 1879, p. 1061.

97 W. Orchard, *Music in Australia, More than 150 years of Development*, p. 155.

98 C. Burton, *The Story of the Swan District 1843–1938*, pp. 51–2.

99 Naturalisation certificate.

Peter Darveniza had arrived in Mooroopna in 1893 to join his uncle, Trojano Darveniza.

100 Tombstone inscription, Mooroopna Cemetery.

PROV, VPRS 7667 [Inward Passenger Lists, Foreign Ports].

The Shepparton News, 4 Feb. 1910, p. 3.

101 James Maranta had five children from his previous marriage.

Naturalisation certificate.

Victorian marriage certificate.

102 *The Bendigo Advertiser*, 14 Apr. 1919, p. 4.

Naturalisation certificate.

Victorian death certificate.

103 *The Maryborough and Dunolly Advertiser*, 2 May 1900, p. 2.

The Riverine Herald, 16 Aug. 1886, p. 3.

Echuca Cemetery records.

The Korumburra Times, 6 Aug. 1894, p. 2.

104 Victorian death certificate.

Huntly Voters Roll for the Year 1873.

The Riverine Herald, 8 May 1877, p. 3.

105 *The Wedderburn Express*, 28 July 1888, p. 2.

106 Ignatio Billich was also known Ignatius or Natale Billich.

Victorian death certificate.

Township of Wedderburn, Parish of Wedderburn, County of Gladstone.

Parish of Wedderburn, County of Gladstone.

The Wedderburn Express, 27 May 1892, p. 2; 19 June 1892, p. 2; 9 Oct. 1900, p. 4.

Victoria Police Gazette, 20 July 1892.

107 PROV, VPRS 7398/P1 [Kew Asylum Case Book].

PROV, VPRS 7399/P1 [Yarra Bend Lunatic Asylum Case Book].

PROV, VPRS 7556/P1 [Yarra Bend Lunatic Asylum Admission Warrants].

PROV, VPRS 7395/P1 [Beechworth Asylum Case Book].

PROV, VPRS 7403/P1 [Ararat Asylum Case Book].

PROV, VPRS 7428/P1 [Sunbury Asylum].

PROV, VPRS 7493/P1 [Index Bendigo (Sandhurst) Benevolent Asylum].

108 Geelong Hospital records.

The Geelong Advertiser, 5 Sept. 1872, p. 2; 11 Aug. 1879, p. 2.

109 Matteo Baillich was also referred to as Bachich.

The Inglewood Advertiser, 7 Jan. 1876, p. 3; 7 Apr. 1876, p. 2.

The St Arnaud Mercury, 12 Jan. 1876, p. 3.

110 *Victoria Police Gazette*, 28 Sept. 1869, p. 211.

111 *The Maryborough and Dunolly Advertiser*, 22 May 1896, p. 2; 25 May 1896, p. 2.

112 The letter to Mattio Marassovich from his sister Ana Mandacovich (Mandaković) was dated 20 June 1897 and the letter from his brother Giuseppe Marasović was dated 18 July 1897. The original letters are currently in the possession of Niel Ross, the grandson of Mattio Marassovich.

113 Some other Croatian pioneers who bequeathed part of their estate to relatives in Croatia were Giovanni Guircovich, John Lussich, Anton Margitich, John Margitich, Joseph Marich, Andrea Petrasich, Antonio Petrasich and Antonio Vidulich.
PROV, VPRS 28/P3, Unit 2413 [254/391].
PROV, VPRS 7591/P2, Unit 892 [254/391].
PROV, VPRS 28/P3, Unit 1251 [184/582].
PROV, VPRS 7591/P2, Unit 661 [184/582].

114 *The Mount Alexander Mail*, 31 Dec. 1906, p. 2.
The Echo (Newstead), 9 Jan. 1907, p. 2.

Chapter 5

1 Croatian pioneers who were still mining at the age of 50 years or older in Australia include: Peter Albich, Cosmo Antich, Vincent Chiorco, Antonio Harlovich, Mathew Hasdovaz, Joseph Marich, Nicolas Marini, George Marinovich, Dominic Milovitch, John Muscardin, Antonio Passalick, Antonio Pavich, Martin Pavilach, Antonio Petrasich, Nicholas Sabadina, Lucas Senjara, George Sersich, Baldosa Trobog, Antonio Vizulin, Luke Yannich, George Zaninovich and James Zibilich.

2 James Esmond discovered gold at Clunes on 1 July 1851. Three months later he discovered the first big find 600 ounces (18.75 kilograms) in Ballarat.
R. Smyth, *The Goldfields and Mineral Districts of Victoria*, p. 446.

3 Victorian death certificate.
Naturalisation certificate.
S. Gill, *The Goldfields Illustrated, The Sketches of S.T. Gill*, p. 10.

4 Most of the Croatian pioneers who settled in Australia came from the Croatian coastline, but Tomo Skalica was born in Slavonski Brod in the inland region of Croatia.
T. Skalica, 'Putovanje u Americi, Aziji, Polineziji u Altantičkom, Južnom, Tihom i Ledonom More od 1851–1855', pp. 145–8, 210–15, 323–6.

5 G. Blainey, *The Rush That Never Ended*, p. 49.

6 G. Blainey, *The Rush That Never Ended*, p. 56.

7 *Reports of the Mining Surveyors and Registrars*, 30 June 1864, p. 31.

8 G. Serle, *The Golden Age*, pp. 22, 80.

9 In 1867 Penninglow and Bersford registered the M. Petrick prospecting claim which was named after Matteo Perich; the claim was located at Mt Pleasant at Sailor Bills Creek.
PROV, VPRS 937, Unit 225 [Perich, M., Wyndham, Burial Expenses, deceased Mattea Perich, 1878].
Registration of Claims in the Jamieson Jordan Sub-Division, Beechworth District (Goulburn Book, Burke Museum).

10 G. Serle, *The Golden Age*, pp. 53, 69.
S. Gill, *The Goldfields Illustrated, The Sketches of S.T Gill*, p. 7.

11 G. Blainey, *The Rush That Never Ended*, pp. 41, 81.

12 According to Serle the gold price was £3 5s in 1852 and from 1853 to 1860 it was £4. In 1865 in areas where there was a concentration of Croatian pioneers for example, Crooked River the gold price varied from £3 17s 6d to £3 18s and in Redcastle–Costerfield from £3 15s to £4 6d.
The McIvor Times, 9 Jan. 1873, p. 2; 20 Mar. 1873, p. 2; 22 May 1873, p. 2.
Reports of the Mining Surveyors and Registrars, 31 Mar. 1865, pp. 29–30, 47–8.
G. Serle, *The Golden Age*, p. 391.

13 Z. Darveniza, *An Australian Saga*, p. 24.

14 R. Smyth, *The Goldfields and Mineral Districts of Victoria*, pp. 541–3, 552–3.

15 G. Serle, *The Golden Age*, pp. 53, 369, 388–9, 391.
G. Blainey, *The Rush That Never Ended*, pp. 60.

16 Today Australia is the world's third-largest gold producer.

17 R. Smyth, *The Goldfields and Mineral Districts of Victoria*, p. 597.

Victoria. Papers Presented to Both Houses of Parliament by Command of His Excellency the Governor. Session 1864–5. Legislative Assembly, vol. 3: Discovery of New Gold Fields, Report from the Appointment to Consider Application for Rewards for the Discovery of New Gold Fields, together with the minutes of Evidence and Appendices. pp. 30–1.
Naturalisation certificate.

18   *The McIvor News*, 23 May 1862, p. 2; 13 June 1862, p. 3.

19   *The McIvor News*, 23 Aug. 1861, p. 2; 8 Nov. 1861, p. 2.

20   *Victoria. Votes and Proceedings of the Legislative Assembly, Session 1862–3*, with copies of Various Documents Ordered by the Assembly to be printed, vol. 2. Reports from Select Committees Gold Prospectors D33 Appendix. Minutes of Evidence Taken Before the Select Committee During Session 1861–2, pp. 11–12, 15–23.

21   *The McIvor News*, 7 Sept. 1860, p. 2; 22 Feb. 1861, p. 2.
Mining Surveyors and Registrars' Reports: Abstract of the Reports furnished by the Mining Surveyors and Registrars of Victoria to the Mining Department for October, 1863, p. 9.
Reports of the Mining Surveyors and Registrars, 31 Mar. 1864, pp. 38–40; 30 June 1864, pp. 45–6.

22   *The Rushworth Chronicle*, 11 Oct. 1957.
J. Flett, *The History of Gold Discovery in Victoria*, p. 9.

23   Bartolomeo Citanich's Croatian mining partners were George Luchinovich, Natale Lussich, Dominic Milovitch, John Pavletich and Louis Spallatrino. In 1869 John Pavletich (Ivan Pavletić), who was born in Bakar, registered the Borsich and Company quartz claim at Graytown which was named after the Croatians, John Borcich and Gasper Borcech, who had registered the Borsich Company alluvial claim in the same area the previous year.
PROV, VPRS 1477, Unit 1 [Registrar of Claims, Redcastle].
Maryborough and District Hospital Victoria, Index to Admissions 1855–1907.
Naturalisation certificate.

24   *The Omeo Telegraph*, 22 June 1888, p. 3; 13 July 1888, p. 2.
Reports of the Mining Surveyors and Registrars, 30 June 1888, p. 28.

25   *The Mountaineer Wood's Point*, 3 Feb. 1865, p. 3.
The Gippsland Times, 8 Feb. 1865, p. 3.

26   *The Victoria Government Gazette*, 1864, p. 2990; 1865, pp. 1510, 1950, 2950; 1866, pp. 228, 1590.
The McIvor News, 19 Oct. 1860, p. 2.

27   Victorian marriage certificate.
The Victoria Government Gazette, 1862, p. 899.
Geological Survey of Victoria, Reports of Progress, no. 4, 1877, p. 49.
E. Dunn, *List of Nuggets Found in Victoria, Memoirs of the Geological Survey of Victoria*, no. 12, p. 59.
The Inglewood Advertiser, 10 Dec. 1875, p. 3; 31 Dec. 1875, p. 2.

28   *The Wedderburn Express*, 23 Oct. 1891, p. 2.
PROV, VPRS 7591/P2, Unit 202 [50/328].
PROV, VPRS 28/P2, Unit 348 [50/328].

29   *The Wedderburn Express*, 11 May 1889, p. 2.
The Inglewood Advertiser, 11 May 1889, p. 2.

30   R. Smyth, *The Goldfields and Mineral Districts of Victoria*, pp. 600–1.
The Wedderburn Express, 11 May 1889, p. 2; 24 May 1889, p. 3; 7 June 1889, p. 2; 15 May 1891, p. 3.
The Inglewood Advertiser, 25 May 1889, p. 2; 11 May 1891, p. 3.
E. Dunn, *List of Nuggets Found in Victoria*, p. 10.
Reports of the Mining Surveyors and Registrars, 30 June 1889, pp. 7, 22.

31   *The Wedderburn Express*, 8 Aug. 1890, p. 3.
E. Dunn, *List of Nuggets Found in Victoria*, p. 52.

32   F. Clune, *Golden Goliath*, pp. 12–13, 16, 21–2, 29–31, 42–5.

33   Matthew Ivancovich spent over 20 months in Australia. Moxley, author of *The Gold Trail*, first became acquainted with Ivancovich in 1895 when they shared a cabin while mining in the same area. The following year, Moxley found out that Ivancovich was present when gold was discovered in California. Ivancovich subsequently drew sketches of the point of the gold

discovery and gave Moxley access to his diary, which also gave details of his travels to Australia. According to Moxley 'Mr Ivancowitsh [Ivancovich] was a well educated man, and a gentleman in every respect. We obtained much valuable information from Mr Ivancowitsh concerning early days in California, the gold discovery in all its details. His father was a Slavonian [Croatian]'.
W. Moxley, *The Gold Trail*.
A. Eterovich, *Croatian Pioneers in America 1685–1900*, pp. 11, 93.

34   S. Korzelinski, *Opis Podrozy do Australii*, p. 114.
S. Korzelinski, *Memoirs of Gold-Digging in Australia*, p. 145.

35   There were also a few occasions Croatian pioneers called their mines Austrian or Hungarian. But all these Croatians kept close ties with other Croatians in Australia.

36   A. Eterovich, *Croatian Pioneers in America 1685–1900*, pp. 66, 103, 114.
L. Antić, *Hrvati u Južnoj Americi do Godine 1914*, p. 297.

37   *Geological Survey of Victoria, Reports of Progress*, no. 11, 1899, p. 18.
J. Flett, *Dunolly Story of an Old Gold-Diggings*, p. 125.

38   *The Dunolly and Betbetshire Express*, 15 Oct. 1878, p. 2.

39   PROV, VPRS 1647 [Mining Registrations, Maryborough District, Korong Division, Register of Claims]

40   *The Dunolly and Betbetshire Express*, 21 June 1878, p. 3; 28 June 1878, p. 2.

41   PROV, VPRS 567, Unit 89 [1602/Dalmatia Gold Mining Co. N.L.].
The Victoria Government Gazette, 1878, p. 1695.

42   *The Dunolly and Betbetshire Express*, 30 July 1878, p. 2.
Geological Survey of Victoria, Reports of Progress, no. 11, 1899, p. 18.
The Dunolly and Betbetshire Express, 29 Nov. 1878, p. 2.

43   *The Dunolly and Betbetshire Express*, 15 Oct. 1878, p. 2; 4 Mar. 1879, p. 3; 13 May 1879, p. 2; 3 June 1879, p. 3.

44   *Geological Survey of Victoria, Reports of Progress*, no. 6, 1880, pp. 24–5.

45   In 1887 an attempt was made to re-open the Dalmatia Gold Mining Company mine. Equipment was purchased and a whim was erected, however, due to the lack of funds the operation was suspended.
Reports of the Mining Surveyors and Registrars, 30 June 1880, p. 31; 31 Dec. 1880, p. 33.
The Victoria Government Gazette, 1879, p. 277; 1880, p. 287.
Geological Survey of Victoria, Reports of Progress, no. 11, 1899, p. 18.
R. Carless, *History of Rheola 1870–1985*, p. 73.

46   PROV, VPRS 1647 [Mining Registrations, Maryborough District, Korong Division, Register of Claims].

47   The Croatian shareholders in the Maximilian Gold Mining Company were Stephen Beriza, Antonio Buzolich, John Buzolich, Vincent Lazarovich, Giacomo Malolich and Theodore Petcovich.
PROV, VPRS 567, Unit 90 [1619/Maximilian Gold Mining Co. N.L.].
The Victoria Government Gazette, 1878, pp. 2221, 2351.

48   *The Dunolly and Betbetshire Express*, 28 Jan. 1879, p. 2; 13 May 1879, p. 2.
The Victoria Government Gazette, 1879, p. 3176.

49   *New South Wales Government Gazette*, 1876, p. 53.

50   PROV, VPRS 1477, Unit 2 [Registrar of Claims, Redcastle].

51   The quartz claim No. 2. Sclavonian in the Maryborough mining district was registered by three miners: Charles Tromp, Matthew Nicholas and Nicholas Oalsen in 1869. From the above surnames there is no clear indication that any of these three miners were of Croatian origin. Hence, this area was most likely previously mined by Croatians from which the name Sclavonian would have originated.
Victorian marriage certificate.
PROV, VPRS 1645 [Registrar of Claims, Maryborough].

52   PROV, VPRS 1615 [Registration of Quartz Reefs, Dam and etc. Inglewood Division Mining Register Maryborough District].

53   Registration of Claims in the Yackandandah South Sub-Division, Beechworth District (Yackandandah Book, Burke Museum).

54   W. Perry, *Tales of The Whipstick, A History of the Whipstick, Neilborough, Sebastian, Raywood, and Myers Creek Gold Rushes*, p. 195.
     Queensland death certificate.
55   *The Gippsland Times*, 15 Apr. 1865, p. 4.
     Reports of the Mining Surveyors and Registrars, 30 June 1886, pp. 29, 45.
56   Yannich had two quartz claims together with fellow Croatian Vincent Popovich near Omeo.
     The Omeo Telegraph, 13 Nov. 1885, p. 4; 4 June 1886, p. 2.
     Reports of the Mining Surveyors and Registrars, 30 Sept. 1883, p. 15; 31 Dec. 1884, p. 41;
     31 Mar. 1885, p. 41.
     Registration of Claims in the Omeo Subdivision of the Mining District of Gippsland
     (Omeo Museum).
     K. Fairweather, *Brajerack Mining at Omeo and Glen Wills*, p. 27.
57   Geelong Hospital records.
58   PROV, VPRS 1477, Unit 1 [Registrar of Claims, Redcastle].
     The Victoria Government Gazette, 1872, p. 1732.
59   *The McIvor Times*, 19 Dec. 1872, p. 2; 20 Mar. 1873, p. 2.
     Shire of Bellarine, Riding of Paywit, rate books.
60   Naturalisation certificate.
     The McIvor News, 20 Sept. 1861, p. 3; 11 Apr. 1862, p. 3; 18 Apr. 1862, p. 3; 27 June 1862, p. 3;
     4 July 1862, p. 3; 5 Sept. 1862, p. 3.
     The Victoria Government Gazette, 1863, p. 1252; 1866, p. 836; 1867, p. 1518.
61   Naturalisation certificate.
     Registration of Claims in the Jamieson Jordan Sub-Division, Beechworth District (Goulburn
     Book, Burke Museum).
62   PROV, VPRS 1477, Unit 1 [Registrar of Claims, Redcastle].
63   Victorian marriage certificate.
     Naturalisation certificate.
64   St Mary's Catholic Church, Castlemaine, baptism records.
65   PROV, VPRS 3719 [Register of Mining Claims, Daylesford].
     Rate book, Shire of Mount Franklin, North Riding.
66   *The Mount Alexander Mail*, 16 June 1913, p. 2.
     The Echo (Newstead), 18 June 1913, p. 2; 25 June 1913, p. 2.
67   Victorian death certificate.
68   St Mary's Catholic Church, Geelong, baptism records.
     Victorian birth certificate.
     The Victoria Government Gazette, 1860, pp. 1134, 1563, 1959, 2210.
     The McIvor News, 28 June 1861, p. 2.
     The Mountaineer Wood's Point, 15 Aug. 1864, p. 3.
     Butler's Wood's Point Gippsland General Directory 1866, pp. 43, 56.
     PROV, VPRS 1477, Unit 1 [Registrar of Claims, Redcastle].
     Sands and McDougall's Directory.
     The Age, 16 Aug. 1886, pp. 1, 8; 17 Aug. 1886, p. 8.
69   Some Croatians who lived in a few Croatian mining communities in Victoria include: Nicolo
     Anticevich, Cosmo Antich, Antonio Bundara, John Bundara, Peter Cussianovich, Antonio
     Harlovich, John Lussich, Natale Lussich, Charles Radovich, Louis Spallatrino and James Zibilich.
70   PROV, VPRS 1332 [Register of Claims, Crooked River].
     PROV, VPRS 1334 [Crooked River, Registration of Water Rights].
71   PROV, VPRS 1477 [Registrar of Claims, Redcastle].
72   *Reports of the Mining Surveyors and Registrars*, 31 Mar. 1864, p. 37; 30 June 1865, p. 47.
73   Victorian marriage certificate.
74   Fortunato Corsano died in Sydney on 9 November 1929.
     H. von Lippa, *Oben und Unten: 20 Jahre in Australien* (Ups and Downs: 20 Years in Australia),
     p. 233.
     New South Wales marriage certificate.
     The Sydney Morning Herald, 11. Nov. 1929, p. 9.

Naturalisation certificate.

75 Some examples of Croatian pioneers who moved from the Victorian goldfields to the New South Wales goldfields include John Muscardin, John Perovich, Francis Petrich, Francesco Vecerina, Antonio Vizulin and George Zenovich.

76 Naturalisation certificate.

77 Between 1891 and 1901 the population of Western Australia increased from 49,782 to 184,124, while the population of Western Australians born in other Australian colonies increased from 6.5 to 40.34 per cent due to the gold rush.
Census of Western Australia, 1891; 1901.

78 Vincent Abbott (Vicko Vranjican) used scientific methods to analyse quartz samples before investing considerable labour into a mine. The first major gold rush in the Murchison River area was in Nannine in the early 1890s and by 1901, Nannine was the centre of 80 mines.
Western Mail, 4 Apr. 1914, pp. 14, 32.
The Murchison Miner, 14 Apr. 1893, p. 3.
F. Buktenica, Jadranski Godišnjak 1942 Adriatic Year Book, p. 109.
N. Smoje, 'Early Croatian Settlement in Western Australia', pp. 241–3.

79 R. Thomas, The Present State of Melbourne and the Gold Fields of Victoria, London, p. 35.
G. Serle, The Golden Age, pp. 85–6.

80 Mathew Hasdovaz's letters revealed that alongside him on the goldfields were Stijepo Bašica, Belin and other Croatians from the island of Mljet.
I. Dabelić, Mlečani u Americi (Mljetans in America), p. 305.

81 G. Blainey, The Rush That Never Ended, pp. 1, 39, 62.
G. Serle, The Golden Age, pp. 371, 381.

82 Henry Morgan's Diary (1852–1908), pp. 118, 120–1, 123–5, 133–5.

83 The Dunolly and Betbetshire Express, 4 Mar. 1879, p. 3.

84 The Victoria Government Gazette, 1902, p. 3979.

85 Joseph Marich was often called Joseph Maurice Mariett in Australia.
The Victoria Government Gazette, 1890, pp. 4046, 4371; 1891, pp. 1871, 2677, 2800, 3233, 3755, 4095, 4267, 4463, 4728; 1892, pp. 89, 92, 712, 1164, 1607, 2206, 2211, 2911, 2915, 3252, 3424, 3564, 3826, 4134, 4138, 4781, 4784.
Naturalisation certificate.
W. Orchard, Music in Australia: More than 150 years of Development, pp. 204–7.

86 The Metcalfe Shire News, 12 Mar. 1892, p. 4.

87 Catholic parish records, Jelsa on the island of Hvar.

88 St Arnaud Mercury, 15 Mar. 1868, p. 2; 22 Mar. 1868, p. 2.
PROV, VPRS 24, Unit 204 [159/Inquest to Deposition Files].

89 The Dunolly and Betbetshire Express, 12 June 1868, p. 2.
Dunolly Hospital Inpatients, 1860–1900.
PROV, VPRS 24, Unit 207 [Inquest to Deposition Files].

90 New South Wales death certificate.
Registers of Coroner's Inquest and Magisterial Inquiries.

91 PROV, VPRS 3719 [Register of Mining Claims, Daylesford].
Castlemaine Hospital (Mount Alexander Hospital) records.
Tombstone inscription, Sandon Cemetery records.
Victorian death certificate.

92 The Gippsland Times, 20 May 1865, p. 3.

93 PROV, VPRS 1615 [Registration of Quartz Reefs, Dam and etc. Inglewood Division Mining Register Maryborough District].
K. Fairweather, Brajerack Mining at Omeo and Glen Wills, p. 24.

Chapter 6

1 Some of the clippers on which Croatians travelled to Australia include Champion of the Seas, Donald Mackay, Oliver Lang, Golden Age and Prince of the Seas.
B. Lubbock, The Colonial Clippers, pp. 10–18, 43, 49, 61–4, 69–70, 75, 87, 96, 101, 167, 347.

2   S. Vekarić, *Naši Jedrenjaci*, p. 334.
    S. Vekarić and N. Vekarić, *Tri Stoljeća Pelješkog Brodarstva*, pp. 41–4, 114, 350.
    Victorian death certificate.
3   *Victoria and its Metropolis Past and Present, Vol. IIA*, p. 240.
    Naturalisation certificate.
4   *The Argus*, 14 Nov. 1848, p. 2; 10 May 1850, p. 2.
    The Sydney Morning Herald, 2 May 1850, p. 2.
5   A. Eterovich, *Croatian Pioneers in America 1685–1900*, pp. 28–41, 121.
6   Gregorio Ferentza was one of the Croatian seamen who left the *Splendido* in Melbourne during
    the gold rush. In 1853 when the *Splendido* landed in San Francisco some of the Croatian crew
    also deserted to seek their fortune on the Californian goldfields.
    The Argus, 3 Jan. 1854, p. 4.
    The Age, 18 Jan. 1856, p. 6; 21 Aug. 1856, p. 2; 11 Jan. 1858, p. 4.
    N. Luković, 'Put Kapetana Visina Oko Svijeta', pp. 34–7.
7   *The Age*, 2 Feb. 1859, p. 4; 4 Feb. 1859, p. 4.
    The Argus, 2 Feb. 1859, p. 4.
    R. Barbalić, 'Istrani – Pomorci na Dalekim Moriman', pp. 103–4.
    PROV, VPRS 38, Unit 3 and 4 [Inward Shipping Reports 1843–1885].
8   Croatian seamen on vessels under the Austrian flag also visited Newcastle, Adelaide, Sydney,
    Port Pirie, Port Victoria, Wallaroo, Port Germein, Hobart, Launceston and Rockhampton.
    The *Ciro* was captained by Marco Martinolich, *Conte Oscar L* captained by G. Ragusan,
    Metta by G. Stangher, *Gange* by Frank Ivancich, *Gehon* captained by A. Cosulich, *Guisto* by
    Deo Radoslovich and *Triade Tarabochia* by G. Paul Tarabochia and G. Radoslovich.
    B. Kojić, 'Lošinjska Brodogradnja, Od Prvi Početaka do Svršetka Drugog Svjetskog Rata',
    pp. 273–4.
    The Age, 20 Apr. 1883, p. 4.
    PROV, VPRS 38, Unit 8 [Inward Shipping Reports 1843–1885].
9   *Victoria Police Gazette*, 9 May 1883, p. 127.
    S. Vekarić and N. Vekarić, *Tri Stoljeća Pelješkog Brodarstva*, p. 150.
    Naturalisation certificate.
10 *The Age*, 18 Aug. 1882, p. 2; 21 Sept. 1882, p. 4.
    Australasian Shipping News, 19 Aug. 1882, pp. 2, 7; 16 Sept. 1882, p. 7; 23 Sept. 1882, p. 3;
    18 Nov. 1882, p. 2; 31 Mar. 1883, p. 3; 16 June 1883, p. 3.
11 *The Age*, 12 May 1883, p. 4.
    Australasian Shipping News, 21 Apr. 1883, pp. 2, 6; 12 May 1883, p. 4; 29 Sept. 1883, p. 2.
12 *The Age*, 25 Mar. 1885, p. 4; 26 Mar. 1885, p. 4.
13 *Australasian Shipping News*, 12 Feb. 1881, p. 4; 14 Apr. 1881, pp. 2, 6; 23 Dec. 1882, p. 2.
    The Age, 23 Jan. 1886, p. 8.
14 A. Cosulich, *Sulle Rotte Dei Capitani Dell'800*, pp. 21, 193–203.
15 *Australasian Shipping News*, 22 Jan. 1887, p. 5; 5 Feb. 1887, p. 5; 5 Mar. 1887, p. 5; 28 May 1887,
    pp. 2, 4; 20 Aug. 1887, pp. 2, 7; 27 Aug. 1887, p. 2; 10 Sept. 1887, p. 3.
    Newcastle Morning Herald, 5 May 1944, p. 2.
16 The Croatian crew on board the barque *Stefano* included: Captain Vlaho Miloslavich, Carlo
    Costa, Giovanni Lovrinovich and Miho Baccich all from Dubrovnik, Baldassare Vukasinovich
    from Gruž and Nicolo Brajevich from Konavle, Martino Osoinak, Gregorio Pavisich and
    Fortunato Bucich from Rijeka, Domenico Antoncich and Giuseppe Perancich from Mali Lošinj,
    Matteo Zanetovich from Kotor and Diodato Vulovich from Dobrota in Kotor, while Croatians
    from the Pelješac Peninsula included Paolo Giovanni Radovich from Potomje, Giovanni Jurich
    from Oskorušno and Tommaso from Kućište. The *Stefano* was built in Rijeka and was owned by
    Miho Baccich's uncle. It had sailed from Cardiff in Wales on 31 July 1875 bound for Hong Kong
    with 1300 tons of coal.
17 G. Rathe, *The Wreck of the Barque Stefano off the North West Cape of Australia in 1875*.
    N. Smoje, 'Shipwrecked on the North-West Coast: The Ordeal of the Survivors of the *Stefano*',
    pp. 35–47.

18 The *Gange* was a three-masted iron barque that had a length of 46 m, breadth 9 m and depth 5 m.
   Australasian Shipping News, 16 Apr. 1887, p. 6; 30 Apr. 1887, pp. 2, 6; 28 May 1887, pp. 2, 6.

19 L. Foster, *Port Phillip Shipwrecks Stage 2, An Historical Survey of Vessels Lost Within a Radius of Ten Nautical Miles of the Head, Outside Port Phillip Bay*, p. 28.

20 *The Argus*, 25 July 1887, pp. 4–6.

21 The chief officer, who was a relative of the owners, was John Hreglich, the boatswain was Giovanni Matesich and the carpenter was Gasparo Glavanich. The other Croatian seamen include: Francisco Dorich, Giovanni Gasparini, Frank Gioffre, Vassilo Lazovich, Martino Matesich, Augustino Pateno, Dominico Pichnich, Giovanni Sablich, Antonio Serwaich, Giovanni Stack and Dominico Tarachia.

22 *The Age*, 30 July 1887, p. 9.
   The Argus, 30 July 1887, p. 11; 1 Aug. 1887, p. 5.

23 Other ships that visited Australia in the 1880s that were built by Martinolić boatbuilders in Mali Lošinj include the *Armida* and *Aurora*.
   B. Kojić, 'Lošinjska Brodogradnja, Od Prvi Početaka do Svršetka Drugog Svjetskog Rata', pp. 266, 271, 274.

24 *The Geelong Advertiser*, 26 July 1887, pp. 2–3.
   The Argus, 29 July 1887, p. 7.
   The Age, 29 July 1887, p. 4.
   The Ballarat Courier, 8 Aug. 1887, p. 4.
   The Queenscliff Sentinel, 13 Aug. 1887, p. 1; 1 Oct. 1887, p. 1.

25 The wreck of the *Gange* has been broken up but is still recognisable by large blocks of concrete that were part of the cargo. The wreck of the *Gange* is protected under the *Commonwealth Historic Shipwrecks Act 1976*. It is situated at latitude 38° 17.72', longitude 144° 36.99'.
   Australasian Shipping News, 13 Aug. 1887, p. 2; 20 Aug. 1887, pp. 2–3.

26 Some Austrian ships and ships that sailed under the Austrian flag with Croatian captains and/or crew which visited Australia prior to the First World War include: *Alba, Albatros, Armida, Aurora J, Ciro, Conte Oscar L, Contessa Hilda, Deveron, Ermina J, Fasana, Francesca T, Francesco Guiseppe I, Gange, Gehon, Genitori Tarabochia, Giovanni S, Guisto, Habsburg, Helgoland, Herradura, Kaiserin Elisabeth, Leopard, Ljubirod, Maratona, Metta, Novara, Osajnaka, Panther, Philadelphija, Ruma, Saida, Sava, Stefano, Stipan, Tiger, Triade Tarabochia* and *Tri Sina*.
   The Sydney Morning Herald, 8 Dec. 1858, p. 5.
   The Argus, 30 Jan. 1891, pp. 4, 7.

27 *The Argus*, 9 Sept. 1880, p. 4.
   Australasian Shipping News, 9 Oct. 1880, p. 3.
   PROV, VPRS 7667 [Inward Passenger Lists Foreign Ports 1852–1923].

28 *New South Wales Police Gazette*, 9 Dec. 1896, p. 433.

29 In 1903 there were 1084 fishermen in Victoria. There were typically two fishermen for each fishing boat. Of the fish they caught 5837 tons were sold at the fish markets. The Geelong (74) and Port Fairy fishing (65) communities each had a similar number of fishermen as the Portarlington and St Leonards fishing community (64), while the Sandringham (19) and Williamstown (23) fishing communities each had about a third of the number of fishermen of the Portarlington and St Leonards fishing community.
   The Geelong Advertiser, 20 Feb. 1875, p. 4.
   Victorian Year Book.

30 E. Wallace-Carter, *For They Were Fishers: The History of the Fishing Industry in South Australia*, pp. 40–57.
   Naturalisation certificate.

31 *The Grafton Argus*, 8 Jan. 1919, p. 2.

32 NAA: B741/3, V/5549.

33 The Latin and Italian word for Zagreb (the Croatian capital city) is Zagabria. In St Thomas' Catholic Church, Drysdale, the godparent for Joseph Zagabria's son, Thomas, was Gregory Pavletich's wife, for Joseph it was Andrew Radoslovich's wife, and for Amelia it was Maryann Paulitish.

34 Interview on 10 August 1998 with Maureen O'Donnell, great-granddaughter of Joseph Zagabria.
PROV, VPRS 7398/P1, Unit 19 [p. 121/Kew Asylum Case Book].
Register and Convictions, Orders, and other Proceedings in the Court of Petty Sessions at
Drysdale.
Victoria Police Gazette, 1906.
The Bellarine Herald, 31 Aug. 1906, p. 2.
Victorian death certificate.
35 *Sands and McDougall's Directory.*
NAA: MP16/1, 1916/310.
36 M. Berson, *Cockburn the Making of a Community*, pp. 142–66.
The West Australian, 10 July 1922, p. 1.
37 *The Port Fairy Gazette*, 24 July 1958, pp. 1–2.
38 *The Bellarine Herald*, 24 Dec. 1908, p. 2; 8 Jan. 1909, p. 2; 5 Feb. 1909, p. 2.
39 *The Belfast Gazette*, 5 Oct. 1877, p. 2.
40 Victorian marriage certificate.
Letters dated 24 May 1995 and 5 July 1995 from Elsie Day; her grandmother's sister married
John Markovich.
Information in letter form from the Tambo Shire Historical Society.
The Banner of Belfast, 8 Dec. 1875, p. 2.
The Geelong Advertiser, 26 Sept. 1885, p. 4.
The Bellarine Herald, 19 Dec. 1896, p. 2.
41 *Victoria Police Gazette*, 6 Apr. 1892, p. 315.
42 Naturalisation certificate.
The Bellarine Herald, 21 June 1907, p. 2; 16 Aug. 1907, p. 2.
43 In 1901 the Victorian Fishermen's Association (Co-operative Fishermen Association of Victoria)
was established and became the main body to represent the Victorian fishermen's interests.
Among their shareholders were Croatian fishermen. For years the Victorian fishermen and fish
retailers had been complaining of the injustices they suffered from the fish auctioneers at the
Melbourne Fish Market.
The Bellarine Herald, 15 Jan. 1898, p. 2.
The Geelong Advertiser, 13 June 1892, p. 2.
Shire of Bellarine, Riding of Paywit, rate books.
PROV, VPRS 28/P3, Unit 1062 [172/829].
44 *The Bellarine Herald*, 26 Oct. 1901, p. 2.
45 *The Port Fairy Gazette*, 13 Mar. 1919, p. 2.
46 A. Eterovich, *Croatian Pioneers in America 1685–1900*, pp. 45–59.
A. Rasporich, *For a Better Life A History of the Croatians in Canada*, pp. 18–19.
M. Vujnovich, *Yugoslavs in Louisiana.*
47 *NAA: MP16/1, 1914/3/476.*
48 B. Morcombe, *Nicholas & Elizabeth Matulick: From Priest, to Paddle Steamers, to Pioneers of the
River Murray.*
49 *Queensland Post Office Directory, Country Directory*, 1896–1897, p. 367; 1900, p. 417; 1901, p. 385.
The North Queensland Telegraph, 11 June 1886, p. 3; 9 Aug. 1888, p. 3.
Queensland marriage certificate.
Queensland death certificate.
50 *Napredak*, 10 Jan. 1948.
Naturalisation certificate.
51 *The Argus*, 15 Sept. 1856, p. 4; 26 Jan. 1857, p. 4; 27 Mar. 1857, p. 4; 12 Aug. 1857, p. 4.
52 From at least 1891 to his death on 2 October 1923 Joseph Catarinich's residential address was
210 Nelson Road, South Melbourne.
J. Bull and P. Williams, *Story of Gippsland Shipping Discoveries of the Early Navigators, Lakes
Steamers, Coastal Windjammers, Shipwrecks and Famous Captains*, p. 28.
Sands and McDougall's Directory.
The Age, 13 Jan. 1903, p. 4; 3 Oct. 1923, pp. 1, 20.
The Argus, 3 Oct. 1923, p. 1.

53 Letter dated 24 January 1997 from Mat Matich, grandson of John Sersic and son of Mate Matich.

54 According to *The Gippsland Times*, Captain John Gelletich was very popular at Lakes Entrance.
Every Week, 29 Aug. 1923, p. 2.
The Gippsland Times, 18 Nov. 1889, p. 3.

55 *The Bairnsdale Advertiser*, 14 Nov. 1889, pp. 2–3; 16 Nov. 1889, p. 2.
The Gippsland Times, 15 Nov. 1889, p. 3; 18 Nov. 1889, p. 3.
The Gippsland Mercury, 16 Nov. 1889, p. 3.

56 *The Observer (Adelaide)*, 31 July 1915, p. 31.
Naturalisation certificate.
South Australian marriage certificate.

57 L. Antić, *Hrvati u Južnoj Americi do Godine 1914*, pp. 90–8.

58 *The Geelong Advertiser*, 9 Nov. 1885, pp. 2–3; 12 Nov. 1885, p. 4.

59 *The Bellarine Herald*, 21 Nov. 1896, p. 2.
The Geelong Advertiser, 24 Nov. 1896, p. 4.

60 *The Bellarine Herald*, 30 July 1898, p. 2.

61 *The Bellarine Herald*, 4 Jan. 1907, p. 2.

62 *The Geelong Advertiser*, 7 Sept. 1867, p. 2; 11 Sept. 1867, p. 4.

63 *The Border Watch*, 6 Apr. 1887.
Register of Coroners' Inquest and Magisterial Inquiries.

Chapter 7

1 After leading a seafaring life Antonio Radovick arrived in South Australia in the 1850s, where he lived before settling in Victoria. Prior to being married he had also lived in New Zealand for two years.
The Southern Mail, 18 Dec. 1890, p. 3.
The Korumburra Times, 12 Dec. 1903, p. 2.
Tombstone inscription, Boroondara Cemetery Kew.
Victorian marriage certificate.
Naturalisation certificate.

2 *Sands and McDougall's Directory*.
Naturalisation certificate.

3 In 1888 Antonio Radovick purchased three adjoining allotments at the corner of what are now Radovick and Commercial Streets where he built the hotel and two shops. Later that year he purchased another three allotments in Radovick Street.

4 *The Great Southern Advocate*, 4 Oct. 1889, p. 2.
The Korumburra Times, 12 Dec. 1903, p. 2.

5 It is estimated that Radovick's Korumburra hotel cost between £7000 and £9000 to construct.
The Great Southern Advocate, 29 Nov. 1889, p. 2.
K. Bowden, *The Early Days of Korumburra*, p. 23.

6 There were at least 16 parliamentarians who attended meetings, banquets or balls in Radovick's hotel.
The Great Southern Advocate, 28 Feb. 1890, p. 2; 9 May 1890, p. 2; 17 Feb. 1891, p. 2;
20 Feb. 1891, p. 2; 31 July 1891, p. 3; 11 Feb. 1892, p. 2; 9 June 1892, p. 3; 19 July 1894, p. 3.

7 *The Great Southern Advocate*, 13 Dec. 1889, p. 2; 20 Dec. 1889, p. 1 to 25 Apr. 1890, p. 1;
2 May 1890, p. 1 to 30 Oct. 1891, p. 1.

8 *The Southern Mail* newspaper operated from one of Antonio Radovick's shops.
PROV, VPRS 28/P2, Unit 675 [90/55].
The Great Southern Advocate, 10 Oct. 1890, p. 2; 15 Nov. 1894, p. 3.

9 *The Great Southern Advocate*, 21 Mar. 1890, p. 2.

10 *The Great Southern Advocate*, 25 July 1890, p. 2; 11 Feb. 1892, p. 2; 18 Aug. 1892, p. 3;
1 Feb. 1894, p. 2; 15 Feb. 1894, p. 2; 19 Apr. 1894, p. 2; 10 May 1894, p. 2; 8 Nov. 1894, p. 3.
The Korumburra Times, 8 May 1893, p. 2; 18 May 1893, p. 3; 23 July 1894, p. 2; 20 Aug. 1894,
p. 3; 10 Sept. 1894, pp. 2–3; 20 Sept. 1894, p. 3; 27 Sept. 1894, p. 3; 1 Oct. 1894, pp. 2–3;
5 Nov. 1894, p. 2.

11   Antonio Radovick was also involved in the Korumburra Gymnastic Club, Korumburra Tennis
      Club and Korumburra Racing Club.
      The Great Southern Advocate, 16 May 1890, p. 2; 30 May 1890, p. 2; 3 Mar. 1892, p. 2;
      17 Mar. 1892, pp. 2–3; 3 Nov. 1892, p. 3; 1 Nov. 1894, p. 3.
      The Korumburra Times, 15 May 1893, p. 2; 11 Jan. 1894, p. 2; 29 Jan. 1894, p. 2; 16 Apr. 1894,
      p. 2; 28 May 1894, p. 2; 23 Aug. 1894, p. 2; 11 Oct. 1894, p. 3; 15 Oct. 1894, pp. 2–3;
      18 Oct. 1894, p. 3.

12   From the first Korumburra Show held in 1894, the Korumburra Agricultural and Pastoral Society
      annually held the Korumburra Show on Radovick's paddock. In 1898 the society purchased the
      land from him. Antonio Radovick operated the publican's booth at the Korumburra Show and
      also won prizes in the cattle, swine, horse and buggy categories of the show.
      The Great Southern Advocate, 24 Feb. 1894, p. 2; 3 Feb. 1898, p. 3.
      The Korumburra Times, 29 Jan. 1894, pp. 2–3.

13   Antonio Radovick helped petition for a school to be built and improved.
      The Great Southern Advocate, 21 Mar. 1890, p. 2; 13 June 1890, p. 2; 21 Feb. 1895, p. 3;
      28 Feb. 1895, p. 3.
      The Korumburra Times, 17 Sept. 1894, p. 3; 21 Feb. 1895, p. 2; 28 Oct. 1903, p. 2.
      PROV, VPRS 795, Unit 1755 [3077/Korumburra].

14   In 1894 the Railway Department and government agreed to purchase 180,000 tons of coal from
      Newcastle at a rate of 60,000 tons per annum for three consecutive years. This angered the
      Korumburra residents, hence they organised to meet parliamentarians to determine why they
      were buying coal outside Victoria rather than from Korumburra. There were also banquets for
      Coal Commissioners and Coal Creek Proprietary Company directors in Radovick's hotel.
      Antonio Radovick continued to manage his hotel till 1899 when he leased it out.
      The Great Southern Advocate, 9 May 1890, p. 2; 17 Apr. 1891, p. 2; 29 Nov. 1894, p. 3;
      24 Mar. 1899, p. 2; 31 Mar. 1899, p. 2.
      The Korumburra Times, 22 Feb. 1894, p. 2; 23 July 1894, p. 2; 6 Aug. 1894, p. 2; 16 Aug. 1894,
      p. 3; 20 Aug. 1894, p. 3; 10 Sept. 1894, p. 2; 24 Sept. 1894, p. 2; 1 Oct. 1894, p. 2; 11 Oct. 1894,
      p. 2; 15 Oct. 1894, p. 2.

15   *The Great Southern Advocate*, 17 Dec. 1903, p. 5.

16   Antonio Radovick was also a director of the Korumburra Butter Factory.

17   Antonio Radovick signed a register for the Austrian Consulate on behalf of the following
      Croatian pioneers: Andrea Bragulin, Antoni Frederick, John Gasparo, Giovanni Lavierri,
      Gregory Pavletich, Nicholas Torchie, Giovanni Vidisich and another Croatian with the given
      name of Vincenzo and an undecipherable surname ending in 'povich'.
      Akten des Ministeriums des Äußern, Administrative Registratur F8/169 Konsulate,
      Melbourne 1880–1918 (November 1882), Österreichisches Staatsarchiv (Austrian Archives)
      Haus-, Hof- Und Staatsarchiv.

18   PROV, VPRS 1332, Unit 2 [Register of Claims, Crooked River].
      PROV, VPRS 3611 [Register of Races, Crooked River].

19   Another of Radovick's Croatian friends in Korumburra was Rocco Zagabria.
      The Great Southern Advocate, 16 Feb. 1893, p. 3.
      The Korumburra Times, 6 Oct. 1904, p. 2.
      Korumburra Cemetery records.

20   J. Flett, *Old Pubs, Inns, Taverns and Grog Houses on the Victorian Gold Diggings*.

21   *The McIvor News*, 7 Sept. 1860, p. 2; 22 Feb. 1861, p. 2; 19 July 1861, p. 2.
      The McIvor Times, 3 Nov. 1871, p. 2; 14 Sept. 1893, p. 2.
      The Colonial Mining Journal, 1861, p. 189.

22   *The McIvor Times*, 8 Dec. 1871, p. 2; 20 May 1880, p. 2.

23   Heathcote Cemetery records.
      PROV, VPRS 28, Unit 229 [35/791].

24   J. Randell, *McIvor a History of the Shire and the Township of Heathcote*, p. 276.

25   *The McIvor Times*, 18 Jan. 1877, p. 1 to 2 Aug. 1877, p. 1; 30 Oct. 1879, p. 3 to 31 Dec. 1879, p. 3;
      3 Dec. 1880, p. 3.
      Victorian death certificate.

PROV, VPRS 1477, Unit 1 and 2 [Registrar of Claims, Redcastle].
26 These hotels in Woods Point were owned by Nicolo Anticevich, Paulo Arnerich, Bartholomew Mercovich and Mattio Marassovich.
27 Victorian marriage certificate.
28 *The Gippsland Times*, 18 Oct. 1864, p. 3.
     Butler's Wood's Point Gippsland General Directory 1866, pp. 9, 22.
29 *The Gippsland Times*, 5 May 1866, p. 3.
30 Township of Woods Point, Parish of Goulburn, County of Wannangatta.
     The Mountaineer Wood's Point, 15 Aug. 1864, p. 1 to 26 Sept. 1864, p. 1.
     New Zealand naturalisation certificate.
31 *The Victoria Government Gazette*, 1861, pp. 120, 580.
32 HAD, baptism records for Gruž, Dubrovnik.
33 Naturalisation certificate.
     Yackandandah Gold Fields Warden's Register.
     Registration of Claims in the Yackandandah South Sub-Division, Beechworth District (Yackandandah Book, Burke Museum).
     The Yackandandah Times, 4 May 1905, p. 2.
34 *The Ovens and Murray Advertiser*, 10 Apr. 1880, p. 8; 17 Apr. 1880, p. 4.
35 *The Ovens and Murray Advertiser*, 2 Oct. 1880, p. 5; 7 Oct. 1880, p. 2; 9 Oct. 1880, pp. 1, 5.
36 *The Yackandandah Times*, 13 Sept. 1890, p. 1 to 8 Oct. 1892, p. 1.
37 *The Yackandandah Times*, 13 Sept. 1895, p. 3; 6 Aug. 1897, p. 2; 4 May 1905, p. 2.
     The Ovens and Murray Advertiser, 6 May 1905, p. 7.
     The Argus, 15 June 1905, p. 3.
     S. Reynolds, *Yackandandah*, p. 38.
38 Naturalisation certificate.
39 J. Randell, *McIvor a History of the Shire and the Township of Heathcote*, p. 275.
     The McIvor Times, 17 Sept. 1869, p. 2; 27 Jan. 1871, p. 2; 10 Mar. 1871, p. 3; 8 Dec. 1871, p. 3; 29 Dec. 1871, p. 2.
40 *The Alpine Observer*, 18 Jan. 1889, p. 2.
41 J. Randell, *McIvor a History of the Shire and the Township of Heathcote*, p. 276.
     PROV, VPRS 1477, Unit 1 [Registrar of Claims, Redcastle].
42 In regional Victoria and New South Wales some Croatian publicans became very prosperous, for example, Pavle Matešić in New South Wales.
     The Mountaineer Wood's Point, 15 Aug. 1864, p. 3.
     The Victoria Government Gazette, 1864, p. 2990.
     Butler's Wood's Point Gippsland General Directory 1866, pp. 43, 56.
43 NAA: B741/3, V/5556.
     The Age, 12 Aug. 1935, p. 1.
     The Argus, 12 Aug. 1935, p. 1.
44 *Sands and McDougall's Directory*.
     NAA: MP16/1, 1916/1035.
     The Wangaratta Dispatch, 19 Feb. 1902, p. 2
45 *The Cyclopedia of Victoria*, vol. 3, 1905, p. 436.
46 Naturalisation certificate.
     Burgess Roll for Borough of Footscray, 1874, p. 445; 1875, p. 489; 1876, p. 550.
     Sands and McDougall's Directory.
47 *The Williamstown Chronicle*, 20 Mar. 1875, p. 2.
48 *Victoria Police Gazette*, 20 Nov. 1878, p. 315.
     Sands and McDougall's Directory.
     The Age, 20 Nov. 1888, p. 1.
49 *Victoria Police Gazette*, 20 Nov. 1878, p. 315; 9 Mar. 1887, p. 76; 16 Mar. 1887, p. 83; 6 Apr. 1887, p. 108.
50 HAR, baptism records for the island of Cres.
     Victorian marriage certificate.
     The Age, 25 Jan. 1883, p. 1.

Sands and McDougall's Directory.
PROV, VPRS 28, Unit 294 [25/166]
51 The several hotels Dominick Leonard managed in Adelaide include: Gothic at 317 Morphett Street (1889–1891); Aurora, 182 Pirie Street (1892); Gouger, 247 Gouger Street (1894–1898); Wharf Hotel, 18 Todd Street (1899–1904); Central Hotel, 74 Commercial Road, Port Adelaide (1906–1909); and Dover Castle Hotel, 47 Archer Street, North Adelaide (1912).
John Burich died in Payneham on 31 October 1907.
J. Hoad, *Hotel and Publicans in South Australia 1836–1984.*
Naturalisation certificate.
The West Australian, 4 Feb. 1909, p. 1.
52 Nikola Barovich was a founding member of the Croatian Slavonic Illyric Mutual and Benevolent Society.
A. Eterovich, *Croatian Pioneers in America 1685–1900,* pp. 22–7.
53 *The Great Southern Advocate,* 9 May 1890, p. 2; 17 Apr. 1891, p. 2; 9 June 1892, p. 3; 25 May 1893, p. 2.
54 *The Great Southern Advocate,* 20 Feb. 1891, p. 2.
55 *The Great Southern Advocate,* 28 Apr. 1890, p. 2.
The Korumburra Times, 11 Jan. 1894, p. 2.
56 *The Great Southern Advocate,* 10 July 1891, p. 2; 24 July 1891, p. 2.
57 *The Korumburra Times,* 22 Feb. 1894, p. 2.
58 *The McIvor News,* 9 Aug. 1861, p. 3.
59 *The McIvor Times,* 23 Dec. 1875, p. 2; 21 Dec. 1876, p. 2; 18 Dec. 1879, p. 2; 24 Dec. 1884, p. 2; 24 Dec. 1885, p. 2.
60 *The Ovens and Murray Advertiser,* 22 Nov. 1879, p. 1.
61 *The Great Southern Advocate,* 17 Jan. 1890, p. 2; 20 June 1890, p. 2; 21 July 1892, p. 2.
The Korumburra Times, 20 Aug. 1894, p. 2.
The Ovens and Murray Advertiser, 2 Oct. 1880, p. 5; 7 Oct. 1880, p. 2; 9 Oct. 1880, pp. 1, 5.
The McIvor Times, 21 Dec. 1883, p. 2.
62 Tombstone inscription, Mooroopna Cemetery.
63 Trojano Darveniza acquired a farm of some 600 acres. He mainly planted grains which were the principal crops grown in the area at the time. However, Darveniza had the unusual foresight to plant grape vines to diversify his farming interests.
Parish of Mooroopna, County of Rodney.
The Leader, 2 Feb. 1889, p. 10.
T. Leavitt and W. Lilburn, *The Jubilee History of Victoria and Melbourne,* p. 40.
64 *The Weekly Times (Supplement),* 12 June 1897, pp. 9, 13.
65 Henri Fortin was award a Diplôme de Grand Prix from France for the valuable assistance he gave Darveniza in the cellar and preparation of the exhibits. In 1896 Trojano Darveniza's wine sales for Victorian consumption were 45,500 litres annually and he exported 27,300 litres outside Victoria. Later, he also sold wine in his Shepparton wine shop.
The Shepparton News, 2 Feb. 1892, p. 3.
The Australian Vigneron and Fruit-Growers' Journal, 1 Dec. 1897, p. 128.
The Weekly Times (Supplement), 12 June 1897, pp. 9, 13.
The Shepparton News, 2 Aug. 1910, p. 1.
66 Some distinctions detailed in *The Australian Vigneron and Fruit-Growers' Journal* in 1897 include the Diplôme of Gold Cross, Brussels; Diplôme de Grand Prix and Grand Diplôme of Honour, Marseilles; Grand Diplôme of Honour, Diplôme of Gold Medal, Stockholm; Diplôme de Grand Prix and Diplôme of Honour, Nice and Toulon; First Grand Prix of Honour, Avignon, France; and many other honours.
The Australian Vigneron and Fruit-Growers' Journal, 2 Dec. 1895, p. 336, 1 Apr. 1897, p. 235; 1 July 1897, p. 25; 1 Dec. 1897, p. 128.
The Weekly Times (Supplement), 12 June 1897, pp. 9, 13.
67 *The Australian Vigneron and Fruit-Growers' Journal,* 1 May 1897, pp. 14–15, 219–20; 1 June 1897, pp. 30–1; 1 July 1897, pp. 40, 45–6; 1 Oct. 1897, p. 96.
W. Bossence, *Tatura and the Shire of Rodney,* 1969, p. 54.

The Shepparton News, 10 May 1892, p. 3; 13 Dec. 1892, p. 3; 21 Nov. 1893, p. 3.
The Victoria Government Gazette, vol. 1, 1898, p. 1135.

68   Romeo Bragato also inspected 103 vineyards in the Ardomona, Toolamba and Mooroopna districts and found 10 phylloxera-infected vineyards.
The Australian Vigneron and Fruit-Growers' Journal, 1 July 1897, pp. 1, 3; 1 June 1899, p. 22; 2 Oct. 1899, p. 118.
D. McLennan, *History of Mooroopna Ardmona & District an Interesting Story of Development 1841–1936*, pp. 107–8.

69   Trojano Darveniza was the executor of Thomas Milovitch's will, so Trojano must have been a trusted friend.
Mooroopna Cemetery register.
PROV, VPRS 28/P3, Unit 183 [118/620].

70   Ivan Roncevich arrived in Victoria in 1927 and lived with the Darvenizas for at least three-and-a-half years. He was working for Darvenizas when his wife arrived in 1929. Ivan Roncevich also brought out from Croatia, Anna Srsen, Toma Hedak and Josip Giljevic who all later became part of the Mildura Croatian Community. When Ante Jerolimov deserted the SS *Carica Milica* at Melbourne on 4 October 1929 he went directly to Darveniza's farm.
NAA: B741/3, V/5466.
NAA: B741/3, V/7627.
NAA: B13, 1929/17857.

71   J. Halliday, *Wines and Wineries of Victoria*, pp. 9–10.

72   Some Croatian pioneers who were miners and later vignerons, include Seraphin Bersica, Ignatio Billich, Stefano Celovich, Frank Entra, George Luchinovich, Theodore Petcovich, Andrea Petrasich, Antonio Petrasich, Joseph Postich, Peter Vranzigan and Vincent Zarich.

73   Some other Croatian pioneers whose fathers were vignerons in Croatia include Matthew Beovich, John Gasparo, Antonio Harlovich, George Luchinovich, Gasper Marohnic, Antonio Petrasich, Antonio Radovick and Nicholas Tadich.
The Nagambie Times, 23 Dec. 1910, p. 2.
Sands and McDougall's Directory.
B. Lloyd and K. Nun, *Bright Gold: Story of the People and Gold of Bright and Wandiligong*, pp. 69–70, 100–1, 110.
Victorian marriage certificate.

74   *The Cyclopedia of Western Australia*, p. 172.
N. Smoje, 'Early Croatian Settlement in Western Australia', pp. 241–3
The West Australian, 24 Sept. 1914, p. 1.

75   HAR, baptism records for Mali Lošinj on the island of Lošinj.
Royal Commission on Vegetable Products, Sixth Progress Report, 1888–91, 19 Sept. 1888, pp. 44–54.
New Zealand naturalisation certificate.

76   *The Australian Vigneron and Fruit-Growers' Journal*, 1 Apr. 1898, pp. 20–6.
The Leader (Supplement), 2 July 1898, p. 4.
The Rutherglen Sun, 2 Apr. 1897, p. 2.

77   *The Australian Vigneron and Fruit-Growers' Journal*, 1 Mar. 1897, p. 212; 1 Apr. 1897, p. 237–8; 1 Sept. 1897, p. 74; 1 Apr. 1898, pp. 203–6; 1 Sept. 1899, p. 91.

78   Romeo Bragato committed suicide in Canada by jumping from an upper storey window following a crisis in his family affairs.

79   Bragato's report and handbook on viticulture in New Zealand are frequently quoted key references on the history of the wine industry in New Zealand.
R. Bragato, *Report on the Prospects of Viticulture in New Zealand together with Instructions for Planting and Pruning.*
D. Scott, *Winemakers of New Zealand*, pp. 23, 25, 45–65.

80   Pokorny, who was president of the Croatian wine association, was one of the founders of what has become Badel, the largest wine and spirits producer in Croatia. Today, Badel alcoholic drinks are sold throughout Australia. At the Adelaide Jubilee International Exhibition of 1887, Maraschino liqueur from Zadar received a first order of merit award.

Official Record of the Sydney International Exhibition, 1879, pp. 867–8.
International Exhibition Sydney 1879, Austrian Catalogue, pp. 69, 71–2.
Sydney International Exhibition 1879, Official Catalogue of Exhibits, Austrian Court, pp. 27–8.
Adelaide Jubilee International Exhibition 1887, Reports of Juries and Official List of Awards, p. 71.

81 *Centennial International Exhibition, Melbourne 1888–9, The Official Catalogue of Exhibits*, pp. 87, 104–5.
Official Record of Centennial International Exhibition Melbourne 1888–1889, pp. 317, 354, 361–2.

82 W. Driscoll and E. Elphick, *Birth of a Nation*, pp. 192–3.

83 Naturalisation certificate.
Parish of Holcombe, County of Talbot.
Rate book, Shire of Mount Franklin, West Riding.

84 Parish of Sandon, County of Talbot.
Parish of Campbelltown, County of Talbot.
PROV, VPRS 627, Unit 87 [7782/31].
PROV, VPRS 392, Unit 2 [Register Leases, Hepburn Division].

85 Naturalisation certificate.
Victorian birth certificate.
The East Charlton Tribune, 13 Mar. 1915, p. 2; 18 Sept. 1918, pp. 2–3.
Parish of Charlton West, County of Kara Kara.

86 *The East Charlton Tribune*, 31 Oct. 1894, p. 2; 21 Nov. 1894, p. 2; 25 Jan. 1902, p. 3.

87 *The East Charlton Tribune*, 24 Mar. 1880, p. 2; 14 Apr. 1883, p. 3; 30 Apr. 1884, p. 4; 10 Jan. 1885, p. 3; 1 Feb. 1890, p. 2; 31 Oct. 1894, p. 2.
The Donald Express, 7 Feb. 1893, p. 4; 10 Feb. 1893, p. 2.

88 *The East Charlton Tribune*, 2 Dec. 1911, p. 2; 18 Sept. 1918, pp. 2–3.

89 *The Korumburra Times*, 19 Mar. 1904, p. 3 to 9 Apr. 1904, p. 3.
The Great Southern Advocate, 24 Mar. 1904, p. 2 to 7 Apr. 1904, p. 2; 21 Apr. 1904, p. 3.

90 HAD, birth records for Vitaljina.
Victoria Police Gazette, 9 May 1883, p. 127.
Conversation on 8 September 1996 with Debbie Brighton, the granddaughter of Natale Radonich.
Electoral roll, 1903.
Sands and McDougall's Directory.
The Age, 25 June 1934, p. 1.

91 Croatian pioneers who came on the same ship as Baldo Cunich to Australia include Paolo Polianich, Steffano Radovick and Rocco Violich. Steffano Radovick joined his relative Antonio Radovick who later became highly successful in Korumburra.
The Burrangong Chronicle, 5 May 1893, p. 3.

92 Nicholas Jasprizza was married twice and had at least six children with his first wife. He was survived by four sons and two daughters. Nicholas Jasprizza was also joined by a brother and a cousin.
The Sydney Morning Herald, 10 May 1901, p. 7; 16 May 1901, p. 7.
The South West News Pictorial, 14 Sept. 1962, p. 1.
The Burrangong Argus, 11 May 1901, p. 2; 15 May 1901, p. 2.
The Burrangong Chronicle, 15 May 1901, pp. 2–3; 18 May 1901, pp. 2, 4.
W. Bayley, *Rich Earth History of Young, New South Wales*, pp. 127, 225.

93 Some other Croatians who settled or worked in Young, include Barisa Batinich, Andrew Cunich, Antony Cunich, Baldo Cunich, Milenko Korljan, Mike Matulich, Kolombo Peric, Nikola Rogulj, George Rusak, Grgo Satara, Ante Vidovich and John Vidovic. Grgo Satara and Kolombo Peric later established their own successful farming enterprises.
The Telegraph, 2 Dec. 1933, p. 1.
The Orange Leader, 19 Jan. 1937, p. 2.

94 *The Slavonic Pioneers of California*, pp. 52–4.

Chapter 8

1 Tombstone inscription, Melbourne General Cemetery.
   Naturalisation certificate.
2 PROV, VPRS 7591/P2, Unit 5 [9/778].
   Sands and McDougall's Directory.
3 *The Victoria Government Gazette*, 1878, pp. 1695, 2221, 2351.
4 *The Age*, 25 Jan. 1886, pp. 1, 8.
   The Argus, 25 Jan. 1886, p. 1.
5 *The Victoria Government Gazette*, 1882, pp. 1658, 1708, 1980, 3124; 1883, pp. 232, 2390, 1885, pp. 2562, 2623, 2789; 1886, p. 91.
   Sands and McDougall's Directory.
6 *Saint Francis' Church, 1841–1941, A Century of Spiritual Endeavour*, p. 110.
7 PROV, VPRS 1647 [Mining registrations, Maryborough District, Korong Division, Register of Claims].
   The Great Southern Advocate, 20 Feb. 1891, p. 2.
   The Age, 14 June 1916, pp. 1, 12.
   Herald-Sun Weekend, 9 Sept. 1995, p. 15.
   Sands and McDougall's Directory.
8 HAZ, baptism records for Supetar on the island of Brač.
   Naturalisation certificate.
9 Register of State School Portarlington, No. 2455.
10 *The Banner of Belfast*, 14 May 1872, p. 2 to 8 Oct. 1872, p. 2; 29 Oct. 1872, p. 1 to 14 Jan. 1873, p. 1.
    Victorian marriage certificate.
11 *The Belfast Gazette*, 21 Feb. 1873, p. 1 to 21 Mar. 1873, p. 1; 7 Mar. 1873, p. 1 to 14 Nov. 1873, p. 1; 21 Nov. 1873, p. 4 to 3 Apr. 1874, p. 4; 10 Apr. 1874, p. 1 to 8 May 1874, p. 1.
12 *The Banner of Belfast*, 12 May 1875, p. 2.
13 *The Banner of Belfast*, 8 Dec. 1875, p. 2.
14 *The Belfast Gazette*, 15 Jan. 1875, p. 2; 5 Feb. 1875, p. 2; 5 Mar. 1875, p. 2; 13 Oct. 1876, p. 2; 5 Oct. 1877, p. 2; 22 Feb. 1878, p. 2; 5 July 1878, p. 2.
15 *The Belfast Gazette*, 14 May 1875, p. 3 to 28 May 1875, p. 3.
16 *The Belfast Gazette*, 11 May 1878, p. 1 to 24 Sept. 1878, p. 1.
17 *The Belfast Gazette*, 23 Dec. 1879, p. 2; 23 Dec. 1879, p. 3 to 13 Jan. 1880, p. 3; 16 Jan. 1880, p. 1 to 15 Oct. 1880, p. 1.
18 *The Belfast Gazette*, 1 Apr. 1881, p. 1 to 5 July 1881, p. 1; 10 Feb. 1882, p. 2; 14 Feb. 1882, p. 2; 28 Mar. 1882, p. 2; 31 Mar. 1882, p. 3.
19 *The Belfast Gazette*, 1 Apr. 1881, p. 1 to 5 July 1881, p. 1.
20 *The Belfast Gazette*, 6 Dec. 1872, p. 2; 24 Dec. 1875, p. 2; 16 Sept. 1879, p. 2; 7 Nov. 1879, p. 3.
21 Register of State School, Portarlington, no. 2455.
    Shire of Bellarine, Riding of Paywit, rate books.
22 *The Bellarine Herald*, 21 Nov. 1896, p. 2; 19 Dec. 1896, p. 2.
    The Geelong Advertiser, 24 Nov. 1896, p. 4.
23 *The Bellarine Herald*, 12 Apr. 1900, p. 2.
24 PROV, VPRS 28, Unit 1331 [102/936].
25 *The Bellarine Herald*, 20 Mar. 1897, p. 2; 6 Apr. 1906, p. 2.
26 *New South Wales Government Gazette*, 10 Jan. 1854, p. 62.
    Victorian marriage certificate.
    Victoria Police Gazette, 10 Nov. 1873.
27 *The Geelong Advertiser*, 1 Jan. 1866, p. 2.
28 According to Smyth, the Albion Quartz Mining Company at Steiglitz was one of the most important mines in Victoria in 1868.
    R. Smyth, *The Goldfields and Mineral Districts of Victoria*, pp. 264–8, 278, 284.
    The Victoria Government Gazette, 1865, pp. 2561–2; 1866, pp. 261, 1591; 1867, p. 2002; 1868, p. 292.

29 *The Geelong Advertiser*, 13 Feb. 1871, p. 2; 5 Sept. 1872, p. 2; 17 May 1873, p. 2; 12 July 1894, p. 2.
Geelong Hospital records.
30 *The Geelong Advertiser*, 9 July 1879, p. 1; 6 Nov. 1880, p. 3; 8 Nov. 1880, p. 3; 1 June 1881, p. 3;
19 July 1889, p. 3; 4 Sept. 1889, p. 3; 2 Dec. 1890, p. 4; 26 Nov. 1896, p. 1; 27 Nov. 1896, p. 3.
31 *The Gulgong Evening Argus*, 5 Feb. 1873, p. 3; 23 June 1874, p. 3; 25 June 1874, p. 4; 9 July 1874,
p. 3; 17 Sept. 1874, p. 3; 1 June 1875, p. 3; 3 June 1875, p. 3.
The Gulgong Guardian, 17 Apr. 1872, p. 2.
32 *The Gulgong Evening Argus*, 25 Aug. 1874, p. 3.
The Gulgong Guardian, 5 Oct. 1872, p. 2; 4 Dec. 1872, p. 2.
33 *The Gulgong Evening Argus*, 27 Feb. 1875, p. 1; 6 Mar. 1875, p. 1.
34 *The Gulgong Evening Argus*, 20 Oct. 1875, p. 2.
35 *The Gulgong Evening Argus*, 18 May 1875, p. 2; 1 June 1875, p. 3; 3 June 1875, p. 3.
36 Naturalisation certificate.
37 *The Gulgong Evening Argus*, 6 Feb. 1875, p. 2.
38 *The Gulgong Evening Argus*, 10 Sept. 1874, p. 2; 22 Sept. 1874, p. 2; 6 Apr. 1875, p. 2;
1 June 1875, p. 2; 27 July 1875, p. 3.
39 *The Town and Country Journal*, 19 Jan. 1884, p. 118.
40 *The Gulgong Evening Argus*, 11 Apr. 1874, p. 3; 5 Sept. 1874, p. 3; 6 Apr. 1875, p. 3; 20 July 1875,
p. 2; 5 Jan. 1876, p. 3.
The Gulgong Mercantile Advertiser, 1 May 1873, p. 3.
The Gulgong Guardian, 2 Mar. 1872, p. 3; 28 June 1873, p. 3.
41 *The Gulgong Guardian*, 22 Jan. 1873, p. 3; 5 Feb. 1873, p. 3.
The Gulgong Evening Argus, 19 Jan. 1875, p. 3.
The Gulgong Argus, 23 Sept. 1876, p. 3; 30 Sept. 1876, p. 3.
The Victoria Government Gazette, 4 Jan. 1884, pp. 2, 41.
42 *NSW Department of Mines Annual Report*, 1881, pp. 49–50.
43 *The Town and Country Journal*, 7 June 1884, p. 1104; 4 Oct. 1884, p. 704.
NSW Department of Mines Annual Report, 1884, p. 61.
44 *The Orange Leader*, 30 Nov. 1908, p. 2.
45 *The Victoria Government Gazette*, 1858, p. 1233.
Victorian marriage certificate.
46 *The McIvor Times*, 23 June 1871, p. 3; 30 June 1871, p. 3; 7 July 1871, p. 3.
47 PROV, VPRS 28/P2, Unit 466 [65/350].
48 *Butler's Wood's Point Gippsland General Directory 1866*, pp. 42, 56.
Maps, Township of Woods Point, Parish of Goulburn, County of Wannangatta.
49 *The Gippsland Miners' Standard Woods Point*, 10 Aug. 1897, p. 1 to 7 Sept. 1897, p. 1.
Naturalisation certificate.
50 *The Gippsland Miners' Standard Woods Point*, 10 Aug. 1897, p. 2.
51 Questionnaire completed on 4 September 1996 by Niel Ross, the grandson of Mattio
Marassovich and a letter from Niel Ross on 20 April 1994.
52 The Croatian surnames in the letters such as Bučić, Mandaković, Marasović, Moro, Pečarević,
Stanić, Tadin, Tomašević and Tomić are all native to the island of Vis.
N. Bezić-Božanić, *Povijest Stanovništva U Visu*, pp. 70, 106, 119, 211, 227, 257, 262, 283, 289, 294,
306, 309–10.
53 The letter to Mattio Marassovich from his sister Ana Mandacovich (Mandaković) was dated
20 June 1897 and the letter from his brother Giuseppe Marasović was dated 18 July 1897. The
original letters are currently in the possession of Niel Ross, the grandson of Mattio Marassovich.
54 Seweryn Korzelinski was a Polish patriot who lived on the Victorian goldfields from 1852 to 1856
and recorded his experiences in his diary. Korzelinski was forced to leave Europe as he was part of
a failed Hungarian insurrection in 1848. He was a major in a Polish division that sided with
Hungary against Austria. On the Victorian goldfields Seweryn Korzelinski worked and made
many friends of various nationalities including Croatians. He subsequently returned to his native
Poland after he was granted an amnesty from Austria.
S. Korzelinski, *Opis Podrozy do Australii*, pp. 8, 94–5, 112–14.
S. Korzelinski, *Memoirs of Gold-Digging in Australia*, 1979, pp. xi, xii.

55 S. Korzelinski, *Opis Podrozy do Australii*, pp. 94–5, 112–14.
   S. Korzelinski, *Memoirs of Gold-Digging in Australia*, pp. 141, 144–5, 150.

56 HAR, baptism records for Lovran.

57 PROV, VPRS 7591/P2, Unit 681 [191/527].
   Sands and McDougall's Directory.
   Naturalisation certificate.

58 *NAA: MP16/1, 1916/1035.*
   The Argus, 11 Sept. 1923, p. 1.
   The Age, 10 Sept. 1923, pp. 1, 16.

59 *Sands and McDougall's Directory.*
   NAA: MP16/1, 1916/1035.

60 *Sands and McDougall's Directory.*

61 Maud Terdich was company secretary of Repco and was one of the first women in Australia to hold that position in a public company. In retirement she directed the activities of the Eye and Ear Hospital Auxiliary opportunity shop.
   The Age, 26 Jan. 1983, p. 8.

62 Letter dated 13 June 1900 written in Croatian in the possession of Mat Matich grandson of John Sersic and son of Mate Matich.

63 Naturalisation certificate.
   Taped interview in October 1993 and 26 January 1995 with Mat Matich, the grandson of John Sersic and son of Mate Matich.
   Victoria Police Gazette, 11 May 1887, p. 146.
   Sands and McDougall's Directory.

64 Interview on 1 and 16 May 1998 with Mate Matich, the grandson of John Sersic and son of Mate Matich.

65 *Sands and McDougall's Directory.*
   The Argus, 21 Mar. 1940, p. 11.
   The Age, 21 Mar. 1940, p. 1; 22 Dec. 1943, p. 6.

66 Naturalisation certificate.
   Taped interview in October 1993 and 26 January 1995 with Mat Matich, the grandson of John Sersic and son of Mate Matich.
   Letter dated 24 January 1997 from Mat Matich, grandson of John Sersic and son of Mate Matich.
   Letter dated 30 July 1914 in the possession of Mat Matich, grandson of John Sersic and son of Mate Matich.

67 Interview on 1 January 1998 and 16 May 1998 with Mat Matich, the grandson of John Sersic.

68 HAR, baptism records for Mali Lošinj on the island of Lošinj.
   Naturalisation certificate.
   Sands and McDougall's Directory.
   Burgess Roll for Borough of Footscray, 1874, p. 46; 1875, p. 24; 1876, p. 47.
   Voter's roll, South Ward of the City of Footscray.

69 Questionnaire completed on 22 September 1996 by Neale Bathols, the great-grandson of George Bathols.
   Letter dated 16 May 1998 by Raymond Bathols, grandson of George Bathols.
   The Argus, 15 Aug. 1927, p. 1.

70 According to *The Nepean Times* of 12 April 1890, Prospero Stanich was a pupil 'To Professor Jas. Gruber, Chief of Imperial Royal University Ward for Disease of the Ear, and Physician of Ear Disease at General Hospital at Vienna. To Dr. Adams Politzer, Imperial Royal Professor of the Vienna University for Disease of the Ear, and Chief of the Ward at the General Hospital for Disease of the Ear. To Professor Dr. Schwartze, Director of the Royal University Clinic for Diseases of the Ear, and Privy Councillor of Medicine, Halle, Germany; and by appointment to his Excellency the ex-Governor of New South Wales'.
   Catholic Parish Records, Hvar on the island of Hvar.

71 *The Nepean Times*, 21 Sept. 1889, p. 1 to 4 Jan. 1890, p. 1; 11 Jan 1890, p. 4 to 10 May 1890, p. 4; 17 May 1890, p. 4 to 2 May 1891, p. 4; 9 May 1891, p. 4 to 18 July 1891, p. 4; 25 July 1891, p. 4 to 23 Apr. 1892, p. 4; 5 Apr. 1890, p. 5; 12 Apr. 1890, p. 5; 19 Apr. 1890, pp. 4–5.

The Sydney Morning Herald, 24 Feb. 1915, p. 9.
The Australasian Medical Directory and Hand book, p. 261.
Prospero Stanich's Probate, The Supreme Court of New South Wales Probate Division No. 69321 Ser. 4.
Naturalisation certificate.
Sands and McDougall's Directory.
Prospero Stanich's receipt to the Westminster Palace Hotel Company Limited Westminster London, 1886.
The seal of the city of Fitzroy, the model ear and photographs are among the possessions Prospero Stanich left to his family on the island of Hvar.
Interview on 12 February 2001 with Dinko Stanić grandson of Ante Stanić on the island of Hvar, Croatia.

Chapter 9

1 John Radich's grandson, Leonard Radic, was a theatre critic for *The Age* for over 20 years during which time he reviewed over 2000 productions. Some of the plays written by him include *The General* (1974), *The Particular* (1974), *Cody Versus Cody* (1980), *Some of My Best Friends are Women* (1983), *Now and Then* (1983), *A Clean Sweep* (1984), *Ground Rules* (1984) and *Sideshow* (1987). He was the editor of *Short Plays for the Australian Stage* (1987) and author of *The State of Play: The Revolution in the Australian Theatre since the 1960s* (1991). Many of Radic's plays have been performed on stage and the ABC has broadcast a number of his radio plays. He wrote the libretto for Felix Werder's opera *The Affair* (1974) which was staged by the Australian Opera at the Sydney Opera House.
Medical Directory of Australia, 1974, p. 133.
Who's Who in Australia, 1959, pp. 162–3.
The Oxford Companion to Australian Literature, p. 637.
D. Thorpe, *Who's Who of Australian Writers*, p. 562.

2 Interview on 9 May 1998 with Arnold Terdich, the grandson of John Terdich.
The Age, 29 Mar. 1929, p. 11.
The Argus, 19 Mar 1929, p. 9; 20 Mar. 1929, p. 5.

3 *The Argus*, 27 Mar. 1928, p. 15; 2 Apr. 1928, p. 23.
S. Priestley, *The Crown of the Road, the Story of the RACV*, pp. 85–6.

4 In the 1964 cliff-hanger grand final, Gabelich stunned football fans with his solo 50 m run and goal that put his side in the lead with only minutes to go. However, his legendary effort was not enough to win the game as Melbourne's backpocket kicked the match-winning goal. Gabelich was a massive ruckman whose huge frame made him virtually unbeatable at throw-ins. He played a total of 161 games for Collingwood from 1955 to 1960 and 1962 to 1966.
J. Main and R. Holmesby, *The Encyclopedia of League Footballers*, p. 150.
The Herald-Sun, 21 Sept. 1964, p. 30.
The Herald Sun News, 20 July 2000, pp. 85–6.

5 Descendants of Croatian pioneers who played football in the VFL include John Catarinich, Trojan Darveniza, Joseph Dobrigh, Laurence Dobrigh, Frank Mercovich, Lee Perussich and Leslie Rusich. Some of the footballers from Western Australia who were of Croatian descent include Adrian Barich, Tony Begovich, Ray Boyanich, Jon Dorotich, Allen Jakovich, Glenn Jakovich, Ray Gabelich, Eric Sarich, Craig Starcevich and Peter Sumich.
J. Main and R. Holmesby, *The Encyclopedia of League Footballers*.

6 *Who's Who in Australia*, 1944, p. 225.

7 In previous chapters we saw that some Croatian pioneers were also active in sports ranging from bowling to boat Regatta races. Another sporting Croatian pioneer was Andrew Radoslovich. According to the *Port Fairy Gazette* his 'sport was bowling, and his interest in this was spread over some sixty years, and even a few months ago [1958], although 93 years of age, he was a familiar figure on the green. As far back as 1909, he was a member of a winning rink of the Association and in 1916 won the Association's singles. He played pennant bowls for years as a member of the Port Fairy team and won numerous trophies in local and district competitions'.

Some of these include winning the Mayor's Trophy, being runner-up in the President's Trophy and the Port Fairy Bowling Club championship.
The McIvor Times, 7 Mar. 1878, p. 3; 26 Aug. 1880, p. 2; 2 Sept. 1880, p. 2; 12 Nov. 1880, p. 2; 26 Nov. 1880, p. 2; 20 Dec. 1880, p. 3; 30 June 1881, p. 2.
The Port Fairy Gazette, 24 July 1958, pp. 1–2; 28 July 1958, p. 2.

8 The president of the Royal Victorian Association of Honorary Justices was a honorary position always given to the Lord Mayor of Melbourne; the vice-president was the highest elected position. In 1901 Douglas Buzolich was among the special guests at the opening of the Commonwealth Parliament.
The Honorary Justice, Sept. 1912, p. 108.
The Age, 8 May 1901, p. 9.

9 *The Age*, 7 Aug. 1976, p. 140; 9 Aug. 1976, p. 25.
Essendon Gazette, 11 Aug. 1976, pp. 1, 3
The Sun, 7 Aug. 1976, pp. 20, 53; 9 Aug. 1976, p. 41.

10 Kaye Darveniza's grandfather, Mijo Darveniza, came to Australia from Croatia in 1900 to join his uncle Trojano. Her great-grandfather Mato came to Australia in 1909.
Medical Directory of Australia, 1974, p. 200.
Who's Who in Australia, 1993, p. 375.
The Age, 14 Aug. 1999, p. 17.

11 PROV, VPRS 795, Unit 1265 [2050/Yandoit].
PROV, VPRS 795, Unit 1109 [1803/Barongarook W].
PROV, VPRS 795, Unit 1755 [3077/Korumburra].

12 *Sands and McDougall's Directory*.
Probate index.
Victoria Police Gazette, 31 May 1899, p. 177.
Electoral roll, 1903.

13 *Who's Who in Australia*, 1985, p. 316.

14 *Newcastle Morning Herald*, 18 Jan. 1908, p. 8.

15 *Newcastle Morning Herald*, 20 Jan. 1908, p. 6.

16 The descendants of Croatian pioneers of Australia who were killed or died of wounds while serving in the AIF include Sergeant Harry Buzolich, Private George Cucel, Private Matthew Cunich, Private Francis Dominick, Private Francis Dubricich, Private Victor Lusic, Corporal George Matich, Private Cosmo Millich, Private Luke Monkivitch, Private Antonio Pavich, Private Joseph Radoslovich, Private Frederick Roderick, Private Eugene Sabadine, Private Anthony Slockwitch, Private Edmund Sticpwich and Private Harry Tussup.
AWM 145 Roll of Honour Cards Army, 1914–1918.

17 Charles Radoslovich, who was orphaned at six weeks old, was adopted by Andrew Radoslovich. His surname prior to adoption was Piller.
The Port Fairy Gazette, 7 Sept. 1914, p. 2.
Taped interview on 16 July 1994 with Miss Ann Piller, the daughter of Charlie Piller who was the foster son of Andrew Radoslovich.

18 AWM 148 Roll of Honour Cards Air Force.
Royal Australian Air Force Register.

19 Leslie Starcevich was born in Subiaco, Perth in 1918. His parents came from Lič in the Gorski Kotar district near Rijeka. He enlisted in the AIF in 1941 and first saw action in North Africa. Starcevich was wounded in Tel el Elsa in 1942. After his recovery he served in North Africa, Papua New Guinea and North Borneo. After the war he returned to Western Australia.
J. Smyth, *The Story of The Victoria Cross, 1856–1963*, pp. 429–30, 434.
I. Grant, *A Dictionary of Australian Military History*, p. 350.
D. Harvey, *Monuments to Courage, Victoria Cross Headstones and Memorials, 1917–1982*, p. 307.

20 Holdsworthy Camp's population peaked in the middle of 1918 when the number of internees reached close to 6000. The *War Precautions Act* and *Aliens Restriction Order* required the registration and control of aliens.

21 *NAA: MP16/1, 1918/2013.*
    Letter dated 30 July 1914 in the possession of Mat Matich, grandson of John Sersic and son of Mate Matich.
22 A. Trlin, *Now Respected, Once Despised Yugoslavs in New Zealand*, pp. 99–133.
    T. Mursalo, *In Search of a Better Life: A Story of Croatian Settlers in Southern Africa*, pp. 98–102.
    A. Rasporich, *For a Better Life A History of the Croatians in Canada*, pp. 75–92.
23 A. Splivalo, *The Home Fires*, pp. 78, 97–8.
24 *NAA: MP16/1, 1914/3/476.*
    NAA: MP16/1, 1915/3/106.
    NAA: MP16/1, 1915/3/379.
    NAA: MP16/1, 1915/3/995.
    NAA: MP16/1, 1916/300.
    NAA: MP16/1, 1916/310.
    NAA: MP16/1, 1916/388.
    NAA: MP16/1, 1916/752.
    NAA: MP16/1, 1916/1035.
    NAA: MP16/1, 1916/1586.
    NAA: MP16/1, 1917/783.
    NAA: A401/1, Catarinich, Catarinich Record of Aliens 6th Military District.
25 The Australian Government gave a payment of 10s per week to the wives of voluntary internees and 2s 6d for every child under the age of fourteen.
    G. Fischer, 'Enemy Labour: Industrial Unrest and the Internment of Yugoslav Workers in Western Australia During World War I', pp. 1–15.
    G. Fischer, *Enemy Aliens Internment and the Homefront Experiences in Australia 1914–1920.*
26 A few of the Croatian-born Australians who served in the AIF during the First World War include Paul Antunovich from Kozice in Dalmatia, Samuel Borich from Podgore and Ante Zurich. Paul Antunovich and Samuel Boric were members of the Croatian Slavonic Society. Many Croatians in Australia had volunteered to join the AIF early in the war but were not permitted.
    NAA: MP16/1, 1916/672.
27 *NAA: MP16/1, 1915/3/983.*
28 *The West Australian*, 18 Aug. 1915, p. 8.
    G. Fischer, *Enemy Aliens Internment and the Homefront Experiences in Australia 1914–1920.*
29 *NAA: MP367/1, 448/6/4947.*
30 The Serbian Government offered potential Croatian recruits from Australia an incentive of 12.4 acres of fertile land in Serbia at the end of the war. However, the Croatians preferred to have the same pay as Australian servicemen or be allowed to enlist in the AIF.
    NAA: MP16/1, 1917/237.
31 Some of the other Croatian families with winery connections in the Swan Valley include: Bakranich, Banovich, Boyanich, Garbin, Kraljevich, Mateljan, Pasalich, Radojkovich, Turkich, Yujnovich, Yukich and Yurisich.
    M. Zekulich, *Wines and Wineries of the West*, pp. 23, 30, 35, 37, 40–5, 51–3, 55, 58, 68, 70–2, 86, 88, 100.
    M. Zekulich, *Wine Western Australia*, pp. 7, 18–19, 23, 26, 37–9, 41–3, 54, 60, 63–7, 72, 80–3, 87–9, 92, 106–8, 110–12, 119, 135–6, 210–12.
    Conversation on 28 August 1996 with Ivan Yurisich, the son of Nicholas Yurisich.
32 I. Kosović and P. Todorić, *Spomen Knjiga o Pomoći Jugoslavenskih Iseljenika Australije Svojoj Domovini od 15.2.1944 do 31.7.1946 God.*
    M. Alagich and S. Kosovich, 'Early Croatian Settlement in Eastern Australia', pp. 235–9.
    N. Smoje, 'Early Croatian Settlement in Western Australia', pp. 241–3.
    M. Berson, *Cockburn: The Making of a Community*, pp. 142–66.
33 Interestingly, only a few Croatians from the Makaraska and Vrgorac districts settled in Australia prior to 1890.
    C. Price, *Southern Europeans in Australia*, pp. 11, 22.
34 Australian Census.

35 C. Price, *The Method and Statistics of Southern Europeans in Australia*, p. 109.
36 Most Croatians who came to Victoria between 1890 and the First World War finally settled in Melbourne.
    List of Croatian members names in various clubs, 1947.
    Naturalisation papers.
37 B. Bunbury, *Timber for Gold, Life on the Goldfields Woodlines 1899–1965*, p. 31.
38 I. Kosović and P. Todorić, *Spomen Knjiga o Pomoći Jugoslavenskih Iseljenika Australije*.
    L. Marković, *Pod Australskim Nebom*, pp. 152–5, 349–59.
39 At the time of the 1934 Kalgoorlie riots almost a quarter of the men working in the mines were non-British (i.e. about 600 of the 2500 men). Some Anglo-Australian miners blamed newly arrived Croatian and Italian miners with insufficient knowledge of English for accidents that regularly occurred in the mines. The Croatian miners did not lose their jobs as a result of the English test as only conversational English involving knowledge of mining was needed to pass the basic English test.
    R. Gerritsen, 'The 1934 Kalgoorlie Riots: A Western Crowd', pp. 42–75.
    The Age, 31 Jan. 1934, p. 9; 1 Feb. 1934, pp. 8–10; 2 Feb. 1934, p. 9.
    The West Australian, 15 Feb. 1934, p. 18.
40 C. Gillgren, 'We and They: Work and Identity of Italian and Croatian Timber Workers in the South-west of Western Australia 1919–1969', pp. 70–81.
    C. Gillgren, 'Boundaries of Exclusion: a Study of Italian and Croatian Immigrants in the Western Australian Timber Industry 1920–1940', pp. 71–82.

Chapter 10

1   The local government areas with the highest number of Croatian-born in descending order are Brimbank in Victoria, Fairfield in New South Wales, Greater Geelong in Victoria, Cockburn in Western Australia and Greater Dandenong in Victoria.
2   L. Paric, D. Boon, A. Henjak, and I. Buljan, *Croats in the Australian Community*, pp. 128, 138.
3   *The Australian*, 18 Sept. 2001, p. 12.
4   Croatians are one of the main ethnic groups in Bosnia-Herzegovina. According to the 1991 Yugoslav Census, Croatians constituted 17.3 per cent of the population in Bosnia-Herzegovina. The 1996 Australian Census revealed that 27.1 per cent of the people from Bosnia-Herzegovina who lived in Australia spoke Croatian at home, while 2001 Australian Census revealed that 19.3 per cent spoke Croatian.
5   E. Kunz, *Displaced Persons: Calwell's New Australians*, pp. 43, 123.
6   From Australian Census data we know that immigration from Former Yugoslavia to Australia peaked in 1970 and 1971, so it is reasonable to suggest that the number of Croatian arrivals peaked in these years. Many of the Croatians who left Yugoslavia in the early 1960s left illegally to escape communism and/or national service.
7   Croatian Students' Association conferences in Australia were held in Cronulla, New South Wales (1986), Mt Eliza, Victoria (1989), Bundeena, Sydney (1990), Shoreham, Victoria (1991), Grose Vale near Sydney (1992) and Ocean Grove, Victoria (1993). More recently the Younger Generation National Conference has been held in Canberra (2000), Geelong (2001) and Sydney (2003).
8   2001 Census Statistics, Australian Bureau of Statistics.
9   According to the 2001 Australian Census, Victoria has 25,555 Croatian speakers corresponding to 0.6 per cent of the total Victorian population. Croatian speakers make up 3.4 per cent of the total population of Brimbank local government area and 1.4 per cent the total population of Greater Geelong local government area. However, the map of Croatian speakers in Melbourne and Geelong (in the colour section of this book) shows the percentage of Croatian speakers is much higher in sections of these local government areas where Croatians have concentrated.
10 In Geelong, the hostel in Norlane was walking distance from Ford.
11 The Australian Capital Territory has the highest concentration of Croatian-born men in the construction industry.

12 Other Croatians who have settled in the Australian outback manage roadhouses, petrol stations, hotels and cattle stations or are gold miners.

13 Tony Santic who was born on the island of Lastovo has also taken the tuna farming industry to Croatia.
BRW, 20 May–14 June 2004, pp. 155, 167.

14 The Croatian old age nursing homes in Australia include Cardinal Stepinac nursing home in Sydney, Villa Dalmacia nursing home in Western Australia, St Anna's Hostel in Adelaide and Croatian Village in Canberra.

15 Statistics on Enrolment and Rank of Croatians in Victorian Schools for Year 12 students from 1975–2003, Board of Studies, 2003.

16 There have been seven Summer Schools of Croatian Language and Culture (Croatian Summer Schools) held in Australia. They were held in Kilmore, Victoria (1984), Perth (1985), Adelaide (1986), Sydney (1987), Canberra (1988), Brisbane (1989) and Geelong (1990).

17 In regional Victoria, Croatian is ranked as the fourth most widely spoken language other than English (after Italian, German and Greek) principally due to a high number of Croatian speakers in Geelong. Croatian is ranked as the most widely spoken language other than English in Port Lincoln and Carnarvon, while it is ranked as the third in Coober Pedy.
2001 Census Statistics, Australian Bureau of Statistics.

18 The renowned artist Charles Billich was born in Lovran, Croatia. After fleeing the Yugoslav Communist regime he studied art at the Volkshochschule art school in Salzburg. Billich then migrated to Australia in 1956. He studied at the Melbourne Institute of Technology and the National Gallery School of Victoria.

19 Croatians have made an enormous contribution to Australian soccer both nationally and internationally. Some of these who were nurtured through the ranks of Croatian soccer clubs in Australia include Mark Viduka, Josip Skoko, Tony Popović, Mark Bosnić, Ned Zelić, Steve Horvat, David Zdrilić, Frank Jurić, Željko Kalac, Joey Didulica, Eddie Krnčević and Josip Šimunić.

20 Croatia's first international soccer match against Australia was in Melbourne on 5 July 1992. However, prior to this, Croatian clubs Hajduk and Dinamo Zagreb toured Australia and played against the Australian national team. In 1976, Toronto Metros-Croatia (from the North American Soccer League), who won the North American Soccer League championship the same year, played against Croatian teams throughout Australia. Croatians in Australia have also had *bocce*, basketball, ten-pin bowling and chess clubs with Croatian names.

21 Table 4: Croatian community-backed clubs in the National Soccer League (NSL) Championship.

Season	Winner	Runner Up
1988		Sydney United
1990–91		Melbourne Knights
1991–92		Melbourne Knights
1993–94		Melbourne Knights
1994–95	Melbourne Knights	
1995–96	Melbourne Knights	
1996–97		Sydney United
1998–99		Sydney United

Prior to 1992 Melbourne Knights was called Melbourne Croatia and Sydney United was called Sydney Croatia.

22 Australian Rules football stars of Croatian background who grew up in Victoria include Ilija Grgić, Val Perović, Marc Dragičević and Brent Grgić. We have already observed other Australian Rules football stars of Croatian background from Western Australia in chapter 9. Max Krilich played first-grade Rugby League for Manly and Australia. He was a busy hooker who was effective running from dummy half and was skilful with the ball in his hands. Krilich captained Manly and is part of a prestigious group of Manly players to have played 200 games for the club. In 1982 Krilich captained the Australian side on the Kangaroo tour of England and

France. The team became the first Australian touring team to go through the entire tour undefeated and was tagged the 'Invincibles'.
Dean Lukin's father was born in Zadar and arrived in Australia in 1956. His mother was born in Australia to Croatian parents. Dean Lukin comes from the Croatian fishing community in Port Lincoln.

23 Many Croatians migrated to Warriewood in the interwar period and their descendants were active in surf lifesaving on Sydney's northern beaches. Croatian descendants have been successful in many other sports in Australia. For example, Tommy Unkovich was a famous jockey during 1943–1945.

24 *The Age*, 5 Nov. 2003, pp. 1–2.
The Australian, 5 Nov. 2003, pp. 1–2.

25 Some examples of Croatian community-backed *bocce* clubs include King Tomislav in Sydney, United Croatia in Perth, Istra Club and Eurobodalla Croatian Association Bocce Club in New South Wales.

26 There are Croatian golf clubs in Melbourne, Geelong, Sydney, Canberra, Brisbane and Adelaide.

27 Senator Stott Despoja was leader of the Australian Democrats from 2001 to 2002.

28 Ljiljanna Ravich worked as a high school economics teacher, high school deputy principal, senior policy officer to a number of ministers before establishing Joint Venture Consulting Group Pty Ltd in 1993. Her parliamentary career commenced on 22 May 1997.

29 Jaye Radisich's paternal great-grandparents were born on the island of Vis. Her great-grandfather, Frank Radisich, arrived in Western Australia in 1914, while her great-grandmother, Domina, arrived in 1922.

30 B. Hills, *Blue Murder Two Thousand Doomed to Die, the Shocking Truth About Wittenoom's Deadly Dust*.
M. Cannon, *That Disreputable Firm the Inside Story of Slater and Gordon*, pp. 140–1.

31 *BRW*, 20 May–14 June 2004, p. 124.

32 Croatian-born Silvio Rivier is a television presenter and producer. He initiated and was associate producer of the documentary program, *When Friends Were Enemies*, which was a finalist in the 1991 AFI Awards and the New York Film and Television Festival.
Eric Bana's and Robert Luketic's fathers were Croatian-born.
Debrett's Handbook of Australia, pp. 785–6.
Contemporary Australians 1995–96, p. 482.

33 *Sunday Magazine Herald Sun*, 23 Sept. 2001, pp. 9–10, 12.

34 Some Croatians who were Australian citizens were killed in police cells in Yugoslavia when they returned to visit their family, for example, Nikola Raspudic and Tony Milicevic. Details of some of these killings were given as evidence in the Australian Parliament.
The Weekend Australian, 8–9 July 1989, pp. 1, 8–9.
The Sydney Morning Herald, 18 Apr. 1973.

35 An example of where the media incorrectly portrayed Croatians as terrorists occurred in 1972 when four Croatians were taken to the Magistrates court in Melbourne on the charge of illegal possession of gelignite which it was alleged they hid in the Warburton ranges in Victoria. One of these, Ivan Mudrinic, surrendered to police with allegations that he was forced into a bombing conspiracy with the other Croatians. The media published articles that portrayed Croatians as terrorists and claimed there was reward for Mudrinic's murder. While awaiting trial, Mudrinic disappeared and later turned up in Yugoslavia where he was treated like a hero. It was then revealed that he was a Yugoslav agent who was paid by the Yugoslav consulate in Melbourne for framing the Croatians. With Mudrinic gone the cases were thrown out of court. However, the media's negative portrayal of Croatians as terrorists had already done its damage. The Australian media no longer freely negatively stereotypes established migrant groups in Australia as they did in the 1960s and 1970s for fear of legal action.
L. Shaw, *Trial by Slander*, pp. 155–64.
The Age, 26 Aug. 1972, p. 3; 23 Sept. 1972, p. 3; 25 Sept. 1972, p. 9; 26 Sept. 1972, p. 3.

36 None of the Yugoslav Consulate or travel agency bombings were ever solved. In 1971 the Yugoslav regime forcibly suppressed a Croatian national resistance movement known as the 'Croatian Spring' which was calling for greater autonomy for the Croatian republic. Many

Croatians claim the bombings in Australia were orchestrated by Yugoslav agents to give Croatians a negative image so there would be no sympathy for the Croatian independence movement.

37 The Labor Government was also keen to please Yugoslavia who was a prominent member of the non-aligned nations with which they wanted to be aligned.
The Age, 21 Mar. 1973, p. 1, 4; 19 Sept. 1973, p. 15.
The Australian, 18 Sept. 1972, pp. 1, 3; 3 Apr. 1973, p. 8; 5 Apr. 1973, p. 6.

38 During the raids on the homes of the Croatians there was excessive force and harassment by the police.
The Sydney Morning Herald, 9 May 1973, p. 14; 18 May 1973, p. 1; 22 May 1973, p. 1; 24 May 1973, p. 8; 20 July 1973, p. 15; 22 Aug. 1973, p. 8.

39 The findings of the Senate Select Committee on Civil Rights of Migrant Australians were never tabled in parliament because of the double dissolution which ended the Select Committee before the results could be tabled. However, a draft of the findings was leaked and published in the *Bulletin*.
With the introduction of multiculturalism and the Labor party becoming more moderate, any Labor anti-Croatian inclinations have long disappeared. Today there are Labor parliamentarians of Croatian descent.
A number of publications were also printed to counteract the negative propaganda unjustly directed towards the Croatian community in Australia. A few of these include: (1) Les, Shaw, *Trial by Slander* (1973), (2) Denis, Strangman, 'The ASIO-Croatian Affair of 1973' in *The Shape of the Labor Regime* (1974) and (3) Douglas, Darby, *Why Croatia?* (1974). In the last decade two masters thesis and two articles have been completed which detail how Yugoslav diplomats, Yugoslav agents, leftist politicians and the Australian media propagated the negative image of Croatians as terrorists in Australia.
The Bulletin, 4 May 1974, pp. 12–14, 17.
J. Batarelo, *The Political Affairs and Discrimination Against Croatian Australians After World War Two*.
M. Ljubicic, Croatians in Australia from Discrimination to Reconciliation 1960–present day.
D. Božin, 'The Great Conspiracy', pp. 481–91.
I. Čizmić, 'The Symbolic Croatian Embassy in Canberra 1977–1978', pp. 492–520.
M. Kovacevic and M. Gladovic, *Articles regarding Croatians in Australia as printed by the Sydney Morning Herald*.
D. Strangman, 'The ASIO-Croatian Affair of 1973', pp. 46–99.

40 *The Australian* showed that Vinko Sindicic, who served 15 years in gaol in Scotland for attempted murder of a Croatian emigrant, was previously sent to Australia to lay the groundwork for a plan to implicate local Croatian nationalists in a manufactured bomb plot. Vinko Sindicic was a high-ranking UDBA officer. He recruited Vico Virkez (alias Vitomir Misimovic), a Serbian who presented himself as a Croatian. Sindicic managed to manoeuvre Virkez into being recruited by ASIO as their source among the Croatian community. Under pressure from the media to find Croatian terrorists, ASIO and the New South Wales Special Branch used dubious evidence to help convict the 'Croatian Six'. *The Australian*, using files from the Australian Federal Police showed that during the trial it was known by the Australian police that Virkez was an UDBA agent. *The Australian* also stated that some high-raking Australian public servants who were UDBA informants/agents had retired once their contact with Yugoslav agents had come to ASIO's attention.
The Australian, 10 July 1989, p. 3; 17 July 1989, p. 12.
The Sydney Morning Herald, 26 Aug. 1991, p. 4; 28 Aug. 1991, p. 3.
The Weekend Australian, 8–9 July 1989, pp. 1, 8–9; 22–23 July 1989, p. 7; 19–20 Aug. 1989, p. 6.

41 In June 1989 *The Australian* revealed there was a cover-up to protect the Yugoslav consul who shot Tokić; a Yugoslav consulate security guard was blamed for the shooting. The Australian police were forced under political pressure to curtail their investigations so the identity of the real shooter could be suppressed.
The Australian, 28 Nov. 1988, p. 1; 29 Nov. 1988, pp. 1–2; 26 June 1989, p. 2.
The Sydney Morning Herald, 28 Nov. 1988, p. 1.

The Weekend Australian, 24–25 June 1989, pp. 1, 4.
'Cloak and Dagger (Croatian Six Conspiracy Case)'.

42 The Croatian language is a language in its own right and differs from Serbian or so called Serbo-Croatian.

43 Croatians from all around Australia came to Canberra to attend this demonstration, many in specially charted buses that departed from various Croatian clubs around Australia. Croatian demonstrations in Australia occasionally made the front page of Australia's leading newspapers. During the early 1990s the slogan, 'Stop War Recognise Croatia', was displayed on banners, posters and stickers across Australia in an attempt to gain support for Australia to recognise Croatia.
The Australian, 2 Sept. 1991, p. 3
The Canberra Times, 1 Sept. 1991, p. 3.
The Age, 6 May 1991, p. 5; 1 July 1991, p. 1; 11 Oct. 1991, p. 10.

Appendices

1 Natale (Božo) Vuscovich was known as 'Christmas', Božo (Natale) is derived from the Croatian word for Christmas which is Božić, while Natale is derived from the Italian word for Christmas.
The Bellarine Herald, 20 Mar. 1897 p. 2.

2. The letter to Mattio Marassovich from his brother Giuseppe Marasović dated 18 July 1897. The original letter is currently in the possession of Niel Ross the grandson of Mattio Marassovich.

Bibliography

Newspapers

The Age.
The Albany Advertiser.
The Alpine Observer.
The Ararat Advertiser.
The Argus.
The Australasian Sketcher.
The Australian.
The Bairnsdale Advertiser.
The Ballarat Courier.
The Banner of Belfast.
The Bega District News.
The Belfast Gazette.
The Bellarine Herald.
The Bendigo Advertiser.
The Border Watch.
The Brisbane Courier.
BRW (Business Review Weekly).
The Bulletin.
The Burrangong Argus.
The Burrangong Chronicle.
The Canberra Times.
The Colonial Mining Journal (Melbourne)
The Daylesford Herald.
The Donald Express.
The Dunolly and Betbetshire Express.
The East Charlton Tribune.
The Echo (Newstead).
Essendon Gazette.
Every Week.
The Geelong Advertiser.
The Gippsland Mercury.
The Gippsland Miners' Standard Woods Point.
The Gippsland Times.
The Grafton Argus.
The Great Southern Advocate.
The Gulgong Argus.
The Gulgong Evening Argus.
The Gulgong Guardian.
The Gulgong Mercantile Advertiser.

The Herald-Sun.
The Herald Sun News.
The Honorary Justice.
The Illustrated Australian News.
The Inglewood Advertiser.
The Korumburra Times.
The Leader.
The Leader Supplement.
The Maryborough and Dunolly Advertiser.
The Maryborough Chronicle.
The McIvor News.
The McIvor Times.
The Metcalfe Shire News.
The Mercury (Hobart).
The Mountaineer Wood's Point.
The Mount Alexander Mail.
The Murchison Miner.
The Nagambie Times.
Napredak.
The Nepean Times (Sydney).
Newcastle Morning Herald.
The News (Adelaide).
The North Queensland Telegraph.
The Observer (Adelaide).
The Omeo Telegraph.
The Orange Leader.
The Otago Daily Times.
The Ovens and Murray Advertiser.
The Pleasant Creek News.
The Port Fairy Gazette.
The Port Fairy News.
The Queenscliff Sentinel.
The Riverine Herald.
The Rushworth Chronicle.
The Rutherglen Sun.
The Shepparton News.
The Singleton Argus.
The Southern Cross (Adelaide).
The Southern Mail (Korumburra).

The South West News Pictorial.
The St Arnaud Mercury.
The Sun.
Sunday Magazine Herald Sun.
The Swan Hill Guardian.
The Sydney Morning Herald.
The Telegraph.
The Town and Country Journal.
The Wangaratta Dispatch.

The Wedderburn Express.
The Weekend Australian.
The Weekly Times.
The West Australian.
Western Mail.
The Williamstown Chronicle.
The Yackandandah Times.
Zora.

Directories, yearbooks etc.

The Australasian Medical Directory and Hand book, including a General Gazetteer and Road Guide, and Local Medical Directory of Australasia, ed. Ludwig Bruck, Australasian Medical Gazette Office, Sydney, 1886.

Bailliere's Victorian Gazetteer and Road Guide, F. F. Bailliere, Melbourne, 1865, 1879.

Butler's Wood's Point Gippsland General Directory 1866, repr. Kapana Press, Bairnsdale, Vic., 1985.

Campbell, A. J., Tourist Guide to Geelong and Southern Watering Places, Henry Thacker, Geelong, 1893.

Debrett's Handbook of Australia, Collins, Sydney, 1989.

Glass, Charles, The Castlemaine Directory and Book of General Information Comprehending Glass's Model Calendar for the two years 1862 and 1863, C. Glass, Bendigo, Vic., 1863.

Maning, F. B. and Bishop, W., Maning and Bishop's Geelong and Western District Directory 1882–83, F. B. Maning and W. Bishop, Geelong, 1882.

Medical Dictionary of Australia, E. G. Knox, Sydney, 1974.

Queensland Post Office Directory, Country Directory, 1896–1897.

Sanders, Emil and Treauore, John, Sandhurst, Castlemaine and Echuca Districts Directory for 1872–3, J. W. Pearson & Co., Bendigo, Vic., 1872.

Sands and Kenny's Commercial and General Melbourne Directory, Melbourne, 1857–1859.

Sands and McDougall's Directory, Sands and McDougall Limited, Melbourne.

Sand's Sydney, Suburban and Country Commercial Directory, John Sands Ltd., Sydney.

Who's Who in Australia, various editions.

General books

Adelaide Jubilee International Exhibition 1887, Reports of Juries and Official List of Awards, H. F. Leader, Government Printer, Adelaide, 1889.

Alagich, Marin, 'Early Croatian Settlement in Eastern Australia', The Australian People: An Encyclopedia of the Nation, Its People and their Origins, ed. James Jupp, Angus & Robertson Publishers, North Ryde, NSW, 1988, pp. 335–7.

Alagich, Marin, and Kosovich, Steven, 'Early Croatian Settlement in Eastern Australia', The Australian People: An Encyclopedia of the Nation, Its People and their Origins, ed. James Jupp, 2nd ed., Cambridge University Press, Australia, 2001, pp. 235–9.

Australians: Historical Statistics, ed. Wray Vamplew, Fairfax, Syme & Weldon Associates, Broadway, NSW, 1987.

Balch, Emily, Our Slavic Fellow Citizens, Charities Publication Committee, New York, 1910, The American Immigration Collection, New York, repr. 1969.

Baldassar, Loretta, Visits Home, Migration Experiences between Italy and Australia, Melbourne University Press, Melbourne, 2001.

Barbalić, Radojica, 'Istrani – Pomorci na Dalekim Moriman', Pomorstvo, no. 4, Croatia, April, 1952, pp. 103–4.

Batarelo, John Vice, 'The Political Affairs and Discrimination Against Croatian Australians After World War Two', masters thesis, School of Modern Languages Slavonic Studies, Macquarie University, 1996.

Bayley, William, *Rich Earth, History of Young New South Wales*, Young Municipal Council, Young, NSW, 1977.

Beovich, Matthew, 'Matthew Beovich's Diary', 22 June 1923, in possession of the Adelaide Catholic Archives.

Berson, Michael, *Cockburn the Making of a Community*, Published by Town of Cockburn, Cockburn, WA, 1978.

Bezić-Božanić, Nevenka, *Povijest Stanovništva u Visu*, Književni Krug, Split, 1988.

Blainey, Geoffrey, *The Rush That Never Ended, A History of Australian Mining*, 3rd ed., Melbourne University Press, Melbourne, 1978.

Bossence, William Henry, *Tatura and the Shire of Rodney*, Hawthorn Press, Melbourne, 1969, p. 54.

Bourke, D. F., *The History of the Catholic Church in Western Australia*, Archdiocese of Perth, 1979.

Bowden, Keith, *The Early Days of Korumburra*, K. Bowden, Korumburra, Vic., 1979.

Božin, Doris, 'The Great Conspiracy', *Croatia/Australia and New Zealand Historical and Cultural Relations*, Most/The Bridge, The Relations Library, The Croatian Writers' Association, Zagreb, 2000, pp. 481–91.

Bragato, Romeo, *Report on the Prospects of Viticulture in New Zealand together with Instructions for Planting and Pruning*, Wellington, 1895.

Buktenica, Frank, *Jadranski Godišnjak 1942 Adriatic Year Book*, Imperial Printing Company, Perth, 1941.

Bull, Joseph and Williams, Peter, *Story of Gippsland Shipping Discoveries of the Early Navigators, Lakes Steamers, Coastal Windjammers, Shipwrecks and Famous Captains*, J. C. Bull and Peter J. Williams, Metung, Vic., 1967.

Bunbury, Bill, *Timber for Gold, Life on the Goldfields Woodlines 1899–1965*, Fremantle Arts Centre Press, Perth, 1997.

Burton, Cannon, *The Story of the Swan District, 1843–1938*, J. Muhling Print, Perth, 1938.

Cannon, Michael, *That Disreputable Firm the Inside Story of Slater and Gordon*, Melbourne University Press, Melbourne, 1998.

Carless, R. L., *History of Rheola 1870–1985*, Back to Rheola Committee, Rheola, Vic., 1985.

Centennial International Exhibition, Melbourne 1888–9, The Official Catalogue of Exhibits, Etc. Commission. Lists of Commissioners, Rules and Regulations, Melbourne, 1888.

Čizmić, Ivan, 'The Symbolic Croatian Embassy in Canberra 1977–1978', *Croatia/Australia and New Zealand Historical and Cultural Relations*, Most/The Bridge, The Relations Library, The Croatian Writers' Association, Zagreb, 2000, pp. 492–520.

Clissa, John, *The Fountain and the Squeezebox (La Fontana e L'Organetto/Funda aš Orginet)*, Picton Press, West Perth, Australia, 2001.

'Cloak and Dagger (Croatian Six Conspiracy Case)', *ABC Four Corners*, 1991.

Clune, Frank, *Golden Goliath*, Hawthorn Press, Melbourne, 1946.

Contemporary Australians 1995–96, Reed Reference, Port Melbourne, 1995.

Cosulich, Alberto, *Sulle Rotte Dei Capitani Dell'800*, Venice, 1984.

Cresciani, Gianfranco (ed.), *Giuliano-Dalmati in Australia: Contributi E Testimonianze Per Una Storia*, Associazione Giuliani Nel Mondo, Trieste, 1999.

Cyclopedia of Victoria, vol. 3, Melbourne Cyclopedia Co., 1905.

Cyclopedia of Western Australia, vol. 2, ed. J. S. Battye, Cyclopedia Co, Hussey & Gillingham, Adelaide, 1913.

Darby, Douglas, *Why Croatia?*, D. Darby, Melbourne, 1974.

Darveniza, Zon, *An Australian Saga*, Southwood Press, Marrickville, NSW, 1986.

Davison, Graeme, *The Rise and Fall of Marvellous Melbourne*, Melbourne University Press, Melbourne, 1978.

Donohoe, James Hugh, *The Forgotten Australians: The Non Anglo or Celtic Convicts and Exiles*, James Hugh Donohoe, Sydney, 1991.

Driscoll, W. P. and Elphick, E. S., *Birth of a Nation*, Rigby Limited, Adelaide, 1982.

Eterovich, Adam, *Croatian and Dalmatian Coats of Arms*, Ragusan Press, San Carols, CA, 1978.

Fairweather, Keith McDonald, *Brajerack Mining at Omeo and Glen Wills*, K. McD Fairweather, Ensay, Vic., 1983.

Fischer, Gerhard, 'Enemy Labour: Industrial Unrest and the Internment of Yugoslav Workers in Western Australia During World War I', *The Australian Journal of Politics and History*, vol. 34, no. 1, University of Queensland Press, 1988, pp. 1–15.

Fischer, Gerhard, *Enemy Aliens Internment and the Homefront Experiences in Australia 1914–1920*, University of Queensland Press, St Lucia, Qld., 1989.

Flett, James, *Dunolly the Story of an Old Gold-Diggings*, The Poppet Head Press, Melbourne, 1974.

Flett, James, *The History of Gold Discovery in Victoria*, Hawthorn Press, Melbourne, 1979.

Flett, James, *Old Pubs, Inns, Taverns and Grog Houses on the Victorian Gold Diggings*, Hawthorn Press, Melbourne, 1979.

Foster, Leonie, *Port Phillip Shipwrecks Stage 2, An Historical Survey of Vessels Lost Within a Radius of Ten Nautical Miles of the Head, Outside Port Phillip Bay*, Victoria Archaeological Survey, occasional report no. 31, Department of Conservation and Environment, Melbourne, 1988.

Gerritsen, Rolf, 'The 1934 Kalgoorlie Riots: A Western Crowd', *University Studies in History*, vol. 5. no. 3, 1969, pp. 42–75.

Gill, Samuel, *The Goldfields Illustrated, The Sketches of S. T. Gill*, Lansdowne Press, Melbourne, 1972.

Gillgren, Christina, 'We and They: Work and Identity of Italian and Croatian Timber Workers in the South-west of Western Australia 1919–1969', *Papers in Labour History*, no. 21, January/February 1999, pp. 70–81.

Gillgren, Christina, 'Boundaries of Exclusion: A Study of Italian and Croatian Immigrants in the Western Australian Timber Industry 1920–1940', in L. Batterham and P. Bertola (eds) *LIMINA, a Journal of Historical and Cultural Studies*, vol. 3, 1997, pp. 71–82.

Grant, Ian, *A Dictionary of Australian Military History*, Random House Australia, Milsons Point, NSW, 1992.

Halliday, James, *Wines and Wineries of Victoria*, University of Queensland Press, St Lucia, Qld., 1982.

Harvey, David, *Monuments to Courage, Victoria Cross Headstones and Memorials, 1917–1982*, vol. 2, K. and K. Petience, Weybridge, England, 1999.

Hills, Ben, *Blue Murder Two Thousand Doomed to Die, the Shocking Truth about Wittenoom's Deadly Dust*, Sun Books, Melbourne, 1989.

Hoad, J. L. (Bob), *Hotels and Publicans in South Australia 1836–1984*, Australian Hotels Association and Gould Books, Adelaide, 1986.

International Exhibition Sydney 1879, Austrian Catalogue, Vienna, 1879.

Jutronić, Andrea, *Naselja i Porijeklo Stanovništva na Otoku Braču, Zbornik za Narodni Život i Običanje*, Zagreb, 1950.

Kiernan, Colm, *Calwell A Personal and Political Biography*, Thomas Nelson, Melbourne, 1978.

Kojić, Branko, 'Lošinjska Brodogradnja, Od Prvi Početaka do Svršetka Drugog Svjetskog Rata', *Anali Jadranskog Instituta*, JAZU, vol. 2, Zagreb, 1958.

Korzelinski, Seweryn, *Memoirs of Gold-Digging in Australia*, ed. Robe Stanley, University of Queensland Press, St Lucia, Qld., 1979.

Korzelinski, Seweryn, *Opis Podrozy do Australii: i Pobytu Tamze od r. 1852 do 1856*, Tom Drugi, Panstwowy Instytut Wydawniczy, Warsaw, 1954.

Kosović, Ivan and Todorić, P., *Spomena Knjiga o Pomoći Jugoslavenskih Iseljenika Australije Svojoj Domovini od 15.2.1944 do 31.7.1946 God*, Centralnog Odbora za Pomoć F.N.R. Jugoslavije u Australia, Sydney, ca. 1946.

Kovacevic, Mladen and Gladovic, Mira, *Articles regarding Croatians in Australia as printed by the Sydney Morning Herald*, Sydney, 1990.

Kunz, Egon, *Displaced Persons: Calwell's New Australians*, Australian National University Press, Sydney, 1988.

Leavitt, Thaddeus and Lilburn, W. D., *The Jubilee History of Victoria and Melbourne*, illustrated, vol. 2, Part 3. Wells and Leavitt, Publishers, Melbourne, 1888.

Leksik Prezimena Socijalističke Republike Hrvatske, ed. Valentin Putanec and Petar Šimunović, Istitut za Jezik Zagreb, Nakladni zavod Matica Hrvatske, Zagreb, 1976.

Little, William, *Guide to Ballarat with Map and Illustrations*, F.W. Niven & Cos, Ballarat, 1890.

Ljubicic, Mirjana, 'Croatians in Australia from Discrimination to Reconciliation 1960 – present day', masters thesis, Melbourne University, 2005 (in progress).

Lloyd, Brian and Nun, Kathy, *Bright Gold: Story of the People and Gold of Bright and Wandiligong*, Histec, Melbourne, 1987.

Lubbock, Basil, *The Colonial Clippers*, 4th ed., Brown, Son & Ferguson, Glasgow, 1955.

Luković, Niko, 'Put Kapetana Visina Oko Svijeta', *Pomorstvo*, no. 4, Croatia, 1947, pp. 34–7.

Main, Jim and Holmesby, Russell, *The Encyclopedia of League Footballers*, Wilkinson Books, Melbourne, 1994.

Marković, Luka, *Pod Australskim Nebom*, ed. Ante Buratović, Izdvački Zavod Jugoslavenske Akademije Znanosti i Umjetnost, Zagreb, 1973.

McLennan, Donald, *History of Mooroopna Ardmona & District an Interesting Story of Development 1841–1936*, repr. Goulburn Valley Printing Services, Mooroopna, Vic., 1984.

Morcombe, Beth, *Nicholas & Elizabeth Matulick: From Priest, to Paddle Steamers, to Pioneers of the River Murray*, South Australia, 2000.

Morgan, Henry, 'Henry Morgan's Diary', 1885–1908, in possession of Rie Arundel.

Moxley, W. A., *The Gold Trail*, Manuscript 855, Oregon Historical Society, Portland Oregon, 1943.

The New Grove Dictionary of Music and Musicians, vol. 5, ed. Stanley Sadie, Macmillian Publishers, London, 1980.

Notes of the Sydney International Exhibition of 1879, Government Printing Office, Sydney, 1880.

Official Record of Centennial International Exhibition Melbourne 1888–1889, Sands and McDougall Limited, Melbourne, 1890.

Official Record of the Sydney International Exhibition, 1879, Thomas Richards, Government Printer, Sydney, 1881.

Orchard, W. Arundel, *Music in Australia, More than 150 years of Development*, George House, Melbourne, 1952.

The Oxford Companion to Australian Literature, ed. W. Wilde, J. Hooton and B. Andrews, 2nd ed., Oxford University Press, Melbourne, 1994.

Paric, Linda, Boon, David, Henjak, Angela and Buljan, Ivana, *Croats in the Australian Community*, Australian Croatian Community Services, Bureau of Immigration, Multicultural and Population Research, Footscray, Vic., 1996.

Perić, Ivo, *A History of the Croats*, CCT–Centre for Technology Transfer, Zagreb, 1998.

Perry, William, *Tales of The Whipstick, A History of the Whipstick, Neilborough, Sebastian, Raywood, and Myers Creek Gold Rushes*, Melbourne, 1978.

Price, Charles, 'The Ethnic Character of the Australian Population', in *The Australian People: An Encyclopedia of the Nation, Its People and Their Origins*, ed. James Jupp, Cambridge University Press, 2nd ed., 2001, pp. 78–85.

Price, Charles, *The Method and Statistics of Southern Europeans in Australia*, Research School of Social Sciences, Australian National University, Canberra, 1963.

Price, Charles, *Southern Europeans in Australia*, published in association with the Australian National University, Oxford University Press, Melbourne, 1963.

Priestley, Susan, *The Crown of the Road, the Story of the RACV*, Macmillian, South Melbourne, 1983.

Randell, John, *McIvor a History of the Shire and the Township of Heathcote*, Shire of McIvor, Heathcote, Vic., 1985.

Rathe, Gustave, *The Wreck of the Barque Stefano off the North West Cape of Australia in 1875*, Hesperian Press, Carlisle, WA, 1990.

Rathe, Gustave, *The Wreck of the Barque Stefano off the North West Cape of Australia in 1875*, Ferrar, Straus and Giroux, New York, 1992.

Reynolds, Susan, *Yackandandah*, Yackandandah Historical Society Inc., Yackandandah, Vic., 1996.

Royal Commission on Vegetable Products, *Sixth Progress Report, 1888–91*, 19 Sept. 1888, Melbourne, pp. 44–54.

Saint Francis' Church, 1841–1941, Century of Spiritual Endeavour, The Fathers of the Blessed Sacrament, St Francis' Church, Melbourne, 1941.

Scott, Dick, *Winemakers of New Zealand*, Southern Cross Books, Auckland, 1964.

Serle, Geoffrey, *The Golden Age, A History of the Colony of Victoria, 1851–1861*, Melbourne University Press, Melbourne, 1968.

Shaw, Les, *Trial by Slander*, Harp Books, Canberra, 1973.

Shaw, Marjorie, *Our Goodly Heritage History of Huntly Shire*, Cambridge Press, Bendigo, 1966.

Šimunović, Petar, *Hrvatska Prezimena – Podrijetlo, Značenje, Rasprostranjenost*, Golden Marketing, Zagreb, 1995.

Skalica, Tomo, 'Putovanje u Americi, Aziji, Polineziji u Altantičkom, Južnom, Tihom i Ledonom More od 1851–1855', *NEVEN*, Zagreb, 1856, pp. 145–8, 210–5, 323–6.

Smoje, Neven, 'Croatians in Western Australia, 1858–1920', *Migrants from Yugoslavia in Australia*, Australian National University, Centre for Continuing Education, 1988.

Smoje, Neven, 'From Starigrad to Sydney, the Story of the Zaninovich Family', *Matica Iseljenički Kalendar*, Croatia, 1989, pp. 116–17.

Smoje, Neven, 'Early Croatian Settlement in Western Australia', *The Australian People: An Encyclopedia of the Nation, Its People and their Origins*, ed. James Jupp, 2nd ed., Cambridge University Press, Melbourne, 2001, pp. 241–3.

Smoje, Neven, 'Shipwrecked on the North-West Coast: The Ordeal of the Survivors of the Stefano', *Early Days Journal of the Royal Western Australian Historical Society*, vol. 8, part 2, 1978, pp. 35–47.

Smyth, John, *The Story of The Victoria Cross, 1856–1963*, Frederick Muller Limited, London, 1963.

Splivalo, Anthony, *The Home Fires*, Fremantle Arts Centre Press, Fremantle, 1982.

Stefanovic, Dan, 'Serbs', *The Australian People: An Encyclopedia of the Nation, Its People and Their Origins*, ed. James Jupp, 2nd ed., Cambridge University Press, Melbourne, 2001, pp. 674–81.

Stenning, Mary, *Croatian and Slav Pioneers, New South Wales 1800's–1940's*, Fast Books, Sydney, 1996.

Stenning, Mary, *Croatian and Slav Pioneers of South Australia and Victoria*, NSW, 1997.

Stenning, Mary, *Croatian and Slav Pioneers of Australia*, NSW, 1999.

Strange, A. W., *Ballarat A Brief History*, no. 2. Historical Briefs Series, Lowden Publishing Co., Kilmore, Vic., 1971.

Strangman, Denis, 'The ASIO–Croatian Affair of 1973', in *The Shape of the Labor Regime*, ed. Les Shaw, Harp Books, Canberra, 1974, pp.45–99.

Sydney International Exhibition 1879, Official Catalogue of Exhibits, Austrian Court, Government Printer, Sydney, 1880, pp. 4, 27–8.

Thomas, R. M., *The Present State of Melbourne and the Gold Fields of Victoria*, London, 1853.

Thorpe, D. W., *Who's Who of Australian Writers*, 2nd ed., D. W. Thorpe in association with National Centre for Australian Studies, Port Melbourne, 1995.

Tkalcevic, Mato, *Croats in Australia: An Information and Resource Guide*, Victoria College Press, Burwood, Vic., 1988.

Tkalčević, Mato, *Hrvati u Australiji*, Nakladni Zavod Matice Hrvatske, Zagreb, 1992.

Tkalčević, Mato, *Povijest Hrvata u Australiji*, Hrvatski Svjetski Kongres u Australiji, Cross Color Printing, Melbourne, 1999.

Tomasevich, J., *Peasants, Politics and Economic Change in Yugoslavia*, Stanford University Press, Stanford, CA, 1955.

Tough, James, *A Short History of St Francis' Church 1839–1979*, the Blessed Sacraments Fathers, Melbourne, 1979.

Vekarić, Nenad, *Naši Jedrenjaci*, Književni Krug, Split, 1997.

Vekarić, Nenad, *Pelješki Rodovi (A–K)*, vol. 1, HAZU, Dubrovnik, 1995.

Vekarić, Nenad, *Pelješki Rodovi (L–Z)*, vol. 2, HAZU, Dubrovnik, 1996.

Vekarić, Stjepan and Vekarić, Nenad, *Tri Stoljeća Pelješkog Brodarstva (Three Centuries of Pelješac Shipping)*, Pelješki Zbornik, vol. 4, Zagreb, 1987.

Verschuer, Mavis, *Echoes of the Past*, J. Kohlen, Perth, 1978.

Victoria and its Metropolis Past and Present vol. 2A. The Colony and its People in 1888, ed. R. L. J. Ellery et al., Mc Carron, Bird & Co., Publishers, Melbourne, 1888.

von Lippa, Hans, *Oben und Unten: 20 Jahre in Australien* (Ups and Downs: 20 Years in Australia) Carl Konegen, Vienna, 1912.

Wallace-Carter, Evelyn, *For They Were Fishers: The History of the Fishing Industry in South Australia*, Amphitrite Publishing House, Adelaide, 1987.

White, Joseph, *The History of the Shire of Korumburra*, The Shire, Korumburra, Vic., 1988.

Wilkinson, John Gardner, *Dalmatia and Montenegro*, John Murray, London, 1848.

Wynd, Ian, *Churches of Geelong*, Geelong Historical Society, Geelong, Vic., 1969.

Wynd, Ian, *Balla-Wein a History of the Shire of Bellarine*, The Council of the Shire of Bellarine, Drysdale, Vic., 1988.

Wynd, Ian, *Geelong The Pivot*, Geelong Historical Society, Newtown, Vic., 1986.

Zekulich, Michael, *Wine Western Australia*, St George Books, Perth, 2000.

Zekulich, Michael, *Wines and Wineries of the West*, St George Books, Perth, 1990.

Croatian migrants overseas

75th Anniversary 1894–1969 St. Nicholas R.C. Church, The First Croatian R.C. Parish in America, Pittsburgh, PA., 1969.

Antić, Ljubomir, *Hrvati u Južnoj Americi do Godine 1914*, Stvarnost i Institut za Migracije i Narodnosti, Zagreb, 1991.

Antić, Ljubomir, *Croats and America*, Hrvatska Sveučilišna Naklada, Zagreb, 1997.

Boka Kotorska, 1871, Petrović, Rade, *Nacionalno Pitanje u Dalmaciji u XIX Stoljeću*, Svjetlost, Sarajevo, 1968.

Božić, Saša, *Kroaten in Wien, Immigranten und Integration im Zusammenhang mehrschichtiger ethnischer Beziehugen*, Jesenski i Turk, Zagreb, 2000.

Čizmić, Ivan, Miletić, Ivan and Prpić, George, *From the Adriatic to Lake Erie: A History of Croatians in Greater Cleveland*, American Croatian Lodge, Inc. Cardinal Stepinac, Eastlake Ohio, Institute of Social Science Ivo Pilar, Zagreb, 2000.

Čizmić, Ivan, *History of the Croatian Fraternal Union of America 1894–1994*, Golden Marketing, Zagreb, 1994.

Čizmić, Ivan, 'Emigration from Croatia, 1880–1914', *Overseas Migration from East-Central and Southeastern Europe 1880–1940*, ed. Julianna Puskas, Studia Historica Academiae Scientiarum Hungaricae 191, Budapest, 1990, pp. 143–67.

Dabelić, Ivo, *Mlećani u Americi (Mljetans in America)*, Dubrovnik, 1993.

Derado, Klement and Čizmić, Ivan, *Iseljenici Otoka Brača, Brački Zbornik 13*, Zagreb, 1982.

Eterovich, Adam, *Croatian Pioneers in America 1685–1900*, Ragusan Press, San Carlos, CA, 1979.

Eterovich, Adam, *Croatians in California, 1849–1999*, Ragusan Press, San Carlos, CA, 2000.

Eterovich, Adam and Simich, Jerry, *General Index to Croatian Pioneers in California, 1849–1999*, Ragusan Press, San Carlos, CA, 2000.

Gaži, Stjepan, *Croatian Immigration to Allegheny County, 1882–1914*, Pittsburgh, 1956.

Glasnik Foruma Hrvatskih Manjina, Hrvatska Matica Iseljenika, Targa, Zagreb, 1996.

Hrvati u Sloveniji, Institut za Migracije i Narodnosti, Zagreb, 1997.

Iseljeništvo Pavla Vidasa Životopis Hrvatskog Iseljenika iz 19. Stoljeća, ed. Tvrtko Mursalo, Hensman Graphics, Johannesburg, 1985.

Jarabek, Richard, *Moravsti Charvati: Dejiny a Lidova Kultura*, Brno, Czech, 1991.

Jelić, Tomislav, *Gradišćanski Hrvati u Austriji*, Analiza hrvatskih naselja u Gradišću, Dr Feletar, Zagreb, 1997.

Katolička Crkva i Hrvati Izvan Domovine, ed. Vladimir Stanković, Vijeće za Hrvatsku Migraciju, Kršćanska Sadašnjost, Zagreb, 1980.

Krpan, Stjepan, *Hrvati u Keci*, Nakladni Zavod Matice Hrvatske, Zagreb, 1983.

Krpan, Stjepan, *Hrvati u Rekašu Kraj Temišvara*, Kulturno-Prosvjetni Sabor Hrvatske Kršćanska Sadašnjost, Zagreb, 1990.

Lakatoš, Josip, *Narodna Statistika*, Tiskon Hrvatskog Stamparskog Zavod, Zagreb, 1914.

Lokos, Istvan, *Hrvatsko-Mađarske Književne Veze, Rasprave i Članci*, Matica Hrvatska, Zagreb, 1998.

Lončarević, Juraj, *Hrvati u Mađarskoj i Trianonski Ugovor*, Školske Novine, Zagreb, 1993.

Lorković, Mladen, *Narod i Zemlja Hrvata*, Matica Hrvatska, Zagreb, 1939.

Los Angeles San Pedro Monuments to Slavic Pioneers, ed. Vjekoslav Meler, CA, USA, 1933.

Mandić, Živko, *Povijesna Antroponimija Bunjevačkih Hrvata u Madžarskoj*, Izdanje Demokratskog savez Južnih Slaveni u Madžarskoj, Budapest, 1987.

Martinic, Mateo, *Voyagers to the Strait of Magellan Yugoslav (Croatian) Immigration to Southern Chile*, Renaissance Publications, Worthington, Ohio, 1990.

Martinić, Mateo, *Hrvati u Magallanesu Na Krajnjem Jugu Čilea*, Književni Krug, Split, 1997.

Mikačić, Vesna, 'Overseas Migration of the Yugoslav Population in the Period between the Two World Wars', *Overseas Migration from East-Central and Southeastern Europe 1880–1940*, ed. Julianna Puskas, Studia Historica Academiae Scientiarum Hungaricae 191, Budapest, 1990, pp. 168–90.

Mursalo, Tvrtko, *In Search of a Better Life: A Story of Croatian Settlers in Southern Africa*, Printpak (Cape) Ltd, South Africa, 1981.

Nejašmić, Ivo, 'Iseljavanje iz Hrvatske u Evropske i Prekomorske Zemlje od Sredine 19. Stoljeće do 1981. Godine – Pokušaj kvantifikacije' (Emigration from Croatia to Overseas and European Countries from the 19th Century to 1981 – An Attempt at Quantification), *Migracijske Teme*, vol. 6, no. 4, Croatia, 1990, pp. 511–526.

Nejašmić, Ivo, 'Hrvatski Građani na Radu u Inozemstvu: Razmatranje Popisnih Podataka 1971, 1981, i 1991,' (Croatian Citizens Working Abroad: Examination of the Census Data of 1971, 1981 and 1991), *Migracijske Teme*, vol. 10, no. 2, Croatia, 1994, pp. 139–56.

Nejašmić, Ivo, 'Hrvatski Građani na Radu u Inozemstvu i Članovi Obitelji Koji s Njima Borave Prema Popisu 1991: Prikaz Prema Novom Teritorijalnom Ustrojstvu Jedinica Lokalne Samouprave' (Croatian Citizens Abroad and Members of the Families Who Live With Them According to the 1991 Census: Depicted According to the New Territorial Units of Local Self-Administration) *Migracijske Teme*, vol. 12, no. 3, Croatia, 1996, pp. 205–18.

Pavličević, Dragutin, *Moravski Hrvati – Povijest – Život – Kultura*, Hrvatska Sveučilišna Naklada, Zagreb, 1994.

Pečarić, Josip, 'Hrvati Boke Kotorske od 1918. Godine do Danas', *Hrvatski Iseljenički Zbornik 1995/1996*, Hrvatska Matica Iseljenika, Zagreb, 1996, pp. 290–300.

Pečarić, Josip, 'Težak Položaj Hrvata u Boki Kotorskoj', *Hrvatski Iseljenički Zbornik 1999*, Hrvatska Matica Iseljenika, Zagreb, 1999, pp. 311–17.

Prpic, George, *The Croatian Immigrants in America*, Philosophical Library, New York, 1980.

Rasporich, Anthony, *For a Better Life A History of the Croatians in Canada*, Mc Clelland and Stewart Limited, Toronto, Ontario, 1982.

Sekulić, Ante, *Bački Bunjevci i Šokci*, Školska Knjiga, Zagreb, 1990.

Šeparović, Zvonimir, *Od Sydneya Do San Francisa Dijaspora ili Rasutnost Mještana Blata na Korčuli Diljem Svijeta*, Zrinski, Čakovec, Croatia, 1982.

Slavonic Pioneers of California, The Diamond Jubilee, 1857–1932 of the Slavonic Mutual and Benevolent Society of San Francisco, ed. Vjekoslav Meler, Slavonic Pioneers of California, San Francisco, CA, 1932.

Smoljan, Ivo, *Sto Godina Hrvatske Bratske Zajednice*, AGM, Zagreb, 1994.

Tjedan Moliških Hrvata, Hrvatska Matica Iseljenika, Targa, Zagreb, 1996.

Tjedan Hrvata iz Slovačke, Hrvatska Matica Iseljenika, Targa, Zagreb, 2000.

Trlin, Andrew, *Now Respected, Once Despised Yugoslavs in New Zealand*, Dunmore Press Ltd, Palmerston North, New Zealand, 1979.

Vujnovich, Milos, *Yugoslavs in Louisiana*, Pelican Publishing Company, Gretna, USA, 1974.

Gold mining

Dunn, E. J., *List of Nuggets Found in Victoria*, Memoirs of the Geological Survey of Victoria no. 12, 1912, repr. Hesperian Press, Perth, 1979.

Victoria. Legislative Assembly. Session 1864–5. Papers Presented to Both Houses of Parliament by Command of His Excellency the Governor, vol. 3. Discovery of New Gold Fields, Report from the Appointment to Consider Application for Rewards for the Discovery of New Gold Fields, together with the minutes of Evidence and Appendices.

Victoria. Legislative Assembly. Votes and Proceedings, Session 1862–3, with copies of various documents ordered by the Assembly to be printed, vol. 2. Reports from Select Committees Gold Prospectors D33 Appendix. Minutes of Evidence Taken Before the Select Committee During Session 1861–2.

Geological Survey of Victoria, Reports of Progress.

Registration of Claims in the Jamieson Jordan Sub-Division, Beechworth District (Goulburn Book, Burke Museum).

Register of Claims in the Buckland Sub-Division, Beechworth District (Buckland Book, Burke Museum).

Registration of Claims in the Crooked River, Beechworth District (Omeo Book, Burke Museum).

Registration of Claims & c, in the Omeo Subdivision of the Mining District of Gippsland (Omeo Museum).

Registration of Claims in the Yackandandah South Sub-Division, Beechworth District (Yackandandah Book, Burke Museum).

Mining Surveyors and Registrars' Reports: Abstract of the Reports furnished by the Mining Surveyors and Registrars of Victoria to the Mining Department for October, 1863.

NSW Department of Mines Annual Report, 1881, 1884.

Reports of the Mining Surveyors and Registrars.

Smyth, R. Brough, *The Goldfields and Mineral Districts of Victoria, with Notes on the Modes of Occurrence of Gold and Other Metals and Minerals*, John Ferres Government Printer, Melbourne, 1869, repr. Queensberry Hill Press, 1980.

Yackandandah Gold Fields Warden's Register.

Croatian baptism and marriage records

Historical Archives Dubrovnik, Croatia = HAD.

Historical Archives Rijeka, Croatia = HAR.

Historical Archives Zagreb, Croatia = HAZ.

HAD, baptism records for Gruž, Dubrovnik.

HAD, baptism and marriage records for Mokošica in Dubrovačka Rijeka.

HAD, baptism and marriage records for Orebić-Stankovići Pelješac Peninsula.

HAD, baptism records for Vitaljina.

HAR, baptism records for Bakar.

HAR, baptism records for the island of Cres.

HAR, baptism and marriage records for Kukuljanovo.

HAR, baptism records for Lovran.

HAR, baptism records for Mali Lošinj on the island of Lošinj.

HAZ, baptism and marriage records for Bol on the island of Brač.

HAZ, baptism and marriage records for Starigrad on the island of Hvar.

HAZ, baptism and marriage records for Supetar on the island of Brač.

Catholic parish records (Župni Ured), Bol on the island of Brač, Croatia.

Catholic parish records (Župni Ured), Hvar on the island of Hvar, Croatia.

Catholic parish records (Župni Ured), Jelsa on the island of Hvar, Croatia.

Catholic parish records (Župni Ured), Rovinj, Croatia.

Catholic parish records (Župni Ured), Supetar on the island of Brač, Croatia.

Official records (including government publications, records from organisations etc.)

(NAA = National Archives of Australia; PROV = Public Records Office of Victoria)

NAA, Series No: A401/1 Item No: Catarinich, Catarinich Record of Aliens 6th Military District (Series No: A456/2 Item No: W3/29/170 War Precautions Act. J. Catarinich).

NAA, Series No: B13 Item No: 1929/17857.

NAA, Series No: B741/3
  Item No: V/5466 Ivan Roncevich.
  Item No: V/5549 Mati Botica.
  Item No: V/5556 Pasquan.
  Item No: V/7627 Jugo-Slav Nationals, Registration of (Yugoslavs).

NAA, Series No: MP16/1
  Item No: 1914/3/476 Franich and Simunovich.
  Item No: 1915/3/106 Christi Franich.
  Item No: 1915/3/379 Capt. J. Catarinich.

Item No: 1915/3/983 Jure Salacan.
Item No: 1915/3/995 Georgo Ivansic.
Item No: 1916/300 Emilius Rossely.
Item No: 1916/310 Jeska Luke Skoljar.
Item No: 1916/388 Jack Lekovich (on parole).
Item No: 1916/672 Gunners Ante Zurich, Paul Antunovich and Samuel Borich (Dalmatians).
Item No: 1916/752 Ivan Franich.
Item No: 1916/1035 Joseph Parquain and Ferdick.
Item No: 1916/1586 Ben Radovic.
Item No: 1917/237 Jugo-Slav.
Item No: 1917/783 List of Germans and Austrians on Parole.
Item No: 1918/2013 Kazia Stefano.
NAA, Series No: MP367/1 Item No: 448/6/4947 Yugoslav.

Asylum
PROV, VA2839, VPRS 7399/P1, Yarra Bend Lunatic Asylum, case book.
PROV, VA2839, VPRS 7556/P1, Yarra Bend Lunatic Asylum, admission warrants.
PROV, VA2840, VPRS 7398/P1, Kew Asylum Case Book, Unit 19, Item No. p. 121.
PROV, VA2841, VPRS 7403/P1, Ararat Asylum, case book.
PROV, VA2842, VPRS 7395/P1, Beechworth Asylum, case book.
PROV, VA2843, VPRS 7428/P1, Sunbury Asylum.
PROV, VA2862, VPRS 7493/P1, Index Bendigo (Sandhurst) Benevolent Asylum.

Mining
PROV, VPRS 263, Korong Division, Register of Claims.
PROV, VPRS 392, Register Leases, Hepburn Division, Unit. 2, p. 25.
PROV, VPRS 567, Unit 89 Item No. 1601 Dalmazia Quartz Mining Company Limited; Item No. 1602 Dalmatia Gold Mining Co. N.L.
PROV, VPRS 1332, Register of Claims, Crooked River, Unit 1, 2, 3.
PROV, VPRS 1334, Registration of Water Rights, Division of Crooked River, Gippsland, Unit 1.
PROV, VPRS 1615, Registration of Quartz Reefs, Dam and etc. Inglewood Division Mining Register Maryborough District, Unit 1.
PROV, VPRS 1645, Registrar of Claims, Maryborough.
PROV, VPRS 1647, Mining Registrations, Maryborough District, Korong Division, Register of Claims, Unit 1.
PROV, VPRS 1650, Registrar book, Majorca.
PROV, VPRS 3611, Register of Races, Crooked River.
PROV, VPRS 3671, Wedderburn Division Mining Registrar, Register of Signature Book.
PROV, VPRS 3719, Registrar of Mining Claims, Daylesford.

School
PROV, VPRS 795, School building files, Unit 1265 File No. 2050, Yandoit
PROV, VPRS 795, School building files, Unit 1109 File No. 1803, Barongarook W.
PROV, VPRS 795, School building files, Unit 1755 File No. 3077, Korumburra

Shipping
PROV, VPRS 38, Inward shipping reports 1843–1885, Unit 3 and 4.
PROV, VPRS 945/P, Release Books of Ships' Crew, Unit 7, Item No. 18.
PROV, VPRS 7667, Inward passenger lists, foreign ports 1852–1923.
PROV, VPRS 11448/P1 Index to Inward Overseas Passengers from British Ports 1852–1923.

Other
PROV, VPRS 24, Inquest to Deposition Files, Unit 207.
PROV, VPRS 24, Inquest to Deposition Files, Unit 296 Item 1021.
PROV, VPRS 570, Shire of Avon Rate Books, North Riding.

PROV, VA 724, Victoria Police, VPRS 937, Unit 225 File. No number. Perich, M., Wyndham, Burial
    Expenses, deceased Mattea Perich, 1878.
PROV, VPRS 627, Land File, Unit 87, File No. 7782/31.

Other public records

Akten des Ministeriums des Äußern, Administrative Registratur F8/169 Konsulate,
    Melbourne 1880–1918 (November 1882), Österreichisches Staatsarchiv (Austrian Archives)
    Haus-, Hof- Und Staatsarchiv, Vienna.
Australasian Shipping News.
Australian Bureau of Statistics, 2001 Census Statistics.
The Australian Vigneron and Fruit-Growers' Journal.
Census of Western Australia, 1891; 1901.
Index to Probate.
Naturalisation certificates.
New South Wales death certificates.
New South Wales Government Gazette.
New South Wales marriage certificates.
New South Wales Police Gazette.
New Zealand naturalisation certificates.
Queensland death certificates.
Queensland marriage certificates.
Register and Convictions, Orders, and other Proceedings in the Court of Petty Sessions at Drysdale.
Registers of Corners' Inquest and Magisterial Inquires.
Tasmanian death certificates.
The Victoria Government Gazette.
Victoria Police Gazette.
Victorian birth certificates.
Victorian Census, 1854, 1861, 1871, 1881, 1891.
Victorian death certificates.
Victorian marriage certificates.
Victorian Year Book.
Western Australian death certificates.
Western Australian probate.

Electoral and voters' rolls
Burgess Roll for Borough of Footscray, 1874.
Electoral Roll, 1903. various electorates.
Huntly Voters Roll for the Year 1873.
Rate Book Shire of Mount Franklin, North Riding.
Rate Book Shire of Mount Franklin, West Riding.
Shire of Bellarine, Riding of Paywit, rate books.
Voter's Roll, South Ward of the City of Footscray.

Churches, schools, hospitals
Castle Hill Catholic Church, baptism records.
Castlemaine Hospital (Mount Alexander Hospital) records
Dunolly Hospital inpatients, 1860–1900.
Geelong Hospital records.
Maryborough and District Hospital Victoria, Index to Admissions 1855–1907.
Register of State School Portarlington, no. 2455.
St Joseph's Catholic Church, Townsville, baptism records
St Mary's Catholic Church, Geelong, baptism records.
St Mary's Catholic Church, Castlemaine, baptism records.
St Patrick's Catholic Church, Sydney, marriage records.

St Thomas' Catholic Church, Drysdale, baptism records.
Swan Hill Hospital records.

Armed Services records
AMM131 Roll of Honour Circulars, 1914–1918.
AWM 145 Roll of Honour Cards Army, 1914–1918.
AWM148 Roll of Honour Cards Air Force
Royal Australian Air Force Register.

Summary in Croatian

U službenim australskim statistikama doseljenici podrijetlom iz Hrvatske u prošlosti su upisivani kao Austrijanci, Talijani ili Jugoslaveni. Stoga je njihova povijest u Australiji uglavnom ostala 'neispričana priča'. Sve do danas vrlo je malo toga objavljeno o životu prvih hrvatskih doseljenika u Australiji. Onih nekoliko Hrvata o kojima je ponešto zapisano, uglavnom nisu bili identificirani kao Hrvati. Razlog zbog kojega je tako malo poznato o prvim hrvatskim doseljenicima, velikim dijelom leži u činjenici da nikada do sada nije urađena cjelovita studija o njihovu životu i njihovu udjelu u izgradnji australskog društva. U ranijim procjenama broja Hrvata u Australiji, njihov je broj također previše umanjivan, što je rezultiralo znatnom prazninom u našem znanju o prvim australskim doseljnicima i o povijesti doseljavanja. Ovom se knjigom namjeravaju bolje osvijetliti životne priče prvih hrvatskih doseljenika – na njihove uspjehe, ali i na promašaje. One ukazuju na činjenicu da su hrvatske pionirske doseljeničke kolonije postojale još u drugoj polovici 19. stoljeća, te da su prvi hrvatski doseljenici itekako sudjelovali u razvoju Australije, znatno utječući na razvoj vinogradarstva, ribarstva i rudarstva. Povijest doseljavanja Hrvata u Australiju i u druge prekomorske zemlje sve do današnjega doba također je u ovoj knjizi kratko opisana. Usporedbom prvih hrvatskih doseljenika s drugim doseljeničkim društvima, priča o naseljavanju Australije i o njenim pionirima stavlja se u širi kontekst.

U drugom poglavlju, opisuje se povijest prvih hrvatskih doseljenika, koji su u Australiju počeli stizati već početkom 19. stoljeća. Već do 1850., Hrvati su živjeli u svim australskim kolonijama. Hrvati koji su doseljavali u Australiju prije 1891. godine stizali su s jadranske obale i otoka, a mnogi su sa sobom donijeli dragocjena znanja stečena u Hrvatskoj. U knjizi se također sažeto opisuju i razlozi njihova doseljavanja u Australiju.

U trećem poglavlju istražuje se gdje su se prvi hrvatski doseljenici u Australiji nastanili, a pruža se i opći pregled njihovih zanimanja te njihova rasprostranjenost na različitim područjima diljem Australije. Najveći broj nastanio se na zlatonosnim

CROATIANS IN AUSTRALIA: PIONEERS, SETTLERS AND THEIR DESCENDANTS

rudarskim poljima, u glavnim gradovima ili u ribarskim gradićima. Mnogi su bili vrlo pokretni pa su putovali diljem Australije, zavisno o tome gdje bi pronašli posao. U ovom poglavlju, hrvatski se doseljenici smještaju u zajedničku sliku useljeničkih pionira Australije, što pomaže proširivanju našega znanja o povijesti naseljavanja Australije.

Kako su Hrvati formirali svoje zajednice i kako su održavali veze s drugim hrvatskim doseljenicima u Australiji, podrobno se obrađuje u četvrtom poglavlju. Jedni su drugima kumovali na vjenčanjima, nazočili pogrebima i jedni drugima kumovali djeci na krštenjima. Prvi su hrvatski doseljenici ponekad prevaljivali goleme razdaljine kako bi održali međusobne veze. Isto tako, zajedno su imali rudnike i druga poslodavstva i živjeli blizu jedni drugima. Mnogi su prvi hrvatski doseljnici i njihovi potomci igrali aktivnu ulogu u australskoj Katoličkoj crkvi, pa se opisuje i njihov udio u razvoju Katoličke crkve u Australiji. Također se opisuje život i doprinos prvih doseljenih Hrvatica.

Peto poglavlje knjige posvećeno je vrlo značajnome doprinosu prvih hrvatskih doseljenika na zlatonosnim poljima: od pronalaženja zlata do drobljenja rude, zapošljavanja rudara i vođenja rudnika. Oni su bili uključeni u sve vidove rudarstva: od ispiranja naplavna zlata, kopanja kvarca, potrage za zlatnim grumenjem do iskopavanja u dubokim rudarskim oknima. Prvi hrvatski rudari slijedili su jedni druge po poljima i rudnicima zlata, a zajednički su i otvarali rudnike od kojih su mnogi nosili imena svojih vlasnika ili imena mjesta u kojima su rođeni.

Životi hrvatskih mornara i ribara u Australiji opisuju se u šestom poglavlju. Hrvatski trgovački brodovi redovito su posjećivali Australiju – neki su ostali i nasukani u australskim vodama. Isto tako i hrvatski mornari na austrijskim ratnim brodovima također su posjećivali Australiju tijekom znanstvenih ekspedicija i međunarodnih izložbi, pri čemu su neki od njih dezertirali i ostali živjeti u Australiji. Male zajednice hrvatskih ribara također su formirane diljem Australije. Tako su Hrvati činili većinu u skupini ribara u Portarlingtonu u Victoriji, pa su ih predstavljali i na pregovorima s parlamentarcima ranih godina dvadesetog stoljeća. Oni su također bili uključeni i u prve spasilačke službe za spasavanje utopljenika i potonulih čamaca. Hrvatski pomorci također su bili i mornari, posada, kapetani i vlasnici brodova koji su trgovali između lučkih gradova u Australiji.

Sedmo poglavlje knjige bavi se hrvatskim doseljenicima kao uspješnim gostioničarima, vinogradarima i farmerima u Australiji. Tako je, na primjer, Antonio Radovick (Antun Radović), gostioničar iz gradiću Korumburra u Viktoriji smatran 'Ocem Korumburre' zbog njegova prinosa izgradnji gradića. Vrhunska vina Trojana Darvenize (Trojana Drvenice) svojvremeno bila su poznata diljem svijeta, a s njima je osvojio više od 300 medalja. Romeo Bragato bio je ovlašteni stručnjak za vinogradarstvo u Vladi Viktorije, a odigrao je vrlo važnu ulogu u razvoju industrije vina kako u Australiji tako i na Novom Zelandu. Nicholas Jaspriza (Nikola Jasprica) postao je vrlo uspješan plantažer trešanja na području Younga u Novom Južnom Walesu, a njegove plantaže trešanja spadale su među najveće na svijetu. Brojni hrvatski pioniri imali su više od jednoga zanimanja. Kopali su zlato, radili kao fizički radnici, mornari, gostioničari, zemljoradnici, ribari, vinogradari. Osmo poglavlje knjige upravo je posvećeno rasponu i raznolikosti života desetorice uspješnih hrvatskih pionira iz toga vremena.

Značajan doprinos kojega su neki od potomaka prvih hrvatskih doseljenika dali razvoju Australije, opisan je u prvome dijelu devetoga poglavlja. Ovo poglavlje je najvećim dijelom posvećeno pregledu povijesti Hrvata doseljenih u Australiju u razdoblju između 1891. do 1945. godine. Posebno su istaknuta glavna područja na koja su naselili i u kojima su stvorili svoje zajednice. Mnogi Hrvati u Australiji bili su internirani kao neprijateljski saveznici tijekom Prvoga svjetskog rata, ali su unatoč tome prikupljali novčanu pomoć za savezničku vojsku, a čak su ustrojili i hrvatsku dragovoljačku postrojbu koja se borila na strani saveznika. Brojni hrvatski doseljenici između dva rata bili su aktivno uključeni u sindikalni pokret i sudjelovali u štrajkovima diljem zemlje. U knjizi su opisani i raznovrsni oblici diskriminacije kojoj su bili izloženi (primjerice, tijekom prosvjeda u Kalgoorlieu).

Pregled doseljavanja Hrvata u Australiju poslije Drugoga svjetskog rata, predstavljen je u desetome poglavlju. U ovome razdobolju je doselio značajan broj Hrvata, a opisana je njihova rasprostranjenost, zanimanja i glavne aktivnosti hrvatske zajednice. Oni su izgradili hrvatske domove, športske stadione, hrvatske katoličke crkve i župe, hrvatske škole i folklorne skupine. Brojni Hrvati i njihovi potomci ostvarili su vrlo značajan doprinos u razvoju australskoga društva, na polju športa, umjetnosti i politike i to je glavna značajka ove knjige koja se u cijelosti bavi poviješću doseljavanja i pregledom najvažnijih postignuća hrvatskih doseljenika i njihovih potomaka u Australiji.

Index

This index is arranged alphabetically, word for word. It includes the Croatian-alphabet spellings of names and places after the Roman-alphabet spellings where these have been used in the text. Page numbers in **bold** are those with the most information, and those in *italic* are illustrations. The coloured pages are noted as *C1*, *C2*, and so on.

A

A1 West All Nations Quartz Mining
    Company, 145
Abbott, Vincent (Vranjican, Vicko), 106, *106*
Abolstein, 5
Aborigines, 115
Abstainer, 129
accidents, 47, 57, 88, 90, 109–110, 133,
    171–172
  Broken Hill, 203
  fishing, 122–123
  Kalgoorlie, 203
ACCS *see* Australian Croatian Community
    Services
Adam, Simone (Adam, Šimun), 159
Adelaide, 7, **57**, 72, 86, 113–114, 130, 215, 268
  boat-building, 217
  Catholic Church, 72, 219
  clubs, 72, 227
  Dabovich, Christopher, 120
  deserters, 113
  Fringe Festival, *C19*
  halls and sporting venues, 268
  hoteliers, 135, 147–148
  Marian procession, *227*
  nuns, 219
  nursing homes, 219
  population, 211
  seamen, 129, 131
  settlers, 57
Adelaide Croatia soccer team, *225*
Adelaide Croatian Club, 72
Adelaide Lead, 46
Adelaide Ship Construction International
    Pty Ltd, 217
Adelong, 106
Adriatic Gulf, as birthplace, 5
Age, The, 84
Agnes, 31
AIF, 169, 183, **197**, 201, 203 *see also*
    World War I
  Bathols, Nicholas, 183, *184*
  Cunich, Matthew, *197*

Dominick, Frederick, 16
Dominick, Percival, *198*
Dubricich, Francis, 57
enlistment, 201
Goidanich, Edward, 74
internees, 202
Lusic, Victor, *9*, *197*
Marassovich, Matthew, 176
Mercovich, Bartholomew, *193*
Millich, Cosmo, *9*
Pavich, Antonio, 197–198, *198–199*
Radonich, Albert, 161, *162*
Roderick, Frederick, 54
Terdich, Alfred, 179
Alagich, Marin, 8
Albany, 58–59, 132
Albatros, 119–120
Albich, Peter (Albić, Petar), 53, 62, 88, 105
Albion Consols mine, 45
Albion Hotel, 147
Albion Quartz Mining Company, 171
alcohol, 87–88, 141
  drinks, 158
  illegal sale, 88–89
  licenses, 154
  sly grog, 144–145
Alexandria, 265
All Nations Hotels, 104, 145
  Caledonia Gully, 145
  Heathcote, 141, 145
  license, 141, 145
  Redcastle, 49, 94, 141, 145, 149
  Woods Point, 145
All Nations mining companies, 175
alluvial gold, 91–92, 95
  Ballarat, 45
  Castlemaine, 28
  Crooked River, 105
  decline, 94
  Moonlight Flat, 47
  Stawell, 47
  Yandoit, 110
Alma, 46, 98

ALP *see* Australian Labor Party
alphabet, Croatian, 6
Alpine Observer, The, 78
Altona, 213, 215
Amherst, 29, 46, 159
Andamooka, 217
Angelinawich, Antonio (Anđelinović), 130
Anicich, Simon (Aničić, Šimun), 114, *114*
Ann Gales, 15
Anticevich, Antonio, 142
Anticevich, Nicholas (Antičević, Nikola),
    55, 69
Anticevich, Nicolo (Antičević, Nikola),
    52–53, 105, 142
Antich, Cosmo (Antić, Kuzma), 62, 177
anti-monarchism and anti-monarchists, 206
antimony, 49, 62, 101–103, 141
Antoniwich, John, 87
Aquinas College, 72
Araluen, 54, 144
Ararat, 74, 175
Archduke Maximilian Dalmatian Reef,
    68, 100, 169
Argentina, 7, 10–12, 14, 81, 132–133
Argentine Navigation Company (Nicholas
    Mihanovich) Limited, 132
Argus, The, 84, 116, 118
Ariel, 170
Armadale, 154–155
  Slavonian vineyard, *155*
Armida, 114, *C2*
Armstrong, Thomas, 133
Arnerich, Mary Ann, 66
Arnerich, Paulo, 19, 51–52, 63, 66, 142, 175
ASIO, 231, 233
associations, 64, 209 *see also* societies
  Giuliano-Dalmati, 2
asylums, 88
athletics, 137, 203
Augustinvich, Michele, 52, 67
Australasian Sketcher, The, 85
Australia, 175
Australia Day, 213, *223*

Australian Capital Territory, 268
Australian Croatian Association Stjepan
    Radić, 267
Australian Croatian Chamber of Commerce,
    238
Australian Croatian Club Ltd, 268
Australian Croatian Club, Hobart, 268
Australian-Croatian Community Club
    Eugen Kvaternik Mount Gambier
    Inc, 268
Australian Croatian Community Services
    (ACCS), 211–212
Australian Croatian National Hall Kardinal
    Stepinac, 226, 267
Australian Croatian Sporting Centre,
    226, 267
Australian Democrats, 229
Australian Football League (AFL), 189
Australian Grand Prix, 179, 187, *188–189*,
    223, C6
Australian Holy Catholic Guild, 78
Australian Labor Party, 32, 187, 191–192,
    229–231
Australian Natives' Association, 137
Australian Soccer Association, 225
Australian Soccer Federation, 224
Australian Vigneron and Fruit-Growers'
    Journal, The, 156
Australian, The, 233
Austria, 5, 9–10, 12–13, 81, 198, 265
    merchant service, 112
    military service, 23
Austrian Consulate, 17, 62, 140, 181
Austrian Creek, 51
Austrians Amalgamated Gold Mining
    Company, 51–52
Austro-Hungarian Empire, 4, 113, 119
Avenel, 49, 154
Avoca, 46
Avondale Heights, 213

B

B, Giuseppe, 40–41, 177
Babare, Matteo, 55
Babich Wines, 203
Babino Polje, 107
Baccich, Miho, 114, *115*
Bačka, 13
Baillich, Matteo, 89
Bairnsdale, 54, 129
Bakar, 18, 21, 30, 32–33, 59, 62–63, 66, 177
Baker, R. Hon, 138
Baladinivinsh, Nicolo, 24
Balch, Emily, 23
Ballarat, 27–29, 45–47, 49, 80, 144, 159, 175,
    214, 267
    clubs, 227
    concerts, 84
    costs, 93, 98
    employment, 216
    Eureka Stockade, 92

population, 28–29, 45
settlers, 46, 105, 159, 167
Ballarat West, 171
balls, 148–149
Bana, Eric, 230
Band of Hope mine, 45
Banner of Belfast, The, 170
banquets, 137, 148, 169
Baric-Ravich, Peter, 55
Barmedman, 109
Barongarook, 31, 192
Barovich, Nikola (Barović), 148
barques, 8, 24, 84, 112–114, 116–118,
    130–131, 160
    from Australian ports, 62
    from UK, 15
    from USA, 97
Baška, 54
basketball, 225
Bassich, Antonio, 63
Bassich, opera singer, 85
Bathols, George (Vidulić, Jure), 22, 25, **182**,
    182, 183
Bathols, Lussina Adelaide, 183
Bathols, Mary Ann nee Jury, 183
Bathols, Nicholas, *184*
Bathurst, 98, 106
Bautovich, Joseph (Bautović, Josip), 50
Bavins, George, 101
Beban, Steffano, 63
Beechworth, 28–29, 51
Bega, 56
Belanich, 65
Belanich, Mark, 40, 66, 110
Belfast Gazette, The, 170
Belfast Oyster Room and Fruit Shop, 170
Belgium, 81
Belgrade, 2
Bell Park, 214, 226, 267
Bellarine Herald, The, 75, 124, 171, 261
Bendigo (formerly Sandhurst), 27–29, 43, 45,
    49, 59–60, 86–87, 98–99
    concerts, 84
    gold production, 47
    population, 28–29
    settlers, 47, 86, 105
    women, 86–87
Benussi and Company, 43
Benussi, Matteo (Benussi, Mate), 42–43,
    111–112
Beovich, Elizabeth nee Kenny, 34
Beovich, Francis, 192
Beovich, Matthew (Beović, Mate), 33, **34**,
    35–36, 84, 169, 192
Beovich, Matthew, Archbishop, 34, 36, 72,
    72–73, 74, 79–80, 187, *220*, 237
Beovich, Vera, Sister, 34, *72*, 192
Bercich, Vincenzo (Berčić, Vicko), 47–48
Beriza, Stephen, 99–100
Bersica, Seraphin (Beršić, Serafin),
    21, 50, 152

Berwick, 214
billiards, 136, 144, 146, 150, 170–171
Billich, Charles, 223, C6
Billich, Ignatio (Bilić), 43, 88
BIMPR (Bureau of Immigration, Multicultural
    and Population Research), 212
Birdwood, 148
birthplaces, 4–5, 30, 44, 55, 183, 239
    see also origins
    Italian forms, 5
Bjelovar, 182
Bjelovučić, Stjepan, Captain, 114
Black River, 96
Blacktown, 205, 209, 214, 219, 227, 268
Blackwood, 45
Blossage, Gaspar, 87–88
Blue Gum Festival, C18
Blue Mountains, 97
Blummer's vineyard, 154
Bobuš, Catte, 180
bocce, 209, 217, 225–226
Bogden, Michael (Bogdan), 173
Boggy Creek, 54
Bogovich, Antonio (Bogović, Ante), 90
Bogut, Andrew, 225
Bol, 16, 147
bombings, 231
Bonacich, Nicholas, 57
Bonegilla, 214
Bonnitcha, Nicholas, 58
Borbeni Radnički Pokret (Militant Workers'
    Movement), 205
Borcich, John, 66
Borsich and Company quartz, 102
Bosnia, 2, C3
Bosnia-Herzegovina, 2–3, 13–14, 212–213
    Croatian Catholic parishes, 81
    humanitarian aid, 236
Bosnich, Mark, 224
Bošnjak, Slavko (Jim), 230
Botica, Mati, 64, 121
Boulder, 80, 86, 110, 131–132, 202–203, 209
    discrimination, 207
    tamburica orchestra, *204*, 209
Brač (Brazza), 5, 29–30, 90, 217
    Arnerich, Paulo, 51
    Beovich, Matthew 34
    Bol, 147
    chain migration, 18
    emigration, 8–9, 12, 17–18
    Florio, Matthew, 16
    Gasparo, John, 33
    Lusic, Victor, 66
    Lussich (Lukšić) families, 19
    Lussich, Natale, 63
    Milna, 57, 167
    Selca, 33
    Sitanich, Nicholas, 66
    Supetar, 34, 170, 261, 265
    Sutivan, 18, 21, 62, 101, 147
    vineyards, 154

Braća Radić, 268, C7
Braća Radić Blacktown Ltd, 268
Bragato, Romeo, 152, *156–157*, 158
Brajkovich, Lennard, 230
Brassey, Thomas, Lord, 156
bravery, 119, 133, 199
Brazil, 7, 12
Brazza *see* Brač
brigantines *see* brigs
Bright, 78
Brighton, 123
brigs, 24, 112, 261, C2
    from Peru, 45
    from East Indies, 59
Brimbank, 213, 230
Brisbane, 58, 211, 215, 268, C20
    Catholic centres, 219
    club, 227
    Corpus Christi procession, C14
    folkloric group, C23
    oyster saloons, 34
    Seventh Day Adventists, 222
    Summer School of Language and Culture,
        C11
Britain, 79, 81
Brkljaca, Dragana, 230
Broadmeadows, 169, 214–215
Broken Hill, 7, 65, 86, 131, 205
    accidents, 110, 203
    Catholic Church, 80
    chain migration, 56
    clubs, 207, 209
    strikes, 206
    tamburica orchestra, 203, *204*
Brookton Hotel, 148
Brookvale, 209
Broughton, 58
Brseč, 40, 103
Brsiza, Steffano, 67
Brunswick, 32–33, 69, 84, 146
Buckland, 7, 27, 51, 67–68, 78, 101, 108,
        110, 144
    Catholic Church, 77–78
    costs, 93
    settlers, 105
Buckland River Riots, 51
Budgeree, 54, 160
Budinich, Nicholas, 180
Buenos Aires, 11, 71, 132
Bull Town, 62
Bundaberg, 58
Bundara Street, 38
Bundara, Antonio (Antun), 22, 52–53, 62, 76
Bundara, John (Ivan), 22, 52–53
Bundara, Kolendin, 22
Bundeena, C8
Bundoora, 214
Buninyong, 45
Bureau of Immigration, Multicultural and
        Population Research (BIMPR), 212
Burgenland, 10, 81

Burich, John (Burić, Ivan), 148
Burke and Wills Hotel, 178
Burnie, 58, 129
Burramine, 50
Burrangong Chronicle, The, 161
Burwood, 38, 67
Busanich, Mark (Busanić, Marko), 40, 66,
        103, 110
bushrangers, 93
Bussanich, Mattio, 100
Buzolich family, *169*
Buzolich and Co, Antonio, 168
Buzolich, Antonio (Buzolić, Ante), 34, 64,
        99–100, **167**, 168
Buzolich, Douglas, 148, 168–169, 187, *190*, 191
Buzolich, Fiovaranti, 100, 167
Buzolich, Janet, nee Bell, 167
Buzolich, John, 99–100, 167
Buzolich Patent Damp Resisting and
        Anti-Fouling Paint Company
        Limited, 34, 168

C

Cabramatta, 205, 209
Cairns, 205, 209, 227, 268
Cairns, Jim, Dr, 231
Calafatovich, Joseph, 69
Caledonia Gully, 145
California, 10, 11, 24, 133, 166
Calin, 147
Callao, 70
Calwell, Arthur, 80
'campanilismo' migration theory, 21
Campbellfield, 214, 226, 267
Campsie, 55
Canada, 1, 7, 10–12, 14, 24, 81, 126
    refugees, 12
Canberra, 197, 211, 217, 219, 223, 234, 236,
        268, C16, C19, C21
    clubs, 227
    'embassy', 229, *234–235*, C15
cane-cutters, 206
Cannaliracusa, 66
Canny, Michael, 82
Carlton, 32–34, 104
Carnarvon, 128, 227
Caroline, 134
Carr, Archbishop, 76
Carson, Alfred *see* Corsano, Fortunato
        Alfredo
Casterton, 31
Castle Hill, 15
Castlemaine (formerly Mount Alexander),
        27–28, 40–41, 105, 177
    gaol, 88
    hospital, 103, 110
    St Mary's, 40, 65, 76, 103
Catarinich, Antonio, 64, 69
Catarinich, John, Dr, 187, 190
Catarinich, Joseph, Captain, 5, 63–64, 69,
        129, *129*, 181–182

Catarinich, Margaret nee McKenna, 64
Catholic centres, 219, 238
Catholic Church, 25, 34, **71–72**, 74–75, 78,
        82, 122, 135, 219–222 *see also*
        individual churches
    Ballarat, 45
    Bright, 78
    Brighton, 123
    Castlemaine, 40, 65, 76, 103
    Clifton Hill, 219
    Croatian language, 80
    Drysdale, 64, 75
    Geelong, 29, 63–64, 170, C14
    Gulgong, 174
    Korumburra, 76, 77, 137
    marriages, 71
    Melbourne, 64, 75–76, 180
    North Fitzroy, 34
    Port Melbourne, 33
    Portarlington, 64
    records, 5
    Shepparton, 86
    St Arnaud, 45
    Sydney, 55, 76, 79
    Western Australia, 80
    Youanmite, 50
    Young, 78
Catholic Family Welfare Bureau, 72
Catholic Immigration Centre, 72
Catholic parishes, 12, 14, 81
Catholic Women's Social Guild, 78
Caversham, 227, 268
Celovich, Antoinette, 96
Celovich, Constantino (or Costa), 96–97
Celovich, Stefano, 43, 66, 89, 96
Cemetery Flat, 99
censuses, 2–4, 13, 140, 211, 223, 233
    Austrian consulate, 17
    birthplaces, 3
    nationalities, 1, 3
    US, 14
    Victoria, 17, 26
    Yugoslavia, 13
Centenary of Federation, C18
Cernić, Vicko *see* Chernich, Vincent
chain migration, 18, 50
Charlton, 45, 74, 160
Charters Towers, 57–58, 105
Chernich, Ellen nee Adams, 56
Chernich, Vincent (Cernić, Vicko),
        55–57, *57*
cherries, 161, 163–166
Chewton, 28
Chile, 10–12, 14, 70
Chillivish, Simon, 24
Chinese diggers, 51
Chreso *see* Cres
Christian Brothers, 80
Church of England, 25, 78
Cibich, Pietro, 113
Cibilić, Jakov (Zibilich, James), 21

Ciro, 113–114, 160
Citanich, Bartolomeo, 95–96, 102
citizenship, 202, 212
Čizmić, Ivan, 8
Clarke, John, 94–95
Clear Creek, 51, 101, 142
Clermont, 173
Clifton Hill, 179, 219, C17
clippers, 111
clothes, 93, 98
Club House Hotel, 174
clubs, 70, 153, 187, 203, 205, 207, **209**, 210,
       213–214, 217, 225–227, 229,
       236, 238
    Croatian Slavonic Society, 203
    Giuliano-Dalmati, 2
    senior citizens, 219
    soccer, 224–225
    sporting, 190, 209
    university, 213
Clunes, 45, 91
coal, 128, 135, 138, 140, 216
Coal Creek Colliery Accident Relief Fund,
    137–138
Coal Creek Miners' Association, 138
Coal Creek Proprietary Co, 148
Cockatoo, 46
Cockburn, 214, 238
Coffey, Mary, 15
Coffin Bay, 120
Colac, 31–32, 159
Collingwood Football Club, 189
Coloper, Annie, 123
Coloper, Stephen (Kaloper, Stjepan), 123, 180
Comandich, Jacomina, 78
Comandich, John, 78
Commercial Hotel, *146*, 147, 175–176
Commercial Travellers' Association of
    Victoria, 168
Commonwealth Police, 231
communism and communists, 206–207
community activities, 71, **209**, 238
community halls, 14, 148, 226
community television, 223
concerts, 84, 148
Constance, 159
consulates, 237
Conte Oscar L, 113–114
convicts, 15
Coober Pedy, 217, 227, 268
Coolac, 15–16, 154
Corbett, Albert, 95
Corio Bay, 133
Corpus Christi procession, C14
Corsano, Fortunato Alfredo (Carson, Alfred),
    105–106
Costerfield, 7, 27, 31, 49, 78, 101,
    103–105, 150
    antimony, 62
    Family Hotel, 49, 141, 149
Cosulich, Callisto, Captain, 114

Country Journal, The, 163
Court of Mines, 94
Covacevich, Prospero, 57
Cravarovich, Matteo (Kravarević, Mate), 21
crayfish, 121, 170
Cres (Chreso), 2, 111, 147
Creswick, 28–29, 45, 85
Crewechich, 99
cricket, 137, *140*, 190, 237
crime, 89, 93
Cristilovich, Gregory, 62, 103
Croatia, 5, 9, 47, 66, 90, 118, 132, 205–206,
    212, 219, 224, 232, 234–238,
    C15, C22
    Austro-Hungarian Empire, 4
    autonomy, 12
    citizens
        as Austrians, 4–5
        as Italians, 4–5
        nationalities, 1–3
    coat of arms, C3
    depressed economic status, 24
    emigration, 11–12, 17
        returned, 12
        women, 56
    Germanisation, 23
    humanitarian aid, 236
    Hungarian control, 4
    invasion, 13–14
    Italianisation, 23
    Magyarisation, 23
    maps, 19
        Portarlington, 30
        Wedderburn, 44
    recognition, 235–237
    refugees from, 3, 12
    refugees to, 10, 13
    repression, 24
    Serbs, ethnic, 2
    wineries, 154
    zadruga, 70
Croatia Deakin Soccer Club, 268
Croatia Geelong soccer team, *216*
Croatia Social and Sporting Club Invermay,
    268
Croatia Whyalla West Soccer and Social Club
    Inc, 268
Croatia, folkloric group, C19, C23
Croatian and Dalmatian Club, 70
Croatian Australian Association,
    226, 237, 267
Croatian Benefit Society, 70
Croatian Bowling Club Jedinstvo (Unity), 203
Croatian Bowling Club Jedinstvo Inc, 268
Croatian Catholic Centres, 226, 267, 268
Croatian Catholic parishes, 80–81
Croatian Catholic Union, 70
Croatian Charitable Society, 70
Croatian Club Adelaide Inc, 268
Croatian Club Caversham Inc, 268
Croatian Club Dr Ante Starčević, 267

Croatian Club Ltd, 267
Croatian Club, Cairns, 268
Croatian Community Centre, 226, 267–268
Croatian Community Centre of Geelong Inc,
    226, 267
Croatian Community Credit Union Ltd, 238
Croatian contingent, 202–203
Croatian Cultural & Educational Association,
    268
Croatian Cultural Week, 238
Croatian Culture Association Bosna St Marys
    Ltd, 267
Croatian Food, Wine and Tourism Festival,
    238
Croatian Fraternal Union, 70
Croatian Hall, 147
Croatian Herald (*Hrvatski Vjesnik*), 223
Croatian House (Hrvatski Dom), 268
Croatian language, 66, 69, 80, 219, 222–223,
    233–234, C10, C17, C24
    Catholic Church, 80
    newspapers, 71
    retention, 14
    schools, 14
'Croatian Six', 233
Croatian Slavonian Benevolent Society, 70
Croatian Slavonic Mutual and Benevolent
    Society, 65
Croatian Slavonic Society, 70–71, 202–203,
    207–208
Croatian Soccer Association of Australia,
    224
Croatian Sporting Club of Port Lincoln Inc,
    268
Croatian Sporting Club Zagreb, 226, 267
Croatian Sports Centre Gold Coast Inc, 268
Croatian Sports Soccer Club Zora, *210*
Croatian Students' Association, 213–214, 235
Croatian Studies Foundation, 234
Croatian Summer School of Language and
    Culture, C11
Croatian Welfare and Sport Club, Coober
    Pedy, 268
Croatian Wickham Sports Club Co-Op, 268
Croatian Youth Organisation, 237
Crooked River, 27, 51–53, 62, 88, 105, 110,
    140, 142
crushing machines and plants, 51–52, 67, 91,
    94, 99–100, 107–108
Cucel, Frank, 32–33, 67, 113, 179
Cucel, John, 33
Cuculić, Tomislav *see* Zuzulich, Thomas
Cunich family, *164*
Cunich, Andrew, 163, *164*
Cunich, Annie Elizabeth nee Jasprizza, *163*
Cunich, Antony (Kunić), 163, *165*
Cunich, Baldo (Kunić), 163, *163*, *165*
Cunich, Leo, *163*
Cunich, Matthew, 197
Curlizza, Jacob (Čurlica), 78
Curzola, 133

Cusack, Rev. Father, 75
Cussianovich, Peter, 105
Cvitanić (Sitanich), 66
Cvitanovich, John (Cvitanović, Ivan), 70
Czech (Moravia), 10

D
D. Buzolich Pty Ltd, 34, *168*, 190, 192
Dabovich, Christopher, *120*
Dalmacija Sydney Croatian Club Ltd, 267
Dalmatia (Dalmata, Dalmacia, Dalmeith), 15, 74, 98–100, 132, 177
 Anticevich, Nicolo, 142
 as birthplace, 5, 9
 Austrian control, 4
 B, Giuseppe, 40, 177
 Celovich, Stefano, 96
 claims' names, 68, 98–99
 coat of arms, C3
 Covacevich, Prospero, 57
 Daylesford, 43
 Darveniza, Trojano, 7, 66
 emigrants and emigration, 10–12, 18, 205
 Francovich, Dominico, 47
 Germano, Antonia, 52
 Harlovich, Antonio 101
 Italian language, 4
 Italianisation, 23
 Italians, 23
 Jasprizza, Nicholas, 7
 Joseph, James, 69
 Lussich, Dominick, 66
 McNish, James, 88
 Milovitch, Dominic, 96
 mines' names, 7, 49
 Nicolich, Francis, 51
 parliament, 23
 population, 22
 Portarlington, 30
 residences' names, 55
 salt monopoly, 23
 Salacan, George, 202
 Spirodine, Tussup, 49
 Vranzigan, Peter, 154
 Yackovitze, Antonio, 145, 154
 Yannich, Luke, 96
Dalmatia Gold Mining Company, 45, 99–100, 106, 108, 167
 shaft, 99, *100*
Dalmatia Quartz Reef, 99
Dalmatin Quartz Mining Company, 101
Dalmatinska Gostiona, 69, 185
Dalmazia Quartz Gold Mining Company, 68
Dalmazia Reef, 68, 99
dances, 148–149, 209, 217, 236
Dandenong, 160, 214–215
Dargo, 53, 62, 77–78
 Inn, 142
Darveniza brothers, 182
Darveniza's winery, 166
Darveniza, John (Ivan), 86, *153*

Darveniza, Kaye, 192
Darveniza, Mary, 86
Darveniza, Mato, 86
Darveniza, Peter (Pero), 86, *153*
Darveniza, Trojano (Drvenica, Trojan), 7, 50, 60, 66, 86, 93, **150**, 151–152, *153*, 159
 chain migration, 50
Davis, Gladys, 134
Davis, J. M., Hon, 134
Daylesford, 27, 41, 43, 50
 Jim Crow diggings, 41
 settlers, 105
De Murska Street, 38
de Murska, Ilma (Pukšec, Ema), 47, 84–85, *85*
Deakin, 227, *229*, 268
Deason, John, 97
Dedo, Stefano, 55
Dee Why, 205, 209
Deegan, Patrick, 133
Defence, Department of, 233
Democratic Labor Party (DLP), 192
demonstrations, political, 156, 232–237, C5, C15, C16, C22
Denmark, 81
deportations, 200
Depression, 12, 182, 205, 208
Derado, Klement, 8
Derado, Klement, 8
Descovich, Ignazio, 148
deserters (from ships), 15–16, 25, 56, 91, 111–113, 119, 131, 160, 171
Dešpoja, Mario, 229, 235
Despot, Vincent, 182
Devcic, Clara (Devčić, Jele), 86
Devonport, 129
dialects, 10
diaries, 7
diets, 93
Dimbulah, 205, 209, 227, 268
discrimination, 187, 201, 208, 231
 fishermen, 126
 Kalgoorlie, 207
 names, 6
 Yugoslavia, 213
displaced persons, 12, 212
 camps, 12
Displaced Persons Scheme, 3, 212
DLP *see* Democratic Labor Party
Dokic, Jelena, 2
Doli, 132
Dominick, Frederick, 16
Dominick, George, 15, *15*, 16
Dominick, Lucy, 33
Dominick, Paul (Domančić, Pavao), 22, 33–34, 38
Doša, 69
dowries, 89
Dragovitch, Cosmo, 177
Drapač, Ljerka, 230
Drvenica, Trojan *see* Darveniza, Trojano

Drmić, Frank, 225
Dromana, 38, 120
Drouin, 136
drownings, 115, 129, 133–134
Drummoyne, 54, 81
Dry Diggings, 43
Drysdale, 64, 75, 122
Duba, 21
Dubricich (Dubrich), Christie (Dubričić), 57, 58
Dubrovačka Rijeka, 21
Dubrovnik, 30, 46, 67, 84, 112, 121, 133, 144
 Bautovich, Joseph, 50
 as birthplace, 5
 Bonnitcha, Nicholas, 58
 Cannaliracusa, 66
 emigrants and emigration, 12, 18, 205
 Geronevitch, Antonio, 94
 Gruž, 142
 Guratovich, Matteo, 57
 Juratowitch, Nicholas, 56
 Lasich, Nicholas, 53
 Monkivitch, John, 31
 Paulussy, Nicholas, 51
 Peru, 99
 Radonich, Natale, 160
 Raicovich, Nicolla, 60
 Rossely, Emilios, 50
 Sabadina, Nicholas, 57
 Voinich, Luka, 173
 Vranat, Peter, 57
Duke of Wellington Hotel, 148
Dundas, 222
Dunedin, 41, 79
Dunolly, 45, 99, 109
Đuratović, Nikola *see* Juratowitch, Nicholas

E
Eaglehawk, 47
East Charlton Tribute, The, 160
Eastern Market, Melbourne, 33
Echuca, 50, 87, 128
Edensor Park, 227, 267
Egypt, 74, 265
Elsie, 133
Elysian Flat, 47
'embassy' in Canberra, 229, *234*, 235, 237, C15
Emerald Hill, 32
emigrants and emigration, 8, 10–11, 13, 17, 205, 212 *see also* migrants and migration
Emma, 97
employment, **215** *see also* occupations *and* self-employment
Emu, 129
Enterprise Gold Mining Company, 175
Entra, Frank (Kentra, Franjo), 51, 101, 142, *142–143*, 144, 149
Epsom, 27, 46, 47, 49, 51, 101, 105, 142

Esmond, James, 91
Eureka Stockade, 45, 92, 159
Europa, 171
Every Week, 129
Excelsior, 130
Excelsior Broom Factory, 81, 81
Excelsior Vineyard, 50, **150**, 151–153, 159
Exford Hotel, 135

F

Fabrio, Louis (Fabrio, Luka), 87
Fairfield, 214
family reunion migrants, 212
farmers and farming, 64, 135, 151, **159**, 217
Farmers' Inn, 170
Federation of Yugoslav Immigrants in
        Australia, 205
Ferentza, Gregorio (Ferenca, Grgur),
        44, 45
Field, Frederick, 141
Filess, Antonio, 68
First World War see World War I
fishermen and fishing, 83, 111, 120–126, 133,
        155, 211, 217
    bravery, 133
    costs, 124
    discrimination, 126
    drownings, 134
    Geelong, 29
    Gippsland, 52
    grievances, 124–126
    Port Fairy, 123
    Portarlington, 30–31, 120
    self-employment, 124
    tuna, 217
Fitzroy, 33, 80, 147
Fiume (Rijeka), 2, 5, 47, 133 see also Rijeka
Flett, James, 7–8, 95
Florio, Girollamo, 16, 74
Florio, Jerome, 30
Florio, Matthew, 16, 74
Florio, Vincent, 29, 134
folkloric dancers, 219
folkloric groups, 14, 209, 217, C4, C6, C7,
        C12, C19, C21, C23
folkloric performances, 238
football (Australian), 59, 137, 189–190, 225
Footscray, 32, 147, 182–183, 213–215,
        226, 267
Forbes, 106
Foreign Affairs, Department of, 233
Fornarich, Antonio (Fornarić, Ante), 147
Fortin, Henry, 150
Four Corners, 233
Fox, Bishop, 80
France, 13, 74, 81
Francis Joseph Quartz claim, 101
Francovich, Anton, 126
Francovich, Dominico, 16, 47, 49, 167
Franich, Fred, 80, 192, 194, 195, 196
Franich, Ivan, 64, 80, 192

Franich, Mate, 64
Franich, Roger, 192
Frank, Francis, 55
Frankfurt, 200
Franktovich, Andrea (Franotović, Andrija),
        7, 49, 94–95, 128
Franziskovic, Vinko, 119–120
Fremantle, 115, 123, 155, 208–209, 214,
        221, 228
    boat-building, 217
    Catholic Church, 80
    Festival, 238
    fishermen, 128, 203, 217
    oyster fishing and saloons, 34, 133
    seamen, 132
    settlers, 58
frigates, 119, C2
Fringe Festival, C19
fruit growers, 159, 216
Fryer's Creek, 43
Furjanić, Michael, 230

G

Gabelich, Ray (Gabelić), 59, 187, 189, 225
Gableish, Nicholas (Gabelić, Nikola),
        58–59, 59
Gago, Gail, 192
Galatea, 62
Gallipoli, 9, 74, 197
gambling, 93, 150
Gamulin, Taddeo (Gamulin, Tadija),
        21, 50, 109
Gange, 84, 113, 116–117, 118–119
Gargurevich, Catherine, 192
Gargurevich, Fanny, 192
Gargurevich, Henry, 192
Gargurevich, John, 192
Gargurevich, Louise, 192
Gargurevich, Maria, 192
Gargurevich, Matteo (Grgurević, Mate),
        21, 33, 53, 108, 192
Gargurevich, Philomena, 192
Gasparo, John (Gašper, Ivan), 33
Gavranić, Tomislav, Dr, 230
Gazettick, Stanislaus, 101
Geelong, 29, 66, 120–121, 128, 140, 219,
        C12, C24
    Benussi, Matteo, 43
    Catholic Church, 72, 74
    clubs, 214
    community activities, 217
    community centres, 226
    concerts, 84
    Croatian language, 80, C17
    Croatian speakers, 214, C9
    drownings, 134
    employment, 216
    Grussich, Mark, 19
    Holy Family Church, C14
    hospital, 88, 172
    Lussich (Lukšić) families, 19–20

miners, 31
phylloxera, 154
population, 28–29, 211, 214
protests, 232
rescues, 133
schools, 214
settlers, 27–29, 49, 159, 171
soccer, 216
St Mary's, 63–64, 75, 170
    Croatian language, 80
ten pin bowls, 226
women, C20
Geelong Advertiser, The, 29–31, 172
Gehon, 113
Gelletich, John, Captain, 129
Gelletich, Nicholas (Jeletić, Nikola),
        129, 130
Gellussich, Francisco (Jelušić, Franjo), 109
Genitori Tarabochia, 114
Georgetown, 101
Gepps Cross, 227, 268
Gercovich, Vincent (Jerković, Vicko),
        45, 46
Germanisation, 23
Germano, Antonia (Germano, Ante),
        52, 66
Germans, ethnic, 12
Germany, 12–14, 81
Geronevitch, Antonio, 49, 62, 94, 141,
        145, 149
Gevirosick, Nicolo, 24
Gippsland, 27, 49, 51–54, 128, 160, 176,
        216, 219
Gippsland Croatian Association Limited,
        267
Gippsland Lakes, 121, 129
Gippsland Miners' Standard, The, 175, 176
Gippsland Times, The, 53
Giuliano-Dalmati, 2
Glamočak, Joe, 217
Glaneuse, 119
Glaninich, Lawrence, 78
Glasgow, 53
Glebe, 54
Glenlyon, 159
Glenorchy, 268
Glinbich, Francesco, 101
Gnječ, Stjepan, Rev, 219
Gobbie, John, 16
godparents, 61, 63–65
Goidanich, Arabella nee O'Sullivan, 74
Goidanich, Edward, Monsignor, 74
Goidanich, Gabriele (Gojdanić), 74
Gojak, 69
gold, 50, 97–98, 103
    Crooked River, 53
    nuggets, 43
        The Opossum, 96–97
        Welcome Stranger, 97
    production, 28, 94
Gold Coast, 211, 227, 268

gold rushes, 2, 24, 54, 97, 101, 104, 106–107, 111, 141, 150
  California, 11
  Mount Alexander, 40
  Otago, 11, 41, 60, 79
  Queensland, 57
  records, 16
  Victoria, 16–17
  Woods Point, 51
Golden Empire, 25
Golden Mile, 106
Golden, Frank, 49, 78, 101, 141, 145, 149
Golden, Mary, 78
goldfields, 21, 24, 42, 60, 88, **91**, 98, 105, 142, 150, 207
  alcohol, 141
  crimes, 93
  Daylesford, 43
  decline, 94
  discoveries, 94
    Bathurst, 98
    Sclavonia Reef, 94
  Gippsland, 52
  Home Rule, 60
  hotels, 135
  Kalgoorlie, 203
  population, 93, 105
  success, 107
  Victoria, 27–28
golf, 190, 217, 226
Good Content Quartz, 102
Good Luck Creek, 53
Good Neighbour Council, *228*
Good Samaritan Sisters, 74
Goody, Launcelot, Father (later Archbishop), 80
Goolwa, 126, 131
Gospa Sinjska, 221
Goulburn Valley, 27, 49–50
Goulburn Valley Wine and Distillery Company, 150
Grafton, 105–106, 121, 144
Graham, Robert, 185
Grandi, John, 64, 67–68, 99–100, 169
Grant, 7, 52, 110, 142
Graytown, 49, 95–96, 104
Grbić, Ivan, 113
Great Southern Advocate, The, 76, 79, 136, 139
Grenfell, 54, 106, 109
Grgich Hills Cellar, 203
grog shops, 141 *see also* sly grog
Grosvenor Hotel, 178
Grussich, John, 64
Grussich, Mark (Grušić, Marko, also Grubšić), 19
Gruž, 142
guest workers, 13
Guircovich, Andrea, 88
Guisto, 113–114
Gulf of Venice, 5

Gulgong, 66, 105–107, 173–175
  Catholic Church, 77
  O'Connell, Daniel, 79
  settlers, 54, 105, 172–174
Gulgong Evening Argus, The, 174
Gundagai, 15, 54
Guovich, Nicola, 24
Guratovich, Matteo, 57
Gwalia, 209
Gwelup, 227, 268

H

Hargraves, Edward, 91, 97–98
Harlovich, Antonio, 101
Harlovich, John, 55
Harp of Erin Reef, 67
Hasdovaz, Mathew (Hazdovac, Mato), 107, *107*
Haskitt, Stephano *see* Posic, Stefano
Hastings, 38, 120, 128
Hawke, Bob, *C21*
Hayes Point, 101
Health and Community Services Union, 192
Health Services Union, 192
Heathcote, 93–94, 102, 144, 175
  All Nations Hotel, 141, 145
Helgoland, 119, *C2*
Hepburn, 144
Herzgovich, Guro, 101
Hesman, Frank, 230
Hibernian Australasian Catholic Benefit Society, 78
Hill End, 54
Hindmarsh–Woodville, 215
Hobart, 7, 58, 132, 211, 268
  Blue Gum Festival, *C18*
  Catholic centres, 219
  club, 227
Hobsons Bay, 111
Holdsworthy Concentration Camp, 200–201
Holy Family, Geelong, 214, *C14*, *C24*
home ownership, 214
Home Rule goldfield, 60, 66, 173
Hong Kong, 3
Honorary Justices Association, *190*
horse racing, 137
Host, Daisy, *132*
Host, Galena Maud, *132*
Host, Peter, 130–131, *131*, 132
Hotel de Roma, 147
hoteliers, 135, 142, 146
  Adelaide, 147–148
  advertisement, *144*
  billiards, 150
  Melbourne, 146
  Woods Point, 142
  United States, 148
  Yackandandah, 144
Howard, John, *C21*
Hreglich, John (Hreljić, Ivan), 118

Hreljin, 7, 39
Hrvatska Zora (Croatian Dawn), *C4*
Hrvatski Dom (Croatian House), 268
Hrvatski Vjesnik (Croatian Herald), 223
Hughes, Billy, 180
humanitarian aid, 14, 236, 238, *C23*
Hungarian Gold Mining Company, 51
Hungary and Hungarians, 5, 10, 12, 23, 81
Huntly, 47, 49, 87
Hvar, 5, 130, 185
  emigrants and emigration, 12, 17–18
  Jelsa, 21, 50, 109
  Pitve, 154
  Stanich, Prospero, 185
  Starigrad, 45–46, 49, 81, 87, 141
  Vranjican, Vincent, 106
  Vrboska, 58

I

illiteracy *see* literacy and illiteracy
Illyria, 5
Immigration Museum, Melbourne, 224, *C17*
immigrants, political, 212
Inglewood, 27, 29, 43, 101, 105
inheritances, 90
Innisfail, 205, 209
intelligence inquiries, 5, 179
International Exhibitions
  Melbourne, 22, 158, 183
  Sydney, 158
internment, 187, **200**, 201–202, 207, *C3*
Invermay, 268
Irish Famine Relief Fund, 78
Irish National Foresters, 78
  Daniel O'Connell Branch (INF), 79
Irish politics, 78–80
Islamic centre, 222
isolation, 88, 226
Istra Social and Sports Club Sydney Inc, 226, 267
Istria, 4, 33, 156
  Brseč, 40, 103
  emigration, 11
  Italian language and rule, 2, 4
  Italianisation, 23
  parliament, 23
  Portarlington, 30
Italianisation, 23
Italians, 12, 53
  Dalmatia, 23
Italo-Croatians, 2
Italy (Molise), 2, 5, 10, 12, 265
Ivančić, Mate *see* Jvancich, Mathew
Ivancich, Frank (Ivančić, Franjo), Captain, 116, 118
Ivancich, Nilla, Mrs, 84, 118
Ivancovich, John, 97
Ivancovich, Matthew, 97–98
Ivanusic, George, 59, 69
Ivanussich, Antonio, 40
Ivanussich, Giovanni, 40, 66, 103

J

Jadran, 213, *C21*
Jadran Hajduk Croatian Club Ltd, 267
Jakovich, Alan, 225
Jakovich, Glen, 225
James and Amelia, 172
Jane, 128
Jane Moorehead, 129
Janjevo (Kosovo), 10
Janjina, 5, 148, 161, 163, 166
Jasprizza, Nicholas (Jasprica, Nikola), 5, 7, 78, 161, *163*
Jassich, Pietro, 19, 62, 103
Jeff Davis Reef, 110
Jeletić, Nikola *see* Gelletich, Nicholas
Jelsa, 21, 50, 109
Jelušić, Franjo *see* Gellussich, Francisco
Jerković, Vicko *see* Gercovich, Vincent
Jim Crow diggings, 41, 43
Joseph Vidulich & Co.'s Pioneer Saw Mill, 126, *127*
Joseph, James, 69
Juratowitch, Nicholas (Đuratović, Nikola), 56
Jurich, Giovanni, *115*
Jvancich, Mathew (Ivančić, Mate), 55, 56

K

Kaiser Gold and Copper Mining Company, 175
Kalgoorlie, 60, 70, 131, 207, 230
    accidents, 110, 203
    Catholic Church, 80
    discrimination, 201, 207
    occupations, 106
    riots, 207–208
    settlers, 86, 88
Kaloper, Stjepan *see* Coloper, Stephen
Karadole, Vice (Karadole), 182
Karamarko, Milan, 230
Karlovac, 11
Kastav, 57
Kaštela, 265
Katamatite, 50
Katnich, Joseph, 128
Kavacevih, Katerina nee Radich, 87
Kazia, Mathew, 123, 128, 180
Kazia, Stefano, 200
Keating, Father, 76
Keilor, 213–214
Kelly, Ned, 93
Kentra, Franjo *see* Entra, Frank
Kerang, 50
ketches, 59, 129, 181
Kew Asylum, 88, 123
King Tomislav Croatian Club Ltd, *228*, 267
Klanjateljice Presvetom Srcu Isusovom
        (Worshippers of the Sacred Heart
        of Jesus), C20
Klaric, Eva nee Host, 131, *132*
Klaric, Mate, 131, *132*
Klaric, Sam, *132*

Klaric, Vincent, *132*
Klokan (Kangaroo), 213, *214*
Koleda, 217, *C12*
Kolonija Dalmacija, 133
Komiža, 44
Korčula, 16, 30, 94, 133, 238, 205
Korumburra, 7, 33, 54, 76–79, 87, 135–140, 148, 169
    Catholic Church, 71, 76
    farming, 160
    population, 135
    schools, 192
    settlers, 54
    St Joseph's, 77
Korumburra Agricultural and Pastoral Society, 137
Korumburra Butter Factory, 137
Korumburra Hotel, 54, 76, *135–136*, 136–137, 148, *149*
Korumburra Progress Association, 137
Korumburra Times, The, 78
Korzelinski, Seweryn, 41, 98, 177
Kos, Jerolim *see* Roderick, Frederick, 54
Kosmos (Kuzma) from Rijeka, 24, **177**
Kosovich, 69
Kosovich, John, 203, 230
Kosovich's Westfield Wines, 203
Kosovo, 10
Kostanjica, 120
Kotor, 12–13, 46, 81, 112
    Kostanjica, 120
    Tripovich, Matthew, 31
    Tivat, 16
    Volich, John, 96
Kovacevic, Maria (Kovačević, Marija), 87
Kraljevica, 16
Kravarević, Mate *see* Cravarovich, Matteo
Krilich, Max, 225
Križari, 219
Krk, 5, 54, 58, 86, 124
Krnčević, Eddie, 224
Kukuljanovo, 32
Kut, 266
Kyneton, 29

L

Labin, 33
Ladies' Benevolent Societies
    Echuca, 87
    Korumburra, 87
    Maryborough, 87
LADO, 217, *C12*
Laisch, N., 62
Lakes Entrance, 52, 78, 120–121, 124, 129
Lakewood, 209
Lambing Flat, 54, 161
Langham Hotel, 146
Lasich, Ellen, 53
Lasich, Nicholas, 53
Lastovo, 2
Lastva, 13

Launceston, 58, 227
Laurenzo, 44
lawn bowls, 147, 225
Lazarawitch, 99
Lazarovich, Vincent, 100
Lazzarovich and Company, 102
Lazzarovich, Spiro, 103, 134
Lekovich, Ellen nee Pavletich, 64
Lekovich, John, 31, 64, 121, *122*
Lenek, *C19*
Leonard, Dominick, 147–148
Leppington, 205, 209
Lesina (Hvar), 5
letters, 5, 7, 70, 148, 176, 179, 264
    alphabet, 6
    Austrian Consul, 181
    Beovich, Matthew, Archbishop, 80
    Calwell Arthur, 80
    Chernich, Vincent, 56
    from Croatia, 89
    Hasdovaz, Mathew 107
    Marassovich, Mattio, 176, 264
    Matich, Mate, 182
    Otago Daily Times, 79
    prisoners of war, 202
    Sersic, John, 180
    unclaimed, 49
    Vuscovich, Natale, 261
Lewis Point Creek, 98
Lewis Ponds, 98, 106
Liberal Government, 231
licenses
    hotels, 136, 141
    miners, 92
life expectancy, 25–26
Light Car Club of Australia, 188
Lightning Ridge, 217
Lindenow, 54
Lindo, *C6*
Lismore, 7
Lister, John, 98
literacy and illiteracy, 6–7, 10, 21, 171
Little River, 100, 121
Little Sisters of the Poor, 76, 171
Little, Thomas, Archbishop, 219
Liverpool (NSW), 200–201, 214, 227, 267, *C3*
Liverpool (UK), 22, 111
Ljubirod, 114
Llewellyn, 58
Loch, Henry, 119
Loftus, Augustus, Lord, 185
loneliness, 70, 87–88
Long Tunnel Mine, 52
Lorenza, 24, 113
Los Angeles, 11, 70
Lošinj, 2, 46, 66, 183
    Albich, Peter, 53
    Corsano, Fortunato, 105
    emigrants, 18
    Mali Lošinj, 126, 156, 182
    Portarlington, 30

Radoslovich, Andrew, 61
  Veli Lošinj, 59, 74
Louis Company Quartz, 103
Louisiana, 10, 133
Lovran, 178
Lovranska Draga, 114
Lower Buckland, 51
Lower Saxony, 5
Lucas, Alfred, 96
Luchinovich, George, 102–103
Lucich, Joseph, 33
Lukene, Simeon (Lukin), 134
Luketic, Robert, 230
Lukin, Dean, 225
Lukšić *see* Lussich
Lusic, 34, 69
Lusic, Julia nee Hurley, 33
Lusic, Matthew, 9
Lusic, Victor, 9, 18, 33, 66, 69, 171, *197*
Lussich (Lukšić) families, 18–19, 21
Lussich and Company Line Reef, 102
Lussich and Company Quartz, 102
Lussich and Party, 62, 102
Lussich, Dominick, 19, 31, 63, 64, 65, 66, 69,
  75, 90, 121, 125
Lussich, Jerome, 20
Lussich, Johanna, 66
Lussich, John, 18–19, 24, 30, 62–66, 63, 69,
  75, 102, 133, 171
Lussich, Kate, 66
Lussich, Katina, 63
Lussich, Mary, 63
Lussich, Natale, 31, 49, 62–64, 66, 93,
  101–102
Lussich Slavich, John, 63
Lussick, Jerome, 18, 63, 128, 148
Luxembourg, 81

M

Macedonians, 3
McIntyre, 44–45, 47, 68, 99, 106, 108, 167
McIvor News, The, 5, 149
McIvor Times, The, 5, 141
Mackay, 126
McNish, James, 88
Macquarie University, 234
Macs Hotel, 147
Madre, 111
Magyarisation, 23
Maidstone, 222
Mail Rest Hotel, 142
Majorca, 46, 49, 82
Makaraska, 205
Maldon, 29
Mali Lošinj, 106, 113–114, 118, 126, 156, 182
Malinska, 5, 86, 124
Manchester Unity, 137
Mandacovich, Ana (Mandaković), 176
Mandaković, Maddalena, 176
Mandelick, James, 47, 60
Manjimup, 209

Mannix, Daniel, Archbishop, 74, 219
Mannum, 126
Manson, Hugh, 63
Manson, Veronica, 63
Maranta, James, 87
Marasović, Giuseppe (Josip), 176, 264
Marassovich, Mary nee Youl, 175
Marassovich, Mattio, 51–52, 70, 89, 141, **175**,
  176, 264
Marassovich's Commercial Hotel, 175
Marcovitch's (Mercovich's) Quartz claim,
  102, 104
Margitich (Margitić), 21, 32, 59, 64, 67
Margitich (Margitić) family, 21
Margitich Anton (Margitić, Ante),
  66–68, 179
Margitich, John (Margitić, Ivan), 59, 134
Margitich, Luka, 62, 67–68, 179
Margitich, Vincent, 64, 122
Marian, Ante, 155
Marian, Joseph (Marijan, Josip), 128, *154*,
  154–155
Maribyrnong, 214
Marich, Joseph (Marić, Josip), 41, 109
Marich, Peter, 109
Marienovich, Marko, 66
Marincovich, Matteo (Marinković, Mate),
  66, 147
Marinovich and Party, 102–103
Marinovich, Michele (Marinović), 62, 102
Marinovich, Norman, Dr, 230
Marinovich, Spallatrino and Company, 103
Marinovitch, George, 62, 103
Marion, Joseph, *154*
market gardeners, 159, 205, 217
Markovich, John (Marković, Ivan), 78,
  124, *125*
Marohnic, Gasper (Marohnić, Gašpar),
  82–83
Marsich, Joseph, 105
Martinolić, Nikola, 118
Martinolich, Giuseppe (Martinolić, Josip),
  113
Martinolich, Marco (Martinolić, Marko),
  113–114
Martinšćica, 111
Marunčić, Nedjelko, 230
Maryborough, Victoria, 27–29, 45–47, 49, 62,
  105, 159
  hospital, 89
  Ladies' Benevolent Society, 87
  wineries, 154
Maryborough, Qld, 58
Mason, F. C., MLA, 136
Matich, Dorothea nee Sersic, 181
Matich, Mate (Matić, Mate), 129, *181*,
  182, 201
Matich, Natale, 66
Matija Gubec Club, Mildura, 153, 205, *206*
Matulick, Elizabeth nee Huggins, 126
Matulick, Nicholas (Matulić, Nikola), 126

Mauritius, 43
Mavorvitch, 65
Mavorvitch, Denis, 103
Mavorvitch, Mary nee Phelan, 103
Mavorvitch, Peter (Mavrović or Maurović,
  Petar), 40, 66, 103, 159
Mavorvitch, Thomas, 40
Maximilian Gold Mining Company,
  45, 99–100, 167
Maximilian Quartz, 96
mayors, 230
Mechanics' Institute, 137–138
Medimurje, 153, 205
Medimurski Club, 205, 226, 267
Melbourne, 7, 29, 114, 140, 146, 205–206, 213,
  221, 223, 267, C15, C17, C22
  Catholic Church, 72, 76, 80
  clubs, 209
  concerts, 84
  consulates, 237
  Croatian speakers, 214, C9
  employment, 215–216
  Fish Market, 124
  fishermen, 120–121, 128
  hoteliers, 135, 146
  Immigration Museum, 224, *C17*
  impressions, 38–39
  International Exhibition, 22, 158, 183
  nursing homes, 219
  oyster saloons, 34
  population, 28, 32, 211
  seamen, 128
  settlers, 27–28, 32, 49, 53
  St Francis, 75–76
  St Patrick's, 219, 222
  University, 213
  wealth, 28, 32
  wine merchants, 148
Melbourne Croatia soccer team, 224, 238,
  267, C13
Melbourne Cup, 225
Melbourne Knights Soccer Club, 224–226,
  238, 267, C13
Mengola, Anton, 126
merchant ships, 111
  from UK, 97
Mercovich, Anthony, 34
Mercovich, Bartholomew (Mirković, Bartul),
  16, 29, 34, 74, 78, 104, *104*,
  145, 190
  descendants, 192, *193*
Mercovich, Bartholomew, Sergeant, *193*
Mercovich, Catherine Teresa, Sister, 74
Mercovich, Francis, *193*
Mercovich, John, *193*
Mercovich, Kate, 78
Mercy, 40
Mersey, 112
Mersuglia, George, 113
Metcalfe Shire News, 109
Methodists, 25

Metrowich, John, 96
Metta, 113
Miarlorick, Charles, 101
Middle Dargo, 62
Midland Catholic Church, 80
migration, 10, 16–17, 56, 106, 206, 219
   'campanilismo' theory, 21
   Asian, 3
   chain, 18, 106, 152, 206
      Broken Hill, 56
      Lussick clans, 21
      Molisan-Croatians, 10
      Mooroopna, 50
   gold rushes, 2, 91
Mihanovich, Cosulich y Zuanich shipping
      company, 132
Mihanovich, Nikola (Mihanović), 132
Mijch, Peter (Mijić), 66
Milach, Frank, 55
Milatovich, Antonio, 112
Milderwick, Nicolo, 24
Mildura, 152, 205–206, 214, 226, 267
   clubs, 209
   employment, 216
   population, 211
Mildura Croatian community, 153
Miles, 160
Militant Workers' Movement (Borbeni
      Radnički Pokret), 205
military service, 23
Milkovitch, Ane (Miljković, Ane),
      86, *153*, *C1*
Mill Park, 214
Millawich, Frank, 64
Millich, Bartholomew, 9
Millich, Cosmo, 9
Millicich, Luca, 158
Millowick, Nicholas, 134
Milna, 57, 167
Miloslavich, Giralomo, 144
Milovitch, Dominic (Milović, Dominik),
      89, 96, 101–103
Milovitch, Thomas, 50, 150, 152, *153*, 154
miner's rights, 92–93
miners, 97, 107
   alcohol, 141
   coal, 138
   communities, 104–105
   diets, 93
   licenses, 92
   opal, 217
Miners' Accident Society, 138
Miners' Association, 137, 148
Miners' Hotel, 142
mining, 5, 29, 45, 63, 67–68, 93, 103
   antimony, 49
   coal, 135
   companies, 45, 67, 91–92, 99, 105, 109,
      167, 175
      accidents, 110
      capital, 52

Kalgoorlie, 208
   names, 51, 52
   Walhalla, 52
   Woods Point, 51
Mintabie, 217
Mitrovich, Niccola, 62, 101, 142
Mladi Frankopani (Young Frankopans),
      218
Mladi Hrvati (Young Croatians), *C4*
Mlican, Vid (Petrasich, W.), 43
Mljet, 107
Modruša-Rijeka, 11
Mokošica, 21, 78
Moliagul, 45, 97
Molisan Croatian Cultural Association of
      Western Australia, 10
Molisan-Croatian language, 10
Molisan-Croatians, 10
Molise, 10
Monkivitch, John (Monković, Ivan), 31–32
Moonlight, 46, 154
Moonlight Flat, 46–47, 87
Mooroopna, 50, 66, 150–151, 182
   chain migration, 50
   District Winegrowers' Association,
      150, 152
   wineries, 154
   women, 86
Moravia *see* Czech
Morning Light, 24
Morning Star Hotel, 146
Morning Star quartz, 101
Morris, Joseph, 84
Morwell, 214, 216, 227
motor sport, 179
Mount Alexander *see also* Castlemaine
Mt Eliza, *C8*
Mount Gambier, 134, 217, 227, 268
Mount Grant, 53
Mount Korong, 47
Mount Livingstone, 101
Mount Lyell Chemical and Manure Works,
      181–182
Mount Moliagul, 99
Mount Morgan, 57, 105
Mt Pleasant, 103
Mountain Creek, 96, 101
Mountaineer, The, 96, 145
Muckleford, 43
Muddy Creek, 142
Mudgee, 54, 172
Murchison, 49, 106
Murchison Miner, The, 106
Murphy, Lionel, Senator, 231
Murphy's Flat, 142
Murphy's Gully, 142
Murray River, 50, 128
Muscardin, John, 99, 100, 106
Musich, 32, 68
Muslims, Bosnia, 2
Myrtleford, 67, 216

N

Nagambie, 59
Napredak club, 207
Narenta, 133
Nar-nar-goon, 59
national day, *229*
National Gallery of Victoria, 223
National Library of Australia, 217
National Multicultural Festival, *C19*
National Soccer League, 224–225, *C13*
nationalities, 1–3
naturalisation, 5, 8, 169, 205–206
Navy, 111, 198
Nellie, 124
Nelson Bay, 217
Nepean Times, The, 185
Neray, 63
Netherlands, 81
Neven, 24, 92
New Bendigo, 109
New Croatia (*Nova Hrvatska*), 223
New Dalmatia Reef, 102
New Morning Star, 175
New South Wales, 14, 16, 18, 27, 78, 105–106,
      144, 206, 231
   arrivals, 106
   clubs, 227
   Croatian language, 222
   farming, 159
   fishermen, 217
   gold rushes, 16, 24, 49, 54, 91–92
   goldfields, 94
   halls and sporting venues, 267
   Murray River, 50
   opal mining, 217
   parishes, 219
   population, 28, 92, 211, 213
   seamen, 131
   settlers, 54
   Seventh Day Adventists, 222
   wineries, 154
New Zealand, 1, 5, 10–12, 14, 24, 26–27,
      70–71, 80–82, 156, 203
   arrivals, 106
   gold rush, 49
   goldfields, 94
Newcastle, 113–114, 132, 219, 268
   club, 227
   employment, 217
   population, 211
Newcastle Morning Herald, 194
News, The, 74
newspaper advertisements, 166, *170*, 175
   Franich, Fred, 194
   Marassovich's Commercial Hotel,
      175, *176*
   Orlovich, 172
   Poschich, 172
   Stanich, Prospero, 185
newspapers, Croatian, 5, 10, 12, 70–71, 223
   Napredak, 207

Nicholovich or Nicholas, Mr, 110
Nicolich, Francis, 51, 52, 103
Nicolich, Ivan, 103
Nicolich, Sarah nee Ryan, 52
No. 1 East Champion Quartz Mining
    Company, 63
No. 1 North Slavonia Reef, 101
No. 1 South, 101
No. 1 South Bristol Reef, 109
Nobilo Wines, 203
nomenclature, 2, 6
Normanton, 144
North Botany, 55
North Carlton, 33, 168
North Costerfield Hotel, 141, 149
North Fitzroy, 34, 76
North Fremantle, 219, 227, 268
North Geelong Soccer Club, 214, 226, 267
North Melbourne, 32–34, 81
North Queensland *see* Queensland, North
North Star Hotel, 168
Northcote Convent, 74, 76
Norway, 81
Nova Hrvatska (New Croatia), 223
Novara, 119, C2
nuggets, 43, 91, 96, 97
nuns, 72, 74, 76, 80, 87, 171, 219
nursing homes, 219, C21
Nyngan, 7

O

Oates, Richard, 97
occupations, 9–11, 91, 110–111, 167, 171–172,
    182, 192, 212, 215–217, 229
    see also employment
  businesses, 33
  gold fields, 91
  gold rush, 16
  in Croatia, 22–23
  Melbourne, 32, 34
  settlements, 27
  Sydney, 55
  women, 215–216
O'Connell, Daniel, 79
O'Connor, 227
Ogulin, 84
Olib, 55
Oliver Lang, 62
Olympics, 223, 225
Omeo, 53, 88, 96, 101
Omiš, 126
Omišalj, 58
Opatija, 33, 88
Ophir, 91, 98, 106
O'possum Point, 96
O'Reilly, Maurice, Monsignor, 74
Orange, 106
Orbital Engine Corporation, 230
orchards, 163, 166, 216
Order of St Andrews, 137
Orebić, 22

origins, 7, 18–19, 21, 98 *see also* birthplaces
Orlovich, Catherine nee Gates, 172
Orlovich, Mattio (Orlović, Mate),
    79, 172–175
Osborne Park, 203, 209
Osijek, 2
Otago, 11, 41, 60, 150
Otago Association, 79
Otago Daily Times, The, 79
Outtrim, 140
Ovens and Murray Advertiser, The, 149
oyster fishing and oyster saloons, 34, 54, 84,
    120–121
  Port Fairy, 170
  South Brisbane, 55
  Sydney, 54–55
  USA, 10, 126
  Western Australia, 133

P

Paddock Hotel, 172–174
Palmer River, 57, 66, 88, 105–106
Panama, 7
Pandrige, Stephen, 67, 101
Pandwick, Pietro, 24
Papawitch, Francis, 109
Parade Hotel, 146, 179
parishes, 81, 219
Park View Hotel, 146
Park, Nicholas, 121
Park, Peter, 121, 144
Parkville, 146
parliamentarians, 138, 148, 192, 229–230
parliamentarians for Croatia and Slovenia,
    236
parliaments, 23
Parramatta, 15, 144
Partisans, 12
Partizanka, 207
Pascoe, Susan, 84
Pasquan, Joseph (Paškvan, Josip), 146, *146*,
    147, 179
Pasquan, Martin (Paškvan, Martin), 25, 34,
    82, 146–147, 178–179
Pasquan, Maximillian (Paškvan), 82
Pasquan's Hotel, 34, 147
Passalick, 65
Passalick, Antonio, 40
patents, 68, 108
Patrick, 124, 171
Paulussy and Company, 67
Paulussy, Catherine nee O'Brien, 67
Paulussy, Ellen, 78
Paulussy, Nicholas, 51, 67
Paulussy, Stephen, 24, 51, 64, 67, 78, 108
Paulussy's Mill, 68, *108*
Pavich, Antonio (Pavić, Ante), 40, 41, *41*, 66,
    103, 197–199, *198–199*
Pavich, Mary nee Hayes, 40
Pavich, Nicholas, *199*
Pavilach, Martin, 64, 65, 66, 103

Pavletich, 32, 68
Pavletich, Annie, 63
Pavletich, Augustina, 64
Pavletich, Ellen nee McMahon, 63–64
Pavletich, Gregory (Pavletić, Grgur), 30–31,
    63–64, 121–122, 124–125, 134, 171
Pavletich, Martin, 34
Pavletich, Thomas (Pavletić, Tomislav),
    33, 41, 79, C1
Pavlinović, Milan, 80
Paynesville, 52, 120–121, 128–129
Pečarević, Gregorio, Father, 264
Pelješac Peninsula, 9
  Anticevich Nicholas, 55, 69
  Calafatovich, Joseph, 69
  chain migration, 18
  Doli, 132
  Duba, 21
  Janjina, 5, 148, 161, 166
  Portarlington, 30
  Potomje, 135
  seafaring, 22
  Trpanj, 23, 45, 102, 104
  Žuljana, 22
Pell, George, Cardinal, 219
Perich, Matteo, 53, 93
Perorish, Guivani, 24
Perorish, Nicolo, 24
Perovich, John, 67
Perseverance Lead, 173–174
Persian, 112
Perth, 33, 58, 148, 203, 214–215, 217, 268
  club, 227
  consulates, 237
  employment, 217
  nursing homes, 219
  population, 211
Peru, 10–12, 70, 81, 99
Petcovich, Theodore, 100
Petersham, 54
Petrasich, Andrew, 43, 44
Petrasich, Antonio (Petrašić, Ante), 43–44
Petrasich, W. (Mlican, Vid), 43
Petrich, Francis, 103
Petrich, Marino, 55, 82, 84
Petrosich, A., 43
Petrovitch, Antonio, 97
phylloxera, 151–152, 154, 156–158
Piller, Charles *see* Radoslovich, Charles
Pioneer Hill, 101
Pittsburgh, 70
Pitve, 154
Pivach, 69
Plancich, 68
Plancich, P., 84
Planter, 170
Pleasant Creek, 47
Pleasant Creek News, The, 47
Plomin, 30, 122
Ploncich, Joseph, 142
Podravac, Vanda, 230

Point Cloates, 114
Point Cook, 202
Pokorny, Franz, 158
Pola, 133
political immigrants, 212
Pollich, James, 40, 101
Polluce, 119
Polorineo, James, 100
population, 10–11, 17, 23, 29, C9
  ageing, 219, 238
  Ballarat, 45
  citizenship, 212
  distribution, 211
  goldfields, 93, 105
  Kotor, 13
  map, C9
  Melbourne, 32
  New South Wales, 28, 211, 213
  South Australia, 92
  statistics, 2–3, 13–14
  Victoria, 17, 28–29, 107, 211, 213–214
  Western Australia, 106
  women, 93
Port Adelaide, 57, 129–131, 147
Port Albert, 52, 59, 120, 124, 128
Port Augusta, 57, 120, 129–130
Port Fairy, 29, 31, 34, 61, 64, 112,
    123–124, 170
  billiards, 150
  fishermen, 120–121, *123*, 126
  newspaper advertisements, 166
  war memorial, 198
Port Fairy Gazette, The, 123
Port Lincoln, 57, 120–121, 128–129, 211, 217,
    227, 268
Port Lonsdale, 116
Port Melbourne, 25, 33, 76, 113, 119
Port Pirie, 57, 131
Port Wakefield, 113, 128
Portarlington, 29–31, 61–63, 66, 140
  billiards, 171
  Catholic Church, 72, 74–75
  discrimination, 201
  drownings, 134
  fishermen, 30–31, 120–122, 124, 126
  Pavletich, Gregory, 63–64
  population, 29–30
  regatta, 124
  rescues, 133
  settlers, 27, 29, 49, 52–53, 59, 63–64, 69,
    76, 102, 123
  St Patrick's, 64
  storms, 133–134
  Vuscovich, Natale, 171
Portarlington Fishermen's Protection Society,
    124–125
Portenia, 112
Poschich, Fortunato (Poščić, Srećko),
    29, 88–89, **171**, 172
Poschich, Raymond, 171
Poschich, Sarah, 171

Poščić, Karlo, 24, 113
Posic, Stefano (Posich, Possech, Powseitch),
    aka Stephano Haskitt or
    John Stanton, 15
Postich, Alice nee Atkinson, 159, *160*
Postich, Francis, 159
Postich, Joseph (Postić, Josip), 16, 74, 159, *160*
Postich, Thomas, 159–160
Potomje, 135
poverty, 87
Prčanj, 13
Premuda, 7, 55
Presbyterians, 25, 79
Price, Charles, 2, 8, 17, 25
priests, 53, 65, 72, 74, 80, 192, 207, 214, 219,
    220, 221
Prime Minister, Department of the, 233
Prince Maximilian Hotel, 167
Prince of Wales Hotel, 47
prisoners of war, 202
professionals, 217
Prolich, Gregory, 101
publicans *see* hoteliers
Pukšec, Ema *see* de Murska, Ilma
Pula, 119, 133
Pulisic, Samuel (Pulišić), 33
Punchbowl, 227, 267
Pyrmont Bridge Hotel, 147

Q

Queen of the East, 24
Queen of the North, 147
Queen Victoria, 185
Queenscliff, 116, 118–119
Queensland, 16, 94, 105–106, 132, 206,
    211, 268
  Clermont, 173
  clubs, 209, 227
  Georgetown, 101
  Miles, 160
  Normanton, 144
  North, 205, 211, 217
    clubs, 209
  population, 211
  settlers, 57–58, 88
  tamburica orchestras, 203
  Townsville, 126

R

Rabasa, Mark (Rabaza), 166
Račišče, 30
Radic, Francesca (Radić), 86–87
Radic, Leonard (Radić), 187
Radich, Eliza nee Duffy, 34
Radich, John, 34, *37*
Radich, Peter, 34
radio programs, 223
Radisich, Jaye, 230
Radnik, 207
Radonich, Albert, *162*
Radonich, Emily nee Vickers, 160, *161*

Radonich, Natale (Radonić, Božo),
    113, 160, *161*
Radoslovich, Andrew (Radoslović, Andrija),
    31, *61*, 64, 113, *123*, 125–126, 171
Radoslovich, Charles (Piller), *61*, 198
Radoslovich, Mary Ann, *61*, 64
Radovich, Charles, 96, 145
Radovick, Antonio (Radović, Antun), 7, 33,
    54, 60, 64, 66, 76, *77*–78, 87, **135**,
    136–139, *139–140*, 148–150, 169
  farming, 160
  tombstone, 38
  tribute, 149
Radovick, Elizabeth nee Gill, 135
Radovick, Steffano, 54, 135, 137
Ragusa (Dubrovnik), 5, 55, 133
Ragusin, G., 119
Raicovich, Nicolla, 55, 60
Raiders Soccer Club Inc, 268
Railway Hotel, 135, 147
Ravenswood, 57
Ravlich, Ljiljanna, 229
Redcastle, 5, 7, 27, 31, 49, 94–96, 101–105
  All Nations Hotel, 94, 145, 149
  billiards, 150
  clubs, 190
  hotels, 141
  Slavonian mine, 141
  Slavonian Reef, 62
Redcastle Reef, 95
refugees, 12, 72, 212–213, 217, 219
  Giuliano-Dalmati, 2
religious denominations, 25
Rerecich, Antone, 59, 128
Rerecich, Giovanni, 113
rescues, 133
Retreat Hotel, 146
Richards, Chas, 125
Richmond, 33, 76, 135
Ridleyton, 227, 268
Rijeka, 2, 5, 23–24, 29, 54, 87, 130, 133, 147,
    171, 177, 180
  Bercich, Vincenzo, 47
  Chernich, Vincent 56
  Descovich, Ignazio, 148
  emigrants and emigration, 11, 17–18
  Fiume, 2, 47
  Gelletich, Nicholas, 129
  Kastav, 57
  Melbourne International Exhibition, 159
  Pasquan, Joseph, 146
  Sersic, John, 180
  ship building, 113
Ringwood, 38
riots, 51
  Kalgoorlie, 207–208
Rismondo, George (Rismondo, Jure),
    16, 33
Riverina, 205, 216
Riverland, 227
Rocchi, Luke, 85–86

Rocchi, Perena (Roki) nee Rastovich
        (Rastović), 85–86
Rocke, Andrew (Roki, Andrija), 128
Rocklea, 227, 268
Roderick, Frederick (Kos, Jerolim), 54, *54*
Roman Catholic church *see* Catholic Church
Romania, 10, 81
Romanik, Vinko, 230
Rončević, Ivan, 153
Rose of Sharon, 129
Rosebud, 38
Rosette, 115
Rossely, Agnes nee Ferguson, 50
Rossely, Emilios, 22, *50*, 152
Rossi, Thomas, 43, 96, 105, 159
Rossich, Frederick, 7, 54–55
Rottnest Island Internment Camp, 200
Rouse, Richard, 173
Rouse's Paddock Gold Mining Company, 175
Rovinj, 16, 33, 43
Royal Australian Air Force, 179
Royal Children's Hospital Appeal, 218
Royal Commission on the Employing of
        Enemy Aliens in Mines, 207
Royal George Hotel, 146
Royal Princess Theatre, 47
Royal Victorian Association of Honorary
        Justices, 168, 190
rugby league, 225
Rushworth, 49
Rutherglen Viticultural College, 156, *157*, 158

S

Sabadina, Nicholas (Šabadin, Nikola), 57–58
Sabadine, George (Šabadin), 60, 66, 173
Sabadine, Joseph, 78, 173
Saida, 119
Sailor Bills Creek, 52, 103
sailors *see* seamen *and* deserters
St Albans, 213, 214, 222, 267
St Albans Saints Soccer Club, 226
St Alipius', Ballarat, 80
St Arnaud, 45, 99
St Brendan's, 86
St Brigid's, North Fitzroy, 34, 76
St Colman's, Fitzroy, 80
St Finbar's, 123
St Francis
        Melbourne, 34, 64, 75–76, 180
        Sydney, 76
St Francis Xavier, Adelaide, 72
St Ignatius, Richmond, 76, 135
St John's, Parramatta, 15
St Johns Park, 219, 267
        club, 227
St Joseph's
        Korumburra, 76, 77
        Port Melbourne, 33, 76
        Townsville, 78
St Kilda cemetery, 66
St Mark's, Zagreb, 218

St Mary's
        Castlemaine, 40, 65, 76, 103
        Geelong, 29, 63, 64, 74–75, 80, 170
        Sydney, 76, 80, 82
        West Melbourne, 82
        Youanmite, 50
        Young, 78
St Marys, 227, 267
St Nicholas, 78
St Patrick's
        Ballarat, 45
        Melbourne, 63–64, 75–76, 78, 80, 219, *222*
        Portarlington, 64, 75
        St Arnaud, 45
        Sydney, 55, 76, 79
St Patrick's Day, 78
St Peter's and Paul's, South Melbourne, 64, 76
St Thomas', Drysdale, 64, 75, 122
Salacan, George, 202, *202*
Sale, 59, 129
Salonika, 202
San Francisco, 11, 65, 70–71, 82–84, 126
San Juan (Sutivan) Quartz, 102
San Juan (Sutivan) Reef, 102
Sandhurst *see* Bendigo
Sandon, 40, 66, 76, 159
Sandringham, 38, 120–121, 123, 180
Santic, Tony (Šantić), 217, 225
Sarich, Ralph, 230, 237
Sarin, Sam, 217
schools, 209, 214
        Catholic Church, 71
        Croatian language, 14, 219, 222, 234, C17
        Holy Family, C24
        summer, 222
schooners, 88, 116, 119, 128–129, 171–172
Sclavonia, 5, 49, 98, 110
Sclavonia Reef, 7, 95
Sclavonian reef, 5, 94–95
Sclavonians, 53
Sclavonians (Slavonians), 4
Scoglier, Jane nee Tyrell, 123
Scoglier, Luke, 113, 123, 180
Scopenage, Antonio, 88
Scott, James, 133
seamen, 56, 112, 120, **128**, 131–133, C2
Sebastopol, 43
Sebenico, 132
Second World War *see* World War II
Selca, 33
Select Committee on Civil Rights of Migrant
        Australians, 231
self-employment, 33, 124
Sellovich, Elizabeth nee Dingle, 46
Sellovich, Luke, 45, 46
Sepich, Matthew, 55, 66
Serbia and Montenegro, 13
Serbs, ethnic, 2
Sersic, John (Seršić, Ivan), **180**, *180*, 181
Sersic, Lily nee Mahoney, 180
settlements, 27, 54, 93, 105, 206

Seventh Day Adventists, 222
shafts, 91–92, 102
        Dalmatia Gold Mining Company, 99, 100
        Maximilian Gold Mining Company, 100
        No. 1 South Bristol Reef, 109
Shamrock Hotel, 47
shareholders, 51, 67, 91, 99–100, 102–103,
        132, 142, 167
Shepparton, 86, 150, 152
Shepparton News, The, 86
shipowners, 132
ships, 62, 67, 111–112, 114, 119, 131, 147,
        159, 171–172, 177, 200, 261–262,
        264, C2
        from Mauritius, 63, 142
        from Trieste, 44
        from UK, 24, 31, 40, 53, 167, 170, 175
shipwrecks, 8, 84, 113–116, *117*, 129, 133
shipwrights, 167
shrines, 221
Šibenik, 132, 181
Siglich, Nicholas, 101, 105
Silovich, Paul, 173
Silver Shillings, 47
silver-lead mines, 56
Simunovich, Marko, 64
Singleton, 56
Šipan, 115
Sitanich, Nicholas (Cvitanić), 66
Skalica, Tomo, 24, 92
Skradin, 182
Slavonia, 4–5, 11, 43, 98–99, 155
Slavonian Benevolent Society, 70
Slavonian Company, 94
Slavonian Reef, Redcastle, 62
Slavonian vineyard, *155*
Slavonic Charitable Society in New Orleans,
        70
Slavonic-Illyric Mutual and Benevolent
        Society, 70, 83
Slavonski Brod, 92
Slocovich, Bogden, 62, 103
Slovakia, 10
Slovenia, 2–13, 81, 219
sly grog, 135, 141, 144–145 *see also*
        grog shops
Smoje, Neven, 8
Smythesdale, 45
Snowy Mountains River Hydro-Electric
        Scheme, 216–217
soccer, 14, 209, 214, *216*, 217, **224**, 225, 227,
        C13, C24
socialism and socialists, 206–207
societies, 61, 65, 70, 217
        benevolent, 87
        Croatian, 10
        historical, 5
        Korumburra, 137
        mutual benefit, 70
        newspapers, 71
        San Francisco, 83

Sofala, 106
  settlements, 105
  settlers, 54
Šolta, 172
South Africa, 1, 7, 10–11, 24, 59, 81
South America, 1, 10, 12, 14, 24, 81
South Australia, 18, 92, 134, 206
  Bathols, George, 182
  boatbuilders, 126
  clubs, 227
  Croatians in, 16
  fruit growers, 216
  halls and sporting venues, 268
  Margitich family, 21
  opal mining, 217
  oyster fishing, 120
  population, 92, 211
  seamen, 129–131
  settlers, 56–57
  wine merchants, 148
  wineries, 154
  Zarich, Vincent 46
South Brisbane, 55
South Johnstone, 205, 209
South Melbourne, **32**, 33, 68–69, 79, 128,
      167, 171
  football club, 190
  St Peter's and Paul's, 64, 76
Spalato, 132
Spallatrino Company, 102–103
Spallatrino, Louis, 102–103, 145
Sparozvich, Matilda nee Bayford, 58
Sparozvich, Nicolas (Sparožvić, Nikola), 58
Sparrow, 134
Spearwood, 80, 86, 123, 203, 209, 230, 268
  club, 227
  street names, 38
Spearwood Dalmatinac Club Inc, 268
Spencer's Brook, 148
Splendido, 24, 45, 112–113, C2
Split, 30, 80, 103, 123, 132, 205, 229, 238, 265
Splivalo, Anthony, 200
Splivalo, August, 126
sport, 137, 149, 187, 190, **224**, 225
sporting clubs, 14
Sportsman's Arms Hotel, 174
Spremnost (Readiness), 223
Spring Creek, 95
Springvale, 214–215, 219, 226–267
Srijem, 13
Stagno, 133
Stamboul, 167
Stangher, G. (Stanger, Josip), 113
Stanich, Ante, 185
Stanić Bardella, Simeone, Father, 265
Stanich, Edith Bell nee Newton, 185
Stanich, Prospero, **185**, *186*, *C1*
Stankovići, 22
Stanley, 142
Stanthorpe, 60
Stanton, John *see* Posic, Stefano

Stanton, Mary, 15
Star and Garter Hotel, *42*, *43*
Starčević, Ante, Dr, 227
Starcevich, Leslie, Pte, 199
Starcevich, Natale, 16, 68, 148
Starigrad, 45–46, 49, 81, 87, 141
Station Hotel, 147
statistics, 1–3, 8, 13–14
Stawell, 28, 47, 48, 144
Steam Hammer Hotel, 147
steamers, 58, 129
steamships, 25, 119 *see also* ships
    from UK, 25
Stefano, 8, 114–115
Steiglitz, 29, 45, 104, 171
Stella, George, 202
Stenning, Mary, 8
Stepinac, Alojzije, Cardinal, 219, 222
Stiglich, Jacob, 33, 54, 64, 71, 76, 79, 140
Stipicich, Nicholas, 62
Stirling, 214
Stirling, Mr, 136
Stjepan Radić club, 227
Ston, 133
Stony Creek, 50
storekeepers, **144**, 159
storms, 133–134
Stott Despoja, Natasha, Senator, 229, 237
Stratford, 142
street names, 38, 54, 139
strikes, 203, 206
  discrimination, 207
Stuart Mill, 45
student conferences, C8
Suburban Hotel, 87
sugar cane, 211, 217
Sumich, Peter, 225
Summer Hill, 219
Summerhill Creek, 98
Sunshine, 213–214, 219, 224, 226, 230,
      267, C4
Supetar, 34, 170, 261, 265
surf lifesaving, 225
surnames, 2, 9, 38, 53, 176
  Anglicisation, 6
  changes, 15–16
  Pelješac Peninsula, 9
  spellings, 6
Susak, 30, 120, 124
Šutalo, Ilija, 8
Sutivan, 18, 21, 62, 101–102, 147, 154
Swan, 214
Swan Hill, 50, 74
Swan Valley, 203, 208–209, 211, 217, 268
  club, 227
Sweden, 13, 81
Swift Creek, 101, 142
Switzerland, 13, 81
Sydney, 7, 34, 78, 114, 135, 147–148, 210–211,
      214, 217–219, 237, 267–268, C6,
      C7, C8, C12, C21

Catholic Church, 76, 79–80
clubs, 209, 227, 228
deserters, 113
fishermen, 120–121
George Street, 120
halls and sporting venues, 267
International Exhibition, 158
King Tomislav Croatian Club, 228
Olympics, 223
political demonstrations, 235
population, 211
seamen, 132
settlers, 54–56, 69, 109
Summer School of Language and Culture,
    C11
Sydney Croatia soccer team, 224, 267, C24
Sydney Olympics, C6
Sydney United, 224–225, 267

T

Tabilk vineyard, 154
Tadich, Nicholas, 16, 67
Tadich, Samuel, 67
Talbotville, 52, 53
Talijancich Wines, 203
tamburica orchestras, 14, 187, 203, *204*, 209,
      209, 219
Tarabochia, Dominic (Tarabokija, Dominik),
      64, 124, *125*
Tarabochia, Eredi, 118
Tarabochia, Mrs, 84
Taradale, 41, 109
Tardy, John *see* Terdich, John
Tardy's [Terdich] Railway Dining Rooms, 34
Tarraville, 52, 120, 123
Tasmania, 16, 58, 132
  clubs, 227
  halls and sporting venues, 268
Taylors Lakes, 213
Temora, 54, 106
ten pin bowls, 226
Terdich Bros, 179, 192
Terdich, Albert, 179, 188
Terdich, Alexander, 179
Terdich, Arthur, 179, 187, *188*
Terdich, Bruce, 179
Terdich, Charlotte, nee Pascoe, 178
Terdich, John (Terdić, Ivan), 34, 67,
      178, 179
Terdich, Maud Frances, 179
Terminus Hotel, 146
Terrey Hills, 227, 267
The Luksic, 128
The Son of Giuseppe, 177
Thingers Reef, 101
Three Bells, 53
Tito, 12, 207
Tivat, 13, 16, 31
Tkalcevic, Mate, 8
Tokić, Joseph, 233
Tom, James, 98

Tom, William, 98
Tomašević Schiopetter, Antonio, 265
Tomasevich, Luka, 169
tombstones, 38, 51–52, 55, 66–67
Tomić, Giuseppe, Father, 265
Torchie, Nicholas, 63, 171
Townsville, 58, 78, 126, 132
Tramontara Moro, Giorgio, 265
Traralgon, 227, 267
Triade Tarabochia, 84, 113–114
Trieste, 5, 23, 44, 112–113, 119
Tripovich Street, 38
Tripovich, John (Tripović), 32, 187, *191*, **192**
Tripovich, Matthew (Tripović, Mate), 16, 31–32
Trnovica, 150
Trobog, Baldosa, 68
Trogir, 88
Trpanj, 16, 23, 45, 102, 104
Tumbarumba, 26
Tungamah, 50
Turner, G., Mr, 138
Tussup, Spirodine (Tušup, Špiro), 49, *49*
Tverdeich, Andrew (Tvrdeić), 55
Tyntynder, 50

U

union movements, 206
United Ancient Order of Druids, 137
United Nations, 237
United States of America, 1, 5, 10–12, 14, 24, 26, 65, 70, 81, 230
   fishermen, 126
   hoteliers, 148
   newspapers, 71
   zadruga, 70
Universal Hotel, 41
Upper Buckland, 51
Uruguay, 12
Ustasha (Ustaša) government, 12

V

Vačani, 181
Vale, R., Hon, 138
Vascovitch *see* Vuscovich
Vecerina, Francesco (Večerina, Franjo), 109
Vekarić, Nenad, 9
Veli Lošinj, 59, 74
Venezuela, 81
Victor's Quartz, 175
Victoria, 14, 16–18, 29, 31–33, 50, 67, 97, 120–121, 128, 134, 187, 206, 219, 230–231, C5, C8, *C17*
   clubs, 209
   coal, 138
   community centres, 226
   Croatian communities, 214
   Croatian language, 222–223
   districts, 27–28

employment, 213, 217
   farming, 159
   gold rushes, 16–17, 24, 28, 54, 91–92
   goldfields, 21, 27
   halls and sporting venues, 267
   map, 28
   north-eastern, **51**
   population, 17, 92, 107, 211, 213, 214
   settlers, 27, 58
   storekeepers, 144
   wealth, 32
   wineries, 154
Victoria Cross, 199
Victoria Junction Gold Mining Company, 41, 109
Victoria Market, 33
Victoria Quartz mine, 47
Victorian Football League (VFL), 189
Viculin, Antonio (Vizulin, Antonio), 63
Vidas, Pavle, 6–7, 38–39
Viduka, Mark, 224, 237
Vidulić, Jure *see* Bathols, George
Vidulich, Joseph (Vidulić, Josip), 78, 126–127
Vidulich, Katherine nee O'Rourke, 126
Vienna, 23
Vincent, John (Vuković, Vicko), 115
vineyards, 15, 150, 155
   phylloxera, 151–152
Virkez, Vico, 233
Vis, 16–17, 84–86, 89, 128, 131, 158, 175–176, 264–266
   Burich, John, 148
   Passalick, Antonio, 40, 44
   Komiža, 44
Visin, Ivan, 24, 112–113
Vitaljina, 160
Vizulin, Antonio, 63
Vlahov, Andrew, 225
Vodanovich, Gerald, 84
Vodanovich, Lena (Vodanović), 84
Voinich, Luka, *173*
Vojaković, Robert, 230
Vojvodina, 13, 81, 212
Volich, John, 43, 96
Voloska, 16, 55, 113, 159
Vranat, Peter, 57
Vranjican, Vicko *see* Abbott, Vincent
Vranzigan, Peter, 154
Vrboska, 58
Vrgorac, 205
Vukasovich, John, 24
Vuković, Ante *see* Wolfe, Antonio
Vuković, Vicko *see* Vincent, John, 115
Vuscovich, 64
Vuscovich, Natale (Vušković, Božo), 6, 19, 31, 63, 69, 76, 120, 124, 126, 133, 166, **170**, 171, 261, 264
Vuscovich, Patrick, 170
Vuscovih *see* Vuscovich
Vuscovitch *see* Vuscovich

W

WA Croatian Community Centre, 268
Waanyarra, 45
Walhalla, 28, 52, 59, 77, 110
Walpa, 54
Walsh, Clara, 78
Wandiligong, 145, 154
Wangaratta, 146–147
Wanneroo, 214
war memorials, 16, 197
Warragul, 147
Warriewood, 55, 205, 209, 225
Warrigal, 129, 181
Waterloo Hotel, 144
Watt. W., Hon, 190
Webster Street Freehold Gold Mining Company, 171
Wedderburn, 27–28, 44, 62, 68, 88–89, 97, 154
   nuggets, 43, 96
   settlers, 43–44, 69, 91, 96, 105
Wedderburn Express, The, 96
Weekly Times, The, 150
weight lifting, 225
Wellington, 129
Wellington, NSW, 174
Wellington, NZ, 60
West Australian, The, 208
West Charlton, 159
West Melbourne, 82
West Wyalong, 106
Western Australia, 8, 16, 33, 59, 78, 84, 106, 115, 128, 132–133, 229–230, 238
   Catholic Church, 80
   chain migration, 106, 206
   clubs, 209, 227
   Croatian language, 223
   Croatian Slavonic Society, 70–71
   discrimination, 201, 207–208
   football, 189
   goldfields, 94
   halls and sporting venues, 268
   hoteliers, 148
   Ivanussich, Antonio, 40
   Molisan-Croatians, 10
   population, 12, 106, 211
   settlers, 58–59, 85–86, 88
   Spearwood, 38, 123
   strikes, 206
   tamburica orchestra, 209
   wineries, 154–155, *155*, 203
Whipsnake Gully, 101
Whipstick, 47, 101
'White Australia', 3
White Horse Gold Mining Company, 175
Whitlam Labor Government, 231
Whroo, 49
Whyalla, 217, 227, 268

Wilkinson, John, Sir, 23
Williams, H., Hon, 138
Williamstown, 120–121, 124
Williamstown Chronicle, The, 147
wills, 5, 90
Wiluna, 209
Wimmera, 129
wine, 156, 203, 211, 217, 230
    production, 154
wine merchants, 147–148
wineries, 135, **150**, 203
Wiskiwitch *see* Vuscovich
wives, 25, 62, 78, 90, 201, 206
    see also women
Wodonga, 214, 227, 267
Wolfe, Antonio (Vuković, Ante), 26
Wollongong, 211, 217, 219, 227,
    268, C7
women, **81**, 84–86, 93, 152–153,
    187, 205, 215–218, C20
    see also wives
    clubs, 209
    marriages, 61
    migration, 12, 56, 65
    occupations, 215–216
    single, 65
Woods Point, 27, **51**, 52–53, 62, 66, 70,
    93, 101, 104, 110, 142, 144,
    175–176, 264
    All Nations Hotel, 145
    settlers, 53, 93, 105
Woolitch, Peter, 173
Woolloomooloo, 54
World War I, 1, 5, 9–10, 126, 181, 187,
    190, 192, 200–203, 207, C3
    see also AIF
World War II, 1, 3, 12, 14, 179, 198–199,
    205–207, 209, 211–212, 215,
    224, 233

Worshippers of the Sacred Heart of Jesus
    (Klanjateljice Presvetom Srcu
    Isusovom), C20
Worsley, 62
Wynyard, 5, 129

Y

yachts, 170, 262, 264
Yackandandah, 51, 143–144, 150
Yackandandah Junction, 142, 149
Yackandandah South, 101
Yackandandah Times, The, 144
Yackovitze, Antonio, 145, 154
Yandoit, 7, 27, 41, 43, 62, 66, 72, 76, 110, 103,
    159, 192
    alluvial gold, 110
    settlers, 40, 91, 103, 105
Yandoit Creek, 159
Yannich (Yanicle), Luke, 7, 88, 101
Yannich, Vincent, 78
Yapeen, 90
Yarrangung, 56
Youanmite, 50
Young, 7, 78, 154, 161, 163, 166
Young, Simone, 230
Yugoslav Immigrants' Association of
    Australia, 209
Yugoslav Settlers' Association, 231
Yugoslavia and Yugoslavs, 2–3, 12–14, 81, 202,
    205, 207, 212–213, 215, 219, 229,
    231, C22
    agents, 233
    break-up, 13
    census, 13
    Communist, 12–13, 206–207, 231, 233–234
    Consulate, 231, 233
    refugees, 74
    secret service, 233
Yurisich, Gregory, 230

Z

Zadar (Zara), 2, 7, 96, 99, 105, 133,
    158–159
zadruga, 23, 69–70
Zagabria, Joseph (Zagabrija, Josip), 31,
    63–64, 122, *122*, 134, 171
Zagabria, Rocco, 54
Zagreb, 11, 153, 230, 237
    cricket club, 237
    embassy, 237
    Melbourne International Exhibition, 158
    St Mark's, 218
    wine, 158
Zagreb, folkloric group, C7
Zan (Zaninović), 69
Zan Bros & Co, 34, 81
Zan family, *81*, *82*, 84
Zan, Clara, 82
Zan, Manda, 82, 83
Zan, Ursula (Zaninović, Uršula), 81–82
Zan (Zaninović), Vincent, 34, 68, 81–82, 84
Zaninović *see* Zan
Zaninovich, George, 66, 82
Zaninovich, Mary, 82–83
Zara, 133
Zara *see* Zadar
Zarich, Vincent (Zarić, Vicko), 22, 46–47
Zero, 59
Zibilich, James (Cibilić, Jakov), 21, 51,
    67, 111
Zlarin, 30, 40, 134, 159
Zrinski, Katarina, 218
Zubrinich, Ivan, 131
Žuljana, 22, 53
Župa, Captain, 111
Zuzulich, Paulina, 90
Zuzulich, Thomas (Cuculić, Tomislav),
    32, 69, 90
Zvijezda (Star) tamburica orchestra, 209